The Old Firm

Frontispiece. It's only a game ... *Glasgow Herald* and *Evening Times*

The Old Firm

Sectarianism, Sport and Society in Scotland

BILL MURRAY

JOHN DONALD PUBLISHERS LTD
EDINBURGH

For my Mother

Reprinted 1985
Second reprint 1985

Printed in Great Britain by Bell and Bain Ltd., Glasgow

Acknowledgements

I started work on this book in 1979, but it had been resting somewhere in my subconscious for a long time before that. In this sense its origins go back to a Glasgow childhood in which football was the dominating passion and sectarianism an accepted fact of life. An accident of history took me and my family to Australia in the mid-1950s, where my enthusiasm for football continued unabated, while religion, at least on the football field, became irrelevant. Another accident of history, in which a televised football match played a key role, took me out of the business world and into that of academia, where my teaching and research centred on French history. My shift from there to a history of The Old Firm was no accident, however, but a calculated decision to make academic capital out of years spent chasing a football, with more enthusiasm than skill. It was also made of the desire most of us have to come to grips with the forces in our childhood that make us what we are. As a Scot who has long been removed from the heat of the religious situation in Glasgow, I hope this history of The Old Firm has the necessary balance of involvement and objectivity to arrive at a judicious appraisal of a problem close to the bone of Scottish life.

In the course of researching and writing this book it has been my great pleasure to incur the debts of many people. I must first thank my university, La Trobe in Victoria, Australia, for granting approval for study leave on a subject far removed from the French Revolution, and far removed, others might think, from respectable academic work. Since then I have been granted funds for further research and in August 1983 was given a subsidy which helped me to attend a Conference at Keele University and return to Scotland to finish the work. The largeness of spirit that makes La Trobe such a fine university is nowhere better represented than in its History Department, where I have been given every encouragement to continue in what for many must have been an obscure topic. In more practical terms my work has been considerably lightened by the the typists in the History Department who, with cheerfulness and efficiency, converted my amateur and heavily scored typing into clean script: to Shirley Gordon, Louise Bennie and Merelyn Dowling my most grateful thanks.

The greatest part of a historian's work, even when he is working on football, is carried out in libraries and archives, and my admiration for librarians and the job they do is rarely diminished. At the Borchardt

Library, La Trobe University, John Horacek and Margot Hyslop have, as always, been unfailingly helpful, but for this book most of the work was done at the Mitchell Library, Glasgow, in conditions that were as close to perfect as any historian could wish: a service as cheerful as it was free from bureaucratic delay, and a staff who not only delivered tome after tome with speedy efficiency, but willingly put at my disposal their knowledge of material relevant to my study: to Joe Fisher and his team at the Glasgow Room, particularly Anne Escott and Helen Bain, my heartfelt gratitude!

When I arrived in Scotland Martin Gilfeather allowed me access to the files on The Old Firm held by the *Daily Record*, and this considerably eased my way into the subject. Of the other institutions I approached for help, the Scottish Football League told me they had nothing worth looking at, but the Scottish Football Association kindly let me read their holdings of Rangers and Celtic Handbooks, and their complete collection of the *S.F.A. Annual*. I wrote to both Celtic and Rangers before arriving in Scotland, explaining the subject of my research: Celtic Chairman, Desmond White, kindly replied to my letter, invited me to see a game at Celtic Park, but was unable to offer any concrete assistance.

One of the delights of football research is that everyone knows something about it, and in this regard I owe thanks to many individuals, most of whose names I don't even know, having done no more than exchange thoughts on the terracings. Others, whose names I do know but are too numerous to mention, include friends, colleagues and acquaintances in Scotland and Australia, particularly those in Australia who have made four academic conferences on the History of Sport such resounding successes. Among discussions conducted with more specific reference to my research I am particularly indebted to: Peter Bilsborough of Stirling University; journalist Gerry McNee and historian Bob Crampsey; my friends from Airdrie, Bill Craig, Big Tam (McAloon) and Wee Tam (Hughes), and my folks from Larkhall — to my late uncle Hugh Graham I owe a particular debt of gratitude for the valuable collection of books on Scottish history which he so generously gave me. To my own family in Adelaide my debts go back over four decades, but they and their Scots exile friends read and commented on various parts of the book, including 'pop' Reid, who was disappointed that there were so few references to Alloa Athletic!

Several people read and criticised early drafts of the manuscript and made valuable comments and suggestions: my colleagues at La Trobe University, historian Alex Tyrrell and philosopher Robert Young; colleagues whom I met by correspondence, Dick Holt of Stirling

University and Tom Gallagher of Bradford University; and my neighbour and friend, Alan Richmond, who was only asked to check certain passages but ended up reading the entire text. To historian and journalist Jack Webster, I am particularly grateful not only for his comments as a publisher's reader, but for his letter of encouragement when that publisher did not follow his recommendations. To John Tuckwell of John Donald Publishers who took the risk, I am grateful not only for his bravery, but for his sharp editorial eye which helped give the final polish and saw the book to press.

Much as I am indebted to the above, there are two people to whom I am more than any others indebted: Roy Hay of Deakin University, and Pat Woods. Roy, renowned economic historian and football fanatic, read the penultimate draft with meticulous care and offered suggestions that amounted to a small chapter in themselves. As a result I re-wrote many passages which strengthened the argument: weaknesses that remain are mine alone. Pat Woods gave me the benefit of his knowledge of Scottish football history and kept me up to date on all Old Firm developments. This book would have been immeasurably poorer without his help.

Bill Murray
La Trobe University

Contents

	Page
Acknowledgements	v
Introduction	1
Part One. The Roots of The Old Firm	5
1. The Beginnings	9
2. The Business Basis of The Old Firm	35
3. The Explosive Mixture: Sport, Politics and Religion	59
4. Catholicism, Scottish Society and the Celtic F.C.	93
Part Two. No Mean City? Glasgow and The Old Firm between the Wars	121
5. Hooliganism in High Places	123
6. Razor Gangs and Orange Walks	143
7. The Riots and the Fans	163
Part Three. Traditions under Challenge	191
8. Two Clubs, Two Traditions	193
9. Sectarianism in the 'Seventies	217
10. Into the 'Eighties	244
Conclusion. Continuity, Change and Challenge	267
Appendix. The Old Firm Monopoly	280
Select Bibliography	282
Index	286

Introduction

To many people casually acquainted with what was once the second city of the British Empire, Glasgow can be summed up in terms of its weather, religion, violence and football, all defied by a pawky good humour that challenges the worst that the environment can produce and suffused with a friendliness that is at odds with the savage sectarianism that has not quite disappeared even today. All these aspects of life in Glasgow are crystallised in the regular encounters of its two major football teams, Rangers and Celtic. These two clubs arguably have, certainly have had, the largest and most consistently faithful band of followers of any two football clubs of any code anywhere in the world. Most of the major cities of the world can boast of local derbies featuring famous football teams, but games between Celtic and Rangers are unique in the bitterness of their religious divisions, and this has ensured the financial success of both clubs for most of this century. The title 'Old Firm' was given to these two teams just after the turn of the century, in recognition of the business aspects of their games, a business, it has later been claimed, that is based on bigotry.

In the history of sport there can be few confrontations that are so closely bound up with the society that produced them as the Old Firm games. In 1988 these two teams will have been playing each other for 100 years, averaging more than four games a year, most of them played before a near sell-out crowd. These games are still supercharged with the tension associated with religious hatred and Ulster politics, and if this often detracts from them as a playing spectacle, it certainly heightens the atmosphere. This tension can break down into violence, and games between these clubs have ended in the worst riots and greatest tragedies in sporting history. Even today, when it is names like Liverpool and Manchester United, Juventus, Bayern Munich, Real Madrid and the giants from South America that dominate the football world, Rangers or Celtic can still reach the top ranks of world competition, and despite the glamour of these bigger clubs, it is doubtful if any of them have a more faithful travelling support than the big two from Glasgow. The reasons for this are complex, but grow out of what the two teams stand for, particularly in relation to each other. Their games are no mere local derby, but a clash of cultures, two world views with Rangers championing the cause of protestantism, Celtic that of catholicism. Today these differences are not so clear cut as they once were, but their appeal is still to the most basic of tribal loyalties. This book seeks to describe and explain this rivalry, set against the society in which it developed. It does so by organising the material around certain themes which are arranged in roughly chronological order: thus the first four chapters use material mainly from the pre-1914 period, the middle three concentrate on the inter-war period, and the final three on the events since the end of World War II.

The origins of the Old Firm rivalry are located deep in Scottish history, in the reaction to the Irish immigration of the nineteenth century, the tensions and expectations that came with the industrial growth of that period and the search for success, if not acceptance, by the Irish community, particularly from the 1890s. By the turn of the century most of the catholic community in Scotland were native born, but they maintained fierce loyalties to both their religion and the land of their fathers. Outside Ireland, it was only in Scotland that a top-class catholic football team was founded by an immigrant community: Celtic were founded in 1887, and their phenomenal success in their first few years effectively destroyed the previously successful catholic teams of Edinburgh and Dundee. But at the same time as Celtic attracted most of Scotland's catholic support, they polarised around themselves the anti-catholic elements in Scottish society. Glasgow Celtic presented one of the most spectacular success stories in the Scottish catholic community at this time, and in a country like Scotland, with a long tradition of anti-catholicism, such success could not be passively accepted. Glasgow Rangers were the club that took up the challenge, and were rewarded with the gratitude, tacit or vociferous, of large sections of the Scottish public, whether or not they were football followers, and if they were, whether or not they were Rangers supporters. Although Glasgow clubs, and drawing their main support from the industrial valley of the Clyde, Rangers and Celtic also attract support from all over Scotland, as well as Ireland and all those countries where there is a collection of Scottish or Irish emigrants. These are the issues that take up the first section of this work.

The second section deals mainly with the period between the two world wars, when the sectarian divide of the two clubs was sharpened with the development of the hardline 'no catholics' practice (if not policy) of Rangers. This was the period when the 'No Mean City' image of Glasgow came into being, and the city became synonymous in some minds with Red Clydeside, razor gangs and rioting football fans. This image, although based on some truth, has been grossly exaggerated. An extensive discussion of the riots resulting from matches involving the two clubs and the general behaviour of their fans is placed in the perspective of the society of this time: the gangs, Orange walks and the more extreme sectarian, political and religious opinions. There are many reasons why Scotland was never seriously threatened by the extremes of Fascism and Communism that were the fate of many other countries at this time, and while football by itself could not be said to have played a major role in reconciling ordinary folks to their lot, it was one of several cultural layers that softened or defused political violence.

The final chapters concentrate on the post-war period. By then the two clubs had long-established traditions, each representative of two dominant aspects of Scottish society: the Irish catholic and the protestant. In this time Celtic, like the Scottish catholic community in general, began to lose the sharp edge of their sectarian image. At the same time, however, the hardline protestant image of Rangers became more clearly defined and increasingly less acceptable with changing world values from the 1960s. The final two chapters look at the attack on Rangers' sectarianism in the 1970s and the prospect for the 1980s, a decade that began with the worst riot between the supporters of the two clubs since 1909 and saw the first ever visit to Scotland by a reigning pope.

It has been said that culture, religion and alcohol are the three great comforters of mankind, and Professor Hugh Stretton has suggested that, other than bread, butter and other economic determinants, 'Men variously need religion, family ties, neighbours; symbols and illusions and allegiances; membership, community, nationality'.[1] If this is so, then it is easy to see why The Old Firm, embodying all these attributes, is as the breath of life to many Scots. It is easy to exaggerate, and to take the worst excess of these games as typical; but on the other hand there is a danger in claiming that sectarianism in Scotland exists only at Rangers/Celtic football matches, or that the sectarianism of The Old Firm has nothing to do with Scottish society. The Old Firm and Scottish society are indissolubly linked, and always have been. Emphasising the religious sectarianism that has played such a conspicuous role in Scottish history is not to say that it has been the most important or even dominant factor in Scottish life, or that other societies are free from sectarianism: but there is something strangely unique about the problem in Scotland, where the power of symbols, names, songs and colours is stronger than in most English-speaking countries. This could be backed up by numerous stories, personally experienced or recorded in memoirs or serious histories, but one must suffice. This was the case of a safety award won by the Yarrow Shipbuilding Company, entitling it to fly the prestigious green and white Safety Council flag over its premises for a

year. It was decided by Yarrow's however, that since the Council did not
have a blue and white flag to fly alongside the official green and white
one, they would have to decline this honour in the interests of safety![2]

NOTES

1. H. Stretton, *The Political Sciences*, New York, 1969, p. 37.
2. Story told in William McIlvanney's assessment of the Old Firm, broadcast
on BBC Radio 4 and Radio Scotland, 15 February 1981.

PART ONE

The Roots of the Old Firm

One of the most remarkable features of the last 100 years has been the spread of association football throughout the world. It has been called Britain's most durable export, and indeed it is still flourishing where the industries it incidentally followed have long since languished. The years before the First World War saw the British Empire at its peak, and even where the imperial red was not splotched across the map of the world, the machines of British industry were hard at work. These machines needed British skills and expertise to work them, and many of these expatriate Britons put as much effort into their leisure as they did into their work. Their main leisure pastime was football. Ironically the only developing countries that did not take up association football as the major football code were the former English-speaking colonies: the USA, Canada, South Africa, Australia and New Zealand. In Europe and Latin America, however, the game took off, usually under the tutelage of British working men, clerks or administrators, and in places like Brazil and Italy the original English names of clubs (Corinthians and Milan) have been preserved.

The connection between industrial development and the spread of the game was no accident: the shift from agricultural to industrial labour brought a changed attitude to the use of energy, for while agricultural labour was usually intermittent, open-air work involving the whole body, industrial workers were generally confined to small spaces, in dark, forbidding worksheds, carrying out soul-destroying work with very little personal satisfaction. Soccer provided one of the great releases for workers in such circumstances: it could be played on a hard surface in a confined space, with only a handful of players; it required no expensive equipment—even none, as a bundle of rags could serve as a ball—and could be enjoyed by the physically small as much as the strong. It was also simple to understand, if difficult to master. As a spectator sport it was also comparatively easy to stage and, since most of the spectators had played the game, it offered itself as one of the great democratic carnivals, one in which no man was the inferior of another in judging the skills of the game or the intricacies of its rules.

For such reasons it quickly became the game of the working class; from crowds of a few thousand in the 1870s top games could bring in over

100,000 just after the turn of the century, and by 1914 football was clearly the most popular spectator sport in Great Britain. It was spreading beyond the insular confines of Great Britain, too, particularly after the First World War, but this growth of the game in foreign fields was one that was shielded from the game's founders by their own arrogance, until the truth was finally forced on them after the Second World War. Then the former pupils showed their one-time masters that the British game was now only one part of a World Game.

In all this expansion of a leisure pursuit into a mass industry, in Britain as throughout the world, the role of Scotland and the Scots was out of all proportion to the size of that small nation and its five million or so inhabitants. In Scotland the game of football has a long history, being recorded back in the times of the first James's and in the early nineteenth century having as one of its great supporters Sir Walter Scott. It was in England that the first football association was founded, however, in 1863, ten years before the Scottish Football Association, but Scots were prominent there, most notably Lord Kinnaird, while it was a Scotsman, William McGregor, who is the recognised founder of the English Football League. Scottish football and Scottish footballers often dominated the game in those early days, whether it were in the formulation of the rules or tactical innovation, and, from the first, English teams, particularly in the north, usually had one or more Scots. Some, like the Preston 'Invincibles', were composed largely of Scots, while the first eleven to play for Liverpool were all Scots. This pattern has never been entirely broken; in the inter-war period, for example, none of the most successful teams played without a Scot: the great Newcastle team of 1926–7 had seven Scots, and Sunderland nine years later had eight. Scottish managers have also been prominent in English football, with names like Busby and Shankly passing beyond the bounds of normal glorification. Similarly Scots keep cropping up in the development of the game abroad, in Europe, in Russia, in South America; and while soccer never became the dominant football code in the colonies, the attempts to get the game going were often made by Scots, and many of the colonial teams had Scottish-sounding names. In the most important game in the Scottish calendar, the International against England, Scotland held the lead in games won right through to recent times—a remarkable feat against a country with eight to ten times the population.

All sorts of reasons can be suggested for the Scots obsession with football, much of it stemming from climate, industrial development and limited choice, but few would deny its reality, particularly in the central industrial belt, and Glasgow in particular. As George Macdonald Fraser puts it in his delightful vignette from *The General Danced at Dawn*, 'The native Highlanders, the Englishmen, and the Lowlanders played football on Saturday afternoons and talked about it on Saturday evenings, but the Glaswegians, men apart in this as in most things, played, slept, ate, drank and lived it seven days a week'. Even today, when football no longer occupies the place it once did, Scotland can still make the world sit up and take notice, whether it be in the brilliant successes brightening up abysmal collapses in the international sphere or the exploits in Europe or England of teams like Rangers in the early 1960s, Celtic's Lisbon Lions, or most recently Aberdeen outclassing the once great Real Madrid in the final of the European Cup-winners' Cup. It is a long time since Glasgow was the second city of the British Empire, and while it might be reconciled to its diminished importance, as Great Britain is to the loss of that long gone symbol of Anglo-Saxon glory, it will never be entirely reconciled to its reduced status in world football.

Scotland's role in the development of the World Game, then, has been outstanding. In Scotland itself the game has centred on Glasgow, and much of the history of the game can be written in terms of the two big Glasgow clubs, Rangers and Celtic—The Old Firm. In the nature of things, as happened in Manchester and Liverpool, Dundee and Edinburgh, Glasgow was bound to produce two great local rivals, and given the nature of the industrial conurbation around Glasgow, it was likely that these two teams would dominate Scottish football. What is not quite so certain is that the nature of this rivalry had to take the form it did. However that may be, the peculiar nature of the Old Firm rivalry was firmly set by the outbreak of the First World War and has continued through to the present day.

Note

It is only in recent years that football as a social phenomenon has been seriously studied. There have been countless books on the playing side of the game, mainly recalling great moments, great players and great teams, and this has tended to be the main theme even of general histories like those of Percy Young and A. Marples. James Walvin's *The People's Game* (London, 1975) was one of the first to set the game against the social and economic background, while Tony Mason's *Association Football and English Society: 1863–1915* (Brighton, 1980) is a superb study of the role of football in the everyday life of ordinary people. For further expansion on my points regarding the role of Scots in the development of the game, while most of this will be obvious to anyone who has read the contemporary literature, one particularly useful source is the invaluable four-volume history of the game by A. Gibson and W. Pickford, *Association Football and the Men Who Made It* (London, 1906). See also Walvin, p. 124 in particular. Gerry Redmond has recently published his study of the role of Scots in the sporting life of Canada. It seems they were prominent everywhere, but for their role in soccer see: G. Redmond, *The Sporting Scots of Nineteenth Century Canada* (London, 1982), pp. 271–5. The quote from George Macdonald Fraser comes from the extract 'Play up, play up, and get tore in' in Ian Archer and Trevor Royle (eds.), *We'll Support You Evermore* (London, 1976), pp. 43–46. In my opinion this and Bob Crampsey's *The Scottish Footballer* (Edinburgh, 1978) are the two most insightful books on Scottish football.

CHAPTER 1

The Beginnings

Glasgow's first International Exhibition took place in 1888, and was acclaimed by the thousands of visitors who marvelled at the cultural and industrial display of the great Workshop of the Empire. Glasgow's second International Exhibition, in 1901, was an even greater success. In the intervening thirteen years the city reached the height of its prosperity,[1] The Exhibition aside, however, 1888 was not a particularly memorable year. The city had fully recovered from the City of Glasgow Bank crash ten years previously, and was back on the full tide of economic buoyancy. The shipyards were busy, the factories operating at full strength, and all around them tenements were being erected to house the labour force that fed them. Unemployment was low and most workers had seen a gradual improvement in their standard of living: many lived in appalling conditions, but most had slightly better wages and more leisure time than ever before. Much of this improvement was rather precarious, and the prospect of unemployment and empty stomachs was always around the corner, but the signs of a changing life style were everywhere, nowhere more so than in the transport revolution that was connecting the farflung suburbs of the city and opening up the borderlands. Cheap transport and the 'short week' encouraged new pattern of leisure: picnics and outings of various sorts, but above all the craze for association football that was sweeping the land, and particularly industrial Scotland. It was the working-class who figured most prominently in these changes, much to the annoyance of middle-class picnickers who found their favourite spots invaded by the uncouth, while the football authorities looked no less anxiously to the future of the game as it threatened to fall under the influence of working-class players and supporters.

In the midst of such far-reaching changes the construction of yet another football ground, in the East End of Glasgow, seemed of no special significance. When the ground was duly completed, mainly by volunteer labour, the catholic community of Glasgow's east end could well pride themselves on the rapid erection of what was to be the first home of the Celtic Football and Athletic Club. On 8 May 1888, the same day as the Glasgow Exhibition opened, Hibernians came through from Edinburgh to honour their Glasgow 'compatriots' by playing the inaugural match against Cowlairs. Just under three weeks later, on 28

May, Celtic played their first game, against the long-established Rangers from the other side of the city. None of the 2,000 spectators at that game could have guessed that they were present at a historic occasion, for that evening marked the first of what was to become the most famous, long-lasting—and bitter—sporting rivalry in the history of football.

When that first game was played between Celtic and Rangers, Queen's Park were still the most prestigious club in Scotland. It was they who had founded the Scottish game back in 1867 and who for years thereafter dominated it, playing for nearly eight years before they lost a goal and ten before they were defeated in Scotland. By the 1880s they were being challenged on many sides, not least by Rangers, who built the best ground in the country in 1887. Rangers' support, too, was the largest, but the team itself had not yet fulfilled the promise of its earlier years. The arrival of Celtic in 1888 was explosive, and within a few years they had changed the face of football in Scotland. The team to suffer most from these changes was Queen's Park, and they did not like it.

It was Celtic who pushed hardest for the formation of the League introduced in 1890 and then fought most determinedly for its inevitable sequel, the introduction of professionalism, three years later. Queen's Park, as champions of the amateur ideal, held themselves aloof from these developments, and as a result saw a steady decline in their fortunes. From that time on, Rangers and Celtic hogged the major honours: Scottish League, Scottish Cup, the local Charity Cup and Glasgow Cup, and for a while the short-lived Glasgow League which was followed by the equally unsuccessful Inter-city League. As a result of these various fixtures Celtic and Rangers could find themselves playing against each other up to ten times a year, with a healthy return at the gate for each encounter. By the turn of the century they could draw £1,000 per game with each other, and ten years later could double this figure. These were enormous returns by the standards of the day, when not many workers would have been earning 30/- a week.

It was the commercial aspects of these games that led to the two clubs being labelled 'The Old Firm', a phrase not without sarcasm, for the sporting press of this time had not altogether overcome its distaste for professionalism and the objectionable moral values that this was presumed to introduce. The *Scottish Referee* in particular deplored what it believed to be a crass interference with sporting values, and it was in this paper, on 15 April 1904, just prior to the Celtic/Rangers Scottish Cup Final of that year, that a cartoon appeared depicting a man carrying a sandwich board with the words: 'Patronise the Old Firm' and signed: 'Rangers, Celtic Ltd'. If this was the birth of the title 'Old Firm'—and the label did

Rangers, Celtic Ltd. *Scottish Referee*, 15 April 1904

not catch on for a few years after, and then only occasionally—the reality went back a whole decade, for it was in 1894 that the management of the two clubs saw the commercial boon in playing each other, and instead of the annual Christmas jaunt into England, decided to stay at home and play each other on New Year's Day. On 1 January 1894 the first 'Ne'erday' game was played, to become 'a feature of the social life of Glasgow as conspicuous and indispensable as the midnight orgie (*sic*) at the Cross or the domestic battening on shortbread and oranges'.[2]

Record gate receipts represented record 'gates', and just before the First World War Celtic and Rangers could attract 70,000 to a league game, as many as all the other first-division games combined. It was apparent that these two clubs were attracting people to their games who didn't otherwise show much interest in football. This was in part because they played the best football; but it was also because they drew on deeper passions than the spectacle of a thrilling sporting encounter tightly contested. For a game of football between Celtic and Rangers reflected the religious and almost racial divisions that scarred community life in many parts of Scotland. Founded by and for the catholic community of Glasgow, Celtic were happy to be known as 'the Irishmen', and following their phenomenal success in the first year after their foundation, the Scottish public cried out for a team to beat them. Queen's Park were at first the great protestant hope, but already their refusal to recognise the changing social conditions in Scottish football had doomed them as a power in the sporting field.[3] And so hopes passed to Rangers, especially when in the 1893–4 season out of six games they defeated Celtic four times and drew with them once. No other team had achieved that feat. Now supporters deserted the less successful clubs of Dumbartonshire, Lanarkshire and Renfrewshire, and made the trek across to Glasgow to watch and encourage the team that seemed capable of stemming the emerald tide.

Rangers

When Rangers honoured Celtic by playing that first game in May 1888, they had already been in existence sixteen years, a career in the rapidly blossoming sport that had seen a spectacular rise to fame and then a collapse into failure and bickering that threatened the very existence of the club. By 1888, however, they were on the verge of recovery, with new headquarters, a new team and a new management.

The Rangers Football Club were founded in early 1872, playing their first game in May of that year 'some two months after the inauguration of the club'.[4] They were founded by a group of lads from the Gareloch, a family with the then innocent enough name of McNeil. Attracted by the new craze on the Glasgow Green, they set out to found a football team; young and keen, they practised six nights a week through the summer and were rewarded with games against the Clyde and Argyle— but not yet the big names like Dumbarton, Vale of Leven, Third Lanark or Queen's Park. The latter condescended to send out their reserve team, the Strollers, refusing to demean their first team by playing against opponents who did not have their own ground to play on. Undeterred, Moses McNeil and his brothers, and the other lads who made up the Light Blues, set out to find a pitch with more dignity and sense of security than a patch at the Fleshers Haugh of the Glasgow Green, where they often had to pay some youngster to stand on the pitch all morning to book it for the game that afternoon. So began the first move that has seen the club go from improvement to improvement, keeping the ground of the Rangers Football Club among the finest in the country. From the Glasgow Green they went to Burnbank, then Kinning Park in 1876. After eleven years there they were evicted, only to set about building the most ambitious ground in Scotland till then. On 20 August 1887 the first Ibrox Park was opened, but even that proved inadequate to cope with the ever-increasing attendances, and in 1899 the club moved to its present site.

Enthusiasm and ambition paid off. In the 1876–77 season Rangers held Vale of Leven to two draws in the Scottish Cup Final, at Hamilton Crescent, the second after a violently protested third goal. The second replay, at Hampden, aroused tremendous interest. There was a continual stream of traffic to that game, as the Scottish Football Association *Annual* reported: 'Thousands of the working-classes rushed out to the field of battle in their labouring garb, after crossing the workshop gate when the whistle sounded at 5 o'clock'. The match was played on a Friday, and some time before the contest began there were 7–8,000 people inside the ground, and as many outside. These were mainly Rangers' supporters. There had been talk of Rangers not turning up for that second replay because of the dispute, but, as the SFA *Annual* for 1877–8 put it, 'with that commendable pluck which characterized them all through the season [the 'young Rangers'] met them at last on Hampden Park'. Rangers lost 3–2, in what was claimed to be the best game played in Scotland until then. Two years later they played the champions from the Vale again, but after another disputed goal refused to turn up for the replay and lost to a walkover. Twice they had reached the pinnacle of the Scottish football scene; their success elsewhere was remarkable and they were even being mentioned alongside Queen's Park as one of the great clubs. When news got back to Glasgow in 1881 that Rangers had been beaten by Nottingham Forest, it was reported in the press that 'many were incredulous and could not realize that there was any English club capable of lowering the colour of the popular blues'.[5]

But the days of success were coming to an end on the home front too. In the middle years of the 1880s the club was accused in some quarters of bad sportsmanship, cheeseparing and selfishness; its committee of riotousness and inefficiency. Many of these accusations came from the *Scottish Athletic Journal* which conducted a virtual vendetta against the club, a vendetta which the rival *Scottish Umpire* declared to be due to Rangers' refusal to buy advertising space in their competitor's journal. However that may be, the record of the club in these years is not a happy one. In 1883 it was kept solvent only by a loan of £30 from president Goudie, and meetings of the committee were marked more by squabbles and bad temper than constructive planning. In that same year the club was asked to play against Dumbarton in a benefit match for the victims of the *Daphne* disaster—at its launching in Linthouse on 3 July 1883 the 500-ton steamer had turned on its side, drowning 146 of the 200 workers still inside its hull. The Rangers' committee insisted on taking out their expenses for the game, and remarked rather sourly on being criticised for this that it was all very well for the big clubs like Dumbarton to play for nothing.[6]

In 1879 Rangers had refused to turn up for the replay of the Scottish Cup Final against Vale of Leven, claiming that they had been cheated of the trophy by a mistake by the referee. In 1884 they were beaten by Arbroath and then claimed that the Arbroath ground was not of the proper dimensions—they measured the bye-line to show it was short by a few inches and·won the protest. Then came another protest against Third Lanark, and when Rangers were beaten by Vale of Leven the *Scottish Athletic Journal* commented sarcastically: 'So far there has been no protest from Rangers'.[7] The *Journal* was having a field day at Rangers' expense, claiming that it had always been the rule of the Rangers to look after themselves,[8] and in September 1885 it reminded its readers that: 'The Rangers last season protested their way from round to round and created in doing so a scandal which shocked the whole football world'.[9] A few months into the next season, the *Journal* published a letter from the Airdrie club, suggesting that Rangers' refusal to arrange a return fixture after a 10–2 drubbing was because they were scared.[10]

In addition to bad sportsmanship the club was condemned for having no humour; it had fallen from its once high state 'through chicanery and trickery' and was regarded with suspicion and dislike everywhere except at Kinning Park.[11] Criticism was extended to the committee meetings and even the club's social functions. Only the band at the December 1884 dance secured the praise of the *Athletic Journal*'s reporter: 'the social tone of the dance was decidedly lower than usual,' he commented, and he claimed that even the club's warmest supporters were complaining.[12] Not altogether surprisingly, then, the club called a special meeting to consider any action it could take against its tormentor.[13] As it happened, the *Scottish Umpire* took up the Rangers' cause, only to be accused of being biased. It replied that this was only to make up for the 'malevolent injustice' in another quarter, and attacked that paper [the *Scottish Athletic Journal*] which had done more to lower the tone of the game by the bickering it had caused among the clubs than even professionalism 'with all its horrors' could do. There was a need for the big clubs, it continued: Queen's Park needed Rangers, just as Abercorn needed Saint Mirren in Paisley or the Harp needed Our Boys in Dundee.[14] For a brief while it looked as though Rangers would lose the support of the *Umpire*, when it castigated them for going ahead with a game against Airdrie despite the ground being covered with six inches of snow. The *Umpire* went straight to the point by saying that Rangers could not complain 'if their conduct is attributed to sordid motives or something of that kind'.[15] Life could be difficult: greed for playing on a snow-covered field, and later cowardice for not playing after a heavy defeat!

By the beginning of the next season, however, all seemed well: the *Umpire* did not repeat its criticisms, and by the middle of 1886 the *Athletic Journal* reversed its attitude to Rangers, making 'a single leap from the depths of unscrupulous misrepresentation to the heights of adoring approbation', as the rival *Umpire* noted. It would not complain too much, however, if Rangers now had two organs.[16] With the press on their side, and a new stadium about to be opened, Rangers entered the year 1887 with their fortunes decidedly on the rise. They moved into their new Ibrox accommodation in what for the time was a blaze of publicity.

At a cake and wine banquet to mark the opening of the new ground, press, local dignitaries, transport authorities and the managing partner of F. J. Braby and Co., who had carried out the construction of the ground, were all there. Tom Vallance proposed the toast to 'the Rangers' Football Club and Ibrox Park', and Provost Ferguson, in answer to the toast to the health of 'The Provost, Magistrates, and Commissioners of Govan', expressed his pleasure in welcoming Rangers into their district. The game

FRED. BRABY & CO., Limited,

ENGINEERS AND CONTRACTORS,

PETERSHILL ROAD, GLASGOW.

RANGERS' FOOTBALL GROUND, GLASGOW (Fred. Braby & Co., Ltd., Pavilion of Galvanised and Corrugated Iron and Wood. Ground Corrugated Iron Sheets fixed to wood framing, thus

Contractors). Grand Stand to seat upwards of 1200 persons. Commodious enclosed with substantial paling formed of their Galvanised and making it strong and unclimbable from outside.

CONTRACTORS FOR PAVILIONS, STANDS, BARRICADES, and other Requisites for Football and Cricket Enclosures.
DESIGNS WITH ESTIMATES ON APPLICATION.

The First Ibrox. SFA *Annual*, 1887–88

was now the game of the people, and he hoped that many young men of Govan would join the club and sustain its well-won reputation. Rangers were a club *par excellence* and he trusted that in the future, as in the past, they would continue to be one of the best clubs in Scotland.[17] The press included illustrations of the new ground, with maps of the district showing how to get there. Such was the demand for the sketch of the new ground that the *Scottish Umpire* had to print an extra 3,000 copies for the unprecedented demand, and made available single copies of the sketch.

Rangers were not quite out of the doldrums, however. The opening game against Preston North End was marred by an 8–1 thrashing and an invasion towards the end by Rangers fans who could suffer the spectacle no longer. In fact Rangers were about to enter one of the worst periods in their history, and even the *Scottish Umpire* was unwilling to conceal the deep malaise that afflicted the club. On 1 May 1888 it reported the dissension running right through it, and deplored the fact that Rangers, with unquestionably the largest following in Glasgow, did not occupy a higher place. It castigated the AGM as 'the most cantankerous ever in the history of the club', adding: 'and that is saying a great deal'. Rangers might have done well on the field, 'but it is certain that in the past they have not taken the proper position in the social and legislative aspects of the game'.[18] *Scottish Sport* took over the attacks on the committee, but at the beginning of 1889 it was able to report: 'The Rangers are on the fair way to recovery! ... What we have regarded all along as the central fault of the "light blues" was an almost idiotic attachment to old and antiquated methods in the conduct of their affairs, and a vexatious lack of enterprise in the furtherance of its interests'.[19]

It is possible, even likely, that the sudden appearance of Celtic on the football scene jolted the Rangers' committee out of their cliquism, intrigue and hair-splitting, but it should also be noted that it was at this time that William Wilton started to make his influence felt on the club, an influence that would be equalled only by Bill Struth, who replaced him after a tragic drowning accident at Gourock on 2 May 1920. Under Wilton, the club builder, Rangers were to know some of their greatest days. In the first season of the new league competition in 1890–91 Rangers shared top place with Dumbarton. In 1894 they won the Scottish Cup for the first time, beating Celtic 3–1 in the final and capping off a great season in which they had defeated the Irishmen four times in six games, losing only once. In the 1896–97 season they won the three main cups—Scottish, Glasgow and Charity, the latter two having then a prestige they have long since lost—and in season 1898–99 they created the unbeatable record of winning the league without dropping a point. From 12 February 1898 to the end of the century Rangers never lost a league game, although in the first game of the new century they fell 3–2 to Celtic at Celtic Park.

By this time they had built one of the finest stadiums in the world, the new Ibrox, the ground more or less as it was known until the complete remodelling of the 1970s. That final year of the old century saw another major change in the Rangers Football Club, when it indicated its faith in the future by becoming a limited liability company. Now the days of open squabbling among committees was over, to be succeeded by boardroom intrigue behind closed doors. Rangers entered the new century with their stormy past behind them: in playing skill, ambition and following there was only one team to match the Glasgow Rangers: the Irishmen from the other side of the city.

Celtic

The Celtic Football and Athletic Club was founded as a charitable

Brother Walfrid. (Pat Woods collection)

organisation, to raise money to provide free dinners, clothing and other relief for the poor of the East End of Glasgow, specifically for the poor of the catholic parishes of St Mary's, St Andrew's and St Alphonsus'.[20] Scotland abounded at this time with Hibs, Harps, Shamrocks, Emeralds and even Emmets, the most successful of whom were the Hibs of Edinburgh and the Harp of Dundee. It was the success of these two clubs that finally impelled some prominent catholic citizens of Glasgow's East End, under the lead of Brother Walfrid and his assistant Brother Dorotheus, to set about forming an Irish football club in the heart of the city. In April 1887 Hibs, holders of the Scottish Cup which they had taken away from the west coast for the first time, had been narrowly defeated by Renton (2–3) in the final of the Glasgow Charity Cup before a crowd estimated at 15–18,000. At that same time, too, a record crowd for the region saw Dundee Harp lose to Dundee Wanderers in the final of the Dundee Burns Charity Cup.

Commenting on the particular attractions of these two games in its editorial of 26 April 1887, the *Scottish Athletic Journal* noted that in each case 'an Irish and a Scotch club was engaged', and estimated that three quarters of the crowd at the Hibs/Renton game had come to support 'the Irish contingent'. It concluded:

> The Irish are nothing if not patriotic and on occasions so momentous as these the vast Celtic population of this city and also of Dundee turn out to give their compatriots an encouraging cheer. People who never witness a football match are attracted to the scene by the political aspect of the game, and not because they are possessed of any enthusiasm for football.

It is doubtful if the catholics of Glasgow were as uninterested in football as the editorialist suggests, but however that may be the only question mark surrounding the foundation of Glasgow Celtic is why it was so long delayed? Edinburgh had given birth to the Hibernians in 1875, and the Harp were formed in Dundee in 1880.

Hibernian were the first sectarian team in Scotland, being founded in 1875 by Canon Edward Hannan, who had it written into the constitution of the club that its players must be practising catholics.[21] The 'second' Hibs, resuscitated in 1893 after the demise of the first Hibs eighteen months previously, dropped the sectarian clause, and since then Hibs have been no more 'catholic' than either Everton or Manchester United. Dundee Harp were a catholic club of distinction, but they went out of existence shortly after the rise to fame of Celtic. Glasgow Celtic, on the other hand, building on catholic support and Irish national sentiment, were to grow from strength to strength.

Brother Walfrid was backed up in his vision of a catholic football club by the enthusiastic support of the builder John Glass, and with other interested catholics they got together on 6 November 1887 to propose the formation of the Celtic Football and Athletic Club. In January 1888 they issued a circular calling for support for the newly founded club, and over the next few months a horde of untiring volunteers put their backs into the creation of a football ground and rudimentary spectator accommodation. The ground was ready by May, and on the eighth of that month 3,000 people turned up to see the Hibs of Edinburgh and

Celtic Park, 1898. (Mitchell Library, Glasgow)

Cowlairs of Glasgow christen the new ground. Rangers, who had refused to perform the honour of opening the new ground, made up for their omission by playing the first game against the new club, and over the next few years the victory against the Light Blues was proved to have been no flash in the pan, as Celtic triumphed throughout Scotland and later throughout the United Kingdom, breaking attendance records everywhere they went.

In the first year of their existence Celtic reached the final of the Scottish Cup, only to be beaten by Third Lanark in the replay of the 'snow final'. Three years later they announced in unmistakable terms that the football scene in Scotland had changed irrevocably when they beat Queen's Park 5–1 in the final of the Scottish Cup: between seasons 1892–93 and 1897–98 they were Scottish League Champions four times in six seasons. In this time they attracted to the game people who had never seen a football match, and as early as 1892 had made their home ground at Parkhead a football stadium large and comfortable enough to attract the big cup games and the internationals. Before long Celtic Park was the major summer venue for athletic meetings, and the club helped promote the new cycling craze by building a cycling track around the ground, thus adding another dimension to its interests. Other initiatives at this time included the first use of goalnets in Scottish football (1892), experiments with electric lights (1893), and the provision of telegraphic and other amenities for the press. Inevitably, but not without a great deal of soul-searching and bitter quarrels, the original ideals of the club became 'sicklied over with the pale cast of gold', and on 4 March 1897 the Celtic Football Club became the Celtic Football and Athletic Club Limited.[22]

Within a decade of their coming into existence, the Irishmen of Glasgow had created one of the finest football teams in Great Britain. Their team played on a ground which had few equals for the time, and it was backed by an ambitious and progressive committee who intended to keep it at the forefront of the Scottish football scene. But like Rangers, Celtic had not won universal acclaim on the road to success. On the contrary, the club had been involved in many controversies and internal dissensions, in addition to suffering what nearly every writer on behalf of Celtic has claimed to be the bitter bigotry of the Scottish football authorities, the Scottish press and the Scottish public in general. It is not so often noted that some of the club's worst problems were created by itself and within its own community.

The first enemies Celtic made were their compatriots from the other side of Scotland who had honoured the club by playing the opening game on the new ground: Hibs were effectively put out of existence by Celtic, whose playing strength was based on the capture of nearly half the players from the Scottish cup holders. These players were actually from the West Coast, and poaching was a common practice in these 'amateur' days, when players were not bound by contracts to a club. Hibs were no better than most other teams in this regard but this did not placate their followers, who let their feelings on the matter be known in no uncertain manner when Celtic played their first game against Hibs in Edinburgh. Three times the pitch was invaded before the match was called to a premature halt. The ruin, however, was approaching. From the peak of success Hibs were dragged down to near and then eventual oblivion, and so, having survived the refusal of the Scottish Football Association to admit them into its competitions back in 1875 because they were not Scots, Hibs were unable to survive the depredations of their Glasgow compatriots and folded up in May 1891. In 'An Open Letter to the Hibernian Football Club', written shortly after the formation of Celtic and following what the writer described as a fluke victory by Celtic over a ten-man Hibs team, a Hibs sympathiser urged the Easter Road committee to show courage in its crisis, concluding:

Now then, lads, go into the season with the proper spirit. Evil deeds never prosper; the duplicity of the founders of the Celtic club will defeat its purpose...

Gentlemen of the committee, have a good heart, and look after your present team well. They will merit your confidence. Members of the club, give your every support to the committee. Irishmen in Glasgow and throughout Scotland, show what you think of the effort to ruin the Hibernians, whose quarters are

EASTER ROAD.[23]

For some time after that relations between the two clubs were strained.

The Renton football club was also badly affected by the formation of Celtic, as they lost their two star players, Kelly and McCallum, to the new club. Indeed it was the promise of Kelly to play for Celtic that ensured the transfer of the Hibs stars, and thus the playing strength on which the success of any club is based. Another star of this time was won over to Celtic by methods which did not meet with the approval of the catholics who made up the following of Carfin Shamrock. For it was from this club that the Celtic officials almost literally stole Jerry Reynolds, the star defender, in a manoeuvre common enough at the time—they sneaked him out of his house under cover of dark and spirited him off before the officials of Carfin could raise the alarm. Writing a serialised history of the club for the *Evening Times* in 1931, 'Veteran' claimed that there were still people in the Carfin district who held bitter memories of that midnight raid.[24]

From their inception, then, Celtic aroused enough antagonism among their fellow countrymen and catholics to be threatened by the formation of the Glasgow Hibernians. The rival club attracted some financial backing, and a start was made on a new ground, but the success of Celtic was too deeply entrenched to be seriously threatened by the rival body.[25] But this was just one other instance of the bitterness that Celtic attracted from fellow Irishmen. Indeed they were so 'freely and fiercely criticized' that the *Glasgow Observer*, the official newspaper of the catholic community, had to come to their defence, sadly admitting that 'the first and busiest throwing stones at the Celts are our own people'.[26]

Celtic's conflict with their 'own people' would be smoothed over with success. When it came to the Scottish football authorities, however, this was an antagonism that success only deepened. Within two years of their inception Celtic were at odds with the Glasgow Association, from which they threatened to resign. The first major blow-up arose out of a disputed goal when Celtic were beaten 3–2 by Queen's Park in the final of the Glasgow Cup in December 1889. Six bottles were thrown from the stand; some of the Celtic team left the field, but were brought back by some older players and the intervention of a Celtic official. In the dressing room after the game two opposing players came to blows, and many of the Celtic team and officials refused to attend the after-match dinner (five years later Queen's Park refused to appear when Celtic beat them with a disputed goal!). Celtic's threat of resignation after this game drew a stinging editorial from *Scottish Sport*:[27] the dispute was over a point of fact, and the Celtic management was giving virtual approval to the conduct of its players.

Nine months later Celtic again thought the referee was against them in a game which they lost to Third Lanark by the odd goal in three. *Scottish Sport* reported how 'for several minutes [the players] sulkily refused to proceed', and its editorial referred to the game as 'a modern Donnybrook ... the worst exhibition we have been unfortunate to see ... pure and unadulterated brutality'.[28] In the end Celtic did not resign from the Association, but they refused to send along their delegate.

The Glasgow Association was fairly big in those early days, but the ruling body was the Scottish Football Association (SFA). Celtic's first major problems with the parent body, in November 1888, ended successfully when their protest against Clyde, who had beaten them 1–0 in a cup-tie, was upheld. Clyde dismissed Celtic's protest as a 'tissue of falsehood from beginning to end',[29] but the SFA agreed that Clyde's late arrival, which resulted in the match being finished in darkness, justified a replay (which Celtic won 9–2). Two years later, however, a major confrontation erupted which did not end so happily for Celtic.

This was the 'Old Renton Affair'. On 31 May 1890 Celtic played against a team of former Renton stars in a benefit match for James McCall, a Renton player.[30] Many of the Old Renton team were professionals, playing in England, and one of them, McCallum, was specifically under suspension in Scotland. When Celtic sought, privately, the advice of SFA president, Mr Park, they were told the match was illegal, but went ahead with it just the same. In the press *Scottish Sport* lashed out at Celtic's 'impudent insult', declared that 'no club can be a law unto itself'[31] and followed this with the admonition that 'if Celtic want professionalism let them go ahead, but while under the rules of the amateur bodies let them abide by them or quit'.[32] The *Scottish Referee*, on the other hand, engaged at the time in vigorous dispute with its rival, claimed that *Scottish Sport's* condemnation of Celtic was because they had ceased advertising with them.[33]

The matter came before the Professional Committee in late August, Celtic being accused of having 'violated the rules of the SFA in their

B

letter and spirit by playing a benefit match and having insulted the
president of the Association in doing so'. The *Referee* continued to offer
some support to Celtic, and although editorial opinion in its rival
castigated Celtic's apparent contempt for the amateur body, contributors
like 'Pertinax' and 'Mugwump' supported the club. The dispute dragged
on, Celtic finally making a somewhat ignominious retreat which implied
that whatever Old Renton had done, at least Celtic had acted innocently
and for the purest of motives: to prove this they listed the charities which
had benefited.[34] As it turned out, the laws of the SFA were not very
clear on the matter and Celtic were merely 'censured'. Kelly and McCall
were suspended, however, for having played with professionals, but their
suspensions were soon lifted. In the end if was the SFA that came off
worst: what they believed to have been effrontery on the part of Celtic
was barely punished, and throughout the affair they were exposed to the
ridicule of some sections of the press. Within three years they would have
to accept final defeat when professionalism was at last made legal.

Despite later claims that the bigots threatened to put and end to Celtic
from the first, it is apparent that neither the SFA nor the organisers of the
charity competitions were willing to kill off the club that was doing
more for the game in a material sense than any other.

Celtic had no qualms about revealing the hypocrisy of amateurism and
forcing the SFA to come to terms with the issue. But just as they were
bringing that issue to a successful conclusion, when professionalism was
legalised in 1893, they were themselves faced by an internal crisis. This
was the dispute among the original members of the club as to whether it
was to remain a charitable organisation or to be converted into a business
devoted to private profit.

The suggestion that Celtic be formed into a limited liability company
was first raised at the AGM for 1893, and thereafter it was brought up at
every subsequent meeting until the proposers were successful in 1897. The
main supporters of the conversion to a limited liability company were the
businessmen, mainly publicans, who dominated the committee; the main
opponents were those who feared that the ideals of the club in regard to
charity would be lost if the businessmen were successful in their aims.
The leaders of this group were often members of the League of the
Cross, the catholic temperance group, who had well-founded fears of the
motives of their opponents. In the catholic press the *Glasgow Observer*
took the side of the temperance groups, and for its pains lost the
advertising revenue from the club. It also lost the use of Celtic Park for
the final of a charity competition it had organised and for which it
provided a cup. The *Glasgow Examiner*, on the other hand, founded on 16

March 1895 as a rival to the *Observer*, wrote scathing attacks in its 'Athletic Notes' column on the bleeding hearts among the 'streetcorner loafers' and 'soup kitchen cranks' who refused to leave the running of the club to those who best knew what was what, and who, if they were allowed to get their way, would soon be demanding that the team selection be by plebiscite.[35]

The author of this weekly column was the leading Celtic official, John McLaughlin, a publican from Hamilton, educated by the Jesuits at Stonyhurst College, and prime mover of the attempt to change Celtic to a limited liability company. On the success of this move he was elected first chairman of the club, a position he held until his death in August 1909. A fiery and forthright orator and journalist, as the gentlemen of the SFA among others well knew, he was happy to heap ridicule on the opponents of limited liability, but not so happy when he was answered in kind. One Frank Havelin, labourer and member of the club with a solitary £1 share, had the effrontery to answer McLaughlin in equally forceful language, and for his pains was taken to court by McLaughlin for £100 damages—more than a year's wages for a labourer—for a 'false and calumnious' statement 'made with the design of exposing him to the hatred and contempt alike of the members of the club and the public'. The sheriff thought otherwise and dismissed the alleged slander with costs in favour of the defender. Of Havelin we do not hear much more in the history of Celtic; of McLaughlin and the publicans we hear a great deal.

The committee members who had struggled to establish the club had good reason to fear that they would lose their influence, and that control by the new directors would see profits going to a 'few moneyed speculators', to the wealthier sections who wanted to 'make a good thing' out of the club. When the issue was raised at the 1893 AGM, it had been reported as an issue of Capital v Labour with 'redoubtable Arthur Murphy' playing the role of Keir Hardie.[36] McLaughlin well fitted the capitalist role. In his battle with the SFA over professionalism two motives underlay his entire campaign: the first, not so clearly spelled out, was that professionalism would keep the money from going to the less wealthy clubs; the other, clearly stated, was that professionalism would make the management masters of the players.[37] McLaughlin was to see the fulfilment of his wishes, and professionalism was in fact to create a virtual feudal relationship between players and management for well over half a century. McLaughlin and the new directors were equally successful in putting the supporters of the club firmly in their place.

One of the first actions of the new directorate was to refuse to honour promises that the brake clubs claimed had been made by the old committee regarding reduced rates for season tickets. This was the first major clash between fans and management, and resulted in a total victory for the latter. These brake clubs were the precursors of today's supporters' clubs, and took their name from the mode of transport to the game: horse-drawn 'brakes' which carried up to two dozen supporters, suitably festooned and always with a large banner identifying the particular brake club and featuring one of the star players. By 1896 there had been enough Celtic brake clubs formed for them to come together in the first of what were to become annual 'socials'.[38] A feature of these early brake clubs which puts them at total variance with later supporters' groups is that they were run under the auspices of the League of the Cross, a strict temperance organisation. This did not endear them to the newly formed directorate: of the seven new directors only John Glass, a builder, was not a publican. But they also believed that the new management were more interested in dividend returns than donations to charity or fulfilling promises made to the club's supporters. It seems, in fact, that committee men Glass and McKay had made promises to the brake clubs regarding ticket discounts for the 1897–98 season, as well as promising refunds for taking up blocks of tickets that had not been selling well in the 1896–97 season. But the promises had only been made verbally and the new directors simply denied that they had been made. A special meeting of all the Celtic Brake Clubs reaffirmed that definite promises had been made, but they were unable to sway the new Board of directors, leaving them with their indignation and empty threats about forming a rival Irish football club. The leaders of the brake clubs claimed to have promises of £5,000 for that purpose, but this second attempt to form a Glasgow Hibs was even less successful than the first.[39]

One other grievance that emerged out of this dispute was an idealism of a more dubious nature: this was the wish of the opponents of the club becoming a company that it should be set up on a sectarian basis—they claimed that 'not half the team are what is commonly termed "the right sort"'. The new directors made it clear that they would continue to employ non-catholics. Whether this was prompted by the fate of Hibs, a genuine wish to avoid the charge of sectarianism, or simply a sound business decision based on the realisation that an all-catholic team would not keep Celtic at the top of the competition and so detract from its drawing power at the gates, cannot be ascertained. The club spoke through the sports writer for the *Glasgow Observer* ('Man in the Know'), who was for many decades an unashamed apologist for the club's every action; he claimed that they would rather have no team at all than 'pay three or four pounds a week to some of the so-called Catholic players, who, by their disgusting behaviour, have been a disgrace to their club; their country and their religion'. But in a more self-righteous tone he claimed: 'To raise the question of religion is singularly out of place when dealing with sporting matters, and I trust that the last has been heard of it in Celtic circles'.[40] However genuine such a wish might have been, the Celtic club, while continuing to play non-catholic players, retained its religious character and its Irish sympathies, and remained inseparably linked with both. As such, too, it ensured financial viability, even if more of this return went into private pockets than needy charities.

Yet however much one may sympathise with the motives of the opponents of commercialisation, and whether or not one sees their fears being realised in the course of events, it does seem that it was the businessmen who were seeing matters in the clearest of lights. Football by the turn of the century was advancing at a rate that could not be halted, and the money people were prepared to pay to see it played was more than could be handled by committees of well-meaning amateurs. There is, too, the eternal irony of charity, that its donors are happy to give, so long as its limits are clearly and severely circumscribed.

The Formation of The Old Firm

In the first few years after 1888 Celtic and Rangers enjoyed a particularly friendly relationship. Their social evenings following matches were convivial affairs, and that same McLaughlin of the rapier pen and acid tongue had equally considerable musical talents that he put at the disposal of Rangers Glee Club and Choir.[41] The two clubs would invite each other to watch English opposition at their respective grounds, and early in 1892 *Scottish Sport* noted that 'the light blues are favourites with the Parkhead crowd'.[42] A year later they travelled together to Edinburgh, and that same journal noted that 'they are getting very pally. And why not?'[43]

The managements of the two clubs had very good reasons to get on with each other. They had the biggest supports in Scotland, and in order to take advantage of the returns from this support it was in their interest to combine against the conservatism of the established authorities. This Celtic did with a brash abandon, but firmly supported by Rangers. Both clubs pitted themselves against the SFA and Queen's Park over the formation of the League, and after its formation stood firm on the need to introduce professionalism. In the autumn of 1893, shortly after the introduction of professionalism in football, they both found themselves in

Scottish Sport

ILLUSTRATED.

No. 1,539.]   FRIDAY, SEPTEMBER 21, 1900.   [No. 25, New Series.

AS RIGHT AS RIGHT CAN BE.

'As right as right can be'. *Scottish Sport*, 21 September 1900

trouble regarding payments to athletes at their respective Sports
Meetings. A sub-committee of the Scottish Amateur Athletic Association
investigating rumours of abuses regarding payments to athletes decided,
among other findings, that: Rangers forfeit their membership of the
Association for 'liberal expenses' paid to athletes at their sports; while

Celtic were censured for their mode of paying the railway fares of a number of athletes who competed at their sports in August 1893. The two clubs fought the punishments, with McLaughlin of Celtic seconding the successful motion of Mellish of Rangers that the punishments be scrapped.[44] Later in the same year their interests coincided to the extent that Rangers' treasurer, J. S. Marr, was styled 'the Celtic's advocate'.[45]

At the same time the two clubs did their best to ensure that they themselves should profit from the big gates each attracted, particularly in the venues for cup games. It had been noted at the time that they preferred to meet each other in the semi-final rather than the final, for then they did not have to share the gate with a third club. Specifically in the discussions over the venue for the Glasgow Cup Final in 1893, Celtic and Rangers agreed between themselves to propose Celtic Park, and that if that was agreed on, then they would divide the stand takings equally. In the event the committee deciding the venue chose Cathkin by 17 votes to 3, it being noted that the two clubs were 'endeavouring to arrange for the monopolization of the combined advantages of finalists and final ground purveyors'. The Celtic representative, William McKillop, frankly remarked that the reason for the proposal was the desire of both clubs to make out of it as much as possible.[46] In 1895 Celtic persuaded Rangers to come to an agreement whereby neither club was to let its ground for less than the total drawings of the stands. The agreement was drawn up on an annual basis with a year's notice of withdrawal under penalty of a £100 fine.[47] The co-sponsorship scheme of 1983 has a long history! A few years later the two clubs would be coming to mutual agreements about the staging of internationals, before the New Hampden eventually took over in 1906.

The two clubs, then, had sound financial reasons to support each other in those early years, as they whittled away at the pre-eminence of Queen's Park and threatened the position of the amateurs in the SFA. For the first three years of Celtic's existence, however, Rangers were singularly unsuccessful in their matches with Celtic, and as playing opponents they tended to be disregarded by them: it was not until February 1893 that they had their first victory over Celtic, when they beat them in the Glasgow Cup Final of that year. Their drawing power could not be overlooked, of course, but in any case the season 1893–94 saw a complete change in the playing fortunes of the two teams with Rangers clearly coming out on top for the first time. On 1 January 1894 they played the first of what was to become the traditional Ne'erday game, and The Old Firm had been formed, although it was still to have the label applied.

'What, you two again!' *Scottish Referee*, 13 May 1904. An article on the same page commented: '... we have a notion that the clubs themselves and the public, not to mention ourselves, would like to see them meet less often, and less seldom monopolize not only gate, but cups'

At the same time the relations between the two teams deteriorated considerably, at all levels. In May 1896 *Scottish Sport* asked testily whether or not it was 'possible for the Celtic and Rangers to meet now, not even in a charity match, without the worst feelings and considerable amount of foulness creeping into the play,[48] and early in the following season, after an exciting draw played before an engrossed 25,000 spectators at Parkhead in October 1896, the reporter for *Scottish Sport* concluded:

> None of the bad blood which unfortunately disgraced more than one of the recent meetings of the two clubs, and even threatened the amenity of a good paying fixture, came to the surface, and it is therefore all the more regrettable that a handful of fools should have sought to cast reproach upon the proceedings by an outbreak of disorder at the close. It was well, however, that they tackled those so capable of dealing with them as the police.[49]

The 'bad blood' was not to disappear, and *Scottish Sport's* warning that if it were to continue it 'would cool the public interest' in their meetings was to turn out to be what historian Bob Crampsey noted as 'one of the most inaccurate prophecies of all time'.[50] Even if they had been merely the strongest clubs in Glasgow at this time, the matches between Celtic and Rangers would have been supercharged with tension, but already the sectarian element was there. In 1896 Celtic and Hibs were top of the Scottish League, prompting *Scottish Sport* to note the dominance in Scotland of two Irish teams and more or less asking where the Scottish team was that could challenge them.[51] Rangers were that team, and bad blood was to prove the basis for one of the most formidable business associations in the history of sport.

At the turn of the century football was irreversibly professional. By that time the annual returns of Celtic had grown from more than £6,500 in 1894 to a British record of £10,142 two years later;[52] and in 1907 a return of £18,884 allowed the directors to pay themselves a dividend of 25 per cent.[53] Rangers were not far behind, with £14,076 in 1908, and shortly thereafter the Ibrox club continually eclipsed its rival at the turnstiles. For both clubs a large percentage of these record revenues was from the games with each other, and the commercial potential of religious and national differences was apparent to both managements. This is not to say that these differences, as yet, were being cynically exploited, but some at least believed that there was a business to be conducted, if not out of bigotry, at least out of conflicting ideologies. Writing for the *Evening Times* in 1940, shortly after he had been dropped by the Celtic management after a 52-year association with the club, Willie Maley went to his first game at Ibrox since he had been sacked.

He commented on the antipathy that formerly greeted him there, remarked somewhat enviously on the impressive stadium that the Rangers support had enabled the club to build, but took consolation in the way that the bitterness that his club and Rangers had fed on had been a great financial boon to both clubs.[54] Bitterness, bigotry or ideology: it is this combined with a sound business sense that sets The Old Firm apart from any other major sporting engagement elsewhere in the world.

NOTES

1. S. G. Checkland, *The Upas Tree: Glasgow, 1875–1975*, Glasgow, 1977, p. 9.
2. *Glasgow Observer*, 6 January 1906.
3. In April 1888 the *Scottish Athletic Journal* took Queen's Park to task for their social exclusiveness, claiming that nothing short of a revolution could restore them to their former pre-eminent position:

> Social distinction in the matter of admitting members must be purged away. It is true the men who upheld the name of the club so gloriously in days gone past had a class connection of a kind, but then they were of the few who played the game. Now everyone plays, and the commonest artisan has the same chance of becoming a great player as the youth who can command a certain social position. [This was not a plea for professionalism, but more for a 'brotherhood of equality and fraternity' such as existed at the Renton club.] We know that in attacking thus the bigotry and sectarianism of the club we are touching one or two of its oldest and ablest members in a tender part, but they must veer round to our way of thinking sooner or later.
> *(Scottish Athletic Journal*, 3 April 1888, p. 17)

4. For some unknown reason Rangers date their foundations from 1873—they even celebrated their centenary in 1973. In fact all early references to the club date its foundation from 1872. The football club calling itself the Rangers played many games in 1872. In the listing of clubs in the official SFA *Annual* Rangers are always listed as being founded in 1872, as in all the early references until well into the twentieth century. This mistake made by club historians has been repeated ever since. It is possible, however, that the club decided to date its foundation from the first general meeting at which office-holders were elected. But this would be a strange procedure: the club was well and truly established in 1872.

The quote used is from a history written by W. Dunlop under the pseudonym 'True Blue', which appeared in the SFA *Annual* for 1881–82, pp. 67–75. This was reproduced in the *Scottish Athletic Journal* (hereafter *SAJ*), 23 August 1887. Another short history of Rangers was included in the SFA *Annual* for 1894–95, pp. 83–86, written by 'Obo'. It is from these accounts that most of this paragraph is drawn.

5. SFA *Annual*, 1881–82, p. 48.

6. *SAJ*, 31 August 1883: letter from Mackay of the Rangers.

7. *Ibid.*, 31 December 1884.

8. *Ibid.*, 4 February 1885.

9. *Ibid.*, 10 September, 1885.

10. *Ibid.*, 14 December, 1886.

11. *Ibid.*, 29 September 1885.

12. *Ibid.*, 17 December 1884.

13. Reported in *Scottish Umpire* (hereafter *ScU*), 7 October 1885.

14. *Ibid.*, 30 September 1885.

15. *Ibid.*, 10 February 1886.

16. *Ibid.*, 21 July 1886.

17. *SAJ*, 23 August 1887.

18. *ScU*, 5 May 1888.

19. *Scottish Sport*, 18 January 1889.

20. Celtic has been much better served by historians than Rangers (see below, pp. 201–04. For the early days of the club W. Maley's *The Story of the Celtic*, Glasgow, 1939, is indispensable. However, it is more a personal recollection than a work of history. The story of Celtic has been serialised in several newspapers from as early as 1912.

21. G. Docherty and P. Thomson, *100 Years of Hibs, 1875–1975*, Edinburgh, 1975, pp. 33, 39.

22. The quote is from J.E. Handley, *The Celtic Story*, London, 1960, p. 62. Morton were the first Scottish football club to become a limited liability company, in 1896.

23. *ScU*, 7 August 1888. On the SFA and Hibs, and Celtic forcing Hibs out of existence, *100 Years of Hibs, 1875–1975*, pp. 33, 42–3.

24. *Evening Times*, 20 June 1931, sports edition. Sixth article in 'Veteran's' 'History of Celtic'.

25. For a while it appeared that the Glasgow Hibs had bought six acres of ground, elected a committee and secured several players whose names had to be kept secret (see *Scottish Referee*, 12 August 1889 and *Scottish Sport*, 9 August 1889). The threat of a rival club was raised again during the dispute with the brake clubs and the new directors in 1897, and again in 1899.

26. *Glasgow Observer*, 12 October 1889. This is quoted *in extenso* in Handley, p. 20.

27. *Scottish Sport*, 17, 20 December 1889.

28. *Ibid.*, 16 September 1890.

29. *Ibid.*, 7 December 1888.

30. The whole episode is fully documented in *Scottish Sport*, see esp. 26, 29 August 1890, 2, 5, 12, 19 September 1890 and corresponding issues of the *Scottish Referee*. See also article, 'The alternative history of Celtic?', by Pat Woods, in *The Celt*, No. 1, August 1983.

31. *Scottish Sport*, 3 June 1890.

32. *Ibid.*, 13 June 1890. Celtic also had troubles with the League: in 1893 they withdrew their reserve team from the Second Eleven competition 'on account of the unfair treatment they received in connection with their Semi-Final Tie with Hearts Strollers last year'.

33. *Scottish Referee*, 1 September 1890. The issue of professionalism also played a part. *Scottish Sport* was an outspoken opponent of professionalism, as was the *Scottish Athletic Journal* which preceded it, yet this journal was prepared to place advertisements for footballers to go south to play in England. Compare this advertisement, in *SAJ* of 5 July 1887:

FOOTBALL—An English Association Club wants good players—Apply, stating record (which must be first class) and terms to Reid, office of this paper.

The advertisement was repeated in subsequent numbers.

34. *Scottish Sport*, 26 August 1890.

35. This whole dispute is superbly documented and commented on by Handley in *The Celtic Story*, pp. 40–57; *Scottish Sport*, 24 January 1896, 21 February 1896. See also the *Glasgow Examiner* of this period for McLaughlin's version of events.

36. *Scottish Referee*, 19 May 1893; *Scottish Sport*, 19 May 1893.

37. *Scottish Sport*, 15 September 1893.

38. See especially *Glasgow Examiner*, 8 February 1896, 19 December 1896.

39. *Glasgow Observer*, 10, 17, 31 July 1897; *Glasgow Examiner* 17 July 1897. The dispute is conveniently summarised by Pat Woods in '1887 and all that— keep politics out of sport', in *Celtic View*, 9 February 1983.

40. *Glasgow Observer*, 17 July 1897 and Woods, 'Keep politics out of sport'.

41. Bob Crampsey gives examples of this early friendship, but implies that it lasted much longer than the first years: *The Scottish Footballer*, p. 20. See also *Scottish Sport*, 9 August 1889, 4 February 1890, 23 June 1891, 6 October 1891, 31 January 1893, for further examples of friendship between the two clubs.

42. *Scottish Sport*, 29 January 1892.

43. *Ibid.*, 31 January 1893.

44. *Scottish Sport*, 2 March 1894.

45. *Scottish Sport*, 21 August 1893.

46. *Ibid.*, 20 January 1893.

47. Handley, p. 43.

48. *Scottish Sport*, 12 May 1896.

49. *Ibid.*, 13 October 1896.

50. Crampsey, p. 20.

51. *Scottish Sport*, 8 September 1896.

52. Handley, pp. 40, 52.

53. *Glasgow Star*, 1 June 1907. In 1897–98 they paid themselves 20%, from then until 1904–05 10%, and in 1905–06 12%. The English Football Association forbade dividend payment of more than 5%.

54. *Evening Times*, 24 February 1940. In his history and in his reports in club handbooks Maley often reveals a mercenary mind.

CHAPTER 2

The Business Basis of The Old Firm

Rangers and Celtic have played each other over 400 times, games watched by about 20 million people in the flesh, and followed through press, radio and later television by countless millions more. The spin-off from these contests is immense. The clubs themselves are in possession of fixed (mainly grounds) and liquid (mainly players) assets in the region of many millions of pounds: Rangers, for instance, have a new stadium (still to be paid for) that cost about £10 million, while Celtic sold Charlie Nicholas to Arsenal in the summer of 1983 for a sum thought to be about £750,000—and that after a steep deflation in the transfer market. In the commercial world these are not particularly vast sums, but in the sporting world they are. In addition, however, there are other industries associated with the game, from field and pavilion supplies on the one hand to custom at the local pub on the other, while the two clubs have been a (mixed) blessing to suppliers of transport of bodies by road, sea and air, and to the owners of the print and electronic media they are the source of news and information that is as important to their customers as their daily bread (or pint).

Glasgow and the growth of football

Football is not just a game: indeed it never has been since the masses started rolling up in their thousands to watch it and pay for the privilege just over a century ago—throughout Great Britain and in most countries going through the throes of rapid industrialisation and the urbanisation that accompanied it. Football was a growth industry in which Scotland, and Glasgow in particular, often led the field.

Within the first years of the new century Glasgow had three of the biggest sports stadiums in the world: Ibrox, Parkhead and Hampden, and in 1909 the *Scottish Referee* was tempted to speculate on the possibility of Glasgow offering spectator accommodation of over half a million: this was to be made up of 300,000 at Hampden, Ibrox and Parkhead; Cathkin (Third Lanark) .was to be extended to hold 100,000 and the new Firhill (Partick Thistle) 60,000. It only needed the 'Bully Wee' (Clyde) to do the right thing and St Mungo (Glasgow) would be tops all round.[1] In view of the eventual fate of Third Lanark and their ground, and the despondency that recently surrounded the fate of Scotland's greatest sports stadium, such optimism rings rather dolefully today. The writer, then, surely wasn't altogether serious, but his flights of fancy had some basis in reality, for until then football had seen continual and spectacular growth.

The first official international between Scotland and England, played at Hamilton Crescent in 1872, was watched by 3,500 people;[2] four years later 16,000 people turned up; and when the big international was switched to First Hampden in 1878 it was watched by 20,000. In 1892 this match went to Ibrox, with 20,000 in attendance; from 1894 to 1904 it was played at Celtic Park, with the exception of 1902, attracting 20,000 to the first game and 63,000 in 1900. From 1906 all the Scotland/England games were held at New Hampden, 102,000 for the first, 121,452 for the second. From that time on, with the exception of the first three games of the 1920s, the big international was never played before less than 100,000 people and in 1937 created the world record of 149,515, a figure that was almost equalled two years later.

The big international against the Auld Enemy has always been the major sporting event in Scotland this century, in contrast to England where the Cup Final has captured the imagination: in 1905 less than 25,000 watched England play Scotland at Crystal Palace, while that same year a record 110,000 saw Spurs become the first Southern professional club to take the FA Cup.[3] In Scotland it wasn't until 1928 that the 100,000 figure was broken for the Cup Final. Not surprisingly this was for an Old Firm game, their first Cup Final encounter since 1909. Rangers won that game 4–0 before 118,115 spectators, ending what for them had been a long drought in terms of Cup success. Before then the highest attendance for the Cup Final had been 15,000 in the 1870s, 18,391 in the 1880s, and 25,897 in the 1890s. Thereafter attendances leapt up: 70,000 for the first drawn final between Celtic and Rangers in 1909, 95,000 to see Kilmarnock beat Albion Rovers 3–2 in 1920. From the 1930s to the early 1970s and the introduction of crowd limits, the Cup Final could usually be counted on to attract over 100,000: in 1937 Celtic and Aberdeen created what must remain the British record when they played before 147,365.

Ordinary club games could not normally match such figures, unless the contestants happened to be Rangers and Celtic. These clubs created a record for a club game in September 1898 when Parkhead was packed with 44,868 fans; an estimated 50,000 saw the Ne'erday game at Ibrox in 1907; and the gates were closed at that ground six years later with 65,000 inside and thousands outside still clamouring to get in. In the boom attendances that came with the first few years of peace after the Great War, in season 1919–20 Rangers' average gate was 30,000, while their four games against Celtic (two League, one Cup and one Glasgow Cup) aggregated 297,000, an average of 74,250. This included 83,000 when Rangers beat Celtic at home in the fourth round of the Scottish Cup. The record attendance for a League game in Great Britain is still the 118,567 who were crammed into Ibrox on 2 January 1939 for the Old Firm fixture. Today, despite the drastic decline in attendances, Rangers and Celtic can still expect a near sell-out for these matches.

The result of this has been a great financial boom to both sides, and the early games between them were as much influenced by financial factors as any other. The *Scottish Referee* cartoon of 1904 with its sarcastic reference to 'The Old Firm' was just one variation of a common theme of the time. Other cartoons would depict managers or treasurers with big grins as they hauled off heavy money bags, or alternatively grim faces close to tears as they looked up to skies that unleashed a combination of rain, hail and sleet: weather conditions not altogether unknown in Glasgow. Journals like *Scottish Referee* and *Scottish Sport* had been advocates of amateurism, and so their cynicism is understandable. But it also fed on the actions and words of managements who allowed spectators to crowd into limited accommodation, permitted games to be played when they should have been cancelled, and who often argued over the division of the spoils.

From the first, as we saw, Rangers and Celtic maintained a close business friendship, but just as teams and supporters were allowing elements of bitterness to creep into the game, greed threatened the peace at managerial level. The first major confrontation came as a result of Celtic's attitude following the Ne'erday match of 1898 when so many fans had been let into the ground that overflows and ultimately break-ins resulted in the abandoning of the game after 60 minutes, with Rangers pressing for the winning goal. Strictly speaking the game then became a friendly, and takings should have been shared. Celtic aroused bitter acrimony when they insisted on retaining the entire stand takings and two-thirds of the ground takings they were due for a League match. Despite the outcry this produced, Celtic stood by their moneybags, and McLaughlin in the *Glasgow Examiner* told the critics of the club what they could do with their complaints.[4]

Similar greed had almost ruined the Scotland v England international two years earlier when 50,000 fans crammed into Celtic Park before the officials heeded the demands from inside the ground to shut the gates. Those inside the ground trying to get a decent vantage point caused

'Nothing succeeds like success'. 'Mr. Secretary Maley: "Leave this to me"'.
Scottish Sport, 24 August 1900

crushing that could only be eased by breaking on to the arena, where
they were pelted by sections of the crowd who thought they interfered
with their own view. The bottles, and the police and soldiers present at
the game, eventually forced the overflow fans back from the cycling
track onto the terracing, and two years later, no doubt remembering the
chaos of the previous fixture, only 40,000 turned up.[5]

The crowds continued to increase, however, and clubs improved their
accommodation to meet the demand. At Ibrox a new wooden terracing
was constructed to house standing spectators, but concern for paying
customers seems to have taken precedence over concern for safety, and
the result was the Ibrox disaster of April 1902. Rangers had won the

right to stage the big international of that year, and 75,000 were packed into Ibrox to see the start of the annual Scotland v England game. Shortly after it began those crushed together in the new stand swayed forward to watch a passage of play, then swayed back, placing great strain on the terracing. Part of the timber flooring at the highest point of the north-west stand gave way and dozens of spectators dropped through a gaping hole, many to their deaths. Spectators then pushed forward in panic, crushing others in their attempt to break on to the park for safety: as a result 25 were killed and over 500 injured. Play was stopped and the players taken from the field, but the Scottish and English authorities decided that it would be best to play the game to a conclusion and so avoid further crowd trouble. For the players, who during the break in play had seen the dead, dying and horribly mutilated brought into the dressing room, what remained was a mechanical charade, which mercifully ended in a draw.

In its account of the disaster, the catholic *Glasgow Observer*[6] could not help making a few nasty inferences. It pointed out that such an international meant an extra £1,000 to the club that housed the event: in this case Celtic's 'splendidly equipped ground, which has stood the test of previous record crowds' was overlooked and 'the Rangers wire-pullers came out on top, and the big match went to Ibrox'. It claimed that there had been complaints about the unsafe nature of the structure ever since it had been opened to the public, and quoted from the *Evening Citizen*:

> Catastrophe, vaguely apprehended, spoken of last week in whispers as a possibility, has unfortunately taken place, and the International Football Association match at Ibrox Park has been marked by an appalling disaster.

It noted that a reader had written to the paper commenting on the vibration of the new structure; claimed, without evidence, that most of those killed and injured were probably people who had never visited Ibrox before—those in the know avoiding the new stand—and concluded that the wonder lay not in the number of killed and injured and the shocking nature of the injuries inflicted, but 'in the multitude that escaped'.

Yet despite the horror that had taken place before their eyes, it was noted that when the game was re-started the fans had climbed back onto the disaster terracing. Some football fans are prepared to take terrible risks to see the game, and most would prefer to take their chances on getting inside the ground, however little chance they have of seeing the game, rather than being left outside. In the many capacity Old Firm games it was not uncommon then—nor is it today—for the disappointed

Ibrox disaster, 1902. *Glasgow Observer*, 12 April 1902

fans to hang around outside, listening to the roars and gauging from the atmosphere how their teams were progressing. By the 1890s football was expanding at a faster rate than the authorities could cope with: if the growth and strength of trade unions in this period was one clear sign of the advent of the common man, with all the hopes and fears this unleashed, another was his incursion into a sport where middle-class administrators feared they might be swamped.

Football and the Working Man

The growth of football as a mass spectator sport was directly related to the industrial revolution.[7] Steam-driven machinery and gas then electrically lit factories dispensed with the seasons: the long nights in winter, the vagaries of the weather, and the uncertain rhythms of sowing and harvest. Now the limits on industrial production were what the human body could withstand or the law would allow. A combination of workers' resistance and enlightened administration gradually improved conditions of work so that ordinary people were able to benefit from cheaply produced goods, with better wages and more leisure time to enjoy them. Improvements came, too, in health and factory conditions, but nevertheless manual labour was long and hard throughout the nineteenth century, and the new time-work discipline meant that the average worker's free time in Scotland was concentrated between five and a half days of grinding work and one day of grim Sabbath observance.

As industrial production gradually took over from agrarian, the drift from country to city accelerated; the population of the industrial centres increased dramatically and, as towns expanded outwards, areas reserved for recreation became scarcer. In these circumstances the discipline applied to industry was applied to leisure, and football, with its meagre demands in terms of quality of pitch and area required, was ideally suited to the new conditions. More than that: to the worker with magic in his feet, football offered a way out of the industrial system; to him for whom the magic was only in the mind it offered a few hours of escapist release.

In the 1850s most workers worked over 60 hours a week, but by the 1870s this had been reduced to a more or less standard 54–hour week, which included *la semaine anglaise*, or the Saturday afternoon off. On the eve of World War I this meant a day that began at 6 a.m. and ended at 5.40 p.m., with two breaks, one between 9 a.m. and 9.45 a.m., and a 'dinner' break of one hour. Work on Saturdays was from 6 a.m. to midday. Office workers usually did not get away until 1 p.m., and most shopworkers had to stay at their counters throughout the afternoon.

The reduction in hours was accompanied by a rise in wages, real as well as actual. In an early study of the wages and conditions of the working class, Professor Leone Levi calculated in 1884 that the working class were on average 30 per cent better off then than they had been in 1857.[8] Weekly wages had risen considerably:

Bulk of builders	30/- to 38/-
Highly skilled artisans	30/- to 40/-
Less skilled artisans	23/- to 28/-
Common labourers	15/- to 20/-

Drawing up an annual budget (50 working weeks) based on a weekly wage of 24/- in 1857 and 32/- in 1884, Levi showed how a deficiency of £3.2.8 in 1857 could become a surplus of £5.19.0 in 1884. This came from some drops in prices as well as better wages, although the cost of living varied in this time: meat, butter and cheese were dearer, while rent was much more expensive, having risen from 4/- to 6/- per week. On the other hand the average worker enjoyed a more varied diet, and bread, sugar, rice and tea were cheaper. Clothing was much cheaper. Levi's 'Workman's budget' included an increase in 'travelling and amusements' from £1 to £3, and in 'sundries', by which he meant 'church, doctor, education etc.', from £2 to £2.10.0. Levi had a serious attitude to life, especially in the way he wanted the working man to lead it. (he considered that Bank holidays and half-day holidays had 'given a taste for a little too much rest',[9] and the purpose of his work was to show that Henry George and the Socialists had it all wrong and that there was nothing to stop the British working man getting to the top by his own labours and careful management of his budget), but his figures, if not his conclusions, have been confirmed by recent economic historians.[10] His calculations leave no room for riotous living, and presuppose constant employment and thrift; but a surplus was possible in the mid-1880s where it had been virtually impossible thirty years previously. This would have produced the odd sixpences that gained entry to the local football match—but not every match, or even every home match, for 6d then was a much bigger slice of his income than the £1.80 being paid by the Scottish fan in 1983.

With the spare time and the necessary cash balance, the working-class Scot was also finding a much greater freedom of movement in the 1890s, allowing a better choice of team to follow. Trains were the first means of mechanised transport, but it was trams that created a revolution in intra-urban travel, as Glasgow spread out to absorb outlying communities. For Glasgow, too, river transport was very important, and Cluthas (river steamers) and ferries had a most important part to play in the early days. Buses and the subway came later.[11]

The rise of the railways was perhaps the most spectacular symbol of the new industrial age, opening up the country wherever the new steel tracks were laid. In the 1880s most people got to the games on foot, and contemporary accounts often remarked on the roads being choked with artisans and others making their way to the game straight from work. But trains played their part, and when Celtic went to Dumbarton in January 1889, thousands were left behind at Queen Street Station, and a thousand or more arrived at the ground too late, to find themselves locked out.[12] Railway officials were quick to adjust to the new demand, and were soon offering 'specials' to take the fans to the games. When Hibs made their first visit to Celtic Park in 1888, their travelling fans had to pay 9/6, 7/- or 4/- for the 65-minute journey; six years later Celtic were advertising 'specials' for their game against Hibs for 2/6 return, the outward journey dropping fans off at Easter Road, the return collecting them from Waverley so that they could enjoy a snack before the trip home.[13]

However, it was the trams that were to provide one of the cheapest and most convenient ways of getting around Glasgow and to its surrounding districts. It was a way out for those in search of relief from cramped streets and polluted air, but it was also a means of drawing thousands of football fans to the big football grounds from the vast population concentrated in the Clyde region. The first horse-drawn tram operated between St George's Cross and Eglinton Street in 1872, and by 1890 the Glasgow Tramway and Omnibus Co. had 233 cars and 2,000 horses. In 1894 Glasgow Corporation took over from private enterprise, introduced electric traction in 1898, and retired its last horse four years later.[14] J. H. Muir, writing his sketch of *Glasgow in 1901*, thought that with the trams the inducement to walk had almost vanished:

> From the start the service has been a great popular and financial success. The cars are large and clean, the horses in their prime. The hours of drivers and conductors have been reduced by half. A halfpenny fare carries one just over half a mile, a penny fare for a mile and three-quarters, while for the maximum fare of threepence one may ride for five miles and a half.[15]

Improvements in service at low cost continued to give Glasgow one of the finest public transport systems in the world. In 1928 Glaswegians could escape to many outlying regions for a maximum of 2d, but even then 'the increase of traffic in our large cities' had become 'a serious problem, both in respect of congestion and mode of transport'.[16]

The electrification of the trams put an end to the river steamers that had been supplying a great service between the centre of the city and Whiteinch. These dozen or so Cluthas (named after the Gaelic word for Clyde) had been plying from Stockwell Bridge since 1884, making eleven stops on their way to Whiteinch, where they arrived forty-five minutes later at a cost of a penny. In the 1890s the north and south of Glasgow were drawn closer together by several ferries, notably the passenger and vehicular ferries which operated between Govan and Whiteinch and served through to the 1960s when they were replaced by the Clyde Tunnel.

The subway system was begun in 1896, but for many years it faced financial problems related to the work under the Clyde, and technical problems related to the method of haulage. In 1923 the Corporation took it over, electrified it, and success was sealed during the Second World War when it was unaffected by black-out restrictions.[17]

To complete the transport network, in 1914 Glasgow Corporation ran a full service of motor buses, bringing an end to the horse 'brakes' that had been so much a part of the football scene until then. Enclosing the top deck must have helped quieten the streets of Glasgow on a Saturday afternoon, but through to the 1980s buses have been the scene of many battles, from vocal exchanges to cowardly attacks on drivers and conductors who took exception to the behaviour of the fans. Indeed the financial blessing of the football supporter has always been a mixed one, providing profits for the buses, trams and trains, but at the price of other passenger's discomfort and often the destruction of property.

Celtic Park was more centrally located than Ibrox, but it was Rangers who were the main beneficiary in the improvements to public transport. John McLaughlin often complained about this, and in 1912, after 40,000 crowded into Ibrox to see the home team draw 3–3 with Dundee, 'Man in the Know', chief sports writer for the *Glasgow Observer*, mused resentfully: 'People sometimes wonder how the Rangers can get such gates at Ibrox, the most remote of all the city grounds'.[18] Rangers no doubt owed much of their good fortune to the tendency of most cities to send their public transport into the wealthier areas, but at the very time Rangers set themselves up at Ibrox there were several transport authorities anxious to establish links with the new ground. By then Rangers were as well supported as Queen's Park, and enterprising entrepreneurs were taking note of the potential source of profits in linking up with Ibrox. At the celebrations preceding its opening in

August 1887[19] it was pointed out that the Joint Line Railway Company had promised to run trains from St Enoch's Station to Ibrox Park for 1½d (although the club had suggested 1d), and that the Vale of Clyde Tramway Company were building new cars which they would run from Paisley Road Toll to Copland Road, with a special line running from Copland Road to the gates of the park for the sum of 1d. The same company would also run brakes from the foot of Queen Street for 2d. The Clutha Company offered to run its steamers to suit the convenience of spectators on their way to the Light Blues' home games. So despite the more central position of Celtic Park, Ibrox was often easier to get to. Even the potential barrier of the Clyde was eliminated, first by ferries, then the subway and later the tunnel: in fact a large percentage of shareholders at the inauguration of Rangers Football Club Ltd at the turn of the century came from Scotstoun, Partick, Hillhead and other suburbs separated by the river. The subway eventually became one of the greatest boons to the Ibrox management, with the Copland Road station dropping fans off right on their doorstep—the subway is of no use to residents on the east side of the city.

In all this Celtic were probably the victims of demographic forces rather than the prejudice of transport authorities, as McLaughlin and others sometimes hinted. It is possible, however, that Celtic did not have as much influence as Rangers in these matters: in 1893 *Scottish Sport* was urging the Celtic executive to bring pressure to bear on the Caledonian Railway Company in order to secure a service of 2d specials from Central to London Road Station, tapping at the same time areas just beyond reach of the ground, such as Paisley Road, Eglinton Street, Gushetfaulds and Rutherglen. It pointed out that Celtic Park was the only big ground 'not supplied with railway convenience'.[20] Three years later the opening of the Caledonian Low Level Railway linked 'all parts of the city' to Dalmarnock Road, which was convenient to Celtic Park, but it was still a ten-minute walk from there.[21] Early in the new century Celtic believed they were the deliberate victims of discrimination by the railway authorities in regard to the amount being charged their supporters for a rail 'special'. As a result they called for a boycott of the railways.[22] By then football and transport were closely interwoven: special services within the city were matched by 'specials' run by railway companies between the major cities. Charter flights to Lisbon and Barcelona were still a long way in the future, but at the turn of the century the idea was already there.

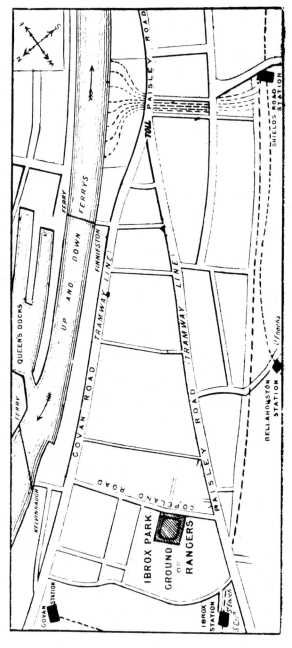

How to get to Ibrox in 1887. *Scottish Umpire*, 16 August 1887

The Press and Football

Transport, then, was an industry whose growth was helped by football and which in turn encouraged the popularity of the game. An even more intimate bond linked the popular press and football. In 1870 the Foster Education Act introduced the principle of free, secular and compulsory education. In part inspired by reformers, it was also a recognition of the fact that industrial society needed a literate workforce, increasingly so as it became more depersonalised. The Scottish Education Act followed in 1872, and although education was not made free until the 1880s, or compulsory until the 1890s, Scotland had had a long tradition of literacy before then. And just as transport got cheaper as demand grew and it became more efficient, so too did the production of newspapers. Conservatives feared the spread of the Yellow Press, as they later would the establishment of radio and then of television, for its seditious political effect. As the popular press became saturated with crime and sport, others might have been relieved that such a diet was more likely to induce a dull apathy or chronic concern with triviality. However that may be, sport, especially football, became an indispensable part of all popular newspapers.

A specialised sporting press was established in Scotland in the 1880s, and before that decade was out many daily newspapers were reserving space for football results, reports of games and predictions of those to come. The *Scottish Athletic Journal* was the first specifically sporting publication in Scotland dealing with football and athletics. It appeared on 1 September 1882, and thereafter came out every Friday, price 2d. Its success was immediate; within a couple of years it was selling 20,000 copies and was able to reduce its price to 1d. By then it was coming out on Wednesdays, to be closer to the weekend football just played, for the concentration of news in the paper was increasingly devoted to football.[23] In September 1886 it expanded from 16 pages to 32.

Such success was not to go unchallenged, and on 21 August 1884 the *Scottish Umpire and Cycling Mercury* came out in similar format and at the same price. Cycling never had the same appeal as football, and both papers relied heavily on football for their news coverage. They might have preferred it otherwise, especially when football threatened to submerge cricket by becoming a year-round game, but they had to follow the demand. For reasons never revealed, the two journals, which had been intense rivals, merged as *Scottish Sport* on 6 November 1888. This came out twice weekly, on Tuesday and Friday, price 1d. Within a short time it was claiming a circulation of 43,000.[24]

The merging of the two journals eliminated one rival, but another soon appeared in the form of the *Scottish Referee*. In appearance the *Referee* was more like the traditional paper with its large format and four pages. It first came out on 5 November 1888, thereafter every Monday 'at noon', costing ½d.

Like *Scottish Sport*, the main concentration in the *Scottish Referee* was on the sporting passion of the West of Scotland: football. These journals, all published in Glasgow, eventually went out of existence, but not because of any waning of interest in football. On the contrary, they failed because they could not rival the daily press, which was able to cover football more regularly, and in particular, in the days before radio, give the quickest scores and match reports.

By the time of the First World War the daily press was becoming the main source of football news, but as early as September 1884 the *Evening News* had issued the first sports special.[25] Looking back on these days from the lofty vantage point of 1890, *Scottish Sport* noted how the evening papers, with the exception of the *Mail* and the *Glasgow News*, had ignored football, but:

> When the evening papers came to see that there was a small gold mine in football, and that a demand existed among the public for the earliest information of the results of matches played on Saturday, a different state of matters prevailed, and 'copy' had to be produced as the match went on and dispatched a few sheets at a time to the printer.

The paper went on to recall the public's reaction when a journalist was sent to London to report Queen's Park's English Cup game against Blackburn Rovers and sent back a column and a half of comment that appeared in the six o'clock edition of his paper:

> The public was incredulous, and many did not believe such a feat possible until they read the morning papers on Monday. The public have since been educated up to this and even greater achievements. Some of the evening papers now send two or three men to London on important occasions in order to supply the craving which exists for detailed descriptions of football matches, great and small.[26]

The craving continued to grow until some papers employed more people on the sports desk than the rest of the staff combined. The famous 'white' edition of the *Evening News*, appearing late on Saturday afternoon, eventually had to compete with the 'green' edition of the *Evening Citizen* and the 'pink' of the *Evening Times*. These papers gave virtually nothing but scores, match reports and league tables. Until the 1950s their sales were easily the best for the week, and could even double the top sales for

The Old Firm at Ibrox in 1898. Before the turn of the century football had found its way into the non-sporting press. Here *The Bailie* gives its impressions of the Old Firm game. Cartoon supplement, 19 October 1898

any weeknight. Many fans were not content until they had read each of the three papers. A marked exception to this was when Rangers or Celtic lost: when they *both* lost there was a marked slump in sales.[27]

If football was the lifeblood of these newspapers, The Old Firm was the lifeblood of football, and any newspaper that valued its sales had to be careful how it reported the affairs of the big clubs. This resulted, particularly in the period before the later 1960s, in a subservience that smothered the talents of good writers who were not allowed to publish anything controversial, other than debating the merits of particular team selections, pronouncing judgements on referees' decisions or condemning the behaviour of the fans. It was not just the big clubs that had to be placated by the omission of controversial material, but the advertisers.

Advertising, like football fans and public transport, or even the capitalist system that it underwrites, has always been a mixed blessing: it has helped create cheaper products but often at the expense of quality. Unlike football teams that often like to see themselves as embodying high ideals, advertisers are less likely to make claims to social responsibility. Newspapers with a crusading bent have often been caught in this bind, some have buckled shamefully before it.[28] The relationship between newspapers, advertising and the two clubs has always been close, as reflected in the *Scottish Athletic Journal's* vendetta against Rangers in the 1880s and Celtic's 'punishment' of the *Glasgow Observer* and *Scottish Sport* for criticising the club in the 1890s. Nevertheless it is advertising that has helped to bring down the price of newspapers and so put them within reach of the common man.

The announcement of the venues for coming matches was one of the first aspects of the advertising side of the press. As other industries grew with the sports craze, so they advertised their wares in the sports and later daily press. Existing industries adapted themselves to the new opportunities created by the need for bigger stadiums, fences to keep out non-paying customers, and turnstiles to let them in at a rate and in such a way that their numbers could be verified. The very nature of the game gave rise to minor industries in clothing and supply of strips, leather for the supply of balls and boots, and nets and goalposts, while grass seed merchants prospered along with the suppliers of grass cutters and rollers. Then came the makers of oils and embrocations which acted as a wonder cure for aching muscles and the hundred and one other ills that quacks thought the sporting body heir to. Increasingly in the 1900s they used a famous player to push their wares, for football players from the earliest years of the game had taken on the aura of stars whose every word was gospel.

Football Mania

As early as the 1880s young lads were trying to touch the clothing of James Kelly, then with Renton, to boast of how close they had got to the great man, and about the same time a Rangers player and committee man reported his horror on finding that in a scratch match being played by some youngsters, each of whom had appropriated the name of some star, his was the name claimed by the dirtiest player in the bunch. Youngsters whose dreams of glory remained in the streets with a tanner ba' were becoming such a nuisance to the authorities that they decided to take action: in August 1892 the first fine under the new Police Act, of 10/6, was imposed on three youths for playing football in the street.[29] For the few whose dreams did lead to glory, the best they could hope for outside the game was managership of a pub, or ownership of a grocery store, tobacconist's or some small business where they would attract customers more concerned about seeing or speaking to the local idol than purchasing whatever wares they dispensed (not that the Glasgow football fan did not take what he received at the pub seriously!).

The whole thing was becoming too much for some churchmen, who feared that the new enthusiasm was deflecting people from the true goal of life—salvation. One minister fulminated against football-playing youths with warnings that there would be no football in heaven.[30] Then there was Nathan Rouse who concluded that since football was not mentioned in the Bible, then it must be the work of the Devil.[31] More often than not it was the swearing, drinking and gambling accompanying football that the men of the cloth railed against, or the evil effects of professionalism. One thing never in doubt was the grip the game had on Scotland's youth. The annual conference of the YMCA in 1890 included among the 'moral and social dangers of the present day in relation to young men': bad literature; betting; billiard playing and cards (the latter prevalent in pubs, streets and trains); shorter hours, which were bad for the character; making pleasure a business; and the 'perfectly sickening' obsession with football. The second last was more specifically related to football, although the other 'dangers' were also part of the football scene.[32]

In 1893, under the heading 'The clerical attack on football',[33] a controversy raged about the effects of the game. This followed the publication in the Glasgow *Evening News* of a letter from a Renton minister who claimed that football had become a craze and even a disease, that its players were being feasted and kept like pet dogs, that young men spent time on football to the detriment of their moral and intellectual nature, and that the game's devotees could speak of nothing else intelligently. In the correspondence that followed, angry letters supported the Renton minister: desecration of the Sabbath was a common theme, for the excitement of the previous day left the congregation fatigued, and they could talk of nothing else, but went over every kick time and time again; they compared notes on Sunday, discussed them again on Monday, and spent the rest of the week wondering about the teams for the following Saturday. Drinking, swearing and gambling were roundly condemned, as was usual, but one writer expressed concern about the physical effects on young lads who worked every day from 6 a.m. to 5.30 p.m. and then instead of relaxing by reading or indulging in social chitchat went out to train. (In fact one Celtic player, having spent twenty-four hours at the furnaces where he was an ironworker, fainted after a match against Linthouse in September 1895.[34]) Of great concern, too, was the increasing manifestation of materialism in sport: a noble trait in one enterprise became a despicable incursion in another.

On the whole the church took the sensible attitude that the game was there to stay and, instead of regarding it as a competitor for young minds, decided to use it as a means to win them over: the leagues organised by the churches and the Boys' Brigade became the most popular and best administered amateur competitions in the country, drawing the best they could from a healthy pastime. It was the 'muscular Christians', after all, who, ball in one hand and Bible in the other, did so much to help organise the game in the new industrial missions. In England several teams, famous today, were founded by individual churches, Everton being the most famous. In Scotland, where Sabbath breaking, drunkenness and pleasure in general were taken more seriously, the role of the church was less direct. Rangers pride themselves on being a Christian club, Queen's Park grew out of the YMCA, and need it be added that Celtic came into being under the auspices of the catholic church?

Whatever the disputes about the merits of the game, or the nature of its grip on the country's youth, its influence as seen in clerical fears, and coverage in the press appeared to be immense.[35] Increased leisure time, however minimal, and improved wages, however far from an ample surplus, put money into a pastime and made it into a business. In the new sporting/industrial economy the rewards to those who could attract most people to their games were considerable. By today's standards, especially since the advent of television and the lure of commercial sponsorship, the financial rewards of sport three-quarters of a century ago might not seem very great, but by the standards of the time they were immense.

THE IBROX TIE.

'Parting at the bank'. *Scottish Referee*, 10 February 1908

The Old Firm Cashes In

Despite the rivalry of the two big Glasgow clubs, they knew that they needed each other. After the first year of professional football, *Scottish Sport* noted the combined income of the two clubs—£12,295.15.2—and concluded that 'Scottish football cannot be described as anything else than a big business'. It noted that Celtic and Rangers had paid something like £3,229.17.8 in wages—enough to support 44 tradesmen at the standard rate of wages for twelve months—yet this amount was paid to no more than 30 players for ten months of doing what was a pleasure. Part of the rub that irked the middle-class journal was that 'many a professional man, many an employer, cannot boast so large an income ...'.[36] Two years later *Scottish Referee* took the trouble to estimate the amount Rangers and Celtic had accumulated from games against each other, especially since 1891, as before then Celtic did not deign to seek out competition with Rangers. The writer calculated that the 33 games between the two clubs had brought in about £12,000. He concluded that 'if the respective managements are not terribly blind to their best interests they will sacrifice a lot to maintain relationships that are so exceptionally remunerative'.[37]

Indeed the two clubs did see this. Before 1910 they played against each other twelve times in benefits for players, six Celts and six Rangers, and when Adams of Celtic was injured in one of these games, Rangers offered their reserve 'keeper to Celtic, and he went on to maintain a blank record in every game he played.[38]

This was a business peace that every now and then threatened to break down, for instance after the abandoned Ne'erday game of 1898 or in the competition for hosting big cup games or internationals. This latter issue came to an end in 1906—unfortunately not for ever!—when New Hampden became Scotland's national stadium. In 1902 Celtic and Hibs refused to play a replayed cup game at Ibrox, and there were other incidents, to be recounted later, that indicated serious tensions between the clubs.

On the whole the business peace won out. If the abandoned riot final of 1909 had gone on to a second replay, as the managements had intended, Rangers and Celtic would have shared over £10,000 for games played with each other that season:

Glasgow Cup (Celtic Park)	£1,198
Glasgow Cup (Ibrox Park)	£1,242
League (Ibrox Park)	£1,725
League (Celtic Park)	£1,081
Scottish Cup (Hampden Park)	£1,958
Scottish Cup (Hampden Park)	£1,710
	£8,914[39]

In the 1911–12 season Celtic had come to the end of their great run of six league championships in a row, and their attendances had dropped so low that their supporters were scolded for this in the catholic press—in one game, against St Mirren, they could not even make the League financial guarantee. Even when Celtic were coasting in to a record six championships in a row, they were losing fans. Tom Maley deplored the poor attendance in a home game against Aberdeen in April 1910 and noted that the Ibrox patronage greatly exceeded that at Parkhead.[40] When the two teams played each other, however, it was a different matter. In the first week of the 1911–12 season, on 26 August, the nine first-division games were watched by 104,000 people, 25,000 of whom were at Ibrox to see Rangers play Morton, while 20,000 were at Parkhead to see Celtic play Falkirk. The following week 104,000 again saw the first division games, the highest crowd for the day being at Shawfield, where 35,000 saw Clyde at the beginning of a good run against Rangers, while 9,000 were at Cappielow to see Morton and Celtic—slightly higher attendances were recorded at Aberdeen, Easter Road and Hampden. The next week Rangers and Celtic were both at home, 30,000 at the former's ground to see Dundee, 18,000 at the latter's ground to see Clyde. Average attendances that week were the same as for the first two weeks. In the last Saturday programme of that year only 63,000 braved the wintry weather, 10,000 of whom went to Ibrox. The New Year's Day programme, however, filled the terracings. Although 71,000 people saw fixtures other than the big match, and so drew in as many spectators as could be expected on a late summer day, 74,000 crammed into Parkhead to see The Old Firm.[41] The game was not a league decider; on the contrary, Rangers were nine points ahead with three games in hand.

The fiscal facts were plain to see: The Old Firm was a sound business proposition, ensuring a guaranteed income regardless of how well or how badly one or other of the two teams was playing. In this century Rangers and Celtic, with a few lapses, have monopolised every aspect of Scottish football (see Appendix). Sound business sense accounts for part of this success, but without the sectarian base that sets The Old Firm apart from other local derbies, the honours in Scottish football and the accompanying monetary rewards might have been spread around a few more clubs. Whether or not this would have been good for Scottish football is debatable, as is the degree to which the management of either of the clubs has, tacitly or otherwise, encouraged this sectarianism: what is beyond doubt is the sectarian nature of the rivalry that gives The Old Firm its unique grip on Scottish football.

NOTES

1. *Scottish Referee*, 30 August 1909.

2. The attendance figures that follow come from: Chalmers Anderson ('Custodian'), *Scotland v. England (1872–1947)*, Edinburgh, 1947; Chalmers Anderson ('Custodian'), *Scottish Cup Football (1873–1946)*, Edinburgh, [1946]; Forrest Robertson, *Mackinlay's A to Z of Scottish Football*, Loanhead [1980]. Estimates taken from contemporary newspapers.

3. B. James, *England v Scotland*, London, 1969, pp. 78–9.

4. *Glasgow Examiner*, 29 January 1898.

5. B. James, pp. 67–8, 70.

6. *Glasgow Observer*, 12 April 1902, p. 7. The *Daily Record and Mail*, in its estimation of the safety of the new stadium, dismissed the doubters:

> As to its safety about which some careful people are concerning themselves unnecessarily, there can be no doubt; the foundations, staging and terracing have been examined by various engineers and show the structure is thoroughly reliable to support the 5,000 tons of humanity which a 70,000 crowd represents ... There is room for thousand upon thousand and no matter where a man may be placed or pushed he will be able to see the game as well from the top story of the huge erection.

(Quoted in J. Burrowes, *Frontline Report*, Edinburgh, 1982, p. 22.)

7. Works on the industrial revolution are innumerable, but for its relationship to sport Wray Vamplew has written many articles in the preparation for his economic history of sport in Great Britain before 1914. See especially his 'The influence of economic change on popular sport in England', *Economic History Review*, vol. 35, no. 4, 1982, pp. 549–67. Also E. H. Hunt, *British Labour History, 1815–1914*, London, 1981; J. Hutchinson, *The Football Industry*, Glasgow, 1982.

8. Leone Levi, *Wages and Earnings of the Working Classes*, London, 1885.

9. *Ibid.*, p. 28.

10. On the improvement in living standards see Vamplew, p. 17; Hunt, pp. 76–7. Levi's conclusions on the 'Relative Improvement of Different Classes of Society' have their own class bias:

> The relative condition of classes in the United Kingdom is by no means immutable. Wealth is attainable by labour and economy, and no class is shut out from the competition. Nay, more, under the British political system there is no right, no advantage, and no avenue to honour, which is not free and open to all alike. Let there be only a perseverance and economy, talent and wisdom, self-mastery and self-restraint, honour and virtue, and the ascent from the lowest to the highest rank, though often rugged and steep, is barred to no one. What is it that the labouring classes should really aim at? Release from labour? A greater amount of political power? Ah, no! The true elevation of the labouring man consists in an increasing energy of his thinking powers, a greater force of moral purpose, a greater culture of the intellect, a greater

refinement of manners and taste, above all in an increasing capacity to repel what is depressing and to attract what is ennobling in his daily intercourse of life.

(Levi, p. 57)

11. See especially the section 'Transport and Communication', by W. C. Galbraith and J. F. Sleeman, in *Glasgow: the Third Statistical Account*, pp. 308–353.

12. *Scottish Sport*, 18 January 1889.

13. Docherty, *100 Years of Hibs*, p. 40, and *Scottish Sport*, 14 December 1894 for advertisement for 'special'.

14. See the delightful series on Glasgow's trams put out by the Scottish Tramway Museum Society, and compiled by Ian Stewart, esp. 'Milestone Events' in *Glasgow by Tram*, 1977, p. 4.

15. J. H. Muir, *Glasgow in 1901*, p. 58.

16. J. Graham Kerr (ed.), *Glasgow: Sketches by Various Authors*, Glasgow, 1928, p. 43.

17. D. L. Thomson and D. E. Sinclair, *The Glasgow Subway*, Glasgow, 1964.

18. *Glasgow Observer*, 7 September 1912.

19. *Scottish Athletic Journal*, 23 August 1887.

20. *Scottish Sport*, 5 May 1893.

21. *Ibid.*, 11 September 1896.

22. Rangers fans were offered seats on the train at 3/6 with no guarantee of numbers, but the railway authorities would not do the same for Celtic. The correspondent complaining about this urged a boycott of a proposed game at Bradford (*Glasgow Star*, 10 March 1906).

23. *SAJ*, 17 October 1884.

24. *Scottish Sport*, 20 November 1888.

25. Crampsey, p. 25.

26. *Scottish Sport*, 28 October 1890.

27. Jack House, 'Changes in the use of Leisure', in *Glasgow: the Third Statistical Account*, p. 611. The catholic press of earlier days, however, was wont to complain that nothing sold papers better than a Celtic defeat.

28. Leading British dailies were warned by advertising agents under threat of removing business not to play up the international crisis in 1938 because it would be 'bad for trade'. H. Wickham Steed, *The Press*, Penguin, 1938, pp. 249–50.

29. *Evening News*, 26 August 1892, p. 4.

30. *Scottish Sport*, 5 July 1889. The other condemned sports included cricket, bathing and swimming.

31. *Scottish Athletic Journal*, 30 November 1886.

32. *Scottish Sport*, 12 September 1890. It should be added that Lord Kinnaird, the aristocratic Scot who did so much for the game in England, was a member of the YMCA and attended the meeting. He was anxious to distinguish between sport and the need to teach people how to use shorter hours and leisure time, and how to keep out the evils of gambling and drink.

33. *Evening News*, March 1893; see esp. 11 March, p. 4.

34. *Scottish Sport*, 24 September 1895.

35. Roy Hay has challenged the influence of football in Scotland in a paper presented to the third 'History of Sporting Traditions Conference', Sydney, Australia, 1979. See 'Soccer and social control in Scotland 1873–1978', in R. Cashman and M. McKernan (eds.), *Sport: Money, Morality and the Media*, Kensington, N.S.W., 1980.

36. *Scottish Sport*, 14 May 1894.

37. *Scottish Referee*, 17 November 1896.

38. This is an oft repeated story, but see G. McNee, *The Story of Celtic: an Official History, 1888–1978*, London, 1978, pp. 229–30.

39. *Glasgow Observer*, 24 April 1909.

40. *Glasgow Star*, 15 April 1910.

41. These attendance figures are taken from the *Glasgow Observer* for the appropriate week.

CHAPTER 3

The Explosive Mixture: Sport, Politics and Religion

No-one watching a Rangers/Celtic game today could come away from it under the illusion that all he had been to was a football match. On the one side of the ground is a sea of green and white, sprinkled with the tricolour of the Irish republic; on the other a mass of red, white and blue scarves set against a vigorous waving of Union Jacks; from one end come rebel songs in praise of the Republic backed up by chants denouncing the UDA; from the other come songs in praise of being up to one's knees in Fenian blood, recalling the glories of the Sash and the victory at the Boyne, and backed up by chants of an uncomplimentary nature about the pope and the IRA. The hatred that fills the air at these games is almost physical in its impact, as Glasgow plays out in bloodless microcosm the tragedy being enacted in Ulster.

Most writers on The Old Firm troubles claim that they began with the arrival of Harland and Wolff from Belfast to establish a shipyard on the Clyde in 1912. Such claims are based on the assertion by Willie Maley in his *The Story of the Celtic* that before 1912 there had been no serious trouble between Celtic and Rangers. In that year, however, 'the rift in the lute appeared, and the Brake Clubs became in the main the happy hunting-ground for that breed termed 'gangster' which has become such a disgrace to our city, and religion became the common battlefield for those supposed 'sports''. He did not mention Harland and Wolff, but 17 years later, then aged 86, he admitted in an interview with Jack House that he had meant them. He claimed: 'These workers had what they regarded as 'religious' ideas for opposing a team which they thought of as entirely Roman Catholic—although even then we were fielding many Protestant players.'[1] This giant shipbuilding firm came to Glasgow with the reputation of having allowed its protestant workers to drive out catholics. As such it no doubt brought many Orange workers to Govan, who in turn took to supporting Rangers. But Maley is not always a reliable witness, and there are many holes in the claim he makes here. He also makes the usual assumption that it is the religion of the players that determines the religious complexion of a club, and is anxious to blame a minority of supporters for attaching their religious bigotry to two teams which are presumably innocent of such taints. In this he has much in common with many other commentators, and both Celtic and Rangers deny the accusation of sectarianism when applied to themselves. For this reason it is necessary to discuss the sectarian nature of the two teams before going on to trace its origins.

Celtic and Religion

The Celtic Football Club was founded for and by catholics, and although it has never been exclusively catholic, it remains a catholic club. It recognises Ireland as the country of its spiritual origins, and although today it has lost all formal contacts with Irish politics, in its early days it was closely associated with the fight for Irish Home Rule. Today the club remains proud of its Irish origins.

It is well known that one of the reasons brother Walfrid, a Marist brother, sought the formation of a catholic football team was to help feed and clothe the poor of the parishes where he worked. But as well as concern for the suffering of the poor, brother Walfrid was also prompted by a fear that protestant soup kitchens might tempt young catholics into apostasy. Moreover he was equally worried about the dangers of young catholics meeting protestants in their place of employment or leisure, particularly during the years after leaving school which he considered the most dangerous so far as 'religious duties' were concerned.[2] A catholic football club, then, could serve the dual purpose of easing the pain in starving stomachs at the same time as it kept young catholics together in their leisure time, free from the temptations of protestants and protestantism. The aims of his helpers may have been more prosaic, but when the circular announcing the formation of a catholic club in the East End of Glasgow was circulated in January 1888, its religious foundations were stressed:

CELTIC FOOTBALL AND ATHLETIC CLUB

Celtic Park, Parkhead

(Corner of Dalmarnock and Janefield Streets)

His Grace the Archbishop of Glasgow and the Clergy of St Mary's, Sacred Heart, and St Michael's Missions, and the principal Catholic laymen of the East End.

The above Club was formed in November, 1887, by a number of the Catholics of the East End of the City.

The main object of the Club is to supply the East End conferences of the St Vincent De Paul Society with funds for the maintenance of the "Dinner Tables" of our needy children in the Missions of St Mary's, Sacred Heart, and St Michael's. Many cases of sheer poverty are left unaided through lack of means. It is therefore with this principal object that we have set afloat the "Celtic", and we invite you as one of our ever-ready friends to assist in putting our new Park in proper working order for the coming football season.

We have already several of the leading Catholic football players of the West of Scotland on our membership list. They have most thoughtfully offered to assist in the good work.

We are fully aware that the "elite" of football players belong to this City and suburbs, and we know that from there we can select a team which will be able to do credit to the Catholics of the West of Scotland as the Hibernians have been doing in the East.

Again there is also the desire to have a large recreation ground where our Catholic young men will be able to enjoy the various sports which will build them up physically, and we feel sure we will have many supporters with us in this laudable object.

Any subscriptions may be handed to any of the Clergy of the three Missions or to the President, Mr. John Glass, 60 Marlborough Street, Glasgow, Dr. John Conway, 14 Abercromby Street, Glasgow, or to J. O'Hara, 77 East Rose Street, Glasgow, or to any member of the Committee, and same will be gratefully acknowledged in course.

The following subscriptions have already been received viz.:

His Grace the Archbishop	20s.
Very Revd. Canon Carmichael	20s.
Revd. F. J. Hughes	20s.
Revd. A. Beyaert	20s.
Revd. A. Vanderhyde	20s.... [3]

Since then catholic representation in the club has remained dominant. Its first patron was the Archbishop of Glasgow, Archbishop Eyre, and subsequent archbishops have assumed a similar role, without necessarily being football enthusiasts.

Throughout their history Celtic have enjoyed the support of the catholic priesthood. Priests were present at the opening exhibition game at Celtic Park between Hibs and Cowlairs, and again when Celtic played their first game, against Rangers: the main newspaper of Scotland's catholics, the *Glasgow Observer*, noted the 'clusters of clergy' who were present at both games.[4] Contemporary cartoons seldom failed to include caricatures of priests among the crowds at Celtic games, and when Celtic were presented with the Glasgow Charity Cup shield for the third successive year in 1894, the support of so many priests for Celtic was commented on by Colonel Merry in his speech inviting the Lord Provost to hand over the shield. He praised the presence at Celtic games of

Sketches at the Match.

The *Referee's* view of a Celtic victory – and the nature of their support. *Scottish Referee*, 24 April 1899

'Catholic clergymen' and invited clergymen of other denominations to identify with the game.[5] Right through to the present time the club admits all men of the cloth into its ground free of charge, regardless of religious faith, but one can be reasonably certain that there were few presbyterians or anglicans among the dog collars that were once so dominant in the stand at Parkhead.

In addition to donating large sums to catholic (and other) charities, Celtic have also allowed catholic causes the use of their ground. In June 1910, for instance, encouraged by the success of several catholic athletes, the club offered Celtic Park free of charge for 'annual athletic meetings to be confined to the parishes of the diocese', with all profits going to 'the sacred cause of charity', specifically the St Vincent de Paul Society.[6] In the 1920s and 1930s open air masses were held at Celtic Park[7] and 27,000 came there on 22 May 1949 to celebrate mass for the centenary of the Catholic Young Men's Society of Great Britain.[8] When the catholic church celebrated the centenary of the Restoration of the Hierarchy in Scotland in 1978, the Celtic management offered the use of its ground to stage the celebrations.[9] Some of the club's supporters showed a commendable absence of parochialism in sharing the sporting triumphs of their team. In 1893 it was reported that committee man Ned McGinn, elated at the club's success in taking the Scottish, Glasgow and Charity Cups in one season (1891–92), wired to Rome: 'We've won the three cups, your Holiness'. Apparently Ned was not too concerned about the pope's manifest problems at that time, most notably the challenge of International Socialism and his attempt to heal the breach with the French Republic, and in a pique at not receiving a reply was only narrowly prevented from moving a vote of censure in the Home Government branch of the Irish National League.[10]

The first committee men and all the club's directors have been catholics, although Jock Stein, a protestant, was offered a place on the Board which he did not take up. The Celtic supporters are overwhelmingly catholic, although not necessarily practising catholics. Celtic players have been mainly catholic, but their best teams have always included protestants, even the odd Freemason: they have also had at least one Pakistani on their books[11] (and this before the Second World War), and for a brief period in the early 1950s there was hope that the Jamaican Giles Heron, the 'Black Flash', might have made the grade. In 1895 a resolution put before the Committee that the first team be restricted to three protestants was rejected. A counter-proposal established that the club sign as many protestants as it wanted. The matter was unsuccessfully raised again in 1897.[12]

Nevertheless the Celtic club has naturally attracted catholics, and its main nurseries have been catholic teams, its main overseas source of players Ireland. In the early days John Glass is said to have looked around on scouting missions for signs of Ireland or the faith in the houses he visited: pictures of Emmet, O'Connell, Parnell and 'other pictures near and dear', and if he found what he was looking for he approached the lad or his parents with renewed courage. On at least one occasion, however, he made the mistake of not looking too closely at a picture of 'ould Ireland', and had to beat a hasty retreat when he saw the bold letters at the bottom: 'No Surrender!'[13] However, while the players are the focus of any football club, they do not determine its policies. This is done by the management and to a lesser degree the supporters, and for Celtic these have been overwhelmingly catholic.

There is little—or no—evidence that the protestants in the Celtic team have ever been made to feel uncomfortable in the matter of religion, but this must have involved a certain tolerance or indifference on their part, for the whole ambience of the club was catholic. The Celtic Handbooks when written by Willie Maley (until 1939) were frankly catholic, as seen on such occasions as the sickness or death of a club member, when sympathy would be extended in the language of the faith: when Frank Kelly, 'worthy son of a worthy father', was killed towards the end of the First World War the wish was expressed that 'the consolation of our Holy Religion may be with all his suffering friends',[14] and when Peter Scarff fell ill in the 1930s Maley asked that he be joined in prayer so that 'He who sends trials may grant him the strength and courage to face the Almighty's Holy Will and meet it as becomes one of our faith'.[15] Maley himself went on an annual pilgrimage to Lourdes, and would on occasions take some of the players with him.[16] When the club went to Aberdeen, a visit to Blairs College, the catholic seminary, was one of the highlights; southern Ireland was the favourite place to visit on summer breaks, and a special dinner put on by the club to celebrate its success in the 1935–36 season opened: 'Let us pray for our Holy Father the Pope'.[17]

The sports coverage of the catholic press is overwhelmingly of catholic sport: this is only to be expected, as other papers cover sport in general and the purpose of the catholic press is to give information regarding events catholic and matters of interest catholic. Indeed one could easily get the impression that the only things Scotch in the early catholic press were the advertisements for whisky. So far as football was concerned, the sports journalists acted as propagandists for Celtic. It was the fortunes of that club which were followed, whether in the *Glasgow Observer* or in the *Glasgow Examiner*, where Celtic president J. H. McLaughlin supplied the football coverage, later Tom Maley, and then the ineffable 'Man in the Know', who, whatever personalities the pseudonym concealed, was consistent in his outrageous bias in favour of Celtic. The *Glasgow Observer*, like most newspapers, deteriorated in quality over the years, especially since the inception of television. Its football coverage virtually ceased in the 1950s, but on the few occasions it raised the subject of football thereafter its interests were still those of the Celtic Football Club.

The biggest change in the Celtic Football Club since their early days has been their diminished social role in the catholic community. Then they provided comfort and excitement to their supporters gathered together in brake clubs, while at other levels of catholic society the Celtic Ball could be advertised in 1895 as the 'only Catholic dance of the season'.[18] Celtic are still the pride of the catholic community, but affluence has weakened the bonds that once united a basically poor people with simple pleasures.

This affluence, too, has severed the club from its origins as a charitable organisation. Certainly the businessmen who took over in 1897 severely dented these fine ideals, but they never dissociated themselves from them. It was said of Tom White, who joined the Board in 1906 and was chairman from 1914 until his death in 1947, that 'he never wavered in his belief that Celtic were founded to cater for the Irish people in the west of Scotland'.[19] The directors certainly did very well for themselves, but whether or not at the expense of charities is doubtful. Certainly in Celtic's first decade catholic charities throughout Scotland and England benefited from their visits. In Stoke in 1892 they were billed as 'The greatest team on earth' when they played in aid of the Hanley Catholic Church Restoration Fund,[20] and the English *Sporting Chronicle* noted the considerable benefits to catholic charities from the Stoke match.[21] Similar praise followed the visit to Manchester to play Ardwick (later Manchester City). There—as elsewhere—'the crowd burst out into wild and prolonged demonstrations of enthusiasm' and hundreds followed the Celtic brake in its 'progress through the streets, cheering lustily'.[22]

By participating in the Glasgow Charity Cup, Celtic were more or less forced to disburse their profits to non-catholic charities, but it has been made a principle by Celtic that they are not an exclusively catholic fund-raiser. Indeed as early as June 1892 the *Glasgow Observer* criticised the club for the 'unfairly small proportion' they gave catholic charities, drawing the criticism from *Scottish Sport* on 21 June 1892 that they were bringing sectarianism into the matter. A year later the *Observer* had more to worry about than distribution of the largesse when the issue of limited liability was brought up. From the time Celtic became a business, charity receded in importance, although it was never to be forgotten. Nevertheless the bonds with the catholic community could only be loosened by this.

Even before then sarcastic remarks had been passed about the motives of the players: Celtic, after all, were possibly the first (only?) amateur football team to go on strike for higher wages (in 1890). The *Irish Weekly Independent* in 1893 remarked sarcastically on 'the brilliant sentiment of Mr Diamond' that the Celtic players 'kicked the ball for faith and fatherland' when everyone knew 'that they kicked for 30s. a week'.[23]

Whether or not the players played for monetary return, they were also playing for faith and fatherland, for the motives (or even faith) of the players were relevant to the countless thousands who followed their progress, whether at matches, through the press or over convivial glasses at pub or social encounter. Many of the players, in any case, were not indifferent to the ideological underpinning of the club: players and directors were intimately and very visibly involved in the politics of the Motherland.

Celtic and Ireland

The Irish origins of the club are even more obvious than the religious, but here the original allegiance has weakened considerably. Celtic play in the colours of the Emerald Isle, their crest is the shamrock,[24] and for most of their history the flag of Ireland, later the Irish Free State, has flown over the ground. When Celtic made their first tour of the United States in 1931, the welcoming committees wanted them to play under the Irish flag and be introduced by the Irish National anthem, for it was as representatives of Ireland and not Scotland that they were seen by the expatriate Irish, who pointed out that Rangers, when they came, played under the Union Jack, rather than a Scottish flag.[25] In the early days the Celts were often referred to as 'the Bhoys' or 'the Irishmen' as much in the catholic as in the secular press; indeed the ultimate accolade for a Celtic player was that he was 'a great Irishman'—and when that renowned Celtic character, Peter Somers, played for Scotland, the catholic press pointed out sarcastically that once you had mentioned his birthplace, then you had mentioned all there was about him that was Scottish.[26] When Belfast Celtic, founded in conscious imitation of the Glasgow club, went out of existence in 1949, most of their supporters' clubs switched their allegiance to Glasgow Celtic[27] rather than another Irish club.

SKETCHES AT THE FINAL.

Celtic v Third Lanark in 1889, the Scottish Cup Final. *Scottish Referee,* 4 February 1889

Celtic were founded by Irishmen like Brother Walfrid, a native of County Sligo, and the men who made up its first committees were the sons of immigrant Irish. Of John Glass, the joiner/builder who was the mainstay of the club in the early years, little is known, except his devotion to all causes Irish. Nor do we know much of Dr Conway, another early committee man, except that he was loved by the poor whose health he tended; but the Colgans were from Belfast, and were big names in the cattle trade; the Shaughnessys were a successful Irish family, prominent in law and the priesthood; the McKillops, three sons of impoverished immigrants who arrived in the county of Ayr in the 1840s, were fifty years later on the verge of being the biggest restaurateurs in Glasgow. The Maleys, the Kellys and the Whites, names synonymous with the history of the club, came from families that were humble, but comfortable. For them and many of their successors, football became the central focus of their lives.[28] The success of Celtic in their first year was one more success story to add to that of hundreds of individual Irishmen.

When Hibs came from Edinburgh to open Celtic Park, they did so to show 'their friendship for their compatriots in Glasgow'. Mr McFadden, a Hibs official, in what was to turn out to be a bitter irony, said that it would 'be a sorry day indeed for the Irish in Scotland when the Irish residents of one city should act in an unfriendly way towards those of another'.[29] The Emerald Isle was the common land, and the ills of the homeland were as real to those born in Scotland as to those who had never left Ireland. At the Celtic half-yearly meeting in December 1891 secretary McLaughlin's report lashed out at the landlord who wanted to increase the rent from £50 a year to £450. 'Being an Irish club,' he said, 'it was but natural that they should have a greedy landlord, and they had one who was working to take a high place among the rack-renters in Ireland.' Tom Flood, moving the adoption of the report, commented on the success of Irishmen in business and positions of responsibility: now they had risen to the top of the ladder in the football world; 'The Celtic team was the pride of the Irish race in England, Ireland and Scotland ...' In seconding the motion S. Henry pointed to the club as 'proof of the ability of Irishmen to manage any concern in which they took an interest': in their club rested 'the fair fame of their nationality'.[30]

If Celtic supporters today can be distinguished by their green and white colours, often with shamrocks and representations of the pope superimposed, changes from the early days have only been of degree and not of kind. The brake club gatherings of the 1890s broke up to the singing of 'God Save Ireland', and at the club's Jubilee Dinner of 1938 'Cead mille failte' was the welcome and 'The dear little shamrock' was

A Celtic brake. *Scottish Referee*, 24 April 1899

the favourite song.[31] At the St Patrick's Day Dinner in 1936 the toasts were to 'The memory of St Patrick' (by Rev. J. Conlon) and 'Our homeland' (by W. Maley), while the words of the Irish Free State's national anthem 'The Soldier's Song' were included in the menu, presumably to bring the proceedings to a rousing conclusion.[32]

No group of Irish expatriates could avoid politics in the late nineteenth century, and the Celtic Football Club, as such a body, were no exception. Irish immigrants and the first generation born of these immigrants were more concerned about the politics of the Motherland than they were about the general politics of their adopted land, and in this they were encouraged by their priests. This was the politics of Home Rule, and while there was a great deal of room for disagreement on how this was to be achieved, there was an overwhelming emotional sympathy for the general concept. The club were involved in such politics from the early days, but informally, through prominent players and officials, rather than officially through the club itself. In this they were perhaps more discreet than their Edinburgh compatriots.

When Hibs beat Dumbarton to take the Scottish Cup to the east coast for the first time, they were fêted in the East End of Glasgow and returned to a tumultuous welcome in Edinburgh where a brake and pair displayed a banner, one side of which saluted the winners of the Scottish Cup, while the other prayed: 'God save Ireland'.[33] There was no concealing the religion or the politics of the Edinburgh club. On a visit to London some of the players spent their free day at the trial of Richard Pigott, involved in forged letters related to a supposed involvement of Parnell in the Phoenix Park murders.[34] Celtic's involvement in politics was less well publicised. But they were involved nevertheless.

Alongside the Archbishop of Glasgow, the first patron of the Celtic Football Club was former Fenian and founder of the National League (1879), Michael Davitt, who was elected patron 'with acclaim' at the annual general meeting of 1889.[35] Davitt, one of the most popular of the nationalist leaders, was invited to lay the first sod of 'real Irish shamrocks' at the new Celtic Park in 1892. He duly appeared, to be received by a speech of welcome from two young lads dressed in Robert Emmet costumes. Whether it was an Orange vandal or a catholic souvenir hunter, the sod was dug up and removed, rousing the wrath of the poet who invoked 'the curse of Cromwell' to 'blast the hand that stole the sod that Michael cut'.[36] When the businessmen took over the club and were faced by a revolt of the brake clubs, who claimed that they had been cheated out of reduced rates on their season tickets, a special editorial in the *Glasgow Examiner* of 17 July 1897, entitled 'Avaunt Factionalism', denounced the charges that Celtic were not an Irish club as 'ridiculous'. The editorialist went on to point out that the Celtic directors had been the chief contributors to every Irish and catholic fund in the city, and reminded his readers that 'they were instrumental in sending a handsome donation from Glasgow toward the Irish Parliamentary Fund. Who else could boast of this?'

This editorial may have been written by Celtic chairman, John McLaughlin, the *Examiner's* fiery sports writer. It is written in his style, but expresses sentiments he was generally less enthusiastic about broadcasting. McLaughlin was the least sympathetic of all the top Celtic officials to the cause of Irish nationalism, and was seldom, if ever, to be found on platforms where that cause was being celebrated. In 1899 he went so far as to speak out against the nationalists and found himself in deep trouble with the Irish community for comments he made in regard to the Boer War. Speaking from the chair at a meeting of the SFA, McLaughlin went out of his way to add his support to a motion which resulted in the SFA contributing 100 guineas towards the establishment of a patriotic fund to help the families of those fighting in South Africa. He claimed to be an Irishman by birth and ridiculed those of his countrymen who opposed the war as 'the ravings of some demented politicians, particularly in the south of Ireland', and questioned whether they represented anyone other than themselves.[37] There was an understandable storm of abuse in reply, most of the critics pointing out that any individual had the right to his own opinion, but McLaughlin was speaking as president of both the SFA and the Celtic Football Club.[38] There were calls for a boycott of the club unless it took action against McLaughlin, and the United Celtic Brake Clubs passed a motion that he be condemned 'in the most emphatic manner' and declared that he would never be given a place of honour in their association.[39] As a result support for the club subsided for a while, and again the threat of forming a rival Irish club was raised.[40] For their part the Board sat tight and rode out the storm. It seems that they did not, despite the demands of letter writers and resolutions of nationalist groups, condemn McLaughlin. It was clear in any case that McLaughlin was a lone voice speaking out on behalf of British imperialism: the other directors were committed to the cause of Ireland, and they and several prominent players were to be found on platforms supporting Irish nationalist causes.

In 1896 William McKillop and John Glass were noted among a large and enthusiastic audience of Nationalists assembled in the Grand National Halls, Glasgow to celebrate St Patrick's Day and make speeches about Home Rule and the release of Irish political prisoners.[41] Later that year these same gentlemen, along with Tom Colgan, were again demanding the release of Irish political prisoners at a meeting held under the auspices of the Glasgow Amnesty Association, the Young Ireland Society and branches of the Irish National League.[42] At a massive meeting in 1901 condemning Lord Rosebery for his betrayal of Irish interests and congratulating 'the gallant Boers who are so nobly fighting the battle of freedom' in South Africa;[43] at St Patrick's Day festivals such as those organised by the United Irish League in 1903[44] or the Ancient Order of Hibernians in 1910;[45] at T. P. O'Connor's tribute to John Ferguson's Memorial in 1907:[46] at all of these the club was conspicuously represented by players as famous as Sandy McMahon, Barney Battles and

John Campbell; directors McKillop, Grant, Colgan and Kelly; as well as other names closely associated with the club, like John Cruden, Arthur Murphy and Frank McErlean.

When Captain Edward O'Meagher Condon, who would have been one of the Manchester Martyrs of 1867 if his American nationality had not won him a reprieve, and the Hon. John O'Callaghan, national secretary of the United Irish League in America, visited Glasgow in 1909, they were met by packed assemblies and standing ovations. At an overflow meeting at the St Mungo Halls, Arthur Murphy chaired the meeting and delivered the opening address, and Celts present on the platform included James Kelly, identified as 'Chairman of the Celtic F.C.', and directors Dunbar and Colgan. At an Irish Club meeting that evening in honour of the 'exiles', there was an even greater number of prominent Celts reported among the notable guests.[47]

Among the many Celtic supporters, players and officials at these meetings Tom and Alex Maley were more frequently reported than brother Willie. But the Celtic manager was no political agnostic. In June 1910 the *Glasgow Observer* reported:

> Mr W. Maley, secretary of the Celtic Football Club, gave a political address in Partick on Sunday last under the auspices of the United Irish League. Although the Maley family are best known by reason of their football fame, the various members of it have always taken a keen interest in politics. Mr T. E. Maley is a constant figure on the Nationalist platforms, and Mr Alex Maley took prominent part some years ago in the affairs of the Pollokshaws branch of the United Irish League, while Father Charles O'Malley, of Ayr, has never suffered his political sympathies to be secreted on the shady side of the bushel.[48]

Along with the Kellys and the Maleys, the name most associated with Celtic is White. Tom White, father of present chairman Desmond, did not join the Board until 1906, when he was appointed to fill the vacancy created by the death of John Glass. At that time he was possibly the youngest director of any football club in Scotland. This success came after a brilliant graduation in law and an enthusiastic commitment to Irish politics and the Celtic Football Club. Prior to his appointment to the Celtic Board he had been a director on the *Glasgow Star*, replacing Joe Devlin as chairman when the famous politician accepted the position of General Secretary of the United Irish League of Great Britain.[49] Later, in 1922, White became a founding director of the *Glasgow Eastern Standard*, and was still with that paper when he died in 1947.[50] White did not allow his position with Celtic to dampen his nationalist ardour, and in 1908 could be found talking on Irish politics at a nationalist meeting at

Barrhead where Quinn, McMenemy, Campbell and Somers—each a current or past star—were present, as well as Cruden and Murphy.[51] At the Condon/O'Callaghan banquet of 1909 he proposed the toast of 'The Irish Party', not just for its promotion of Irish interests, but because it 'indefatigably safeguarded the educational interests of the Catholics of Great Britain'.[52]

Possibly the most prominent of all the Celtic officials involved in politics was William McKillop, foundation committee man, and MP for North Sligo, who died in 1909 and was sent to his grave with a papal blessing from Rome at the request of His Grace the Archbishop of Glasgow.[53] But the link between Celtic and Irish politics is most clearly seen in the person of John Glass, whose untiring efforts to found the club and then establish it were duly recognised in Maley's *The Story of the Celtic* and by the club itself when it granted him 300 fully paid shares when it became a limited liability company. When John Glass died in June 1906, his obituary appeared not in the sports, but in the political pages. Apart from the energies devoted by Glass to Celtic, he had been a founder and member to his last day of the O'Connell branch of the Irish National Foresters, a foremost worker for Catholic Union, a silent worker for the United Ireland League and a treasurer of its Home Government Branch.[54]

And while Celtic players were prominent in lending their names to Irish political causes, Irish politicians were happy to associate themselves with Celtic. Michael Davitt was the most notable of these, but there were others. That same report from the *Irish Weekly Independent* that made sarcastic remarks about Celtic footballers playing for 30/- rather than for 'faith and fatherland', also commented on the club attracting to Glasgow politicians like Davitt, Sheehy and Matt Bodkin 'to kick a ball before a crowd of gaping Scots'. A rather ambiguous remark about the 'Celtic purse' hints that they received donations for their appearances,[55] although one would have thought the publicity would have been worth enough by itself. Indeed the much publicised support of Davitt for Scottish football rings rather discordantly alongside his professed dislike of Gaelic football.[56] This is the more remarkable in that the game so fervently followed by Irish nationalists on Scottish soil was barred on native Irish heath by the Gaelic Athletic Association, a sporting body much more committed to politics than either Celtic or Rangers.

T. D. Sullivan, MP and composer of 'God save Ireland', the virtual Irish national anthem for fifty years, saw his first Celtic game in November 1892. He was fêted by the club, cheered by the players, and in his turn sang a verse of his own song.[57] Charles K. D. Tanner, Irish nationalist MP and Mayor of Cork in 1890, accompanied Davitt to Celtic Park at its inauguration in 1892, and when Celtic went down to London to play London Caledonians in 1894, he congratulated them on their victory.[58] On subsequent visits Celtic were entertained by Joe Devlin, one of the main forces behind the revitalising of the Ancient Order of Hibernians after 1886.[59]

The granting of partial independence to Ireland by the creation of the Irish Free State in 1922 took some sting out of the political issue in Scotland. In the football columns of the *Glasgow Observer*, however, 'Man in the Know' continued to lash out at the blue-noses and the Black and Tans. He claimed, reporting The Old Firm game of November 1922, that the Celtic spirit was seen at its best in Kevin Barry

> who has been adopted by the Celtic Brake Clubs as their patron saint. It was fine to hear the boys on the north terracing peeling out—
>
> > In Mountjoy one Monday morning
> >   High upon the gallows tree
> > Kevin Barry gave his young life
> >   For the cause of Liberty.
>
> And right well they sang it too. The best the rival male voice choir on the south bend could produce was a doggerel parody on a Salvation Army hymn ...[60]

'Man in the Know' was not a member of the club, but he had been associated with it since its inception. His judgements, made in the catholic press, could only reflect the attitudes of the club; certainly it had the means to silence him if it wanted to.

The club has less control over the actions of its supporters or even Supporters' Clubs. In the early days the brake clubs could be used for political purposes, and at the fifth annual festival of the United Celtic Brake Clubs (1900) Bailie John Ferguson, seeing the number of young men and boys present, urged them to be 'true to Ireland as their fathers had been'.[61] These days, however, the club would denounce in the severest terms any attempt to associate the club with Irish nationalism. The Kearny Branch of the Glasgow Celtic Supporters' Association is on the other side of the Atlantic and so even further out of the club's reach. It is also near the centre of the most sympathetic support for the IRA outside Ireland. So perhaps it is not surprising that some propaganda for that cause should appear in some of its official publications.[62] In that case the Celtic management could do little, but it is not altogether surprising that Celtic should attract such associations.

In the early days of the club some political activists were concerned that the Glasgow Irishman's obsession with football was taking his mind off more important matters,[63] and Michael Davitt is said to have admitted that if he saw too many Celtic games 'he would foreswear politics for football so much had it impressed him.'[64] The politics of Irish nationalism was not fought out in and around Parkhead, and the nationalists, within the Celtic club as in the community at large, were bitterly divided among themselves, as the tragic civil war following partial independence was to show. But to the general cause of a free Ireland there was a strong commitment by Celtic and their supporters, albeit romantic and in writing rather than in conviction and fighting. If the Irish in Ireland were oppressed by the English, the Irish in Scotland suffered from the arrogance, if not bigotry of the Scots, and this drew them together in a community where common religion and nationality often transcended economic ills or class grievances. Celtic in those early days, and for a long time thereafter, were the proud symbol of what appeared to be a closely knit community. They entered the sporting scene at the same time as many catholics were making their presence felt in Scottish society, in business, in some of the professions and in local politics. Part of the surge of optimism that carried catholics forward at this time was the success of their football team, where every victory was notched up against their detractors, where every cup or flag won was a slap in the face to the Scottish Establishment. This was a challenge, however, that had to be met. And it was, in the Rangers Football Club.

Rangers and Sectarianism

It is the proud boast of many Rangers fans that theirs is the bluest of blue, most staunch and loyal protestant club in Scotland. This has not been discouraged by the Board, who have been accused of maintaining a practice of discrimination against catholics. Certainly no Board member has been a catholic; nor have any of the managers; but it has been said that the ban also applies to the administrative and cleaning staff, and pools agents have been known to be dismissed when it was found out they were catholics.[65] Above all it applies to players, and rumours—one of them confirmed—abound of the fate in store for any Rangers player unlucky enough to fall in love with a catholic girl. Glasgow Presbytery's newspaper *The Bush* compiled a dossier on Rangers but its contents have never been released, in part to protect the careers of past and present Rangers. *The Bush* left no doubt about its revelations in a stinging front-page editorial emblazoned: *The Blue Barrier*, and opening: '"Are you a catholic?" that's the big disqualifying question to an applicant for any job at Ibrox'.[66] The attack by *The Bush* is just one of many over the past decade, but that controversy is one that is best left to a later chapter. All that need be said here is that under pressure to sign a catholic after the Birmingham riot of October 1976, manager Willie Waddell declared the end to a policy that Rangers said had never existed, while in November 1983, following the resignation of manager Greig and an appeal by sections of the press for Rangers to end their sectarianism, Chairman Rae Simpson insisted that Rangers had never been a sectarian club.

To be a protestant club in a protestant country is hardly something to be ashamed of; most clubs in Scotland are in fact protestant in the sense that most of their officials, players and supporters are nominally at least non-catholic Christians. With Rangers the case is somewhat different. The view has been encouraged among Rangers fans that the club will have nothing to do with catholics. At least since World War I they have not knowingly signed a catholic player. Most Rangers fans and shareholders have been quite happy with this situation, a hard-core element rejoices in it. The Rangers Football Club, then, is widely regarded as not only protestant, but anti-catholic and therefore sectarian. The forces behind this policy and its vociferous support from the terracing are clear in some people's minds: 'Get stuck intae them Orange-Masonic bastards' is a fervid exhortation that can often be heard from a Celtic fan during the occasional silences that descend on an Old Firm match. If neither Freemasonry nor the Orange Order is the force it once was, the Rangers Football Club remains indissolubly linked in many minds with both.

There are few institutions that have been subjected to more ill-informed speculation than Freemasonry. Much of this stems from the secrecy that surrounds its meetings and the belief, not without some basis in fact, that the brotherhood looks after its own and in this way has gained strongholds in many businesses. At least until fairly recently many catholics were wont to blame 'the grip' for blocking their promotion prospects. In fact Freemasonry is not necessarily anti-catholic, although the order has been condemned by the papacy and no catholic can be a practising catholic and an active Mason at the same time. There are many Masons who are happy to include catholics among their intimate friends, but Catholicism and Freemasonry have a long history of antagonism. In the eighteenth century, when the brotherhood still included many catholics in its membership, the papacy condemned it on at least three separate occasions, mainly because it was believed to propagate the subversive notions of liberty, equality and fraternity. In the nineteenth century Freemasonry tended to become more of a middle-class stronghold, concerned about the advancement of the individual through useful job contacts rather than the liberation of mankind through freedom, justice and fraternity. By then catholics were banned from entering it, under pain of excommunication: Freemasonry was regarded as a rival religion at the highest levels, as a devil cult at the more imaginative. On the other hand Masons, professing belief in the Great Architect, could be Buddhists, Muslims or merely Deists, but not, because of the potential conflict of the confessional, Roman Catholics. The antipathy between Freemasonry and Catholicism is quite clear, although until recently the bitterness was being eased. Pope John Paul II, however, in his efforts to return the church to a more mediaeval purity, has renewed the strictures on catholics becoming Freemasons although he has removed the punishment of automatic excommunication.

In Scotland there are more Freemasons per head of population than in the rest of the United Kingdom. In Scotland, too, the mutual antipathy of Masons and catholics is probably much greater, a reflection in part at least of the divisions between protestant and catholic communities. The Rangers Football Club has close links with the Scottish business classes, and both of them operate in milieus in which masonic influences are strong. If Rangers do have a policy of excluding catholics, it is not one that even the most masonic business enterprise would be allowed to continue with today, despite having the means of doing so. In the past this was tolerated, today it is illegal. But then, are Rangers a business? Or merely a football club trying to live in the past? If Rangers do have a blanket ban on the employment of catholics, one might well wonder how such a ban could be imposed other than by an institution like Freemasonry. However, none of this is 'hard' evidence.[67]

In the official histories of the club written by John Allan and Willie Allison one can detect certain phrases and images that can be construed as masonic. In *The New Era*, for instance, Allison talks of 'the clasp of a loyal Ranger', 'secrets ... were sacred to him', 'as the compass his heart was true' (p. 19); 'sacred trust', 'shrine of football', 'true in their conception ...' (p. 25); 'stronger because of the trials overcome' (p. 28); 'a sacred trust', 'no true Ranger has ever failed in the mission set him' (p. 29). And after several repetitions of 'true' and 'loyal' on p. 126 we have 'good and true follower of the club', the 'sacred trust' that is the Rangers Football Club, and the 'mystique of Ibrox'.

One of the principles of Freemasonry is a commitment to silence,[68] a reflection of the secrecy that binds members together. It is this that has given rise to outlandish rumours about the aims of Freemasonry and what happens at its meetings, but it is true that one of the virtues insisted on by Freemasons is silence in the face of controversy. This has certainly been a policy followed by Rangers in the many disputes they have been involved in, but even in more mundane matters no-one could accuse anyone associated with Rangers of garrulousness, and reporters have often been grateful for any words beyond the statutory 'no comment'.

A second aspect of Freemasonry is loyalty to the established government. Freemasons in Scotland would insist that theirs is a protestant country and so they have a duty to that government, which is the government of Great Britain. Through acceptance of the Union Jack as their symbol and the queen as the object of their devotion Rangers' allegiance, ironically for a club which would like to see itself as Scottish, is primarily to Great Britain. At Rangers Supporters' Clubs the queen is toasted, and alongside her the national bard, though Burns's inclusion is more likely to be for his masonic associations that his frequent anti-monarchical outbursts. One other aspect of Freemasonry is the bond of brotherhood that binds its members even when they have ceased to have an active interest in the organisation. Few clubs have retained the loyalty of their staff in the way Rangers have—and this includes managers Symon in 1967, White in 1969, Wallace in 1978, and Greig in 1983, who left at other than their own pleasure.[69]

In the final analysis the link between Freemasonry and the Rangers Football Club can only be inferred. Whether or not these links are formal, it is doubtful if those between Rangers and the Orange Order are. But they are more visible. Relations between the Orange Order and the Masonic Order are not always the most cordial, and it is to the embarrassment of many Masons that the two orders are frequently lumped together. In Scotland a common bond is their attitude to catholics, but while Freemasons are not openly anti-catholic, the Royal and Ancient Order rejoices in being the arch-enemy of the Roman Harlot and all her acolytes. What happens at Rangers' Board meetings remains with the Board, but there is no blanket of secrecy surrounding the feelings of some fans on the terracing, whose songs and slogans echo the faith of the Orangemen of old.

The Orange Order is openly and unashamedly anti-catholic. Founded in Ireland in 1795, it was established in parts of Scotland and other areas of Great Britain where there were large pockets of Roman Catholics, and has a devoted if declining following. Many Orangemen do not fulfil the requirement of the Order that they be practising Christians, and fewer still would care to pay attention to its condemnation of foul language, but none would be unaware of its attitude to catholics. This typical oath, from an American Orange Lodge, may have a familiar ring in regard to the employment practices of the Rangers Football Club:

[that] I will not employ a Roman Catholic in any capacity if I can secure the services of a Protestant; that I will not aid in building or maintaining by my resources, any Roman Catholic Church or institutions of their sect or creed whatsoever, but will do all in my power to retard and break down the power of the Pope; that I will not enter into any agreement with a Roman Catholic upon the subject of this Order, nor will I enter into any agreement with a Roman Catholic to strike or create a disturbance whereby the Roman Catholic employees may undermine and substitute the Protestants; that in all grievances I will seek only Protestants and will counsel with them to the exclusion of all Roman Catholics, and will not make known to them anything of any nature matured at such conferences; that I will not countenance the nomination in any caucus or convention of a Roman Catholic, for any office in the gift of the American people, and that I will not vote for, nor counsel to vote for, any Roman Catholic, but will vote only for a Protestant; that I will endeavour at all times to place the political position of this Government in the hands of Protestants (Repeat). To all of which I do most solemnly promise and swear, so help me God, Amen.[70]

Derek Johnstone is one player who has expressed his surprise at Rangers' attitude towards catholics, but accepts it, leaving such matters to the management.[71] Perhaps more typical would be the attitude of former player, Doug Baillie, now a reporter with the *Sunday Post*, who says the question never arose, but he wasn't silly enough to believe that if he had been a catholic he would have been playing with the club.[72] Danny McGrain tells how his very name was enough to discourage the Rangers' scout who came to look at him,[73] so that one of Scotland's finest full backs had to make do with a team that had prestige as a football playing team but which, to a fanatical Rangers' supporter, had nothing else. Rangers have signed South Africans, Danes, Swedes, Icelanders (even Australians) and prefer to think of their Irish signings as Ulstermen[74]— but they have ignored the many talented catholic footballers who have come on the market.

Like the supporters, Rangers' players have been known to sing party songs in post-match celebrations,[75] and when the European Cup Winners' Cup was paraded around Ibrox in 1972 a senior police officer on duty that night was disgusted to find the Rangers players joining in wholeheartedly with the Orange songs and chants.[76] Jock Wallace, when manager of Rangers in the mid-1970s, is reported to have invited the players on their way up the tunnel before home games to cry out the password 'No surrender!', adding: 'Aye, and don't say it if you don't mean it'.[77] In the early 1950s Rangers' Jimmy Smith, accompanied by 'Tiger' Shaw, was happy to be photographed at a Burns' Supper sporting a tie with King William of Orange emblazoned across its ample breadth.[78] It is hardly surprising, then, to hear that Old Firm games can be played in an atmosphere of hatred, although this is seldom mentioned by players in their generally rosy memoirs.[79]

So just as protestants in the Celtic club must every now and then tolerate or accept the religious undercurrents, so the indifferent Rangers' player must tolerate or accept the undercurrents of Orangeism or anti-catholicism. And just as Celtic offered Parkhead for the centenary celebrations of the Restoration of the Catholic Hierarchy in Scotland, so Rangers have not objected to their ground being used for the annual divine service of the Grand Lodge of Scotland before the 'walk' to mark the anniversary of the battle of the Boyne.[80] As noted earlier, when Celtic went to North America in 1931 they were under pressure to play under Irish colours, just as Rangers were expected to play under the Union Jack, rather than specifically Scottish symbols. When Rangers left for that tour of North America in the summer of 1930 there was a large and excited crowd to see them off. Writing in the official Rangers' history, John Allan recorded the vow of the Rangers players at that farewell: 'We mustn't let these *loyalists* down'.[81]

The Orange backing for Rangers is most clearly seen in the terracings. The symbols of Rangers fans feature King Billy on his white horse, the songs include 'Boyne Water', and less charming ditties like 'I'd rather be a darkie than a Tim ...' Rangers supporters' clubs rejoice in names like The John Greig Loyal, the Strathleven Loyal, the Motherwell Orange and Purple, and their pick-up points are often Orange or Masonic lodges. Large contingents of Ulstermen come over to Scotland for the more important games, and one of Rangers' most ardent sympathisers, however unwelcome he may be, is Pastor Glass, who fell out with the Orange Order because it lacks his standard of ideological purity. The Order itself recognises the allegiance of many Rangers fans, and when a section of them cheered the injury to John Thomson of Celtic at The Old Firm game of 5 September 1931, an injury from which he never recovered, the Order thought it necessary to publicly disown them.[82]

Again just as hawkers selling IRA propaganda set themselves up outside Celtic Park and young Celtic supporters wear scarves with IRA emblems, so it is outside Ibrox Park that the same work is done on behalf of the UDA. When the Sunday *Observer* ran a colour supplement on 'The Defenders of the Ulster faith' in December 1979, the son of Dundonald Brigade Commander Jock McKitterick proudly posed wearing what could be taken to be his Rangers scarf and standing beside a plaque bearing the Red Hand of Ulster.[83]

'Staunch', 'loyal' and 'true blue' are terms of praise for any Ranger: loyal to the colours and true to the cause. When Rangers made their declaration against sectarianism in October 1976 it met with the disapproval of many of these fans, and the failure to act on that declaration is claimed to be because the club is captive to them.

Rangers' Catholics

In a radio broadcast at the time of The Old Firm troubles of 1949, well-known sporting journalist John Macadam asserted that '... a few moronic fanatics have persisted in sticking Catholic and Protestant labels on to Celtic and Rangers, and it is no good telling them that all along Rangers have signed Catholic boys when they wanted them for football, and it's been the same with Celtic'.[84] Thirty years on, one might think Macadam's use of adjective misplaced, but at the time it caused no more than a small flutter in the catholic press.[85] There is no official ban on signing catholic footballers at Ibrox—it is most unlikely that there is an article to this effect in their constitution or the minutes of the club.[86] Nevertheless the unwillingness of Rangers to play catholics is long-established. In the history of the club no more than about ten catholics have ever played for Rangers, and only four of these for the first team, while only one stayed with the club for more than two years. This was Archie (Punch) Kyle, pinched from under the noses of Celtic in 1904 from Parkhead Juniors. He stayed with Rangers until 1908, when he went south to Blackburn before coming back to play for Clyde and St Mirren.[87] Kyle was a very good player, who represented Scotland in two League internationals.

The only other catholics who played for Rangers and made a name for themselves were Kivlichan, Mainds and Murray, all of whom were signed at the time when Rangers were desperately trying to break the run of a Celtic team on its way to a record six championships in a row—between 1904–05 and 1909–10. Kivlichan is the best known of these. He played for Rangers while a student at Glasgow University, from which he graduated with a degree in medicine. He was with Rangers only for the 1906–07 season, after which he transferred to Celtic, but in that time scored winning goals for both teams. Colin Mainds played for Rangers at the same time as Kivlichan before he moved to Third Lanark in 1907. Tom Murray proved to be as much a bird of passage. He arrived from Aberdeen in 1908 but then moved on to Newcastle the following year.

Before this Pat Lafferty had played for Rangers in 1886, J. Tutty in the

1899–1900 season, and Tom Dunbar in the 1891–2 season. Dunbar is better known because he was the brother of Michael Dunbar, who became a Celtic director. The rest of his career was spent in the Celtic reserves, and he was one of the players called up after the Celtic three-man 'strike' of 1896. Joe Donnachie played for Rangers during and just after the First World War. Also John Jackson, who was said to be a catholic, signed for Rangers in May 1917, but he didn't play for them. He moved to Celtic in September of that year where he played twenty-six League games before moving south in 1919. At the time of the Jackson transfer, Rangers, as in 1906–07, were anxious to break the Celtic strangle hold, Celtic having won their fourth successive championship. A petulant 'Man in the Know' hinted at how Rangers were so desperate to beat Celtic that they were 'grabbing more First League players than they can find places for at a time when other clubs have to carry on with any kind of substitutes'. In the same 'Notes on Football' it was claimed that there were enough players around who wanted to stay at Ibrox 'just long enough to share in a victory over Celtic'.[88]

Since then only two catholics have played for Rangers. Of these, the South African Don Kichenbrand, was not a practising catholic, and the other, Laurie Blyth, was a mistake.[89] Unfortunately for the latter it was a mistake that possibly could have cost him a career as a professional footballer. He was signed by Rangers for the 1950–51 season, and at the end of the 1951–52 season, at a time when other clubs were giving out frees by the barrowload, he was the only Rangers player released,[90] although he himself was told that he had to go because Rangers were cutting down on playing staff. One of the ironies of the Blyth case is that he is now a protestant. His father, who was known to the Rangers scout, had been a protestant, but what the scout did not know was that he had married a catholic and his son had gone to a catholic school, a factor which somehow escaped the usually vigilant scout who signed him. Rangers went on with the deal even when they later discovered his educational background—at St Joseph's, Dundee. But the lad was never given a chance: as often as not he was left on the bench. Although he was not a regular attender at chapel, when he went to a Roman Catholic church to be best man at his brother's wedding, the atmosphere was decidedly frosty thereafter. From Rangers he went to Dunfermline, but his heart was no longer in the game, and he quit shortly thereafter.

It would appear, then, that Rangers had no hardline policy before the First World War. Yet as early as 1890 a minor furore was aroused in the Rangers camp when a certain Wylie was accused of lying down in a match against Celtic, and so favouring his 'co-religionists'. After some heated moments the matter was settled—and Wylie himself cleared when it was established that not only was he untarnished with the stain of romanism, but was indeed a 'member of the Established Church choir', and though 'a little strange in his ways' he was 'at heart a thorough light blue'.[91] A storm in a teacup no doubt, but none the less an indication of a certain strength of feeling inside the Rangers club at that time. One other factor that helped steer Rangers in an all-protestant policy, possibly encouraged by the examples of Kivlichan, Mainds and Murray, was revealed to a young catholic lad called Brown, who was given a trial with Rangers in 1912. When he asked why Rangers never signed catholics, he was told that the experience of the club was that any catholic footballer was only interested in playing for Celtic. As a result: '. . . we made a rule that if we knew the player was a Catholic we would not approach him'.[92] There is no doubt some strength in such an argument. Not only were Celtic the catholic club up until then, they also happened to be the best club in Scotland. It is also an indication that in 1912, as in 1890, although there was no ban on signing catholics, Rangers did not go out of their way to sign them.

If few catholics have ever played for Rangers, there are few players who have moved between the two clubs. Dunbar and Kivlichan I have mentioned. In the pseudo-amateur days Jack Hendry moved from Rangers to Celtic, probably the first to do so. He replaced Mick McKeown when the latter, playing hard to get with Celtic, no doubt for higher wages, had his resignation accepted. Hendry, who played a couple of games for Celtic before moving to England, is reported to have said that he would 'play for no other *Scotch* club next season but Rangers'.[93] As mentioned earlier, Tom Dunbar also played for the two clubs at this time. George Livingstone played for Celtic, Manchester City and Rangers in the first decade of the century.[94] The most celebrated case, however, is that of Alex Bennett, a star forward with Celtic between 1902 and 1908, who went on to star in a famous partnership with Smith on the Rangers wing thereafter. Bennett's transfer caused a sensation at the time, but not overtly because he was going from Celtic to Rangers. He had been determined to leave Celtic at least one season before he actually did, and successfully covered his ultimate destination until the last minute.[95]

An even more significant shift from Celtic to Rangers was that of a player who was to become a Rangers director when his playing days were finished. R. G. Campbell had been a star with Queen's Park when the Celtic directors proudly announced that they had secured his transfer to Parkhead in August 1905. His stay with Celtic was not a pleasant one, however, and he barely saw the rest of the year out. He did not strike form and suffered the abuse that the fans save for such crimes; it is apparent that this heart was not with Celtic, and after a certain amount of self-righteous murmuring by the Celtic officials he was allowed to go to Rangers in January 1906.[96]

It is hardly surprising that few players have moved directly between the two Old Firm teams: no major football clubs are going to allow themselves to be weakened to the benefit of their closest rivals. But even when it comes to individuals playing for both Rangers and Celtic at an interval of time, such occasions seem to be few and far between. David Taylor played with Rangers between 1906 and 1910, then for six games as a defender in the Celtic championship side of 1918–19: in the meantime he had played for Bradford City and Burnley. Another case is David McLean, who scored 29 goals for Rangers in that first post-war season, although he had scored only 6 goals for Celtic in 27 league games between 1907 and 1909: in the intervening period he embarked on an odyssey that took him to several clubs. Tully Craig played for Celtic for three years before going to Alloa; from there he went to Rangers in 1923, where he won five caps: he was the last player to move between the two clubs until Alfie Conn moved to Celtic from Rangers via Tottenham Hotspur in 1977.

There have also been some Rangers and Celtic players who have played for the other side in friendlies, and Rangers and Celtic have often played in a combined team against a 'select', usually as a benefit for a player, or to assist a special appeal. In the special rules operating for competition during World War I, Scott Duncan, later to become a Rangers regular, but then having trouble making their first team, played two games for Celtic—as a soldier he did not need his club's permission to play the two games.

The Origins of Rangers' Sectarianism

The arrival of Harland and Wolff Shipbuilding Company at Govan in 1912 no doubt played its part in developing the anti-catholic attitudes of Rangers,[97] but it was hardly crucial. Rangers have always had strong links with the shipbuilding industry, a more or less natural outcome of their geographical location, and it is reasonable to suppose that a large number of their supporters have always been workers in the shipyards and related industries. It is also well known that the shipyards have been a stronghold of protestantism, carried to its most extreme in Harland and

Wolff. As early as 1886 the Rangers secretary Walter Crichton was able to offer employment at the John Elder works as an inducement to potential players.[98] He did so through a foreman at the works. This was a connection maintained by Bill Struth: during the Second World War he was in a position to keep Willie Woodburn and Billy Williamson close to Ibrox through arrangements made between himself and sympathetic contacts in the yards.[99]

It is doubtful, then, if the arrival of Harland and Wolff introduced a new element, although it might have reinforced a developing trend. For a start the total number of Northern Ireland workers, and the number of these who were bigoted Orangemen, could not have been all that significant. Only 3,566 immigrants came from Ireland to Scotland between 1913 and 1920 inclusive. Certainly many Ulstermen came over *before* this period, however, as the same source says: 17,327 in the period 1900–1920 and only 3,655 from Ireland outside Ulster.[100] Not all of the Ulster Irish were protestants, although it is likely that those who were had Orange sympathies.

The Rangers hardline policies probably developed at this time. The early management, although including men of breadth and humanity like James Henderson as first president, and although he was succeeded by a man of equal if not greater stature in Sir John Ure Primrose Bart., were clearly aware of the financial benefits they could gain from their challenge to Celtic, and the clearer the religious lines in these games, the better for rivalry.[101]

The rigid observance of the 'no-catholics' policy seems to have coincided with the rule of Bill Struth. Clearly he did not oppose it. Struth's role at Ibrox coincided with the catastrophe of the depression that blighted the lives of so many working-class families between the two world wars. Until the end of the First World War and for a brief time thereafter there was work for those who wanted it; thereafter employers had a constant pool of unemployed from which to draw. The power of the foreman grew, the vulnerability of the unskilled was starkly revealed. Emigration was one solution, especially for skilled native Scots; the catholic Scoto-Irish were proportionately unskilled, and suffered accordingly. The directors, management and foremen of the heavy industries in Scotland were nearly all protestants, often Freemasons, sometimes Orangemen: in each case their sympathies went to the native Scots; that is to say Scots by name and religion, for they would not have considered a catholic a true Scot.

This clannishness, looking after 'one's own', was rife in the industrial sphere, and was reflected in the Rangers Football Club. Their success at this time was barely challenged: they could pick and choose players as the captains of industry appointed and dismissed employees.[102] More to the point, in doing so they were showing themselves as champions of the protestant cause, and for this they warranted the gratitude, tacit or acclaimed, of protestants throughout Scotland. From this time on any mention of catholics in connection with the Rangers Football Club was either accidental or based on hearsay.

Two such cases involved former Celtic player Tom McInally, and Barney Battles, son of the famous Celt of the same name. McInally, then with Third Lanark, was reported in March 1925 to have been involved in a transfer deal whereby two Rangers, Kirkwood and Chalmers, went to Third Lanark, while he came to Rangers to help them in their bid to win the elusive Scottish Cup. He is said to have visited Ibrox but did not sign because of financial considerations.[103] The 'authoritative source' mentioned in the *Glasgow Eastern Standard* report was not revealed, nor is it certain that McInally was a catholic. If Barney Battles followed the faith of his father, then he was indeed a catholic, for his father was a Celtic star who was also a prominent political activist, and who died prematurely in 1905. The young Battles had begun his career in the United States with a Boston club, and it was while playing with them that he was spotted by the great Tommy Muirhead, who had taken a break from Rangers to help the American club in 1925. When Rangers toured the States in 1928, the bubble had burst for soccer players in search of the pot of gold. Wages that had been as high as $3,000 in 1923 had dropped to $900. The Rangers tour unsettled many of the soccer emigrants, among them Battles. He returned to Scotland, and appeared at Parkhead during the 1928 close season, claiming that Rangers had made him 'a marvellous offer'. Rangers denied this, and eventually he was signed by Hearts.[104] It is likely that it was either McInally or Battles that John Rafferty was referring to in a 1972 article where he claimed that there was 'irrefutable evidence' that in the late 1920s Struth was 'prepared to sign a Catholic player but was dissuaded from doing so by the other players who wanted to have everybody in the club of the same religion'. Unfortunately Rafferty gave no indication of what this 'irrefutable evidence' was, but it is interesting to note that anti-catholic feeling was shared so strongly by the players.[105] If Rangers were interested in Battles, then he was the last catholic they were interested in, unless we include Wilf Mannion—but interest in the brilliant English inside-forward ended when it was pointed out that he was a catholic and that if Struth signed him, he would be 'departing from a long term policy'.[106] By the 1940s the practice was well established: applauded by some on the terracing and upheld without a quibble by the Board, it was, until recently, passed over in silence by the press and the Scottish football authorities.

In fact the real origin of sectarianism in Scottish football lay in the very formation of the Celtic Football Club and their unprecedented success. The success of Celtic at this time coincided with a resurgence of catholic militancy both in local matters and Irish national affairs. Every country with a large immigrant population went through these same problems, but in Scotland there was a combination of features that made them more volatile than in any other country outside Ireland. It was from these factors, deep in the nature of Scottish society, that the Celtic Football Club sprang, and from it the rivalry we know as The Old Firm.

NOTES

1. Maley, *The Story of the Celtic*, p. 29; interview with Jack House in *Evening Times*, 3 February 1955, p. 14.

2. This fear of apostasy is brought out in an article on brother Walfrid, in the *Glasgow Observer*, 24 November 1900, p. 5. See also Pat Woods, '1887 and all that', *Celtic View*, 2 February 1983.

3. Maley, pp. 7–8.

4. *Glasgow Observer*, 12 May 1888, 2 June 1888.

5. *Glasgow Herald*, cutting in Glasgow City Archives, M.P., 26.221.

6. *Glasgow Observer*, 18 June 1910, p. 3.

7. J. Cooney, *Scotland and the Papacy*, Edinburgh, 1982, p. 89.

8. *Daily Record*, 23 May 1949.

9. Glasgow *Evening Times*, 14 March 1978.

10. *Scottish Referee*, 7 August 1893, quoting from the *Irish Weekly Independent*.

11. See the photograph of Abdul Salim in A. Breck's *Book of Scottish Football* (*Scottish Daily Express*, 1937), p. 12; Maley claims Celtic had a Jew on their books (*The Story of the Celtic*, p. 33) and Freemasons (told to J. Macadam and reported in *Charles Buchan's Football Monthly*, August 1960, p. 20). One of their early players, goalkeeper Duff, was said to be an Orangeman, and more recently Bertie Peacock.

12. Handley, *The Celtic Story*, p. 168. See also below, p. 000.

13. *Glasgow Observer*, 7 July 1909.

14. *Celtic Handbook*, 1919–20.

15. *Ibid.*, 1933–34, p. 19.

16. J. McGrory (with G. McNee), *A Lifetime in Paradise*, Glasgow, 1975, pp. 30–1; Maley is also prominent in a front-page photograph in the *Glasgow Observer*, 22 July 1938 heading a procession of the Blessed Sacrament on the return from the annual pilgrimage.

D

17. McGrory, p. 88.

18. *Glasgow Examiner*, 23 November 1895, p. 4.

19. *Evening Citizen*, 5 March 1947.

20. *Scottish Sport*, 4 November 1892.

21. *Ibid.*, 11 November 1892, quoting from *Sporting Chronicle*.

22. *Ibid.*, 30 December 1892.

23. Quoted in *Scottish Sport*, 7 August 1893.

24. Described as a four-leafed shamrock in '*Texaco*' *Grandstand*, vol. 2, Scottish Football League, Division One, London, 1971, p. 8.

25. *Glasgow Observer*, 23 May 1931.

26. *Glasgow Star*, 8 April 1905. The *Star* had secured the services of Somers to report on the Scotland/England international.

27. M. Tuohy, *Belfast Celtic*, Belfast, 1978, p. 49; M. Brodie, *The History of Irish Soccer*, Glasgow, 1963, p. 236.

28. The history of these Scots–Irish catholics warrants a fuller study. What I have gleaned from occasional snippets in the newspapers and some articles merely whets the appetite.

29. *Glasgow Observer*, 12 May 1888.

30. *Scottish Sport*, 15 December 1891.

31. *Glasgow Observer*, 18 June 1938, p. 3.

32. Part of this is mentioned in McGrory, p. 88.

33. 'The Hibernian Football Club', by 'Tirconnell', in SFA *Annual*, 1887–88, pp. 63–7.

34. Crampsey, *The Scottish Footballer*, p. 20.

35. *Scottish Sport*, 21 June 1889.

36. Maley, *The Story of the Celtic*, pp. 15–6.

37. *Glasgow Examiner*, 25 November 1899. Pat Woods brought this issue to light in an article in *Celtic View*, 9 February 1983, 'Keep politics out of sport'.

38. *Glasgow Examiner*, 2 December 1899 (incl. letters to the editor); *Glasgow Observer*, 2 December 1899, 9 December 1899.

39. *Glasgow Observer*, 9 December 1899.

40. *Ibid.*, 23 December 1899.

41. *Glasgow Examiner*, 21 March 1896.

42. *Ibid.*, 16 May 1896.

43. *Glasgow Observer*, 28 December 1901, p. 12.

44. *Glasgow Star*, 28 March 1903, p. 8. T. P. O'Connor the main speaker.

45. *Glasgow Observer*, 19 March 1910, p. 11. Joe Devlin the main speaker.

46. *Glasgow Star*, 2 February 1907.

47. *Glasgow Observer*, 2 October 1909, p. 8.

48. *Ibid.*, 11 June 1910, p. 8. O'Malley was the family name in Ireland, probably changed to make the name more acceptable in a new environment. Only Charles, the eldest brother, kept the original name.

49. *Glasgow Star*, 30 June 1906.

50. *Glasgow Eastern Standard*, 8 March 1947.

51. *Glasgow Observer*, 14 November 1908, article headed: 'Celts in Politics/Nationalist Meeting at Barrhead'.

52. *Ibid.*, 2 October 1909, p. 8.

53. *Glasgow Observer*, 28 August 1909.

54. *Ibid.*, 9 June 1906, p. 16; *Glasgow Star*, 9 June 1906 (front page), 16 June 1906.

55. *Scottish Referee*, 7 August 1893.

56. Letter from Bernard Meehan, Acting Head of the Manuscripts Department, University of Dublin (*Celtic View*, 23 March 1983) in response to Pat Woods' articles on the early history of the club. He was unable to find any reference to Celtic in the large collection of Davitt papers, but enclosed for publication an account by *The National Press* (Dublin) of the Davitt visit to Celtic Park.

57. *Scottish Sport*, 22 November 1892. Written just after the 'Manchester Martyrs' episode of 1867, it served as an Irish national anthem for half a century.

58. See Meehan letter in *Celtic View*, 23 March 1983.

59. See article by Tom Maley in *Glasgow Observer*, 10 June 1911, p. 10.

60. *Glasgow Observer*, 4 November 1922.

61. *Glasgow Observer*, 24 November 1900.

62. Each year this club has a Celtic personality as its guest of honour: it was Bobby Murdoch in 1981. The menu for the 17th Annual Banquet has one full page 'in memoriam' to Mr and Mrs John Duffy, pointing out that they were from 'Rebel Derry'.

63. Handley, *The Celtic Story*, p. 39.

64. *Celtic Handbook*, 1933–4, p. 35.

65. *Evening Times*, 15 October 1976.

66. *The Bush*, no. 51, September 1978.

67. It is significant that perhaps the only article to criticise the club for its masonic associations is an 'underground' publication: see the article 'Falling Masonry' in *Foul book of football*, London, 1976, pp. 90–91.

68. The following two points are taken from an article in the *Sunday Mail*, 29 June 1952, p. 9. The article was sparked by a Church of England clergyman who was reported to have said that you could not be a Christian and a Mason at the same time. The issue was also brought up in the catholic press, where two catholic converts, Gilbert Harding and Mr Maude Q.C., one with many relations who were Masons and the other an ex-Mason, claimed that Freemasonry was not a menace to the church. The eminent members of the Catholic Brains Trust were howled down for their stupidity in failing to see the evil of the brotherhood. The issue was covered in several issues of the *Glasgow Observer* in September 1952. Perhaps some of the most surprising responses to the *Mail* article were from indignant wives of Masons who claimed that their marriages had been ruined by the demands made on their husbands.

69. In April 1982, however, sacked physiotherapist, Tom Craig, threatened to take his case to court, and more recently, in September 1983, Derek Johnstone's

wife told the Glasgow *Evening Times* (9 September 1983) of her bitterness at the way the club had treated her husband. Not earthshaking stuff, but it is unlikely that such criticism would have been published in the Scottish press even ten years ago.

70. *Glasgow Observer*, 9 November 1895, p. 5.

71. D. Johnstone, *Rangers: My Team*, London, 1979, pp. 92–5.

72. *Sunday Post*, 17 October 1976, p. 28.

73. Danny McGrain, *Celtic: My Team*, London, 1978, pp. 7–12.

74. Cf. Allison's description of Billy McCandless in the official history: 'Billy, like all Ulstermen, was never more noble, more inspired or more in his element as when the fight grew white-hot. Not for the bold Billy the easy way out in any game.' (*The New Era*, p. 268).

75. Ralph Brand reported this in an article in the *News of the World*, 17 October 1965.

76. *Scottish Catholic Observer*, 22 October 1976, p. 9.

77. Article by Ian Archer in the *Glasgow Herald*, 22 August 1983, in a profile of then Rangers manager John Greig.

78. Newspaper photograph in the author's possession: date and title unknown.

79. It should be noted that Celtic's Bobby Lennox, a veteran with twenty years' Old Firm experience, says in his autobiography that although he had experienced bitterness against Celtic, this was by teams other than Rangers, and that while he had been called 'a Fenian so-and-so and that sort of thing', such remarks had never been made by a Rangers player (Bobby Lennox with Gerry McNee, *A Million Miles for Celtic*, London, 1982, p. 45). Given the tension surrounding these matches, it would be surprising if both teams were not under the strictest instructions to avoid any sectarian remarks.

80. See *Glasgow Herald*, 6 July 1970 (with photograph). Also *The Scotsman*, 8 July 1966. Ibrox was also used by the Boys' Brigade to celebrate their centenary year (1983). This is an innocent enough organisation in most eyes, and many protestant Scots have spent happy years in its ranks. Catholics, banned by their church from attending the obligatory monthly Brigade church service, effectively could not become members. An extreme protestant attitude was that of the novelist, R. W. Campbell, who was said to despise 'anyone who was not a white, Scottish, Boys' Brigade member' (R. D. Elliott, 'The Glasgow novel', PhD, University of Glasgow, 1977, p. 329).

81. J. Allan, *Eleven Great Years: the Rangers, 1923–1934*, Glasgow, 1934, p. 59.

82. *Glasgow Observer*, 12 September 1931. Maley's response to the accident was scarcely much better than that of the cheering fans: when asked by a journalist whether it had been an accident, he replied: 'I hope so' (McGrory, *A Lifetime in Paradise*, p. 46).

83. *Glasgow Herald*, 27 April 1984, pp. 1, 11. See also fn. 37 p. 162. For a graphic depiction of the extremism that has attached itself to the two sets of supporters see the photos in the German *Stern* magazine (15 October 1981) of Celtic fans with tatooed arms portraying the Celtic Football Club, the Crucifix

and the Sacred Heart, and Rangers fans no less tastefully decked out in jackets with the club colours and Union Jacks as well as drawings of Prince Charles and Lady Diana. The photos might not have lied, but the accompanying article included some of the most incredible nonsense ever written about The Old Firm.

84. B.B.C. Home Service, 24 September 1949. Reported in *Glasgow Observer*, 7 October 1949, p. 7.

85. In the *Glasgow Observer* under the heading: 'Did Catholics Play for Rangers?'. It was from the response to this, beginning with the issue of 14 October 1949, that much of my information on Rangers' catholics comes. I checked all the names mentioned in the 1949 correspondence against contemporary newspapers, and was surprised to find out how accurate most of the information was. Pat Woods has further checked these lists and other sources to finish what is virtually a complete survey of Rangers' catholics.

86. The club refuse public access to their records.

87. In fact Kyle had been signed provisionally for Celtic, and played a few games for them as a 'provisional' (*Weekly Record*, 10 July 1915, article by J. McMenemy). The last reference I have seen to him was when he was given sixty days with hard labour for trying, with another ex-internationalist, to bribe the captain of Bo'ness United in 1924 (*Glasgow Herald*, 5 June 1924).

88. *Glasgow Observer*, 22 and 29 September 1917.

89. Allan Herron says this of Kichenbrand (*Sunday Mail*, 17 October 1976, p. 47). Blyth was given some publicity as a result of the attacks on Rangers' sectarian policies since 1969. See for example *Daily Express*, 3 June 1969; *Daily Record*, 16 October 1976; *Glasgow Herald*, 16 October 1976.

90. See *Sunday Mail*, 4 May 1952, p. 12.

91. *Scottish Sport*, 16, 19 September 1890.

92. *Glasgow Observer*, 14 October 1949, p. 7; Joseph Clark, a relation of Tom White and son of a prominent member of the Holy Cross R.C. congregation, Glasgow, is said to have been approached by Rangers, but he held out and signed for Celtic (*Glasgow Observer*, 27 January 1912, p. 9).

93. *Scottish Sport*, 6 May 1890, p. 9.

94. McNee, *The Story of Celtic*, p. 229.

95. When he wrote his memoirs for the *Weekly Record* (weekly from 1 May 1926 to 7 August 1926) in 1926 he spoke at length about his signing for Rangers, and the public interest that this aroused, but said nothing of religion. It is more likely that this silence was more a matter of incidental press censorship than innocence of religious undertones.

96. *Glasgow Star*, 5 August 1905; 19 August 1905; 28 October 1905; 20 January 1906.

97. It seems, for instance, that Harland's Ulstermen had an annual celebration of their arrival in Govan. The *Govan Press* of 24 March 1922, under the heading 'Harland's Ulstermen's Night Out', reported the 'tenth Scottish–Ulster social evening of the staff of Messrs Harland and Wolff's Glasgow works'. Mr James Smyth in the chair, head foreman riveter, proposed the health of their great employers and launched into further paeans in their praise.

98. *Scottish Athletic Journal*, 10, 17 and 24 August 1886.

99. See *Rangers News*, 10 May 1972, article on Willie Woodburn: 'When war broke out, Willie, like many other Rangers was fixed up with job in the Clyde shipyards so his career was not affected'. Williamson said in the *Rangers News* of 29 March 1972: 'Bill Struth fixed up many of his players with jobs in the shipyards so he could keep them together, and when I reported to Ibrox he told me he had a job for me as a checker in some yard. But I was already at Jordanhill Training College and carried on with my course until I was called up a few months later'. Celtic players also missed war service because they were in 'reserved' occupations.

100. J. E. Handley, *The Irish in Scotland*, Glasgow, no date, pp. 340–1.

101. Willie Maley, *Evening Times*, 24 February 1940.

102. See Cooney, *Scotland and the Papacy*, pp. 18–19: 'For young unemployed Catholics, this was the era of "What school did you go to?" "Were you in the Boys' Brigade?" and "Who was your Sunday school teacher?"'

103. *Glasgow Eastern Standard*, 14 March 1925; *Daily Record and Mail*, 12 March 1925 (article by 'Waverley').

104. *Glasgow Observer*, 14 July 1928, p. 10.

105. J. Rafferty, 'The People at Sport' in A. M. Dunnett (ed.), *Alistair Maclean Introduces Scotland*, London, 1972, p. 217.

106. *Glasgow Observer*, 21 October 1949, p. 7. Of course rumours have continued to abound about some Rangers players who were said to be catholics or, what is just as bad in some eyes, had catholic associations. At the time of the Birmingham declaration it was revealed that a 21-year-old American, Hugh O'Neill, whose family had come from Paisley and whose father was a catholic, had played a couple of games in Rangers reserves that year. He came from Kearny, hotbed of expatriate Irishmen, and it was said that his departure for Rangers had been strongly opposed by them. But no-one actually said that he was a catholic, and his mother was a protestant (*Daily Express*, 21 October 1976; *Evening Times*, 21 October 1976). However that may be, Rangers certainly did not use this signing to ease the pressure they were coming under at that time. Nor did they enlarge on a rather enigmatic statement made by Hugh Taylor in the *Daily Record* the day after the story broke. Taylor claimed that 'Other famous Rangers, if the truth be known, had catholic backgrounds: it was believed that one of the greatest Rangers, Torry Gillick, was brought up in the same environment' (22 October 1976). If there was any truth in these rumours Rangers do not seem anxious to expand on them: one can only speculate on whether the rumours are without basis or whether Rangers are embarrassed by them. See also below, pp. 233–40 for further discussion of the reaction to the Birmingham declaration.

CHAPTER 4

Catholicism, Scottish Society and the Celtic F.C.

There are few countries where the Protestant Reformation was more complete than in Scotland. There every sign, sound and sight of popery was removed from the reformed creed, worship and buildings of the reformed faith; there the adherents of the old faith were hounded with the zeal that only religion can inspire, until only a handful of catholics were left in isolated pockets in the Hebrides, the Highlands, around Aberdeen and Banffshire, and in odd clans like the McDonalds of Glengarry. The culture of catholic Scotland was cleansed out, to be replaced by the austere calvinism of John Knox; the licentiousness and ostentation of the hierarchy were replaced by the severe and uncompromising morality of the presbytery; the authority and intolerance of the papacy gave way to the despotism of a democracy based on the Bible and supervised by the Holy Beagles of the Calvinist Inquisition. If Scotland gained in intellectual freedom, it lost something in aesthetic values, but few Scots would have exchanged their literacy for a love of the arts, which they came to see as corrupt and corrupting. The religion of the Stuarts was the main stumbling-block to their restoration and it was this more than his character defects that doomed the pretensions of the Young Pretender in the 1740s. Even when catholicism had ceased to be a threat, it continued to be hated; Senex tells us that in Glasgow of the 1790s, when the total catholic population of Glasgow was 39, there were 43 anti-catholic societies,[1] and the burgess's oath to that city at the turn of the century included an explicit renunciation of 'the Roman religion called Papistry', making it possible for a Jew, a Muslim or a Hindu to accept the oath, but not a catholic.[2]

If anti-catholicism survived in the absence of catholics, it thrived on contact with them. Throughout the eighteenth century there had been a constant traffic across the small stretch of sea that separates Scotland from northern Ireland. Much of this was in connection with the cattle trade, and those who remained in Scotland were absorbed into Scottish society. With the first signs of the industrial revolution this began to change. The catholic population in Scotland throughout the eighteenth century was probably never greater than 40,000, or 3% of the total. Throughout the nineteenth century the catholic population steadily increased:

1827	80,000	4%
1851	146,000	5%
1900	446,000	10%

In overall percentage figures this is a significant but not a dramatic increase;[3] however, the immigrants did not spread themselves evenly throughout the population. The immigrants of the eighteenth century had come as farm labourers, those of the nineteenth came as labourers in the service of the new industrial expansion. Before the 1840s they arrived in search of work and a living wage; from the Famine on they came as exiles driven from their homeland to avoid death. Set apart from the native population by their clothing, their accents and their customs, they accentuated their differences by clinging together in an environment that was at best strange, at worst actively hostile. In 1841 Wigtownshire had the highest percentage of Irish-born in its population—nearly two thirds—but it was the coal and iron industries of the Clyde valley that made the heaviest demands for labour, and it was there that the immigrants congregated:

Lanarkshire	13.1%
Renfrewshire	13.2%
Glasgow	25%

Within the counties the concentrations were even more significant:

Coatbridge	43.9% rising to as high as 60%
Airdrie	35.6%
Hamilton	31.1%
Motherwell and Wishaw	28.4%
Paisley	24.0%
Clydebank	24.0%
Greenock	31.0%

For many of these immigrants, Scotland or the other parts of Great Britain to which they were forced were just stepping off points on their way to America, where they became more easily integrated into the burgeoning economy of a nation with new frontiers still to be conquered. In Great Britain, especially in places like Cardiff, Liverpool and Manchester where the natives saw them as a threat to their jobs, hostility rose with the numbers: the Stockport riots of 1851, for instance, resulted in several deaths and forced hundreds of Irish to flee their homes and sleep in the fields for weeks. In the Glasgow region, where the concentration of immigrants was even greater and the natives no more welcoming, the situation was worsened by the inclusion among the immigrants of a higher number of protestant Irish, descendants from the Plantation of Ulster and members of the Orange Lodge. The first Orange Walks were held in Scotland in 1821, and 1822, and the majority of members were drawn from these Irish immigrants. These first marches were accompanied by the disorder that was to mark them with various degrees of violence over the next century and more.[4] Nevertheless sectarian violence in Scotland in the middle years of the century was not as bad as in parts of England, particularly Stockport, and the Restoration of the Roman Catholic Hierarchy in 1878 was carried out peacefully, in marked contrast to the hysteria that had greeted it in England in 1850. Scotland's economic buoyancy accounts for this in part, and it has also been suggested that the leaders of the Scottish churches were too involved in their own internecine quarrels after 1843 to have time for external ones.[5] But to say that sectarianism in Scotland in this period was not as serious as in England is not to say that it did not exist. Moreover economic expansion does not last forever, and the growth of the Irish community in Scotland continued at a much greater pace in regard to the overall population than it did elsewhere in the United Kingdom.

If the immigrant Irish had been able to graft themselves on to even a small but flourishing native plant, their progress to security might have been easier. Unfortunately it was often the case that Scots catholics looked no more kindly on their Irish co-religionists. In the 1780s, long before the Irish came to swell the catholic population of Scotland, the vicars apostolic Hay and Geddes specifically requested in their pleas for more priests to be sent to Scotland that none of them be Irish. Highland catholics have in general managed to retain friendly relations with their protestant neighbours. Even those who were forced to leave their native heath were more easily assimilated into those other parts of Scotland to which they were driven. In Greenock, for instance, where Highlanders and Irish congregated in large numbers, 'there was a marked contrast between the easy integration of the Highlanders and the far slower and more difficult assimilation of the Irish'.[6] Again schemes to assist distressed Highlanders, such as the building of the Glasgow–Edinburgh canal and the Caledonian Canal, in fact employed a greater number of Irish.[7]

For some time the native Scots catholics maintained top place in the hierarchy, albeit as Colm Brogan has remarked, like impoverished country gentlemen who had inherited a fortune from a chain of fish and chip shops.[8] Inexorably the numbers began to tell, and eventually the shamrock replaced the thistle on the baptismal font of the pro-cathedral at Glasgow and Saint Patrick's Day took over from Saint Andrew's Day as a day of rejoicing. Catholicism in Scotland was thus confirmed as an alien creed. It was the religion of Rome or the religion of Ireland: in neither case was it Scottish.

It was, moreover, the religion of the lowest classes. In England some aristocratic catholic families had survived the Reformation, and so catholicism retained a certain social cachet. In Scotland they were eliminated, and in the second half of the nineteenth century 'well-bred' Scottish catholics were either new arrivals or converts. This did not make catholicism more respectable in the eyes of wealthy Scots, rather the converts were regarded as double traitors: to their class as well as their religion. One of the features of Scottish anti-catholic bigotry is its intensity among the so-called respectable classes. Beginning with the literary outpourings of *The Bulwark* and of *The Scottish Protestant* from the 1850s and continuing through prominent members of Glasgow University and spokesmen for the Church of Scotland at the highest levels, there has been an unbroken outpouring of anti-catholic vituperation.[9] The Rangers Football Club is part of a long tradition.

Two Communities: Cultural Apartheid

In a rather rosy assessment of the assimilation of the Scots–Irish, the historians of the Church in Victorian Scotland, Drummond and Bulloch, claim that by the turn of the century the catholic population of Scotland was well on the way to assimilation, and that the danger of the West of Scotland in particular going the way of Ulster was overcome; that despite 'the segregation of schools and some tensions at the lower levels of industrial employment no ghetto mentality appeared'. They go on to claim that the second generation of immigrants ceased to think of themselves as Irish, and that any surviving rivalry found an outlet, not in religion, but football.[10] In fact relations between the two religious communities at the turn of the century amounted to a virtual state of apartheid; and The Old Firm, far from reflecting reality merely at the 'lower level of industrial employment', was the cultural expression of divisions that ran right through the two communities. Had the immigrant Irish arrived with the best will in the world, their situation would have been desperate enough, coming as they did with their poverty and disease and uprooted from the only life they knew; but instead they came with a culture and set of beliefs that set them completely apart from the native Scots. And no more than the native Scots protestants could they look to their leaders for guidance in the matter of tolerance, for the immigrant catholics belonged to a Church which demanded absolute obedience not only in religious beliefs, but in politics and social relations. The catholic church was not interested in assimilation, which it saw as an unmitigated evil, but in the preservation of the faith among its flock and the inculcation among them of their duty to convert Scotland to catholicism. The effects of this were felt well into the second half of the twentieth century.

Even without the strictures of the Church, it was the most natural thing in the world that the immigrant Irish should seek out the companionship of their compatriots and take up residence near them, even if this meant forming a ghetto. When they needed comfort and leadership they went to the one source from which it was available: the priest. To these people, illiterate in one of the most literate societies in Europe, the priest was their political leader as much as their spiritual guide. With him they would eventually erect their own churches and schools, form their own clubs and societies and generally carve out a life of their own in their new home. The priest might be kindly or tyrannical, but he was always respected and often loved. Native Scots saw this devotion to the priesthood in a different light from that of the children of the immigrants. They refused to see that the priests had won their reputations by their genuine concern and active work on behalf of their parishioners; they chose instead to see this obedience as the authority of Rome weighing down on the flock, and the accusation levelled at the native Irish, that they were made up of a priest-ridden peasantry, was as easily levelled at the urban immigrant.

One of the main duties of priests in Scotland was to guard their parishioners against 'denationalisation', and the columns of the *Glasgow Free Press* in the 1850s and 1860s often inveighed against the danger of association with protestant Scots who would 'poison and corrupt our hearts [and] make us cold and indifferent about our religion and duty to God'.[11] As we have seen, this was a dominant motive in the founding of Celtic in Glasgow. In Dundee, as W. M. Walker has shown, priests dominated parochial life and exerted an influence that was socially conservative and suspicious of secular influences.[12]

It was this fear on the part of the catholic church that contact with protestants and protestantism would lead to apostasy on the part of the catholic that led to the *Ne temere* decrees (1907), requiring the protestant partner in a mixed marriage to swear that he or she would bring the children up as catholics. For parents who feared the dilemma faced by children who were liable to fall in love it was safer that members of the opposite sex met 'only their own kind'. A further institutional barrier to protestant/catholic interaction was introduced in 1918 when, under pressure from catholics who had been concentrating their political efforts on municipal elections, the Education (Scotland) Act was passed. However just in terms of easing the burden of catholics paying double to keep their children free from secular and humanist interests at school, this act had incalculable social effects. Thereafter there was no economic pressure for catholics to send their children to a state school. For the few who wanted to do so for other reasons, as Father Sydney MacEwan's mother, a teacher, herself well knew, there was the immediate risk of the sacraments being withdrawn. In her case she simply refused to seek episcopal permission. Young Sydney went to Hillhead High, incidentally contributing a fine argument in favour of integrated schools.[13]

With all these influences at work it was easy for Scottish children of the two faiths to grow up in complete ignorance of one another, feeding on rumour and believing the most outrageous lies about each other. Protestants could look with some fear and awe at the procession of catholics to Chapel on Sunday mornings, and feel envious when, their religious observance over, catholics were free to break the Sabbath without as much as a solitary thunderbolt descending to punish their wickedness.[14] Neither at school nor at play need they mix. That great Scottish institution, the Boys' Brigade, was denied to catholics because of the duty to attend church parade once a month. Catholics founded their own Boys' Brigade, but it seems that it was not a great success. By the turn of the century catholics lived in a 'self-enclosed social world, in which the Church had duplicated every movement of Protestant and secular social service and charity'.[15] Catholics had their own clubs, their own sports, and after 1887 they had their own football team to follow.

The cultural and social gulf dividing protestants and catholics was one that could be lived with, and if properly observed, there was little need for conflict and none for violence. When it came to politics and job hunting this was not the case, especially in the nineteenth century.

The catholic church does not pretend to stand apart from politics, and in the century before 1890 it issued several ringing denunciations of democracy, liberalism and all political ideologies that put the people before God. By the 1890s its fear of socialism forced it to think of the poor and the seductive baits being offered by the enemies of property. This directed the Church towards a more realistic approach to the Social Question, which however conservative in intention and paternalistic in effect, eventually paved the way for catholics to join the Labour Party without fear for their eternal souls. But in the latter part of the nineteenth century, and until the creation of the Irish Free State in 1922, the dominant political issue for all Irish catholics in Scotland was Home Rule. As we have seen, this was a cause that was embraced, however discreetly, by the Celtic Football Club. It was a cause, too, to which some protestants were attracted. However, Home Rule for Ireland was not an issue that excited the sympathy of most Scots, who, if they found the Irishman's religion detestable, saw his politics as irrelevant.

More immediate than the conflict over religion or politics was the conflict over jobs. For the same reasons as the bosses welcomed the Irish, they were hated by the natives. The Irish were accused of accepting lower wages, and as the trade union movement got under way they were accused of acting as strike-breakers. There is contradictory evidence on this last point,[16] and exaggeration on the other, but regardless of the facts later discovered by historians, and the exaggeration of the time, the native Scottish workers did have some reason to be worried. For those Irish who saw Scotland as a temporary stopover on the way to America, money in the bank was the main aim, and in such circumstances catholics were unwilling to conform, for instance, to the Union strategy of 'the wee darg', a form of 'go slow' or 'work to rule'; for this they might be denounced for working too hard! Since most catholic Irish came from an agricultural economy, where barter prevailed, many accepted low wages unaware that they were undercutting other workers. Union power is strongest when there are more jobs than men to fill them; despite the industrial expansion of the nineteenth century this was not always the case, and in times of recession the immigrants were a ready target for the frustration of the unemployed. Even in good times the threat of 'bringing in the Irish' could be an effective weapon in weakening the bargaining power of the workers.

The catholics were not alone in weakening the trade union movement of course. Neither the protestant unionists nor the catholic unionists had the support of their Church, the Church of Scotland being as suspicious of organised labour and the threat it represented to established society as the Church of Rome. In terms of cynical exploitation of sectarian differences, however, Orange bosses were without peer.[17] Of course there were not many big catholic employers in the nineteenth century, and even well into the twentieth. Sectarianism in Scotland, with its underlying appeal to nationalism on both sides, has served as a convenient diversion from class differences.

Whatever the contribution of the immigrant Irish to working-class political organisation, there can be no denying their contribution to the industrial progress of Scotland in the second half of the nineteenth century. It was they, very often, who took on the dirtiest jobs: navvies on the railway networks and other giant construction works such as the Loch Katrine reservoir, then in the mines of central Scotland and the factories springing up everywhere, such as the jute mills in Dundee. From such positions they started the race to respectability behind the native

Scot; often they didn't even bother to join in, for 'getting on' was not imprinted on the minds of young Irishmen as it was in the land of John Knox and Samuel Smiles. Many would break through, and by the turn of the century middle-class catholics were well on their way up the social ladder, but the working-class catholics as a whole tended to be left at the bottom of the economic slag-heap. Even into the twentieth century when middle-class catholics were making inroads into most professions and previous protestant strongholds, working-class catholics of Irish descent did not do as well as their protestant equivalents. Discrimination was only part of this picture: education was more important, being tied as it was to catholic religious values. Priests and parents were equally determined that catholic children be educated in catholic schools, and the former were wary of the challenge to their authority that might come from reading that was not strictly controlled. Moreover many catholic parents (and very often priests) were poorly educated and so attached little importance to education themselves.

Cut off from protestant Scots, as they were by religion, politics, cultural pursuits and job opportunities, the Scoto-Irish were faced by a social snobbery that verged at times on racial arrogance, caricatured on occasions as the Apes so beloved of some (mainly English) Victorian cartoonists.[18] Far from being assimilated, which they would not have wanted in any case, the Scoto-Irish at the turn of the century were living in virtual social and cultural apartheid.

Clearly, then, Celtic and Rangers did not create sectarian division, but were instead among its consequences. A series of historical factors came together to ensure that religious antagonisms in Scotland would be more bitter and divisive than elsewhere outside Ireland. For the same reasons religious antagonisms in English football have not developed into sectarian divides. Everton and Liverpool appear not to have encouraged the sectarianism that some of their supporters associated with the two clubs, and eventually the two managers were happy to see the remnants wiped out,[19] while the catholicism of Manchester United has never been loudly proclaimed.[20] Liverpool, Manchester, Birmingham and Cardiff all had large Irish communities, but none of them produced an Irish football club as strong as Edinburgh Hibs or Dundee Harp, let alone Glasgow Celtic. In historical developments great events seldom emerge out of trivial incidents, but in the history of football clubs a single, energetic individual can often play a dominant and influential role. In Scotland deep historical currents met an energetic group of individuals who happened to be fanatical football enthusiasts, and the result was Glasgow Celtic, the most explosively successful club in the history of the game.

THE SCOTTISH "YELLOW PERIL."

A Catholic View of the Orangemen. 'The "Yellow Peril" of Scotland made itself felt in some of the mining villages of the West of Scotland, on Saturday last, when the "Loyal" Orangemen of Anderston invaded Auchinstarry and Kilsyth, and left a trail of wounded women and children behind them' *Glasgow Star and Examiner*, 22 April 1905

Contrary historical currents determined that there should be a reaction to this success, and this turned out to be Rangers. Thereafter the clubs could have maintained religious affiliations without becoming sectarian, but determined individuals in both clubs and larger historical forces were to ensure that this would not be the case.

St. Mungo — 'Go in and win my children the flag will not go out of the family whatever happens.'

The *Referee's* view of an Irishman. *Scottish Referee*, 17 February 1905

Celtic/Rangers and Social Status[21]

That Celtic and Rangers represent a microcosm of a particular aspect of Scottish society is reflected in the social composition of the two clubs. Celtic's first Board of Directors (1897) was made up of six publicans and one builder; the first Rangers Board (1899), by contrast, was made up of two wealthy employers (a carriage hirer and a house factor), some white collar workers (cashier, commission agent, manufacturer's clerk and insurance secretary) and one skilled tradesman (a fitter). Celtic's earliest patrons were the Archbishop of Glasgow and a radical politician; Rangers, on the other hand, had Sir John Ure Primrose (who later became chairman), and he was succeeded by the millionaire grandson of the founder of Burmah Oil, Sir John Cargill.

The contrast is no less striking when the social composition of the nominal owners of the two clubs, the shareholders, is considered. Although 224 people held original shares in Celtic, 92 per cent of these shares were held by only 50 people, and of that number 43 per cent of the shares were held by people in the wine trade, usually publicans. Of these major shareholders, 'managers' and 'agents/salesmen' of various types represented 19 per cent each; the next major occupational category was 'professional' (7 per cent), closely followed by shopkeepers (6 per cent) and skilled or semi-skilled workers (5 per cent). Among these major shareholders there was also one clerk and one 'labourer'.

The spread of all Rangers shareholders is much wider. Of their original 752 shareholders, about 75 per cent had only a single £5 share. Of the bigger shareholders, people claiming to be 'manufacturers/merchants/managers' had substantial holdings, but there was no dominance of a single group such as the predominance of publicans with Celtic.

When the entire range of the shareholders of both clubs is considered, the differences are equally striking. This reduces the total Celtic shareholding in the drink trade to 14 per cent, but it is still twice the equivalent figure for Rangers. Rangers had much larger percentages of shareholders in the managerial (8:1), professional (12:6) and clerical (21:5.5) brackets; Celtic in shopkeepers (4:17) and 'labourers' (0.4:11). For both clubs the biggest occupational groupings are skilled and semi-skilled: 39 per cent for Rangers, 37 per cent for Celtic. Of Rangers' shareholders in this category, however, 31 per cent were in skilled jobs, mostly associated with shipbuilding (such as riveters and welders) and allied industries. Only 8 per cent were classified as 'semi-skilled'. Separating semi-skilled from labourers among the Celtic shareholders is more difficult, as 'gas workers' or 'iron workers' could be either, but even if these are taken to be semi-skilled (and not 'labourers'), the figure of 37 per cent divides into 19 per cent skilled and 18 per cent semi-skilled.

Two other statistics are worth pointing out: of the Rangers' shareholders, 4 per cent claimed to be foremen of one sort or another, none among the Celtic shareholders did. On the other hand only 0.5 per cent Rangers shareholders admitted to being 'labourers', while 11 per cent of Celtic shareholders accepted this lowly title. It might also be noted that one Celtic shareholder claimed to be a 'gentleman', against three for Rangers, in both cases about 0.5 per cent.

Both clubs increased their shareholdings soon after they had become limited liability companies, but most new shares were brought up by existing shareholders.

These figures are not very surprising. The liquor trade and other retail outlets were among the few opportunities available to newcomers, especially in the case of catholics whose Church was never very strong in its condemnation of drink. Of the Celtic shopkeepers, four shareholders were pawnbrokers, another outlet associated with poor immigrant groups. The concentration of forge workers, gas workers and labourers is no doubt directly related to the Parkhead Forge, and the Glasgow Gas Supply Company which provided so much work for those who lived near Celtic Park. At this time almost all of the Celtic shareholders lived within a small radius of the ground. Nor is it surprising that Rangers' shareholders, both at white collar and blue collar level, were concentrated in the field of shipbuilding. Rangers drew their shareholders from a wider geographical distribution than Celtic, but the vast majority came from the more fashionable south and west of the city.

These figures, had they been available to the public then, could only have served to reinforce what prejudiced eyes could see for themselves. The managers and professionals of the Rangers could look down on the publicans of the Celtic; their clerks might even cock a snoot at their shopkeepers; their foremen and skilled workers would almost certainly have regarded themselves as superior to the ironworkers, gasworkers and labourers of the immigrant Irish. All in all we can see here the basis of that arrogance that has been a feature of the 'We Arra People" brigade ever since.

Prejudice or Paranoia?

While arrogance stands out as one of the features of the Rangers club and its supporters, paranoia belongs peculiarly to Celtic. Nearly every writer on behalf of the Celtic Football Club, from the first journalists in the *Observer*, the *Examiner* and the *Star*, directors in articles contributed to official handbooks, Maley in *The Story of the Celtic* and Kelly in his *Celtic*, as well as historians like Handley and the most recent history of the club by Gerry McNee: all have complained about how Celtic has had to suffer the wilful prejudice of the Scottish football public, the press and the Scottish football authorities. These comments apply in particular to the early days, but most Celtic supporters will tell you that they apply even today. Celtic supporters, like the catholic community in general, have generally been unable to recognise their own part in generating the prejudice that they have undoubtedly had to face. By a too easy cry of 'Foul!' they have enveloped themselves in a persecution complex instead of seeking explanations for the antagonism they aroused.

The crudest expression of this fear is the belief that every referee in Scotland has it in for Celtic, but the villain that has occupied centre stage has usually been the Scottish Football Association, castigated in no uncertain terms by McLaughlin in the 1890s, Willie Maley throughout his long career, and Sir Robert Kelly when nearing the end of his in the 1960s.

Football authorities, like authorities everywhere, tend to be conservative. The debate over professionalism in Scotland, as elsewhere, was marked by hypocrisy, but in Scotland it was more protracted. Full credit must go to McLaughlin of Celtic for cutting through the shamateurism and bringing payment into the open, but the indignation of the Association at being forced to accept professionalism, which many of its members found abhorrent, however hidebound it may have been, was not necessarily bigotry. In the Old Renton affair, Celtic played against professionals knowing they were flouting the rules. Celtic's disputes with the Glasgow Association verged on simple bad sportsmanship, although it should be pointed out that most clubs in those days were less bound to accept the decisions of the referee, and every year the SFA was plagued with protests, so much so that someone was eventually moved to write 'A Protest against Protests'. Nevertheless Celtic were not the easiest club to live with in these early days, especially from the point of view of those who made the rules and wanted to see them observed.

Accusations of press bias eventually led to the strike in 1896 by three Celtic players who refused to take the field unless a particular journalist was banned from the ground. Clubs are as sensitive to criticism today as they were then, but perhaps they are more prepared to accept that newspapers have a role to play, and it is not that of public relations officer for a particular club. In the 1880s the *Scottish Athletic Journal* ran a systematic campaign against Rangers, but this was eventually patched up, and from then until the 1970s Rangers, with the brief exception of Cyril Horne in the 1950s, have certainly had little to complain about. Celtic have, but I have found no evidence of any *systematic* campaign against them, particularly on the grounds of their religious affiliations.[22] If the press came to exult in a Celtic defeat, part at least of this can be explained by the wish to see the tall poppies cut down—and from the first year of their existence there was no taller poppy than Celtic. In the weeks before the three-man strike of 1896, Meechan and Battles in particular came in for some harsh criticism by the *Scottish Referee*. But this was for rough play which the reporter pointed out was unnecessary with such talented players.[23]

Newspapers have to find news and report it, and they should not flinch from controversy. In its early years Celtic were engaged in several incidents which, though normal for the time, did not improve their reputation in the eyes of those who suffered: the poaching of players from Hibs which effectively put them out of existence, albeit temporarily; the kidnapping of Jerry Reynolds; the disputes with the authorities. Then there were the fierce disputes that preceded the formation of the Limited Liability Company. The club tried to ban reporters from its annual general meetings where these disputes were aired, but reports of the near fracas into which they sometimes degenerated did find their way into the press. Perhaps some newspapers ascribed the acrimony at these meetings to Irish temperament, but the newspaper that reported them in greatest detail was the catholic *Glasgow Observer*, for which it was punished by the removal of club advertising. No-one could accuse that paper of anti-Irish feeling. In fact the Celtic dispute was a reflection of a wider quarrel within the catholic community in which the Home Rule branch of the United Irish League, which was dominated by publicans, was being attacked by the *Glasgow Observer* whose proprietor (Diamond) and editor (D. J. Mitchel Quin) were teetotal and puritan. Both groups, however, supported the Irish MPs and were opposed to Sinn Fein.[24]

For a while it looked as though a decided racism was creeping into the *Scottish Referee*, when its cartoons depicted the Celtic player with the dumb look of a creature emerging from a peat bog, while the Rangers equivalent had the noble stature and intelligent eyes of the Aryan, but these cartoons were of short duration.[25] Occasional reports meant to be of a humorous type would have a Celtic supporter speak in the broadest accent of 'Ould Oireland', but the only paper that made a regular feature of this was the *Glasgow Observer*. For this it was severely castigated by its

THE LEAGUE CHAMPIONSHIP.

Apes and Aryans. *Scottish Referee*, 3 February 1905

religious rival, the *Examiner*, which demanded that the same treatment be meted out to that paper as had been meted out to the theatre group that had tried to put on *The Shaughraun* in San Francisco.[26] *The Shaughraun*, a play written by that prolific dramatist, Dion Boucicault, had been 'run off the boards' for what was seen to be an insulting representation of the Irish.

It would be a tiresome and profitless task to list every accusation of bias and try to assess its justification or otherwise. Every club has bad luck with referees on occasions, and every now and then bias might play its part, but on the whole the breaks work themselves out. This is not to deny a more subtle bias which is marked by an assumption of superiority and hence righteousness. Rangers have probably benefited from this, but it has not stopped even their official spokesmen complaining of prejudice: John Allan, for instance, protested in *The Story of the Rangers* that Celtic's six championship triumphs were rewarded with a shield presented by the League, whereas in regard to Rangers' triumphs between 1898 and 1902 'the League did not so much as present a barren compliment'.[27] His nephew, Willie Allison, over forty years later, noted that referees often made decisions that 'left us puzzled and perplexed'.[28]

No-one would take accusations of bias against Rangers seriously, but while it is impossible to make a calculation of pluses and minuses on every dispute, it is important to analyse the climate out of which such accusations arise. As has been suggested above, Celtic were as much the creators as the victims of feeling against them. In two areas in particular they were both sensitive and vulnerable to criticism: the dominance in the club of publicans and the accusation that it introduced religion into sport.

Celtic were dominated by publicans in the early days, and this was a source of great soul-searching within the club itself, but individuals like Frank Havelin and groups like the League of the Cross had to give way to the more hardheaded McLaughlin and those who wanted the club to be run as a business. Long before this, however, *Scottish Sport* took the club to task for associating the players with the drink trade, mixing moral outrage against the evils of alcohol with the evils of being paid for playing a game, for in the pre-professional days managership of a pub was one of the means by which clubs could attract star players.

In its editorial of 31 October 1890 *Scottish Sport* commented on the 'black spots upon the fair economy of football', and singled out 'one of the most hideous and objectionable' as 'the prostitution of the game to suit the business interests of publicans'. The matter that provoked this diatribe was the refusal of the Licensing Court to grant a licence to William Groves, the Celtic star forward, and the editorial wasted no time in placing the Celtic club squarely in its sights:

... the Parkhead club must now occupy a very anomalous and unenviable position in public opinion. We can compare the club to nothing but a modern Frankenstein; some of its aspects are most fair, others are most repulsive. On the one hand the club dispenses with the lily hand of charity succour to the sick and portion to the poor; on the other hand it watches indifferently, if it does not encourage, its young men throwing themselves recklessly into a business of which every tendency is towards moral ruin ... It is wrong that a business, such as the publican business, should feed and support itself to the detriment of a fair and honourable sport; it is iniquitous that a club professing charity and many kindred virtues should tolerate, far less countenance, the adoption of the public-trade by its players ... The player-publican, with isolated exceptions, is nothing but a decoy, and a most miserable, money-grubbing decoy at that.

The editorialist went on to describe a scene like something out of Dante's *Inferno*, with 'filthy human beings' and the stench of 'equally filthy' tobacco, where a crowd mad with drink and enthusiasm refused to drink a drop that was not poured by the hero of that afternoon's game.

Lest this attack on Celtic be thought to be impugning religion, the writer hinted that Archbishop Eyre had condemned the practice, and concluded:

We do not desire that religion should suffer by what we have written on this matter, or what we may write, but we expect that religion, should it so far forget itself as to neglect its functions, will not, at least, shake hands with the devil and encourage him in his work.

Three weeks later the editorialist returned to the fray 'booted and spurred', lashing out at the effect on the morale of the game and payment 'through the till'. Once again Celtic and Groves were mentioned, with strong insinuations, without actual charges, that Celtic or individuals acting for the club were supplying Groves with the capital (£500) as a means of securing and retaining his services:

We admit it with sorrow that football in some quarters is doing its level best to encourage the drink traffic. Unhappily in the quarters we refer to and which, for obvious reasons, we need not name, the clubs are almost entirely governed by publicans, who find that it pays them immensely to interest themselves in football. It behoves everyone, therefore, who loves football for football's sake, to denounce this damnable prostitution of the game.[29]

By and large the religion of the Celtic club was played down, although it did cause some concern among the sporting establishment of the day. Before the foundation of Celtic, *Scottish Sport* had commented on the Irish who turned out to see Hibs and Dundee Harp, people who were not in the least interested in football, but were inspired by a patriotic pride in the triumphs of these Irish teams. The same paper billed the semi-final of the Glasgow Cup between Queen's Park and Celtic in November 1888 as: **Scot v Celt**. This was an 'international' match, and the report praised the aim of Celtic to 'do honour to the Emerald Isle, from which they spring', and their patriotism that did honour to the Old Country:

> The Scot is no less patriotic than the Celt, and knowing a great political significance was attached to this great cup-tie, the Queen's Park were drawn from a much larger constituency than usual.

The Celtic support outnumbered Queen's Park's, who won the game 2–0,[30] but it should also be noted that the number turning up on that day to support Queen's Park was much greater than usual.

The match itself was not without incident, and at one stage Celtic supporters seized and pummelled Gillies, the linesman. *Scottish Sport*, however, merely commented that 'The Celtic club, like many of its neighbours, is not blessed with a quiet and unassuming following', and commented sympathetically on the difficulty the club was having in getting policemen to come to their games.[31]

A year later, as a result of the Glasgow Cup Final against Queen's Park, which Queen's won through a disputed goal, the reporter was less inclined to look for excuses. He commented that the Irish were as clannish as the Scots, but did not take adversity so philosophically:

> The patriotism of the Irish and the Scotch was appealed to, and I fear the religious element was not absent. The introduction of religion into sport is to be deprecated on every ground ... How much, then, of the unpleasantness that characterized the game can be apportioned to race and how much to religion would be difficult to determine ... [the] Celts have tarnished their reputation as sportsmen and as players.[32]

When Dundee Harp tried to re-form their once famous combination, *Scottish Sport* said outright that it deprecated the decision of the management to run the club under the patronage of the Church:

> We do not believe in clubs formed on sectarian lines; it does the cause of religion more harm than good, and it brings the charity and humanity of sport into a narrow channel for the outflow of intolerance and the coarser feeling of our everyday life. The Harp, by following the lines of the Celtic, are introducing into Dundee and the north of Scotland a phase of football which we happen to know does not have the sanction or support of some of the finest and most catholic minds of the Romish Church.[33]

In these attacks on Celtic there is some hypocrisy, and a great deal of snobbery, but there is also a moral concern with a justifiable basis. Celtic were a religious and a political club, and as such they did introduce a religious and political element into football as Hibs had done before them. But in view of the nature of Scottish society at this time, a club like Celtic was inevitable and even desirable; it provided a focus for the Irish/catholic community which was a potential source of good—if the footballing public saw this as a threat, Celtic could hardly be expected to apologise for it. If the Celtic supporters were noisy and at times violent, they shared this with most other clubs of the time. The game then was in transition from a middle-class to a working-class game, but it was still being controlled by middle-class authorities and reported by middle-class journalists. The criticism that the *Scottish Sport* doled out as a result of the abandoned New Year's Day game of 1898 between Celtic and Rangers smacked of sheer snobbery. The reporter referred to the crowd as 'the very scum of the city, drunken and brutal in their behaviour and language' and, in a statement that reflects on the improvements we have seen in the streets of Glasgow over the last eighty years, claimed that there was more fighting and bloodshed than in 'an entire evening's walk through the city on a pay Saturday'. These 'specimen of the slums' were not really football followers, but people 'with a prejudice' might be tempted to criticise the low unsportsmanlike character of the frequenter of Celtic Park. The Celtic club itself was to be exonerated from all blame, and the reporter concluded that if there had been enough police provided—especially mounted—there would have been no trouble.[34] Unlike Queen's Park, Rangers and most older clubs, which had begun with a middle-class management and whose early teams were mainly middle class, Celtic arrived on the sporting scene, as did the immigrants to Scotland a generation or two earlier, like intruders at a garden party: with the largest support in Scotland they announced to all and sundry that football was no longer a middle-class preserve.

Closely tied to the working-class incursions was the issue of professionalism. Only those with financial security can be expected to play for nothing, and it ill befits those whose money comes from investments and sinecures to condemn others for accepting pay for mere games. The rewards to the professional footballer of this time were a small return on the pleasure they gave, the risks they took and the effort they expended. It was money well earned, and despite the fears of the traditionalist, the game lost little in sportsmanship by introducing this commercial element.

The castigations of *Scottish Sport* in regard to Celtic's connections with the publican's trade, however, were based on moral outrage at a real evil at the heart of Scottish society. Glasgow was not alone in this, and working-class drunkenness was merely more visible than that of the rich, although it had a more disastrous economic effect. But this does not diminish the gravity of the problem. It was natural to see the publican as central to this evil, as he was the one who profited from it; J. H. Muir in his sketch of *Glasgow in 1901* commented that 'the publican must bear in mind that he is a social pariah only because he is a social parasite'.[35] He was condemning the pubs for their 'perpendicular drinking' and not the religion of those who owned them.

Most football clubs at this time had associations with the drink trade, and had on their boards directors who were pub owners;[36] but apart from Falkirk with three directors connected with the drink trade on their original board (out of seven) and Partick Thistle with 75 per cent of its shareholdings in the hands of publicans—in this case belonging mainly to one man—none had such close associations as Celtic. Protestants drink and get drunk, but in doing so they incur the wrath of their church; in Father Mathew and the League of the Cross, catholics have a temperance tradition, but drinking is treated much more indulgently by the catholic hierarchy than by the spokesmen for the protestant churches. Drink, too, probably caused greater economic and social havoc among catholics than it did among protestants. This has been noted by many writers on catholic affairs, and the Liverpool Irishman, John Denvir, who could boast of the Irishness of Britain's Irish when he wrote their history in 1892, had to admit in his *Catholic Times* that 'drink, more than poverty, has been the curse of the Irish'.[37] It is not without accident that the liquor trade was dominated by catholics, or that the Celtic Football Club should have similar associations: but it is not altogether surprising either that they should suffer some of the social opprobrium attached thereto.

Celtic, then, like the catholic community in general, fell foul of the 'respectability' of many Scots protestants for a variety of reasons: for their politics, their social status and their connections with the drink trade. Much of this was plain snobbishness rather than prejudice, although the one can easily lead to the other, often leaving the latter intact when the original reasons for the snobbery have disappeared. Catholic historians have catalogued the bigoted outpourings of protestant fanatics from James Begg to Pastor Glass, and are justifiably incensed at this. Few have looked to the features of catholicism that have sustained the suspicions of more moderate protestants: religious differences in regard to divorce and contraception; condemnation of mixed marriages; failure to observe the Sabbath; toleration of drink and gambling; papal authority and suspicion of the confessional. In general they fear in catholics their devotion to religion as seen in their obedience to the priest and attendance at mass and condemn them for laxity in what they consider the more important moral matters like drink, gambling and 'respectability'. Perhaps there is some envy too of a religion which despite everything seems more humane and less censorious of human frailty. Even Brother Clare, better known as James Handley, who has written so well on the history of catholicism in Scotland and is author of one of the best histories of Celtic, seemed unaware that part at least of the resentment felt by Scots protestants did have some justification. Willie Maley and Bob Kelly are two Celtic stalwarts who have written books which seethe with the injustices they believe their club has suffered, and the latest history, by Gerry McNee, repeats all the accusations from the previous books, and suggests that the old prejudice is still alive and spitting.

Maley and Kelly belong to a generation when the ghetto mentality was still strong, and while some of the factors that perpetuated it are still with us, McNee might have taken a more critical look at the claims of some of his esteemed predecessors. Celtic have suffered from bigotry, perhaps most obviously in the Flag Flutter of the Fifties (see pp. 183–186), but it is instructive to take one episode described in Kelly's *Celtic*, and look at it more closely.[38] This emerged out of an incident between Quinn and Craig in an Old Firm match played at Parkhead in March 1905, deliberately selected by Kelly to show how badly treated Celtic were in those days.

Rangers were leading 2–0 with eight minutes to go when Quinn, then at the height of the powers that give him claim to be Celtic's greatest ever centre-forward, was held by Craig, Rangers full-back, and appeared to kick out in retaliation or to get free. As a result Quinn was ordered off. An invasion of the pitch by enraged Celtic fans brought the match to a premature halt, and Celtic conceded the game to Rangers. The referee claimed that Quinn kicked Craig and stamped on his face; Quinn denied the charge, and Craig acted as a witness on Quinn's behalf. Craig himself was not injured. Nevertheless the SFA stood behind the referee and suspended Quinn for four weeks. Celtic appealed on Quinn's behalf and took libel action against a Glasgow newspaper that had accused Quinn of violent play. The appeal was dismissed but the result of the libel action was in Quinn's favour, although all he gained was a shilling damages and no costs.[39]

At least one later witness claimed that Quinn definitely kicked Craig, and although the absence of damage to Craig's face is significant, it is far from unknown for footballers to stand up for each other in nasty

[SPECIAL.]

IRISH FOOTBALL TRIUMPH.

GLASGOW CELTS WIN SCOTTISH CUP.

RECORD GAME AT HAMPDEN PARK.

Grand Play by Celtic Forwards: Quinn Scores Thrice.

BY "MAN IN THE KNOW."

Quinn, 'Irish' superstar of 1904. *Glasgow Observer*, 23 April 1904

incidents on the field. The crowd break-in probably made the SFA all the more determined that punishment be meted out.

As a footnote to his story of the Quinn/Craig incident, Kelly notes that a public subscription was arranged and a gold watch presented to Quinn 'in recognition of the bad treatment he had received'. In fact if Kelly had gone into that matter further he would have found out that the subscription and gold watch referred to another incident involving Quinn that took place two years later, in which the part he played was decidedly ambivalent and the role of Celtic in defending him was not of the most glorious.

This second incident also took place against Rangers, this time in a Ne'erday match at Parkhead in 1907. On this occasion Quinn was ordered off for kicking Hendry of Rangers in the face while he lay on the ground. Quinn's own testimony virtually justified the referee's action in ordering him off, for he claimed that he had been incensed at Hendry fouling a much smaller Celt and rushed in with the intention of wreaking revenge. At the last second he decided against this and jumped over Hendry. What no-one denied was that one of the Celtic players had hit Hendry in the face, which was covered in blood. Nevertheless the Celtic club took up Quinn's case in an attempt to discredit the SFA for its punishment of Quinn, which they claimed was a punishment not of the player 'but of his nationality and his creed'.[40]

The *Glasgow Star and Examiner*, under the chairmanship of young Celtic director Tom White, made it into a *cause célèbre*,[41] donated £10.10.0 and announced that the Celtic directors had donated two guineas each to compensate Quinn during his eight-week suspension. The players chipped in 10/- each, but donations from supporters, all listed in the columns of the *Star* over the next few weeks, were a bit slower. The rival *Observer* virtually ignored the whole affair. In the event the *Star* subscription raised £255, more than adequate compensation for the four weeks' wages lost by 'the greatest footballer Ireland has ever produced or Scotland ever seen'. To mark the presentation a gala concert was held at St Mungo's Halls, but despite its size thousands were left outside. The proceeds of the concert, given free by the performers, went to various charities, Quinn received his cheque and his wife was presented with a gold watch.

Kelly's account of the Quinn/Craig incident makes great play of the attempt to close Celtic's ground as a result of the behaviour of their fans, and indicates that throughout the club's career it has been under this threat. In fact Celtic then as now were too valuable to everyone concerned with the game to be expelled, and at the time of the two

Quinn incidents there was a clamour from the smaller clubs against the favouritism that they believed was bestowed on the powerful. Moreover there was a campaign afoot to stamp out rough play. About the time of the second Quinn incident a Fatal Accidents Inquiry into the death of William Walker of Leith Football Club in a game against Vale of Leven found that Barr of the Vale was not culpably responsible, but added the rider that the SFA enforce its rules about rough play. It was also revealed in a footnote to this controversy that none other than J. H. McLaughlin, the Celtic president and then vice-president of the SFA, moved for the closure of Underwood Park, Paisley in 1898, for behaviour on the part of the Abercorn fans that was no different from that of the Celtic fans who attacked the referee at Celtic Park in 1905.[42]

Celtic, like the catholics they represented, suffered from the gibes and intolerance of other Scots, but looking inward to their ghetto, they could only exaggerate such examples out of all proportion. One result is that a virtual reflex reaction from the second Quinn case resulted in funds pouring in from eminent catholics in Scotland as well as donations from the United States, and others from Belfast and other parts of Ireland. Quinn was the superstar of his time, and no doubt Celtic followers had good reason to idolise him, but support for his involvement in the Hendry incident reflects less on the justice of the case than on the degree of paranoia that had developed in some catholic communities at that time.

NOTES

1. Cited in Colm Brogan, *The Glasgow Story*, London, 1952, p. 184.

2. 'Senex', *Old Glasgow and its Environs*, Glasgow, 1864, p. 257. 'Senex' was reporting on the 'shameful' persecution of catholics in the eighteenth century (pp. 257–9).

3. There have been several demographic studies of the Irish in Scotland. In addition to J. E. Handley, *The Irish in Scotland*, see: James Darragh, 'The catholic population in the twentieth century', in the *Glasgow Observer* Special Supplement: 'Scottish Survey: 1878–1955' and his later article in *The Innes Review*, 'The Catholic population of Scotland: 1878–1977', reprinted in David McRoberts (ed.), *Modern Scottish Catholicism: 1878–1978*, Glasgow, 1979.

4. The work on the Irish emigration is vast, but the history of the Orange Order in Scotland has still to be written. For a general history of the Orange Order see: Tony Gray, *The Orange Order*, London, 1972. For an excellent short account see: Taylor Downing (ed.), *The Troubles*, London, 1980, pp. 56–7, 126–7

and *passim*. For examples of civil disorder in Scotland involving Orangemen, see Alan B. Campbell, *The Lanarkshire Miners: a Social History of their Trade Unions, 1775–1874*, Edinburgh, 1979, Chapter 7 on 'The Irish'.

5. 'Protestant extremism in Glasgow and Edinburgh, 1930–38: its growth and contraction', unpublished paper by Tom Gallagher, kindly supplied by the author.

6. Hunt, *British Labour History*, p. 170.

7. *Ibid.*, p. 162.

8. Brogan, *The Glasgow Story*, p. 186.

9. Handley gives many examples of this in *The Irish in Scotland*, as do most catholic writers, but see especially: Ross, 'The development of Scottish Catholic Community', pp. 41–2, 48–9, in McRoberts, *Modern Scottish Catholicism*.

10. A. L. Drummond and J. Bulloch, *The Church in Victorian Scotland, 1843–1874*, Edinburgh, 1975, pp. 77–8. Drummond and Bulloch, like the sociologist John Highet who wrote the section on 'The Churches' for the *Third Statistical Account*, seem to share a very narrow view of what constitutes a catholic or a protestant; for them this seems to necessitate church attendance and knowledge of respective dogma, rather than a shared community of beliefs based on what they believe 'their' church expects of them. The latter have a religious faith, however unsophisticated.

11. Campbell, *Lanarkshire Miners*, p. 192.

12. W. M. Walker, 'Irish immigrants in Scotland: their priests, politics and parochial life', *The Historical Journal*, xv, 4 (1972), pp. 649–67. For the Irish in Scotland, in addition to Handley, see McRoberts, *Modern Scottish Catholicism*.

13. Father S. MacEwan, *On the High C's*, Glasgow, 1973, p. 39.

14. There is a superb evocation of the image of catholicism as seen by a young Scots protestant in Gordon Williams' novel *From Scenes Like These*, London, 1968, pp. 232–4. On the other hand Alan Spence's *Its Colours They Are Fine*, Edinburgh, 1983, has descriptions of a Glasgow boyhood in the late 1950s in which the portrayal of Orange or merely anti-catholic, bigots is sensitively and objectively sketched. For such types Ibrox and the Rangers Football Club were their main objects of devotion, hatred of catholics their highest ideal.

15. Sheridan Gilley, 'Catholics and Socialists in Glasgow, 1906–1912', in K. Lunn (ed.), *Immigrants, Hosts and Minorities*, Folkestone, 1980, p. 165.

16. See especially Campbell, *The Lanarkshire Miners*, p. 194. It might also be pointed out that football grounds were popular spots for taking up collections for unions (Crampsey, p. 15). Celtic and Hibs were particularly generous: the Bridgeton weavers gained £25 in one collection at Celtic Park; the biggest crowd Airdrie had ever seen gathered to see Hibs play the local team in a benefit match for local miners in bitter dispute with the pit owners—as a result their debts were wiped out (Docherty, *100 Years of Hibs*, p. 42). Ian Ward, 'Irish Immigrants and Scottish radicalism, 1880–1906', in I. McDougall (ed.), *Essays in Scottish Labour History*, 1978, pp. 65–89; Ian S. Wood, 'John Wheatley, the Irish, and the Labour Movement in Scotland', *Innes Review*, Autumn 1980, pp. 71–85;

Tom Gallagher, 'Catholics in Scottish politics', *The Bulletin of Scottish Politics*, no. 2, Spring 1981, pp. 21–43.

17. Campbell, *The Lanarkshire Miners*, has several examples of this; see especially pp. 235–8.

18. See especially L. P. Curtis, *Apes and Angels: The Irishman in Victorian Caricature*, Newton Abbot, 1971.

19. There is a strange silence surrounding the religious associations of the two big Liverpool clubs. They were a reality, although none of the club histories seems willing to acknowledge this, and Tony Mason, in his comprehensive social history of English football, *Association Football and English Society, 1863–1915*, Brighton, 1980, never raises the subject. A BBC radio programme in 1981, 'The Merseyside Miracle', claimed that protestants once supported Liverpool, while catholics supported Everton, but then went on to discuss contemporary affairs. Arthur Askey raised the subject in his autobiography. The famous comedian tells the hoary old story about two football fans returning home from a match where 'Liverpool, the Protestant team' beat 'Everton, the Catholic team' by 6–1. Pat says to Mike, 'Aye, there'll be some sad hearts in the Vatican tonight' (Arthur Askey, *Before Your Very Eyes*, London, 1975, pp. 33–4). Handley claims in his history of Celtic (p. 27) that Everton, 'like Celtic, owed its success to immigrant support, the Irish in Liverpool rallying wholeheartedly round it'. Before the 1960s very few catholics played for Liverpool, while several catholics did play for Everton. John Smith, wealthy brewer and chairman of Liverpool, indirectly praised both his own and the Everton club for getting rid of sectarianism. He claimed that: 'Twenty years ago I wouldn't have dared put a Catholic in to manage a pub in a Protestant area. Liverpool could have gone the same way as Belfast, or Glasgow, over religion. But when you've got streets, offices and shops, even families divided down the middle—Red or Blue—they haven't the time or energy for other divisions', Brian James, *Journey to Wembley*, London, 1977, p. 145; see also pp. 155–6, 161. To have got rid of sectarianism means it must have been there in the first place. It should be added, however, that one could read all of the official Rangers histories and believe that that club was innocent of sectarianism.

A massively detailed study of democracy and sectarianism in Liverpool has recently appeared, but unfortunately it is rather narrowly political and makes not a single reference to football. It would appear from this book that sectarian strife in Liverpool, at least before 1939, was as bad as in Glasgow. The absence of references to football in a book claiming to be a social history of Liverpool is a serious omission; in a book claiming also to be about sectarianism it is astonishing. For the reasons stated above I very much doubt that the Liverpool clubs remained untouched by sectarianism: P. J. Waller, *Democracy and Sectarianism. A political and social history of Liverpool, 1868–1939*, Liverpool, 1981.

20. It was said of Manchester United that they did not have to hire scouts, as every priest in the country did that job for them: G. Green, *There's Only One United*, London, 1978, p. 48. More recently, with the sacking of Sexton,

speculation about his replacement raised the issue again. Busby, McGuinness, O'Farrell, Docherty and Sexton are, or are believed to be, catholics. Two names mentioned in regard to Sexton's replacement were also catholics: McMenemy of Southampton, and McNeill of Celtic.

21. Most of this section is taken from data on the two clubs held at the Scottish Companies Register, Edinburgh. Wray Vamplew has been gathering similar information for a much larger project, an economic history of sport in Great Britain before World War 1. Much of this has been presented at various conferences and published as part of the proceedings. On shareholding in Scottish football teams see his 'Ownership and control in gatemoney sports: Scottish football before 1915', in *Canadian Journal of History of Sport*, vol. 12, no. 2, December 1981, pp. 56–83.

22. The collection of newspapers in the Glasgow Room of the Mitchell Library is extensive, but incomplete; in particular it often does not have the Saturday evening sporting editions. Most frustrating too is that its collection has been vandalised by one or more persons who obviously had an interest in The Old Firm. Nevertheless what remains is more than one individual could read in its entirety.

23. *Scottish Sport* was in general, but not consistently, more sympathetic to Celtic than *Scottish Referee*. In 1894 the former would contrast the 'play' of Celtic to the 'dash' of Rangers. In 1896 the latter condemned Celtic for the resort to force on the part of some of their players who were 'often guilty of unnecessary charging and the stupidity of their conduct is heightened by the fact that in ability they have no need to adopt such tactics' (16 November 1896); Battles was later advised to try 'A little less pugilism and a little more football', and it was noted that Doyle's 'tackling ability has sadly deteriorated' (23 November 1896). Pride was one of Celtic's main faults, another article in the same issue claimed, and their fall would do them as much good as a Rangers' win would be good for the game. It was the reporter for the *Referee* (and its parent body the *Evening News*) that the strikers wanted banned. The *Referee* did show more partiality to Rangers, most flagrantly in the comparative reactions to the Celtic break-in of 1905 (against Rangers) and the Rangers break-in of 1912 (against Clyde). Handley and Kelly cite these examples *in extenso*.

24. Gilley, p. 167. Gilley, however, does not mention the *Examiner*, which supported the Home Rule Branch.

25. See especially *Scottish Referee*, 6 January 1905, 3 and 17 February 1905.

26. The *Observer* had a regular column where Riley, the Celtic supporter, discoursed in a thick accent with Rogan of Queen's Park.

27. John Allan, *The Story of the Rangers*, Glasgow, 1923, p. 205. Celtic have often complained about how their achievements have been ignored.

28. W. Allison, *Rangers: the New Era*, Glasgow, [1966], p. 66. See also pp. 72, 174, 230–1.

29. *Scottish Sport*, 21 November 1890.

30. *Ibid.*, 20 November 1888.

31. *Ibid.*, 23 November 1888.

32. *Ibid.*, 17 December 1889.

33. *Ibid.*, 5 December 1890.

34. *Scottish Sport*, 4 January 1898.

35. Muir, *Glasgow in 1901*, p. 178.

36. On this see the tables drawn up by Vamplew, 'Ownership and control in gatemoney sport: Scottish football before 1915'.

37. Hunt, *British Labour History*, pp. 161, 171.

38. R. Kelly, *Celtic*, Glasgow, 1971, chapter entitled 'Quinn case', pp. 37–42.

39. *Ibid.*, p. 42.

40. *Scottish Referee*, 4 and 11 January 1907; *Glasgow Star and Examiner*, 12 January 1907 and subsequent numbers.

41. The subscription was mentioned in the issue of 12 January 1907 and lists of donations were recorded every week thereafter to 9 March 1907, where details of the presentation are given.

42. *Scottish Referee*, 4 and 11 January 1907, 22 February 1907.

PART TWO

No Mean City? Glasgow and The Old Firm between the Wars

To many people, especially those who have never visited it, Glasgow is a city of poverty, poor housing and brawling gangs. Although based on some truth, this is a most misleading picture, and it has been the despair of individuals trying to attract business to the city that concentration on the violent side of life in Glasgow scares off potential investors. This image took shape, if it was not exactly invented, in the period that interrupted the two world wars of the twentieth century. In 1919 the tensions surrounding the 40 Hours Strike, its feared link with Bolshevik revolution in Russia, and the presence of troops to quell anticipated trouble, gave rise to the label 'Red Clydeside'. The worst fears were never realised, and most of the Red Clydeside leaders went on to Parliament and even ended up with titles. But the label stuck. In 1935 McArthur and Long's *No Mean City* helped equate Gorbals with Glasgow and pictured its streets as swarming with razor-wielding youths. The book became an immediate bestseller and has been regularly reprinted ever since. Throughout this time, too, football matches involving Rangers or Celtic were looked on with some trepidation by local authorities and football fans who were more interested in the game itself than the undercurrents that always threatened to sweep away its ostensible purpose.

Working-class radicalism, gang fights and riotous football fans have all been aspects of life in Glasgow, but they have been exaggerated, as much by Glaswegians who take a perverse pride in their reputation for toughness, as by outsiders—be they Scots or foreigners—who find it easy to extend the grim exteriors of many of the buildings and rough speech of most of the inhabitants to a predisposition to criminality. Today the reputation of Red Clydeside has faded, although it was revived, albeit briefly, during the heroic failure of the Upper Clyde Shipbuilders' 'work-in' of 1971. Putting matters in perspective, Iain McLean has recently demolished the political mythology surrounding Glasgow with his *The Legend of Red Clydeside* (Edinburgh, 1983): 'The most revolutionary thing that ever happened in Scotland at that time was when J. S. Clarke's wife made Davy Kirkwood wash the dishes—which he'd never done before' (p. 239). Fear of the gangs is recurrent, usually with references back to

121

the 1930s when they were believed to be most dangerous. As regards Rangers and Celtic football fans, most people believe that until recently they were worse than they ever were. The violence of the gangs and the riots and brawls in or around football grounds where The Old Firm are playing are real enough, and for any innocent inadvertently caught up in them a frightening experience, but they should be placed in a wider historical and social context to be seen in their proper perspective. Part of that context is manifestations of bigotry from the so-called 'upper' ranks of society, another is that of the environment from which most working-class violence springs. Violence at Old Firm games, while it need have no direct connection with either of these, is nevertheless closely associated with them.

CHAPTER 5

Hooliganism in High Places

Bigotry, particularly in Scotland, is not the monopoly of any one class. In Scotland its most obvious expression is on the terracing at Old Firm games, but it manifests itself in many other ways, no less pernicious for being less glaring or expressed in a polished accent. And bigotry is itself a form of hooliganism. It is not to diminish the gravity of hooliganism, be it by Rangers, Celtic or other fans to say that it is part of the society that has helped nurture it: anyone who has seen the victim of a flying bottle or watched a group of thugs attack a youth who happens to be wearing a scarf of a different colour is rightly repelled by such senseless brutality. Nor is it any compensation for the victim of a boot in the face to know that the boot was worn by a kid from a deprived environment. In such cases the outraged letters to the editor urging that the hooligans be caged, birched or otherwise put out of action are understandable. But they offer no solution.

A better society might go some way towards that solution, but societies take decades to change and there can never be unanimity as to which changes represent improvement. In the case of Rangers and Celtic there is, in theory, a change that would be easy to make and which would remove the most objectionable aspect of hooliganism at their games: the elimination of sectarianism. Again in theory Rangers and Celtic could, by a change in attitude, have become the agents for great reforms in Scotland, since the two clubs, arguably, have had a more formative influence than any political party over Scotland's male youth, while the opinions of a Morton or a Meiklejohn, a Quinn or a Gallagher, would have carried much more weight than any minister or schoolteacher. Like most football clubs in Great Britain, however, Celtic and Rangers for most of their histories have tended to see their fans as little more than income at the turnstile (later pools, shops and other spin-offs) or vocal backing on the terracing. More than most they have been captives of society; albeit willing captives for the most part, profiting from an ideology that has fitted in comfortably with their capitalist ethos.

For these reasons it ill befits the managements of the two clubs, as was frequently done by Struth and Maley between the wars, to berate the swearing and rough behaviour of their fans without taking positive action to encourage improvement. In this they were no better than the leaders of their particular society in this period; indeed the hooliganism exhibited by the crowds at Rangers/Celtic games pales in significance beside the verbal hooliganism of some groups and individuals with claims to being the leaders of the two main religious communities in Scotland.

Scotland, Ulster and Orangeism

It has been said that the name 'hooligan' comes from an Irish family called Houlihan, who were prominent troublemakers in London in the late nineteenth century: it might have been more appropriate, perhaps, if Lord Randolph Churchill had lent his name to such an expression. Playing on protestant fears and hatreds to further his own political ends, he helped set the pattern in 1886 for today's crisis area when he moved to Belfast to stir up fears about Gladstone's first Home Rule Bill. Writing to his friend James Fitzgibbon, Lord Chief Justice of Ireland, on 16 February 1886, Churchill said that he had decided some time previously that if Gladstone went for Home Rule, then he would play the Orange card, which he hoped would prove to be the ace of trumps. The result was a summer of sectarian violence unparalleled till then in that violent city. A prime source of the trouble was the shipyards, where there were only 200 catholics in a workforce of 3,000. The majority were Orangemen, who believed that Home Rule would mean that they would lose their jobs to catholics. This was the fear that Churchill played on. When Salisbury was defeated in January 1886 and Gladstone told Queen Victoria that his policy was to grant Home Rule to Ireland, Churchill left for Ireland where he was greeted at Larne harbour by enthusiastic supporters. Later he addressed a meeting at the Ulster Hall where he claimed that Gladstone was about to plunge a knife into the heart of the British Empire and suggested that 'now may be the time to show whether all those ceremonies and forms which are practised in your Orange lodges are really living symbols or idle and meaningless shibboleths'. He was neither condemned nor held responsible for the riots which followed in the summer of that year, riots which his son, Winston Churchill, later described as 'savage, repeated and prolonged'.[1]

In 1911 the House of Lords' veto was removed on the Home Rule issue, and it looked as though a very moderate extension of Home Rule to Ireland would be granted. This time it was Bonar Law, the Conservative leader, who dealt the cards. The son of an Ulster Presbyterian clergyman, born in Canada and educated in Glasgow, he did not allow this wealth of geographical experience to broaden his intellectual horizons in any way. At a Unionist rally at Blenheim Palace on 12 July 1912, he repeated the rhetoric of Churchill: 'I can imagine no length of resistance to which Ulster can go in which I would not be prepared to support them, and in which, in my belief, they would not be supported by the overwhelming majority of the British people'. A short time later, Edward Carson, standing on the steps of Craigavon, read the Ulster Covenant, out of which was born the Ulster Volunteer Force. It was signed by nearly half a million people, some in blood it is said, and pledged to defend Ulster and the whole of Ireland against Home Rule, 'using all means which may be found necessary to defeat the present conspiracy to set up a Home Rule Parliament in Ireland'.[2]

Big names in powerful places lent their support, including £30,000 from Rudyard Kipling, while the Army indicated whose side it was on when it refused to take action against officers who said (in what has been called the 'Curragh Mutiny') that they would refuse to take action against the Ulster Volunteer Forces. This was in March 1914. In the following month the Ulster Volunteers landed 35,000 rifles at Larne in Co. Antrim, and concealed and distributed them with the connivance of the authorities. War diverted attention to more pressing problems than Home Rule, but the Easter Rising of 1916 brought the issue back to the forefront. When the war in Europe ended, war in Ireland moved from isolated skirmishes to full-scale combat. The British government introduced into the conflict the infamous Black and Tans, battle-hardened and often selected for their feelings on the sectarian issue. They met atrocity with atrocity, urged to greater effort by encouragement from high office. On 12 July 1919 Carson claimed to be 'sick of words without action', and the result was the onslaught on Londonderry which resulted in five days of rioting. At the same time Unionist leaders in Belfast called on the shipyard workers to drive out the 'Fenians' with revolvers: the military stood by while catholics were driven from the shipyards and had their houses burned. It seems that the plans had been laid earlier to clear the yards of all catholics.[3]

The settlement of January 1922 solved the problem, at least so far as most protestants were concerned. The creation of a separate Ulster eased their fears, which the catholics had done little to allay, of Home Rule being Rome Rule. When catholics who thought the truce a sell-out turned on those who accepted the Treaty as the best possible under the circumstances, many protestants could take some satisfaction in watching the Irish kill the Irish with even more ferocity than had marked the Anglo-Irish conflict.

Events in Ireland had very few direct repercussions in Scotland. There was no obvious response in Scotland to the Ulster Covenant of 1912, the

Easter Rising came when minds were otherwise occupied, and after the war there were only two events of major significance that reflected the troubles in Ireland: the arrest of sixty IRA men for illegally drilling on Carman Moor, near Polmont, and an attempt to free Irish prisoners in the Duke Street shoot-out of May 1921, when a police inspector was killed.[4] Moreover the number of catholics who had died in the Great War could not be ignored. Among the victims of that catastrophe were many Scotsmen of Irish descent, including Peter Johnstone, a Celtic player who died in France, while one of the first soldiers to win a Victoria Cross was former Celt, corporal William Angus of the HLI.[5] Throughout the war the *Glasgow Observer* never wavered in its loyalty to Great Britain, and constantly publicised the heroic deeds of Scots catholics.

The Easter Rising of 1916 did introduce a troubled note, coming as was intended in Britain's moment of peril, but it was at first denounced by most catholic Irish: in Scotland the *Glasgow Observer* condemned it in sorrow and not a little anger. If it had not been for the vindictiveness of the British authorities, that is how reaction to the Rising might have remained, but the government chose to act without mercy towards the rebels, and made martyrs of men who had been greeted even with hatred by some of their compatriots. In Scotland the *Glasgow Observer*, too, revised its initial opinion. Later the well-publicised atrocities of the Black and Tans on the one hand and the Irish Volunteers (known as the Irish Republican Army from about 1919) on the other reinforced opinions formed out of the Rising and its aftermath.

The creation of the Irish Free State, however, took the heat out of the sectarian question in Scotland. Now the vast majority of Scots of Irish descent could concentrate on more purely Scottish affairs, and indeed many turned their energies to the support of the Labour Party: affairs in Ireland could become more a matter of nostalgia than a living injustice. The Education Act of 1918 was also clear proof that Scotland was not impervious to catholic demands, with benefits both spiritual and material to every catholic family in Scotland. Certainly some Scots could look on this latter reform with some alarm, but at least the way was clear for leaders in the two communities to effect some sort of reconciliation. Alas, while the majority lived in suspicious ignorance of each other, vocal minorities chose conflict rather than compromise.

The Sectarian Issue in Scotland between the Wars

In 1923 a report to the General Assembly of the Church of Scotland was published on 'The Menace of the Irish Race to our Scottish Nationality'. The writer claimed that Scotland was on the verge of committing 'race suicide', as its culture was swamped by the floods sweeping over from Ireland. The writer was no solitary fanatic, unfortunately, but spoke as a prominent voice in the Scottish Presbyterian community. The General Assembly seemed genuinely troubled by the 'menace of Romanism', and a few years later George Malcolm Thomson, in *Caledonia, or the Future of the Scots*, claimed that the Scots were a dying race, being replaced in their own country by a people 'alien in race, temperament and religion'.[6] In October 1926 the *Scots Observer* opened an eight-year career dedicated 'To the greater glory of God and the temporal welfare of the Scottish nation'. It came out weekly, price 2d, and in its second number, on 9 October, Rev. Duncan Cameron raised the issue of 'Scottish Nationality and Religion: Problem of Irish Immigration'. The main problem as he saw it was that the Scots were emigrating, while their place was being taken by immigrants from the Irish Free State. These Irish immigrants were either drifting into the slums or they were creating them; one seventh of the population, they were one third of the criminal population; intemperate, devoid of self-reliance, they were all too ready to seek public aid and charitable assistance. They were a serious problem to the statesman, the despair of the social worker, and an element in the State that was inaccessible to Scottish ideals and influences. The only solution open to a Scotland without leadership and cohesion, with so many of its numbers emigrating, was government controls. The Christian minister therefore advocated two measures familiar enough today: first there should be strict limits to immigration; and second there should be a statutory obligation on all parish councils to return to their native land all paupers who had not been three years resident in the parish.

The fears of the fanatics in the Church of Scotland had no basis in statistics,[7] but they did have an emotional basis on which they continually fed. The Roman Catholic Church of the inter-war years was as committed as ever to its duty to convert Scotland to the true faith. The *Ne temere* decree had been a defensive reaction against apostasy, but the 1918 Education Act was a potential springboard to action. The doors of the universities were now open as they never had been before, and at a prize-giving address at St Aloysius High School in late 1921 the catholic convert and Professor of Greek at Glasgow University, Professor Phillimore, urged that education be used as the means of converting Scotland. The universities were open to capture, he claimed, undefended cities with no more than 200 of their 5,000 students catholics. Now they had to face the missionary energy of the greatest missionary race in the world. Similar themes were taken up by W. E. Brown, Lecturer in British History at Glasgow University.[8]

At the local level priests went about their work, many no doubt praying quietly, like Bruce Marshall's fictional Father Smith, for the souls of the heathen, but others, like Bishop Graham, could raise a few hackles with remarks about the protestant religion being no better than that of the 'heathen Chinee'.[9] At the same time minor controversies would flare up now and then, such as protestant indignation about local catholic church halls being used for gambling, or attempts by catholics to have public parks opened at 1 p.m. on Sunday, a time, it was noted, when catholics who had been to Mass had completed their religious worship, while protestants had the whole Sabbath to keep holy.

In the 'twenties the two communities grew in parallel, if not apart. The activities of the Orange Lodges continued with vigour, as did Freemasonry: 25 per cent of the masonic lodges in the United Kingdom were in Scotland, and about 10 per cent of the adult males were members.[10] At a more junior level, the Boys' Brigade and the Scouts expanded as never before: the former was barred to catholics, being tied to the protestant churches. But even the Scouts, with their more general commitment to Christianity, were looked on with suspicion by the catholic church, which did not approve of catholics joining organisations that did not have its specific approval. The catholic church was pursuing its own programme of Catholic Action and, coinciding with the reign of Pius XI (1922–39), as John Cooney has shown, drove its separate roots deep into Scottish society. Educated catholics, particularly lawyers and doctors, created their own 'mafia', and various other Leagues, Guilds and Societies provided services that kept catholics free from their protestant equivalents—for instance the Catenian Association promoted the interests of catholic businessmen and professionals, the Caledonian Society prayed for Scotland's conversion, while the Knights of St Columba and the Hibernians 'gave catholicism secretive wings comparable to the Masons and the Orange Order'. The success of catholic 'lay apostles' in 'christianising' their environment was recognised by the Vatican in the late 1930s, success being seen in 'the proliferation of Guilds such as the Transport Guild, the Don Bosco Guild of Catholic Teachers, the Guilds for dentists, workers in pharmacy, postal workers, police, nurses, lawyers, doctors and the very strong Miners' Guild'. It was claimed that only one other diocese, an American one, was more successful in this regard than Glasgow.[11]

Catholics and protestants were thus kept apart, catholics in particular living in their own closed world. Journalist Pat Bolan later claimed that the first time the outside world burst into his 'self-contained catholic parish' was with the miners' strike of 1926, when families came together to protect the victims of eviction. He tells of the kindly old parish priest who helped the poor where he could, but was so far removed from the reality of the problem that he would open his Lenten sermon to a congregation near starvation with the words: 'At this time, dear brethren, it behoves us all to retrench our superfluities'.[12] Kindly or whatever, the priest still reigned over his flock with a grip that no protestant minister could aspire to. A young Irish catholic lass got a job with a Jewish family in the Gorbals, looking after their wee girl. Without thinking about it, she taught the child her prayers, and when she went on a fortnight's holiday the Jewish parents were astonished to find their child saying Hail Mary and God bless this and that. They realised it had been an innocent mistake, and laughed about it; but the local priest was not so amused as he told the young girl to 'keep on with the good work'.[13] The priests themselves were under strict discipline. When Father Sydney MacEwan, one of Scotland's finest tenors, was invited to sing as a Gentleman of the Chapel Royal, a position that would have taken him to Windsor Castle and St James's Palace, after three weeks' singing with the Anglican church of St Margaret's he was elated. But he had to refuse. The Anglicans had not concerned themselves about his religion, but when he confessed about his participation in Anglican services his priest told him immediately: 'You must give this up at once'. He was participating in 'false religion'.[14]

Throughout this time the catholic press offered the faithful a refuge from the secular fare of the daily newspapers. The *Glasgow Observer* concentrated on things Irish and catholic, and included virtually no material that was purely Scottish. In fact catholic journalists at this time showed scant respect for the country that was their home,[15] and 'Man in the Know' in the sports pages of the *Glasgow Observer*, with his contempt for the Rangers supporters and warm praise for Celtic fans and their singing of political songs, was perfectly in tune with the general tenor of the paper. Indeed in March 1920 the proprietor of the paper, Charles Diamond, was sentenced to six months' gaol for an article he had published, 'Killing no murder', which discussed the ethics of tyrannicide. This was shortly after an assassination attempt on the Irish viceroy, Field-Marshal French. Catholics might have thought the sentence severe, but the *Scotsman* thought it lenient, and this opinion would no doubt have been shared by the majority of Scots protestants, whose opinions about the loyalty of the Scots–Irish would have been confirmed, especially when a year later the inquiry into the Duke Street shoot-out revealed a widespread underground activity on behalf of the IRA.[16]

In the meantime the defenders of Scotland's culture against subversion and swamping by an alien religion and nationality continued to voice their fears and demand that Scotland make a stand in face of the menace. In the midst of so much nonsense, the *Glasgow Herald* emerged as a pillar of common sense. In March 1929 it commissioned an inquiry into the Irish in Scotland and published its findings over five issues.[17] The first report considered the question of Irish immigration against its historical background, and concluded that the 'flood' of immigration was no more than a 'trickle', and this had been the case since the turn of the century. Addressing himself to the question of the dole in the next issue, the writer concluded that the Irish were not living off poor relief, and that Scotland was not being invaded by sluggards and malingerers. On the issue of population increase the writer showed that the birthrate among poorer protestants and catholics was much the same, although middle-class catholics and artisans tended to have larger families than protestants. The implications of this for the future, the writer considered in the next issue, were not serious. The final article turned to the more emotional issue of the preservation of Scottish nationality, a matter less easily discussed in terms of demographic facts and historical objectivity. The writer rather aptly pointed out that it would be a weird sort of joke to invite all the Irish over to build the railways, the reservoirs, the jute mills, the ships, and then tell them to go home when they were no longer needed. The writer took up the question of racial attacks on the Irish. It had been claimed that if the natives were being replaced by a superior race, then they would be compelled to resign themselves to this, but this was not the case. On the contrary, 'A law abiding, thrifty and industrious race is being supplanted by immigrants whose presence tends to lower the social conditions and to undermine the spirit of independence which has so long been a characteristic of the Scottish people'. The *Herald* writer disagreed, and quoted Professor Gregory's work to show that improved economic conditions and basic social reforms were a much more worthwhile approach to the problem than immigration restrictions.

But while the *Herald* writer dismissed race as a barrier, he did point to the segregation which he claimed to be imposed by the catholic church: RC strictures on 'mixed' marriages; written contracts on bringing up children; duty of RC's to attempt to convert non-RCs; interference of priests in non-religious matters. He appealed, again drawing on the work of Professor Gregory and some of the correspondence generated by the 1926 controversy, to the Roman Catholic Church to show good faith and abandon its policy of segregation, beginning with the education laws—otherwise the other side would develop a counter movement, 'and the end of such armed neutrality is war and disaster'.[18]

The articles produced a series of letters to the editor, most of which were sensible and well balanced, playing down alarmist views and expressing a desire for peace between the two communities. Unfortunately they also revealed what no-one would have disputed: there were in fact two separate communities. A letter from 'J. O'D. Derrick'[19] pointed out how he and other catholics had been cold-shouldered in non-denominational organisations when they were anxious to contribute, and asked in exasperation why they were criticised for not joining more in Scottish life. For him at least the education issue was a red herring and the racial one an invention that would disappear if the problems of unemployment and land distribution could be solved.

On the other hand the catholic *Glasgow Observer* showed a curiously ambivalent attitude. It praised the *Herald* for demolishing the delusion of the Irish invasion,[20] and praised the conclusion that fidelity to the faith accounted for the increase in catholics in Scotland.[21] But then it went on to extol this as a matter for triumph, praising the high birthrate in the catholic community and its implications for the future. It could only have reinforced protestant prejudices about the irresponsible fertility of catholics and the ominous purpose that lay behind this. In practical terms the *Observer's* uncompromising attitude was even more sadly calculated to defeat the aspirations of those hoping to draw the two communities together: it roundly condemned the appeal to catholics to give up their segregation policies as 'an invitation to apostatize'.

The Vatican and Catholic Leadership

As the newspaper of the catholic community in Scotland, the *Observer* was one of the main interpreters of Vatican policy. This it did in the spirit of ultramontanism, or complete submission to the dictates of Rome: indeed when Diamond, its proprietor, died in 1934, he was compared to Louis Veuillot, one of the greatest propagandists for right-wing catholicism that the Church had known. In pursuing such policies the *Observer* spoke also for the bishops and priests of the Scottish hierarchy, whose 'notorious anti-intellectualism' left them 'unprepared for the theological awakening at Vatican II'.[22] The result was that ordinary Scottish catholics were burdened with a leadership that was conservative not only in matters of morals and spiritual observance, but also in politics and social reform. In the nineteenth century the main enemy had been democracy, in the twentieth it was socialism. Ironically these were fears that the catholic hierarchy shared with its enemies on the other side of the religious fence, but such was the sectarian hatred that it did not bring them together in face of the common enemy.

Throughout the nineteenth century the catholic church had been a staunch supporter of the rights of property, and the rights of those with wealth to do with it as they wished—albeit with pious reminders about the virtues of good works and the duties of charity. The rise of international socialism from the 1890s in particular gave a semblance of reality to fears about the envy of the have-nots, and sincere catholic socialists like John Wheatley found it increasingly difficult to gain acceptance for their belief that a just social order did not contradict the teachings of the Church. Wheatley maintained his faith despite abuse directed at him from leaders in the Church—his views were distorted in the catholic press and riots were instigated by priests which resulted in attacks on his property and threats to his life.[23] Yet Father O'Brien, who denounced Wheatley from his pulpit, was a man who was passionately devoted to the interests of the working class—not just catholics—and the large personal sum he expended on their welfare in the early 1920s won him the admiration even of the local Orangeman, King Lawson.[24] But while O'Brien denounced socialists whose solution to the problem of poverty went beyond charity, he was in turn condemned by the archbishop when he started to use church building funds in addition to his private wealth to feed starving miners. Archbishop Mackintosh forced him to resign his parish in 1922. Wheatley managed to retain his beliefs and stay inside the church, but others left, some like Harry McShane to join the Communist Party.[25]

In 1917 the worst fears of the leaders of the western nations, and not just the catholic church, were realised when news of the Revolution in Russia made a reality of what until then had been a mere threat. The spectre of Bolshevism, now given flesh and blood as well as daggers and guns, raised fears so grave that the atrocities of Orangemen were taken off the front pages of the *Glasgow Observer* and the machinations of the Freemasons were also relegated to the inside. It was such fears that were behind the rise to power of Mussolini in Italy and Hitler in Germany. Such concerns were reflected in the major catholic newspapers of this time, and reached almost fanatical proportions when the Civil War broke out in Spain in 1936.

Meetings of Fascists in Scotland, mainly Scots of Italian origin, were favourably reported in the *Glasgow Observer*, while Mussolini was particularly warmly praised for his attempts to suppress Freemasonry. In 1933 the full evil of Hitler's intentions was not apparent, and it was only in January of that year that he came to power. He was accorded mild censure in the *Glasgow Observer*, but it was the Jews who came in for the worst abuse. If the Jews felt hurt at Hitler's attitudes, then the solution was in their own hands, it declared in 1931. The Jews had to get rid of their own black sheep, for it was they who had looted and burned the convents and nunneries in Spain, supplied by Moscow funds, while the plunder of the Church in France had profited mainly Jews. Moreover the persecution of Christians in Russia, and the plunder of the Christian churches there, had largely passed into Jewish hands. With little evidence to support this, the writer concluded: 'These facts are unhappily incontrovertible'.[26]

When it became apparent that the Hitler regime had not only come to stay, but intended to carry out policies that were incredible in their sheer barbarity, troubled consciences reacted with the consoling thought that Nazism was a barrier to Bolshevism. However, while such spirits could close their hearts to Hitler's treatment of political 'deviants', it was rather more difficult to accept his oppression of religious minorities. The catholic church's attitude to these victims, and its professed Christian principles, received a particularly nasty jolt when catholic Austria was swallowed up in March 1938 by the Nazis. Shortly after that the *Glasgow Observer*, commenting on the attacks on Jews in France, noted how that country had 'suffered badly from Jewish–Masonic liberalism' and 'crooked politicians', but admitted that 'neither of these evils' was sufficient excuse for an outburst of anti-semitism. It noted that a pogrom against Jews 'fosters the worst kind of nationalism'. Adopting a loftier tone, the writer pointed out that catholics must not allow themselves to be carried away by mass propaganda, and that their law of charity embraced 'Jews and negroes and all unpopular minorities'. He was pleased to note, then, that some French catholics, in particular Jacques Maritain, were taking an active part in protecting the civil liberties of the Jews.[27] Catholics in Scotland might rightly have felt angry at being treated as an 'unpopular minority' in the country of their birth, no matter how secure their civil rights, but the record of their own church in regard to the toleration of beliefs that differ from catholicism is not a very happy one.

The *Observer's* sympathy for 'unpopular minorities', and its willingness to overlook 'evils' like 'Jewish–Masonic liberalism', were based on charity rather than justice, but even charity was not to be extended to the Popular Front government elected to power in Spain in February 1936. Fascism in Italy and Nazism in Germany were dealt with fairly lightly by the catholic press, but this was not to be the case with Spain's left-wing democracy. When Franco's Falangists provoked the Civil War in July

1936, the catholic press engaged in a systematic campaign on behalf of General Franco. Issue after issue publicised the atrocities of the 'anarchists' that were matched by details of the heroic exploits of Franco and his Falangists. As Fascist divisions from Italy moved in to help Franco, while Nazi dive bombers perfected their aerial techniques for the bigger battle yet to come, the democracies stood paralysed: the Republicans could look for support only to the volunteer International Brigade and the active intervention of Soviet Russia. Perhaps the latter was proof enough for the catholic press that it had right on its side: it was not seen that way by all catholics, however, and the blatant propaganda that issued from its pages caused many to leave the official church.[28]

The leaders of the catholic church, then, beginning with the papacy, but acting right through the 'respectable' and educated sections of public life—university, press and pulpit—displayed no more tolerance and understanding, in their own way, than the Churchills and the Carsons in the matter of Ulster. The social effects of the church's beliefs, whatever relief they may have brought true believers, were divisive and potentially disastrous.

Scotland has never gone the way of Ulster, and it is unlikely that it ever will. Religion has helped divide the working class, but no major political figures have cynically exploited the issue as was done in Ulster, where the Unionist Party and the Orange Order achieved a dictatorial grip. With the events of the late 1960s and 1970s so close to mind, and the bitter intransigence of the protestant authorities in Ulster that was a major cause of these tragedies, it is too easy to overlook the real fears and suspicions of Ulster protestants when Ireland was divided in 1922. Some commentators have pointed to Eire to show that protestants had nothing to fear from Irish Home Rule, that protestants there have never been persecuted. This may be true, but it is easier to tolerate a small minority than it is a large one. That minority, too, has had to forego some of the basic ideals of liberal democrats, and this right down to the present day. The Irish Republic was a catholic regime in every sense, one in which the position of the Church was so assured that it didn't need any written guarantees. By the 1937 Constitution the State acknowledged the 'special position' of the catholic church, but no concordat was ever negotiated or even suggested. In finances the Church remained a voluntary body; bishops were appointed by Rome from a list drawn up by the Irish hierarchy; the clergy were forbidden to participate in politics. In all this the Church had no complaints: not only did it have the subservience of the politicians, but it had the support of the people in a way few other churches, catholic or otherwise, could boast, and the power of the priest was backed up by the apparatus of the State: divorce, contraception and other aspects of catholic morality were written into the laws of the land, and censorship was freely applied to the press or any other media that expressed opinion contrary to the teaching of the Church. Above all the Church had a unique grip on education, approached only in the Netherlands, Quebec and Scotland. But it went beyond even the Scottish system, for education was not just denominationally controlled, but clerically controlled. And even at university level the principle of separate education for catholics applied.[29] The religious grip on Irish politics has slackened slightly since 1937, but the result of the referendum on abortion in September 1983, and the publicity surrounding it, were not a good omen for moderates on both sides who see a compassionate secularism as the only basis for the unification of that tragically divided island.

Scotland is not Ulster, of course, but no other country has such close links with it, both geographical and historical. Certainly the catholic church seemed to be doing its best to persuade the bigots that their fears were justified, but in times of reasonable economic and social security the rhetoric of the extremists was fairly harmless. The 1930s, however, were not a period of economic or social security, and the protestant extremists in particular had their greatest opportunity to make political capital.

Sectarian tensions in the Thirties

Virtually the entire inter-war period in industrial Scotland was one of depression, with the problem of unemployment spiralling after 1929. But the system of government in Britain was never seriously threatened. A major reason for this, no doubt, is that however drastic conditions were for many workers, they were often better off than they had been before the war, and some economic historians would stress that 80% of Glasgow was at work for most of this period.[30] Moreover, neither national nor local government had been so remote in Great Britain as in many continental nations: Glasgow, in particular, was developing a fine reputation for municipal socialism, and many community enterprises were free from backdoor political manipulation. The energy of young Scots that was not expended on productive labour had many other outlets. On the protestant side there were the Orange and Masonic Lodges, the Boys' Brigade and other church activities, while the catholics had their equivalent bodies. Of a more neutral nature were the British Legion and Rotary clubs, which helped encourage political passivity and hence conservatism. For the more impecunious there were other forms of relief: public libraries offered shelter from the weather during the day, and at night cinemas and dance halls offered cheap forms of entertainment. Increasingly throughout the 1930s radio added a new dimension of pleasure for those who wanted to stay at home; for those who liked the outdoor life Glasgow had one of the cheapest tramway systems in the world. Above all, of course, though only for the male population, there was football: to be played or watched in streets or parks, or followed with religious intensity at Celtic Park or Ibrox. Or at away games: unemployed fans would walk great distances—from Glasgow to Kilmarnock and even as far as Dundee—to see their teams play.

None of these distractions solved the real problems of the day: unemployment, poor housing and poor diet. In his novel of a Trans-America foot race in 1931, Tom McNab has his hero, Hugh McPhail, battling it out for the big prize, a few months after the athletic Scot had been playing 'sixpence a man' football matches on Glasgow Green. McNab comments on how McPhail and thousands of unemployed like him had seen the spine of their life vanish, and with it the core of their belief in themselves; for 'These men *were* what they worked at. Nothing in their recreation or their family life could ever make up for that loss'.[31] Nevertheless these distractions made the life of dedicated socialists that much more difficult. By the same token they made life difficult for right-wing extremists. Fascism in Scotland never got a grip, and, by contrast with Europe, the most extreme right-wing political bodies were anti-catholic. Two of these were the Scottish Protestant League in Glasgow and Protestant Action in Edinburgh, the former putting four councillors into Glasgow Corporation by 1934, while the latter increased its support in the east as its counterpart in the west declined: it became the second largest party in Edinburgh, with 31 per cent of the vote and returning a maximum of nine councillors.[32]

The leaders of these right-wing groups do not appear to have been a very inspiring lot. John Cormack of Protestant Action was finished when the *Glasgow Weekly Herald* published a letter from him just as they received it, complete with errors of punctuation and grammar: to be a fanatic was one thing, to be a semi-literate was another.[33] Forrester and the Protestant League came to an even more dismal end. Enraged by the visible evidence of a fact of history which most Orangemen (and catholics) prefer to ignore—that the pope and King Billy were political allies—he went over to Belfast with a group of Protestant Leaguers where he slashed a painting in the Stormont Parliament depicting the

The National Crisis, 1931. Press comment on the apparently greater importance being placed on sport than on a political crisis. The National Government had just been formed to meet the deepening Depression. *Evening Times*, 5 September 1931

pope blessing King William of Orange for defeating James II at the battle of the Boyne in 1690.[34] The longest-lasting of the right-wing extremists was Alexander Ratcliffe, son of an east-coast minister who was elected to the Glasgow town council seat of Dennistoun in 1931, winning it from the Tories, although he lost it in 1934. Throughout this time, indeed from 1930 to 1945, he ran a newspaper called variously the *Vanguard* or the *Protestant Vanguard*, in which he stigmatised the Gorbals as 'Jew-land', and in the summer of 1939 he paid a visit to Germany where he was well received. But he was above all anti-catholic, and on the eve of the Battle of Britain he was bewailing the fact that there was no Hitler in Scotland to get rid of Popery there. Britain's success in defying the Luftwaffe destroyed any hopes he might have entertained of becoming Hitler's gauleiter for Scotland and putting into practice the wishes of those who in the 1920s and 1930s had wanted to get rid of Scotland's catholics. Amid such talent Pastor Glass emerges as an intellectual giant.

Despite this, these right-wing extremists deserve more study than they have usually been given—Ratcliffe and Cormack did far better electorally than the more charismatic Oswald Mosley in the 1930s. They had little to offer that was new, reflecting instead existing prejudices, and when

Ratcliffe gave his support to the Scottish Democratic Fascist Party of W. Weir Gilmour and Major Hume Sleigh in 1933, it was mainly because the Party refused to allow catholics to become members and indeed included in its programme the expulsion from Scotland of all religious orders, the repeal of Section 18 of the 1918 Education (Scotland) Act, and the prohibition of Irish immigration to Scotland. When these articles were deleted from the SDFP's charter later in 1933, Ratcliffe abandoned it.

Nor did he join forces with the other major anti-catholic forces, the Unionists and the Orange Order. He accused Unionists in the Orange Order of having sabotaged an Orange and Protestant Party formed in 1922 because it threatened Tory interests, and his friendly relations with the Ulster Unionists suffered with the Forrester incident in May 1933— the picture slashed by Forrester in the Stormont parliament had been a gift of the Ulster Prime Minister, Lord Craigavon. Ratcliffe was too much of an individualist, and also too devoted an anti-catholic, it would seem, to have any long-term success with an established party—one that had to at least give the impression of tolerating individuals or groups it found repugnant.

The press gave Ratcliffe and his Scottish Protestant League little support. For the most part they chose to ignore their activities, out of distaste for what they stood for, or out of unwillingness to give them any publicity. When this could not be avoided, newspapers like the *Daily Record*, the *Glasgow Herald* and the *Evening Citizen* were hostile, and when his demise came they welcomed it. Ratcliffe had his own *Vanguard*, of course, and on at least a couple of occasions gained access to the columns of the left-wing *Forward*. The only material support he seems to have gained came from his visit to Germany in 1939, but throughout the war he continued to publish the *Vanguard* from an address in Bearsden, a wealthy district on Glasgow's western border. In the final count Ratcliffe had little to offer: the depression years gave him his opportunity, and he could count on a certain amount of sectarian feeling, but for reasons suggested earlier, Scotland's religious divisions ran counter to the growth of any would-be Fascist party.

Paradoxically, too, the Education Act of 1918 that has done so much to maintain sectarianism in the Scottish community can also be said to have been a means of stifling its more extreme manifestations. Because that Act gave catholics full state funding for their religious schools, they did not see the need to form a separate party, around which sectarian feelings might have polarised at the political level. Instead they stayed within the Labour Party. But while in this way they lost some of their separate identity, they maintained their own cultural institutions, not least of which was the Celtic Football Club. By the 1930s its management had long since lost any interest or given up any involvement in politics and were thoroughly committed to the social status quo. Similarly the Rangers Football Club was linked more to Unionism and Orangeism than to the more extreme sectarianism of the Scottish Protestant League. Both clubs, however, offered a release for sectarian hatreds in the relatively harmless atmosphere of a football match. If at the same time this helped sustain sectarian hatred, the two clubs were not alone, for while Ratcliffe and Co. loudly rattled their empty drums, church and university continued to add their own hysteria.

The Assembly of the Church of Scotland raised the bogey of Irish immigration throughout the 1930s, although the 'floods' had become a seepage by 1938. In 1930 the Unionist and Professor of Law at Glasgow University, Andrew Dewar Gibb, launched a vitriolic racial attack on the Irish in Scotland in a book entitled *Scotland in Eclipse*; and in 1938 the Scottish Nationalist, John Torrence, wrote a pamphlet, *Scotland's Dilemma*, in which he warned of the dangers of Irish immigration, which if not controlled would inevitably result in 'a race-conflict of the most bitter kind'.[35]

As always, such extremists were matched by fellow spirits on the other side. In 1936 that famous convert, Compton Mackenzie, wrote *Catholicism and Scotland*, which saw Scotland's true traditions in pre-Reformation days, praised the Irish for never having given up their nationhood while the Scots had sold out to England, and made the purely religious claim that the Real Presence of God on his altars was more precious to Scotland than the real presence of a Parliament in Edinburgh.[36] Another convert, the prominent writer Peter Anson, wrote *The Catholic Church in Modern Scotland* the following year. In his final chapter he made no doubt about the duty of catholics to convert Scotland to the Faith, and talked of the difficulties of clearing 'the dense forests of ignorance'.[37] He was very pessimistic about the success of conversion, however, and saw the only hope in immigration and the offspring of the descendants of those exiled Irish immigrants who were winning Scotland back to the 'Faith of its Fathers'.[38] Having thus ensured that he would arouse the antagonism of even the most moderate Scottish protestant, Anson concluded by raising the spectre of communism, and called on catholics and protestants to stand side by side in the fight against the rising tide of paganism.[39] These last two books were written at least partially under the influence of the events of 1935 in Edinburgh. In that year Scotland's capital saw sectarian riots of a kind more disgraceful than any that dishonoured the terracings of Ibrox or Parkhead—more disgraceful in that many of the victims were women and children, while the excuse for the riots was a purely religious one. They also highlight the fact that bigotry in Scotland is not the monopoly of any one class or geographical region.[40]

The first major riots of that year, instigated in large measure by Cormack's Protestant Action, were in June, when at the Usher Hall, Edinburgh the freedom of the city was granted to the Prime Minister of Australia, Joseph Lyons. Demonstrators gathered outside and protested inside against the insult of giving the freedom of the city, not to an Australian, but to a catholic. The Scots are nothing if not selective in their prejudices, for they said nothing about the granting of civic freedom, at the same ceremony, to the Hindu Maharaja of Patiala (*in absentia*), and to the Tory, Lord Tweedsmuir. Appetites thus whetted, the mobs rolled up in force to protest at the first-ever Eucharistic Congress to be held in Scotland, in July 1935. Buses bringing in women and children were stoned, and riotous tumult greeted the Catholic Young Men's Society Civic Reception at the City Chambers and again on the Sunday at the Cathedral. In an official statement Archbishop McDonald deplored the treatment of catholics in the months prior to the riots; he claimed that catholic citizens had been subjected to a campaign of vilification, calumny and savagery, particularly at their place of work; priests could not appear in the street without being 'subjected to unspeakable indignities', sworn at, spat on and molested.[41] The archbishop's statement was prompted in part at least by reports in the English press about 'exaggeration' of the riots. We should note, however, the extent of the violence he had to bear before he felt impelled to speak out, indicating that for a long time before that most serious grievances had been silently borne.

Clearly, then, the riots between warring fans at Celtic and Rangers matches were no creation of the game itself, but rather a reflection of a condition much larger than a football field and a weekly encounter. Clearly, too, there were more hooligans outside the game than inside it. And just as clearly the literary hooliganism of the so-called respectable sections of Scottish society was of a type less justifiable and every bit as reprehensible when words were translated into action. The cries of outrage when football crowds riot are none the less understandable, but less so is the hypocritical indignation of those whose condemnation falls selectively on groups whose violence is merely more obvious.

NOTES

1. These incidents have been recounted many times: the quote above comes from A. Boyd, *Holy War in Belfast*, Tralee, 1969, pp. 119–23. Churchill, of course, was not involved in any of the events that directly resulted in the riots, but has sentiments more typical of the attitudes that allowed the explosive situation to develop. The word 'hooligan' seems to have been coined in 1898, although its origins are not clear. See G. Pearson, *Hooligan. A History of Respectable Fears*, London 1983, pp. 74–9, 83–4, 255–6 n. 3.

2. Both quotes from T. P. Coogan, *The I.R.A.*, London, 1980, p. 23.

3. *Ibid.*, pp. 44–5.

4. *Evening Citizen*, 24 January 1955. Another was seriously injured.

5. J. McShane, 'The Story of Celtic', *Scottish Field*, July 1967, pp. 24–7, 46. Willie Maley, in a series appearing in the *Weekly News* between May 1936 and 29 August 1936, mentions Willie Angus but says that he was only briefly on Celtic's books (18 July 1936). Peter Johnstone, a more prominent Celt, died in France (*ibid.*, 25 July 1936).

6. Cited in Handley, *The Irish in Scotland*, pp. 338–9.

7. See esp. *ibid.*, pp. 340–2.

8. *Glasgow Herald*, 21 December 1921. Without naming Phillimore, Handley (p. 336) waxes ironical about the response evoked in the press and protestant pulpits by the professor's remarks.

9. *Daily Record and Mail*, 27 June 1923.

10. C. Harvie, *No Gods and Precious Few Heroes*, London, 1981, p. 100.

11. Cooney, *Scotland and the Papacy*, pp. 89–90.

12. *Ibid.*, p. 90.

13. B. Kay (ed.), *Odyssey*, Edinburgh, 1980, p. 6.

14. McEwan, *On the High C's*, p. 122.

15. Roberts, *Modern Scottish Catholicism*, article by O. D. Edwards, 'The Catholic Press in Scotland Since the Reformation'. 'Scotsmen who read the Catholic press might indeed wonder whether the Irish had any loyalty to Scotland' (p. 167); 'Protestant Scotland implied that Catholicism was alien; the Scottish Catholic press literally was' (p. 173).

16. *Glasgow Observer*, 14 May 1921, p. 6.

17. *Glasgow Herald*, 20, 21, 22, 23, 25 March 1929. This series is well summarised in Handley, *The Irish in Scotland*, pp. 344–351.

18. *Glasgow Herald*, 25 March 1929.

19. *Glasgow Herald*, 30 March 1929.

20. *Glasgow Observer*, 23 March 1929, p. 3.

21. *Glasgow Observer*, 30 March 1929, p. 4.

22. Cooney, p. 61, but see the entire chapter 'Romanisation', pp. 51–61.

23. See especially Ian S. Wood, 'John Wheatley, the Irish and the Labour Movement in Scotland', in *The Innes Review*, Autumn, 1980, p. 78.

24. Cooney, p. 90. S. Gilley, 'Catholics and Socialists in Glasgow, 1906–1912', pp. 192–3, considered the riots 'a storm in a teacup'.

25. McShane's autobiography, written with the help of Joan Smith, has some particularly interesting insights into the life of a young catholic in Glasgow in the early decades of this century: *No Mean Fighter*, London, 1978.

26. *Glasgow Observer*, 26 September 1931, p. 8.

27. *Glasgow Observer*, 7 May 1938, p. 8.

28. *Glasgow Observer, Scottish Survey*, and *Scottish Catholic Herald 1878–1955* (Special Supplement); article by A. G. Hepburn, 'Political and industrial relationships', although Hepburn, whose article seems to be more a warning about the dangers of communism, does not express the issue in these terms. See also Pat Bolan's comment in Cooney, p. 91.

29. In addition to more general works, much of the above is extrapolated from: J. H. Whyte, *Church and State in Modern Ireland: 1923–1970,* Dublin, 1971, 1974.

30. Information supplied by Roy Hay, Deakin University.

31. Tom McNab, *Flanagan's Run*, London, 1982, pp. 36–7.

32. Harvie, p. 100. For a fuller discussion of protestant extremism, however, see Tom Gallagher's various articles. In particular, he has written an excellent paper on the Scottish Protestant League and Protestant Action, which is as yet unpublished: 'Protestant extremism in Glasgow and Edinburgh 1930–38: its growth and contraction'. I am indebted to Tom for keeping me informed of his findings in such matters.

33. Cooney, p. 20.

34. Gallagher's unpublished paper. Gallagher, however, does not identify Forrester as the man who slashed the painting: this is in Harry McShane, *No Mean Fighter*, p. 206. Most of what follows on Ratcliffe and the SPL is from Gallagher's unpublished paper.

35. Handley, *The Irish in Scotland*, p. 352.

36. Compton Mackenzie, *Catholicism and Scotland*, London, 1936, esp. pp. 185–8.

37. P. F. Anson, *The Catholic Church in Modern Scotland*, London, 1937, p. 211.

38. *Ibid.*, p. 214.

39. *Ibid.*, p. 216.

40. In his unpublished paper on protestant extremism Tom Gallagher refers to the Edinburgh riots as a 'bizarre throwback to the Porteous Riots of the 1740s or to the 1780 Gordon Riots in London'. But he does show that the riots did not take place in a political vacuum; that Cormack was more extreme in words and action than Ratcliffe, achieved more success than Ratcliffe did in municipal politics, and of course managed to drum up a much more violent riot than any that took place in Glasgow.

41. *Glasgow Observer*, 13 July, 1935, p. 1.

CHAPTER 6

Razor Gangs and Orange Walks

There is no major city in the world that has not had trouble with violent youths, just as no major football club has been free from problems caused by its more violent supporters. It would appear that both have similar causes, notably boredom and a search for excitement in an urban environment that has been unable to offer either useful employment or a sense of identity between the community and its disadvantaged members. It seems likely, though it awaits proof, that street gangs are made up of the same people who get involved in brawls at football matches. Whether or not this is the case, there are many common factors between the gang youth cult and football support, both in the values that hold them together and in the middle-class fears that break out every now and then in 'moral panics'.[1]

No Mean City

As a tailpiece to their bestselling novel, the authors of *No Mean City*, an unemployed baker from the Gorbals and a journalist who beat into shape the manuscript the Gorbals baker had dumped on his desk, claim that they did not draw 'an exaggerated picture of conditions in the Glasgow tenements or of life as it is lived amongst the gangster element of the slum population'. To reinforce this assertion they list ten cuttings from newspapers between December 1929 and August 1935. The last quotes the heading: 'GLASGOW'S NAME A BY-WORD', and claims that extracts of the same kind could be quoted *ad nauseam* from the Glasgow and national newspapers of these years.

Whether or not Glasgow was already a byword for violence, McArthur and Long's novel certainly helped to make it so. The novel itself emphasises the terrible housing conditions, and even carries a brief message through the words of the long-suffering Lizzie, the Razor King's wife, shortly after he had been kicked to death by a crowd of aspiring successors:

> Johnnie [the Razor King] has come through a hellova lot, when you think of it. He was no' a well-educated fellah or anything like that, but, aw the same, the crowd of mugs that have ministers and priests and aw that looking after them, wid have had *naebody* looking after them at aw if it

> wisny for the likes o' Razor King. Whit does it matter to the heid yins
> what happens in Gorbals or Bridgeton or Garngad or Anderston, or any
> other bliddy slum in Glasgow for that matter, so long as we keep quiet? Do
> they care hoo we live or whit we dae or whit kind of derrty hoose we
> have? No bliddy fears! They need wakin' up once in a while, and it's
> fellows like Razor King that makes them remember we're alive.[2]

But the novel dwells on the sordid: as one contemporary reviewer put it,
it was like visiting a farmyard and then reporting on a dungheap as the
visit to the farm.[3]

No one could deny the appalling slums that disfigured many parts of
Glasgow then, as they had done for the best part of a century and which
would plague the city for decades to come, but while some might
shudder in horror at the lives lived by the slum-dwellers, others, like
George Blake, could condemn those governing Glasgow who had
allowed landowners and property-owners to divide and subdivide their
dwellings and sites, producing 'warrens in which the impoverished
detritus of the old industrial order multiplied and festered', and marvel
that 'the maintenance of decency in such conditions is much more than a
simple social duty; it is a feat'.[4] More recently G. G. Robertson in his
Gorbals Doctor gives his story of what life in the Gorbals was really like
between 1923 and 1935 with one chapter setting out to destroy 'The
Gorbals myth'. The doctor did not deny that violence of various sorts,
particularly wife-beating, was endemic, but he emphasised that neither
'the policeman nor the ordinary citizen had any fear of threat to life as he
moved about the Gorbals area at any hour of the day or night'.[5]

Robertson was a doctor who worked in close co-operation with the
police, and so was in close contact with the less savoury aspects of
Gorbals life. Two books[6] have come out in recent years giving glimpses
of that life from a different perspective, from two post-war youths from
similar backgrounds, whose different talents took them in opposite
directions. Jimmy Boyle's *A Sense of Freedom* shows how a talented
youngster took to crime and ended up in gaol; in Pat Crerand's *On Top
with United*, the ex-Celtic star, then playing with Manchester United,
describes a youth where fighting was a way of life in a respectable
working-class environment, and where his particular talents took him to
Parkhead and the glory of playing for his country at Hampden.

There was another youth whose fame has become part of the folklore
of Glasgow. He came from Bridgeton on the other side of the river, and
when he died in July 1962, aged 56, a crowd of 1,000 gathered outside
his tenement home in Brook Street, Bridgeton for his funeral, later
stopping traffic as they formed a large funeral cortège from there to

Riddrie cemetery.[7] The deceased was 'King Billy' Fullerton, in his latter days a peaceful citizen, but still remembered as the man who founded the best known of the Glasgow gangs: the Bridgeton Billy Boys, remembered at least wherever Rangers Football Club is playing as the fans take up to the tune of 'Marching through Georgia':

> Hello! Hello!
> We are the Billy Boys
> Hello! Hello!
> You'll know us by our noise
> For we're up to our knees in Fenian blood
> Surrender or you'll die
> For we are the Bridgeton Billy Boys.

As he is remembered on the terracings, so it is fitting that his gang saw birth at a football match. For it was as a young lad of eighteen that Billy Fullerton had the misfortune to kick the winning goal against Kent Star on the Glasgow Green, in 1924. The result was assault by hammer and a strategic retreat. The call went out that a great wrong had to be righted, and since the perpetrators of the wrong were catholics, there was an immediate response, from the Airdrie and Coatbridge areas in particular. Within a matter of weeks the Billy Boys had been formed, with a gang membership of up to 800. For the next ten years at least they were prominent at Orange Walks and at Rangers football matches. If they were not attacking, or being attacked by, rival gangs at 'walks', where banners and the big drum were the prize trophy, they were picking fights before, during or after the exploits of their sporting heroes. The Billy Boys were the biggest and best known of the gangs who had their heyday in the years between the wars, but particularly in the early 1930s. With their protestant base they set up a non-sporting parallel to The Old Firm, and with their big day of the year on the Twelfth of July they had a perfect venue for close season swagger and parade.

The Recurring Theme

Fights between rival countries, towns and communities are as old as mankind; so too, no doubt, are fights between rival youths within communities. With industrialisation and urbanisation young men were thrown together to form their own hierarchies and sub-cultures. Glasgow, with its tightly packed tenements built to house the workers for an unprecedented industrial development, was a natural breeding ground for lively youth activities. Its streets and backyards became the main playground for many youngsters, providing the terrain for a variety of games, from kick-the-can to 'keepie-uppie', headers and scratch football matches with a worn tennis ball. The street corners served as meeting places for older youths, and the crowds gathering there, at tenement entries or under the light of street lamps at night were a constant reminder of the reality of industrial depression and the unemployment it brought about. In Glasgow depression and poverty were more visible than in most other cities of comparable size.

A major problem in tracing the history of gang warfare, as of football hooliganism, is that most of the evidence comes from old folks whose memories have been distorted with time, and newspapers with a middle-class bias reporting what is essentially a working-class phenomenon. As Lizzie noted in her brief epitaph on Razor King, the 'heid yins' were happy enough to leave the slums alone while violence was not too obvious and did not threaten the more 'respectable' sections of society. Only when it became spectacular did it generate 'moral panics', which might tell us more about the state of middle-class consciences than life in the slums. Nevertheless, there do seem to have been periods when gang warfare assumed significant proportions, most notably in the 1930s and the late 1960s.[8]

The troubles of the late 1960s brought a few reporters from England to take a look at Glasgow's problems, and in the days before Brixton and Toxteth gave new dimensions to the havoc that can be wrought by rebellious youths, delivered their varied judgements on life in Glasgow. Of the four major reports, that by the *Daily Telegraph* was the shallowest.[9] It ran an article in its magazine supplement which revealed that Glasgow had a colour problem: Blue and Green. It told of a tough Gorbals publican who claimed to be scared of the gangs then running wild, for they were different from the gangs of the old days, the days of the Razor Kings, when the sources of gang conflict were clearly defined: religion, family feuds or plain protection rackets. The reporter also interviewed some members of the Tong gang, one of the many terrorists 'living in the shelter of the Welfare State'. He claimed that Glasgow had the worst gang problem in Britain and was among the top six in the world (alongside Mexico City, New York, Chicago, Palermo and Bogota), but his conclusions were probably as hasty as his research, which had him talking about Carlton for Calton, and Bear's Den for Bearsden.

The *Sunday Times*[10] report was more accurate: it headed its story 'Glasgow belongs to the knife' and opened up with statistics on violence, claiming to show Glasgow way ahead in proportion of violent crime. However, it finished on a more friendly note, emphasised the kindliness that predominated, and wondered that there were so many law-abiding citizens in the conditions Glaswegians had to put up with. The *Observer*[11] report of May 1968 headed its story: 'Where violence is as casual as the smile of a pretty girl', and opened with fulsome praise of a great city 'with a character as strong and pleasing as its national drink', before settling down to the less pleasing facts. Religion was inevitably mentioned, and comparison made with Liverpool and Cardiff where sectarian strife had disappeared, whereas in Glasgow football matches between Celtic and Rangers required a major police operation. Its conclusion was optimistic, was kind enough to say that 'Glasgow is splendid to look at', and suggested that if Glasgow had a rash across its face, then this was a common symptom of change in the human body.

A *Guardian* report a year later[12] looked at one of the practical efforts to combat the gang problem, and while it did not mention sectarianism as such, religion still had a predominant place. This was a sympathetic report on the Easterhouse project, where Graham Noble and Archie Hind had been the main organisers of recreational activities of the gangs 'pacified' by entertainer Frankie Vaughan. If it was critical, it was of Glasgow Corporation which had refused to support the project, and of Bailie James Anderson, the city's police convenor, who resigned as a trustee of the project because he thought there were more direct methods that were a better answer to the problem. The religious element in the problem was suggested by Noble, whose quote gave the article its sub-heading: 'John Knox is not dead, he is alive and stirring up trouble in Easterhouse'. According to Noble, the legacy of Knox and his Calvinism was a repression of normal feelings, and violence was the outcome of an inability to speak or act openly with the opposite sex. There is no doubt a great deal of truth in this, although we must assume that catholics, too, have come under the influence of Knox, albeit subconsciously. However that may be, the project was based on ideas as old as the gangs: the kids ran the centre themselves, while Noble and Hind sought to divert the essential need to feel loyalty and express affection into less destructive channels.

The gang menace seems to have come in various waves or phases. In the 1890s it was the Penny Mob that ruled the streets, in this case Townhead and the East End. Their name came from the amount they levied on shopkeepers for the fines incurred by their love of fighting, mainly with fists and belts, but also stones, paling stakes and wash-boiler lids. In the early 1900s warfare raged between the San Toy Boys and the Tim Malloys, and occasionally spread to the public at large. About the same time gang troubles spread to the south side, where some of the gangs said to be inspired by 'lurid literature' were the Mealy Boys, McGlynn Push, Village Boys, and the Gold Dust Gang.

It was in 1916 that the gangs next made the headlines, with subs like 'Glasgow Apaches on Warpath', a headline indicating the influence, or at least knowledge of, the gangs who had been terrorising Paris. In fact the Glasgow gang did not call themselves the Apaches, like their Parisian counterparts, but the Redskins, and it was to them that many acts of terror were attributed, even long after they had been broken up. Most prominent, along with the Redskins, were the Kelly Boys, with lesser gangs like the Brig Ahoy, Death Valley Boys and Beehive Boys. Among the factors encouraging the gangs at this time were streets darkened because of the war, and the depletion of the police force because so many had volunteered for war service. The gangsters themselves were aged mainly between fourteen and seventeen. Just before the war knuckledusters were popular as weapons and were used in disturbances outside Ibrox Park in 1912. During the war primitive coshes were used, while the organisation of the gangs was indicated by the use of whistles to summon members to combat. Some shopkeepers made a profit out of selling knuckledusters (on sale at 6d and 10d each), but others were terrified by the threat of having their shops smashed, either because they did not pay a gang levy or gave information to the police.

One writer blamed the rise of the gangs on free education, claiming that hooliganism had been unknown when parents had to pay for their children's education out of their own pockets: now these parents were neglecting their responsibilities, and it was they who should be in the dock. A more popular explanation, and one familiar enough across the generations, though in different guises, was the effect of 'movies'. The influence of the new craze can clearly be seen in the names of the gangs, but the Penny Mob and other gangs had flourished without the benefit of Hollywood. Many writers to the press were aware of this, claiming that the gangs had always been there, and that in view of the living conditions the wonder was that 'tens of thousands of city working lads are so well behaved'.[13]

The years after the war were marked by violence at many football matches, but in 1920 the *Evening Times*[14] reported that organised hooliganism had ceased to exist in Glasgow, although there had recently been an attempted revival with the Baltic Fleet, a gang which had come to the attention of the press in 1916. Late in that year the troubles in Ireland were reflected in an 'Up Dublin!' riot on the Albert Bridge, but the *Evening News*[15] pointed out that this was no worse than a normal Saturday night fracas, and commented that a portion of the Irish community always carried out its faction fights in Glasgow. But while there was always a group that was 'agin the polis', the *News* added that 'most of our Irish fellow citizens knew that Glasgow was not Dublin'. For the rest of the 'twenties Glasgow was in the grip of an economic depression, and witnessed sporadic gang problems, notably those brought to light by Sillitoe: the Razzle Dazzle, the Parlour Boys or the Beehive Gang of 1924, the last associated with organised crime, and the Albert Bridge Street brawl of 1928 between the South Side Stickers and the Calton Entry, in which Tate of the Calton gang was killed.[16]

It was in 1930 that the activities of the gangs once again passed from being a nagging nuisance to being branded as a menace, with old tags like 'reign of terror' being brought into use again. This was the year, too, in which Rev. J. Cameron Peddie arrived from Aberdeen to take up his post as minister of Hutchesontown Parish Church in the heart of the Gorbals. Like others who lived there, he did not find the people of the Gorbals as black as they had been painted, but rather 'friendly, kindly, appreciative, battling hard against poverty and unemployment'.[17] They were concerned about their families, especially the future of their kids, and approached him about this. Peddie's solution was to found clubs run by the youngsters themselves, in which the virtues of loyalty and co-operation were turned to more productive ends. His success seems to have been most impressive, with 30 clubs eventually being founded with a total membership of around 4,000. He himself was appointed honorary leader of each of the clubs.

The event which brought Peddie most dramatically into contact with the gang problem was one which followed a replayed Cup Final between Rangers and Partick Thistle in 1930. The route home from Hampden to Bridgeton, even without a detour, is through what was the catholic area of the Gorbals. The result on this occasion was the Crown Street fracas, in which the Billy Boys met the South Side Stickers and the Liberty Boys with bottles, sticks, bricks and 'other weapons'. The street was thick with heaving bodies holding up traffic, while innocent bystanders crowded into shops for safety and others enjoyed the spectacle from the safety of their tenement windows. Eventually the street was cleared, but thanks only to the efforts of the police, mounted and on foot. There were only four arrests as a result of this 'Alleged gang fight: Sequel to Cup Final Discussions', as the *Evening Citizen* cautiously reported.[18]

The Gang 'Menace'

One of the results was a spate of articles on the gangs. The *Evening*

Citizen sent 'a special investigator' to discover 'The Truth about the Glasgow gangs', and his findings were disclosed over four issues.[19] This investigator played down the 'menace' of the gangs and suggested that 'scare' was more appropriate. He believed that the gangs were part of the social order, and those he talked to, made up of boys between seventeen and twenty-one, were generally in search of amusement, often provoked into fights by police who harrassed them for loitering. In their search for amusement they might often come into conflict with each other, but there was nothing criminal in their activities. Razor-slashing was the subject of exaggerated stories of the gang menace—he recounted the story of two children who set a street in panic when they were seen to be playing with their father's razor. The reporter included a fair amount of romanticism in his report, but most of it was good sense, and it does seem likely that he spent some time with the gangs.

Most trouble began in a cinema or a dance hall, he claimed. These were the main centres of popular entertainment, along with football, throughout Britain at this time. They were to indoor entertainment what football was to outdoor, and in Glasgow were indulged in with the same wild passion.[20] Unlike football, they were enjoyed by both sexes; but like football they could be the scene of vicious brawls. Here the excuse for the fight would most likely be a girl and would be fought on the spot, but more serious fights would be pre-arranged with bottles, sticks and any other weapon to hand being used: occasionally razors would be brought into play. The *Citizen* investigator claimed that politics was not normally a source of dissension, but a General Election or the Orange Walks could present a glorious opportunity for a battle.

The writer also claimed that religion was absent in these disputes, except as a point of demarcation; that most gangs were a mixture of 'both' religions, and that the strongest and leading catholic gang, the Calton Entry, had a protestant as its leading fighter. Peddie also played down the role of religion, although some other investigators placed it high on the list of causes.[21] As a church minister, Peddie probably had a rather narrow view of religion, judging it by church attendance rather than as a tribal rite creating a division from birth so strong as to send people to spill blood over it.

In the Gorbals, as elsewhere in Glasgow, most children were born to be brought up either as catholics or protestants. Pat Crerand claims that the first thing he learned there was that the world was made up of protestants and catholics—there were no neutrals.[22] Religion is barely mentioned in *No Mean City*, but this is as much as anything because it was assumed as a fact of life that you were either a catholic or a protestant. Early in the novel Razor King, then plain Johnnie Stark, is talking to Mary on their way back from their first date:

> 'Do you know, Mary,' he said, 'that you were about the best dancer at the National the night? And you a prodisant, the same as me'.
> 'Ach! Ye're just kiddin'!' she replied defensively. 'There's lots of good Catholic dancers too. Still … I widny feel that I was right married unless a minister did the marrying and aw that, wid you, Johnnie?'[23]

This division was no invention of the Glasgow working class, but something thrust upon them by the leaders of opinion in press and pulpit, and perpetuated by the segregated education system.

Peddie was in a predominantly catholic area, so it is likely that the sectarian element was not so strong. But there could be no denying the religious basis of the Billy Boys, and catholics among them would have been as rare as inside Ibrox stadium or even behind the goal at its east terracing. On the other hand the basically catholic inspiration of gangs like the Coburg Erin, McGlynn Push or even the McGrory Boys is apparent from the names. It could well be true, however, that the Calton Entry, a catholic gang, had a protestant as its star fighter, just as the ranks of the Celtic Football Club have been open to talent, with many protestants among their most famous players.

It should be noted, too, that Peddie was always careful to keep religion in the background, for too many schemes had been ruined by over-zealous ministers using table tennis as a pathway to God, giving rise to the derisory call: 'We waant nane o' yir ping-pong'. Peddie had the help of the press, police and local councillors, either tacit or anonymous—the police actually allowed two gang members leave from prison to take part in a football match he helped organise. But if it had been suspected that Peddie was in league with any of these authority figures he would have lost their support immediately. The police in particular accepted Peddie's refusal to give away names of any gang member guilty of criminal conduct. Informers were criminals of the worst sort according to gang morality, loyalty was their cardinal virtue.

When Peddie turned his attention to the gang problem in the middle of 1930 he was not on his own, although it seems he was the most effective. The *Evening Citizen* of 9 August of that year praised his efforts under the heading:

Southside Stickers
Gangsters new Slogan
Brotherhood and Good Citizenship

but an issue of a week later remarked on the work being done by a Rev.

F

Sydney H. Warnes in the Bridgeton district, with the approval of the Glasgow Presbytery.[24] About the same time the Scottish Education Department instituted a system of continuation classes on a less formal basis, while an anonymous Glasgow businessman claimed to have a hundred per cent success rate with gangsters he looked after on release from gaol.[25] On the other hand came Chief Inspector Sillitoe and his 'Cossacks' intent on bringing the gangs to heel. He arrived in Glasgow in 1933 from Sheffield where he had been introduced to the virtues of the razor in gang fights, and it was this experience that he brought to bear in his role of Chief Constable in Glasgow. He was less anxious to see the positive side of the gangs, as he believed that too much sympathy had been spent on the weak-willed who slid into senseless violence while those who survived the same environment and went on to make good were overlooked.

Sillitoe was an authoritarian, with the authoritarian's certainty of his (or her) own righteousness and ability, but he harboured no religious prejudices. He caused a furore when he threatened to put an end to Old Firm games, and for his trouble received a death threat that resulted in his checking all suspect mail for parcel bombs. It seems that his high-profile police presence at Ibrox and Parkhead, together with a no-nonsense approach to troublemakers, eliminated some of the more violent features of these games.[26] He did not solve the problem, of course: that is beyond any mere law-enforcing body. For the same reason his claim to have 'solved' the gang problem, although not without some substance, is rather exaggerated.

Despite catholic accusations of bias in regard to the police, it seems that Sillitoe's main energies were expended in attacking protestant gangs. Indeed it is with the break-up of the Billy Boys that he saw the return to law and order. He sought and received the support of the magistrates, who imposed stricter penalties, and thus encouraged, his police got to work. The major episode involving 'Sillitoe's Cossacks' was a well-prepared ambush of the Billy Boys on their way to stir up trouble near Celtic Park, but the most picturesque was that involving 'Big Tommy from the Toll'. The latter arrested Fullerton and then fought off Fullerton's cronies single-handed, leaving behind many a cracked or bruised skull, as the evidence that followed in court showed; witnesses aroused the curiosity of the judge as they claimed: '... and then Big Tommy from the Toll hit me and that is the last I remember'. The magistrate asked if the oft-mentioned Big Tommy was in the court and if he was, would he stand up. Sergeant Morrison stood up and the magistrate nodded his understanding as he thanked the huge police officer and asked him to resume his seat.[27]

One other claimant to the taming of the gangs was Major Malcolm Spier, a pioneer in the Boy Scout movement, war hero and former chairman of Toc H and the Glasgow Conservative Club.[28] At public school he had learned the effectiveness of a good caning, and thought that what the gangsters needed was a 'jolly good hiding'. Using his influence at Barlinnie, to which he was admitted as a Boy Scout visitor, he decided to try out his theories about the need to hurt and humiliate on none other than the leader of the Billy Boys himself. This was in 1929, while Fullerton was in gaol for brawling. The punishment was administered in the privacy of the major's own office, and took the form of a spanking by clothes brush in which the major 'certainly did not spare him'!

None of the accounts mentioned above agree on the details of Fullerton's escapades, particularly in regard to dates, any more than Fullerton's own account, also published in the *Citizen* articles. These accounts, too, are written from memory, and don't always square up with contemporary accounts. There are certain constants, however, which apply in particular to the inter-war period, but no doubt to later periods as well: most of the gang members were young, usually in their teens; they were either unemployed or under-employed; they lived by a strict code of ethics that needed direction rather than denunciation; they did not make a business out of their activity; and their victims were usually members of other gangs, although shopkeepers sometimes had to support the levies of gang fines and the damage that accompanied gang battles; drink, religion, football and personal insult, particularly over a girl, were often among the immediate causes of a bloodletting.

There can be no doubt that it was the slums and the lack of job opportunities that spawned the gangs: the streets were more salubrious than a fetid single room or room and kitchen, while three months in Barlinnie was like rest and recreation for some of the gang members, since it gave them the chance of decent food and accommodation, something they were not used to in their tenement homes. In a time of up to 30 per cent unemployment, in areas of congested tenements, there were not enough boys' clubs to go around, or not enough of the right type. Peddie's success lay in keeping the authorities in the background, for most of these kids were profoundly suspicious of school, church and police force, and there were not enough men of Peddie's rare compassion mixed with common sense to go around. So while the slums remained, and regular employment ceased even to be a dream, the police were left to deal with the immediate problem of protecting the public. In the third article of a series dealing with the gangs, the *Weekly Record*[29] had an ex-gangster claim that kindness wouldn't kill the gangs, but that fear works wonders, and was the only thing the gangster respected. Peddie and Sillitoe both had their role to play, but it was the war that finally broke the gangs, providing a more glorious field to commit acts which previously had earned them only gaol or the contempt of the public.[30]

Fullerton, Fascism and the Orange Order

Fights between rival gangs were endemic throughout the inter-war period in Glasgow, and a football match between Celtic and Rangers was often the scene of some brawling or other, but the most predictable occasion for a large-scale riot was the annual Orange Walk. In Scotland, unlike Ulster, the Orange Order never became tied to the Unionist Party, some of its members have been known to vote Labour, and at the General Strike of 1926 some Orangemen came out in support of the pickets.[31] Nevertheless the links between the Orange Order, the established church in Scotland and conservative politics, though informal, are real enough. Similarly the links between the Billy Boys, the Orange Order and Rangers Football Club, though informal, were real enough. The Billy Boys provided a great deal of the colour behind their favourite's goal at Ibrox, and bawled out the songs, chants and slogans that urged their favourites on, but they were equally at home on Scotland's Glorious Twelfth, when they did not have the distraction of a football match.

The annual celebration of William of Orange's victory over the catholic James II at the River Boyne in 1690 has been a regular feature of the Scottish calendar since the 1870s, and in this century, particularly in the inter-war period, the Orange Walks have offered the major occasion for a close season sectarian set-to. The Orange Order was founded in Ireland in 1795,[32] but the first Walks were not held in Scotland until 1821 and 1822. Thereafter they were sporadic, falling under various bans for the violence they provoked. It was only after bans were lifted on street parades in 1872 that they became an annual event. In the 1880s, with the threat of Home Rule in Ireland, the Order strengthened its position and started building many Orange Halls; its Walks became a barometer of the state of economic and sectarian tensions.

The Walks themselves can be a colourful and festive occasion, not without a little incongruity, with the bowler hats and umbrellas in staid contrast with the brightly coloured banners, sashes, white gauntlets and aprons. The songs are tuneful, the marchers a mixture of jauntiness and military stiffness, and if the leader knows how to twirl his mace he can set off a splendid spectacle. In recent years numbers at the marches seem to have dropped off and the marchers in some eyes look somewhat decrepit, but in their heyday they were an awesome sight, filling the streets with their followers and the air with their music. Backed up by the rhythmic rattle of the side drums and the more menacing beat of the big lambeg, the message of the songs would be sung out to the accompaniment of flutes, fifes and accordions: praise to King William, honour to the Sash and death to the Fenians. With up to 50,000 in full regalia the marchers could take up to an hour to pass a given point, and for every marcher in the procession there were others swept along by the occasion, not active supporters, but by the same token not repelled by the sentiments being expressed.

A public park would serve as the assembly point for speeches reminding the gathering of the foundations on which the glories of the British Empire were based: the principles of the Reformation, the freedom that was the antithesis of romanism and which was indissolubly linked with national prosperity. Speakers and the assembled multitude would offer prayers to God and renew oaths of loyalty to King and Empire, vow undying support for their Irish brethren resisting Home Rule, before 1922, and the Ulster government thereafter.

After the formalities the picnic atmosphere would continue, with sandwiches and lemonade for some, and more fortifying refreshments for others. Fired by the speeches and fuelled by the refreshments, the return home could take a different turn, as the marchers stepped up their rhythm and drummed out their chants as they approached known catholic areas. In the years between the wars there was no Twelfth in Scotland when trouble in varying degrees of violence did not break out.[33]

The first provocation, of course, was the march itself, but the press of the time was more likely to see the provocation elsewhere: the windows of tenement homes where the catholic occupiers had painted the woodwork green and 'flaunted' green curtains; youths who jeered at the marchers and others who waved green handkerchiefs; Irish flags deliberately hung from the windows. In the tenements, there could be found missiles of various kinds, from bottles and stones to buckets of water and worse. If required they could be used with deadly effect.

In such a situation only the presence of the police could prevent an all-out riot, and usually they managed to restrict hostilities to isolated skirmishes. Taunting youths might directly challenge the marchers, sometimes the marchers would break ranks to attack their taunters;

missiles might fly from tenement windows to be answered in kind. Even after the marchers were in their trains and coaches for the last part of the journey home, isolated fights would continue throughout the night. The papers the following day had the material for their headlines:

> 1923:   Tense Scenes at Orange Walk
>   Glasgow Marchers Badly Injured
>   An Ugly Situation
>
> 1925:   Glasgow Orange Day Riot: 50 Arrests
>   Many Casualties in Big Orange Parade Clash
>   Bandsmen Use Instruments as Weapons in Pitched Street Battle
>   Man Shot in Garngad Midnight Melee
>
> 1927:   Battle Outside Public House
>   Police in Action with the 'Billy Boys'
>   Ambulance Kept Busy
>   Many Arrests Follow Orange Walk
>   Rival Factions' Fierce Skirmish in Springburn
>   Attempt to Seize Partick Banner
>
> 1930:   Scottish Orange Day Tragedies
>   Demonstrators Pelted with Rain of Bottles
>   Clashes with Police

And so on through to 1939, when the Walk passed without incident, minds by then being filled with more serious matters.[34]

The Orange Order in Scotland was never received formally into the Establishment the way it was in Ulster, where membership of the Lodge was a prerequisite to political power and where a prominent politician could declare pride in this membership as more important to him than that of prime minister. In Scotland this cross-class alliance was never so strong: the presbyterian ministers who are Orangemen have never been more than a small minority of the Church of Scotland ministers, and most upper and middle-class Scots treat the Order with a certain snobbish disdain. But as always in Scotland, residual and deep-seated anti-catholicism means that the Orange Order can never be entirely damned, for while its members and their methods might not be approved, their motives were worthy of some commendation. The apparent unwillingness of the Rangers' Board to condemn the sectarian hatred of so many of the club's followers could be construed in this sense, although whether this is a more charitable view than the more common one that such criticism would chase them away from the turnstiles, is another matter.

In the overall perspective Fullerton was a minor figure, and while he and his gang earned the glory that came with spreading fear in some circles and respect in others, they earned little else. But they had a potential which was appreciated by some politicians who did not shun violence as a means to achieving their ends. In his more peaceful old age Billy Fullerton admitted that he had joined the Fascist Party and became a section commander with 200 men and women under his command. He recalled how he would lead them into Communist marches in order to seize their big drum for his flute band, but ruefully claimed that to that day he could not give a definition of what Fascism was. Fullerton could not have been as naive as this would suggest, for there is a consistency in his allegiances that reveals a fairly well developed ideology.

For a start the Billy Boys were committed, as their membership card and rules stated, 'To uphold King, Country and Constitution ... to defend other Protestants'. This is perfectly in line with conservative thinking in Great Britain, and in 1926 the Tories put this into effect when they hired the Billy Boys to act as strike-breakers during the General Strike. For their efforts they were awarded certificates that many of them treasured for years afterwards. Fullerton also admitted that his gang was hired by politicians to break up meetings organised by their opponents.[35] This was done, he said, as long as the meeting to be broken up did not have the same aims as the Billy Boys. Clearly he would not have been doing this work on behalf of Liberal or Labour politicians. More likely he would have been in the pay of capitalists subsidising anti-socialist propaganda in the working-class districts, such as the West of Scotland Economic League. One of the subscribers to this and other Tory funds was Sir John Cargill, patron of Rangers, and described by Patrick Dollan when he wrote for *Forward* as 'the patron saint of Tory Capitalism in the West of Scotland'.[36] There was no link between Cargill's business interests and the gangs or even between Rangers and the Orange Order. But the club has never been thought of as tolerant or sympathetic to strugglers, being always on the side of the Big Guns, and so it naturally attracts certain personality types. It is for such reasons that the first club in Scotland to have its supporters accused of racism is Rangers. This is certainly undeserved, and shocking to most Rangers fans, but even before the controversy over this issue in August 1983, when black players in the West Bromwich Albion team were heckled, and a visitor from Sierra Leone wrote to the *Glasgow Herald* to complain of the abuse he had been subjected to in the Ibrox stand, two Scottish journalists had referred to the association of some Rangers supporters and rightwing racism.[37]

As for Billy Fullerton, he might well have added racism to round off his array of prejudices, for in addition to his other pursuits he founded, in the Foundry Boys' Hall, London Road, Bridgeton, a branch of the Ku Klux Klan, whose aims were the same as those of the 'senior' Billy Boys. Perhaps, however, it was to be the catholics of Glasgow who were to fill the role of the negroes of America's Deep South. Neither the Ku Klux Klan nor the Fascist offshoots of the Billy Boys caught on, however, emphasising the ultimately harmless nature of the Glasgow gangs. Indeed, in view of what was happening elsewhere in Europe in the 'twenties and 'thirties Scotland's problems relating to violence were comparatively minor. The streets of Glasgow were never filled with black shirts such as those who took Mussolini to power or the brown shirts who acted as Hitler's thugs; they were free from the leagues, openly Fascist or merely anti-democratic of the sort that weakened France and left it for the Nazis to walk through in 1940; nor did Glasgow have to suffer the guns and killings that rocked Chicago. There are many reasons why Fascism never took root in Scotland: a comparatively minor one, but one with a rather ironical twist, is that the union of anti-Socialist forces which was the strength of Fascism in Italy, Germany and Spain was weakened by sectarianism, for much as the catholic hierarchy and powerful business interests hated Socialism, they often hated each other even more. So despite the efforts of some politicians to divert the energies of the gangs into more lethal pursuits, they were more often expended in street fights, sectarian marches and football matches.

NOTES

1. Since I wrote this chapter Geoffrey Pearson's *Hooligan* (London, 1983) has been published. This 'History of respectable fears' adds weight to many of the points I am making. Pearson sets out to destroy the belief of the 'law and order' advocates that street crime and hooliganism are the product of permissiveness, and represent a decline from some 'golden age', usually about twenty years previously. Using a vivid and impressive range of historical sources, Pearson shows that successive generations have voiced identical fears of social breakdown and moral degeneration.

2. A. McArthur and H. Kingsley Long, *No Mean City*, Corgi edition, 1978, p. 245. There have been several works in more recent years dealing with the life of ordinary folk in Glasgow and the industrial conurbation that surrounds it: Peter McDougall's *Just a Boy's Game* caused a furore when it was televised by BBC1 on 8 November 1979 because it concentrated on the violence of razor-wielding youths in contemporary Greenock (unnamed); Alan Spence's collection

of stories, *Its Colours They Are Fine*, evokes some splendid pictures of working-class life in Glasgow from the late 1950s from a more varied point of view. In 1983 the Third Eye Centre brought out the first collection of poems dealing solely with Glasgow, aptly entitled *Noise and Smoky Breath* and edited by Hamish Whyte. For a fuller appreciation of such themes, however, Geddes Thomson's anthology of poetry, prose and drama of the West of Scotland, *Identities* (Edinburgh, 1981) is an excellent appetiser for the rich fare that the cultural gourmet can sample without straying very far from the centre of Glasgow. The violence and brutality of much of *No Mean City* reappear in many of these works, but taken as a whole they present a picture in which the sordid and the sentimental are balanced by the straightforward honesty and good humour that are the characteristics of most people. Some of the most ordinary aspects of life in Glasgow have been retold with great humour by Billy Connolly: the scatological emphasis of much of Connolly's material is probably more his own than his characters', but his portrayal of certain Glasgow situations and characters is brilliant. Albert Kane's *The Glaswegian*, Braunton, 1983 is some sort of personal rêverie. Sean Damer has written a sociological treatment of aspects of life on the Broomloan Road estate, which runs alongside the western stand at Ibrox: 'Wine alley: the sociology of a dreadful enclosure', *Sociological Review*, 22 (2), May 1974, pp. 221–48. Dealing more specifically with the 'orange and green' theme, Anthony J. McCaffrey has written an as yet unpublished anthropological thesis (MA) which he submitted to the University of Durham in 1976: 'The Scottish mind: Glaswegian social structure and its relationship to the Scottish character'. Peter Bilsborough has recently had accepted his MA thesis submitted to the University of Stirling, June 1983, 'The development of sport in Glasgow, 1850–1914'.

3. 'Hieronymus' in the *Glasgow Observer* (16 November 1935, p. 4), who claimed to be a priest who had 16 years' experience in the district. *The Scotsman*, 31 October 1935, p. 15 referred to it as an 'exceedingly sordid novel', the work of an unemployed baker which was undistinguished, but useful for its vivid first-hand knowledge. The reviewer also saw it as a warning to rescue slum dwellers from their sub-human conditions as much for society's sake as for those who suffered directly.

4. G. Blake (ed.), *The Trials of Patrick Carraher*, London, 1951, p. 23.

5. G. G. Robertson, *Gorbals Doctor*, London, 1970, pp. 128–37.

6. P. Crerand, *On Top with United*, London, 1969, pp. 28–34; J. Boyle, *A Sense of Freedom*, Pan edition, 1977.

7. *Glasgow Herald*, 26 July 1962, p. 5. See also the poem, 'King Billy' by Edwin Morgan in G. Bruce (ed.), *The Scottish Literary Revival*, London, 1968, pp. 108–9, and more recently in *Noise and Smoky Breath*, pp. 54–5.

8. A series of articles on how Rev. J. Cameron Peddie 'broke the Glasgow gangs' appeared in the *Evening Citizen*, 7/10/11/12/13/14 January 1955; this was followed by a series on Fullerton and the Billy Boys, 16/18/19/20/21 January 1955. It seems that the *Citizen* was anxious to steal the thunder of Sir Percy Sillitoe's *Cloak without Dagger* (London, 1955) which appeared that same year.

Sillitoe has a chapter on the gangs, in which he emphasises the use of force in quelling them, with no reference to the work of Peddie. I used these as a point of reference to check contemporary accounts, and it is on this that most of what follows is based. There have been several articles in newspapers and journals, based mainly on sensationalism. James Patrick's *A Glasgow Gang Observed*, London, 1973, is interesting for what it sets out to do, but is slipshod in its historical account. The best short account is by J. A. Mack in *The Third Statistical Account (Glasgow)*, pp. 644–50, based, however, mainly on the *Citizen* articles and Sillitoe's *Cloak without Dagger*. There is an excellent study of working-class youths in England in: S. Humphries, *Hooligans or Rebels? An oral history of working-class childhood and youth, 1889–1939*, Oxford, 1981. See also Pearson, *Hooligan*.

9. *Daily Telegraph*, 4 October 1968.

10. *Sunday Times*, 31 December 1967. This article includes a comment by J. A. Mack that, unlike the pre-war, the post-war gangs were made up of teenagers rather than adults. This is not borne out by what I have read: the gangs of the inter-war years were generally aged between seventeen and twenty-one, with a few younger and a few older. The *Times* article also quoted figures to show that with a fifth of the population of Scotland, Glasgow was responsible for a third of its violent crimes.

11. *Observer*, 19 May 1968.

12. *Guardian*, 10 April 1969.

13. Most of the foregoing comes from cuttings in the Glasgow Scrapbook, vol. 14, pp. 93–118, vol. 17, p. 96 held in the Mitchell Library.

14. *Evening Times*, 19 January 1920.

15. *Evening News*, 21 June 1920.

16. N. Lucas, *Britain's Gangland*, London, 1969, pp. 1–14.

17. *Evening Citizen*, 7 January 1955.

18. *Evening Citizen*, 17 April 1930.

19. *Evening Citizen*, 4/6/7/8 August 1930.

20. With the opening of Green's Playhouse in 1927 to seat nearly 4,500 patrons, Glasgow had the biggest cinema theatre in Europe. It also had the largest number of dance halls per head of population in Britain. The dancing craze is well portrayed in *No Mean City*, but right through to the demise of Barrowland even casual acquaintance with the city brought home this particular obsession. In latter times, however, one would be less likely to see two males dance with each other as proof of their masculinity!

21. A special investigation by Mr Robert Spence, ex-MP, was carried out on behalf of the Scottish Temperance Alliance. He gave as a major cause the excessive zeal on behalf of the two football teams, Celtic, 'supported by Roman Catholics', and Rangers, 'supported by Protestants'. He thought that unemployment was the major cause of the problem, however, while drink played only a small part—perhaps what one would have thought a disappointing conclusion for a temperance group, but they claimed to be pleased with this finding. The investigator also put the age of the gang members at fourteen to

twenty years. See report in *The Scottish Temperance Reformer*, 15 August 1930, p. 162.

22. Crerand, p. 28.

23. *No Mean City*, p. 31.

24. *Evening Citizen*, 14 August 1930, p. 1. The issue of two days later commented on the 'admirable work' of Peddie.

25. *Evening Citizen*, 12 June 1930, p. 1, under the headline: 'Another Scheme for Wiping Out the Gangs'. The businessman claimed that police reports would show that Glasgow in 1912 had more serious problems with the gangs and that 'the root of the problem is unemployment, of course'.

26. A. W. Cockerill, *Sir Percy Sillitoe*, London, 1975, pp. 153–4, tells of the threat to close Old Firm games and the death threat. A more pointed appraisal of Sillitoe's personality and 'gangbuster' reputation is in J. P. Bean, *The Sheffield Gang Wars*, Sheffield, 1981, pp. 121–9, 132–4.

27. *Third Statistical Account*, pp. 647–8; Sillitoe, p. 133.

28. *Evening Citizen*, 20 January 1955, p. 4.

29. *Weekly Record*, 12 July 1930.

30. Many served and died as Commandoes in the Second World War, *Third Statistical Account*, p. 649.

31. C. Harvie, *No Gods and Precious Few Heroes*, London, 1981, p. 100.

32. A history of the Orange Order in Scotland has still to be written. T. Gray's *The Orange Order*, London, 1972, deals mainly with the Order in Ireland. The most extensive treatment of the Order or rather its activities in Scotland is in Handley's *The Irish in Scotland, passim. The Scotsman* published two very good articles on the Order in Scotland: 'Close-up', 8, 9 July 1966.

33. Most of the foregoing is based on a survey of the papers in this time, but is also influenced in part at least by childhood folklore. Peter McDougall's *Just Another Saturday*, shown on Scottish Television in 1976, was an excellent portrayal of The Twelfth in Glasgow; Hector MacMillan's play *The Sash*, published by Molendinar Press, Glasgow in 1974, is a more savage portrayal of the hero Bill MacWilliam's preparation for his big day of the year.

34. Headlines from, respectively: *Sunday Mail*, 8 July 1923; *Sunday Mail*, 12 July 1925; *Sunday Mail*, 10 July 1927; *Sunday Mail*, 13 July 1930.

35. *Evening Citizen*, 19 January 1955. At one stage Fullerton and his two 'lieutenants' had £1,200 in a Bridgeton bank. This princely sum possibly came from the pockets of the politicians rather than the gang members' subscriptions of 2d weekly (if they could afford it). Fullerton used half the money on his flute band and a trip to Belfast, but lost the other half when one of his lieutenants absconded with the money while he was in gaol.

36. *Forward*, 29 June 1935.

37. Most of the resultant letters to the *Glasgow Herald* further condemned the club, some tried to defend it, and inevitably a couple had to drag in Celtic's foulmouths (*Glasgow Herald*, 5, 9, 10, 12, 17, 18 August 1983). (I myself visited Ibrox shortly after this controversy and couldn't help noticing that one of the supporters standing in front of me was a black, and he attracted no abuse

whatsoever—but then he was rigged out in Rangers' colours.) John Fairgrieve, in Nuremberg to cover the 1967 European Cup Winner's Cup Final between Rangers and Bayern Munich, visited the stadium made notorious by the rallies of 1935, and was met by a Jew who wept as he likened Rangers fans to Nazis chanting 'Juden Raus'. But later a remark by one of Fairgrieve's colleagues about 'Bloody animals' in references to the Rangers support brought the matter back into perspective they were enjoying themselves, Fairgrieve replied, 'They're not too bad' ('We arra people' in Archer and Royle, *We'll Support You Ever More* pp. 201–3). Brian Wilson has accused Rangers fans of using National Front slogans, specifically in the graffitti left behind at Eindhoven after a Rangers' European Cup game ('Crossfire' broadcast on BBC, 28 November 1978). Writing to *The Scotsman* on 18 June 1980, James Gillespie raised the issue of racialism as a subject that had been overlooked in the various inquests into the recent Hampden riot. He was referring to the foothold the National Front had found in Scotland by allying with extreme protestant (or anti-Irish) organisations in public demonstrations, concluding that the National Front had identified their fellow travellers and that its 'sponsorship for a member of an Apprentice Boys of Derry Club in the Glasgow Central by-election seems to complete the jigsaw'.

CHAPTER 7

The Riots and the Fans

Riots at football matches are as old as the game itself: the early games were in effect legalised riots. From the days when rival villages faced up to each other the size of the sides has gradually been reduced to the dozen or so who made up the public school teams, finally settling for eleven a side halfway through the nineteenth century. As the size of the teams was reduced, so the rules were modified and 'the murdering practice' of football gradually became more civilised. With the formation of the Football Association in 1863, handling and hacking were outlawed, and while the game remained a pretty rough physical affair for a long time thereafter, and most teams featured a hatchet man whose skills were not necessarily with the ball, the robust style of the game stayed much the same until the invasion by the 'continentals' in the 1950s.

While violence as a normal part of the game on the field has diminished, violence off the field has not; although the pattern, like that of the 'gang menace', seems to have been an alternation between periods of calm and periods of turbulence in Scotland at least. The most spectacular riots in the history of football in Britain involved both Rangers and Celtic. One was at the Scottish Cup Final played at Hampden Park in May 1980; the other was at the same stadium, at the same stage of the same competition, seventy-one years previously. A major difference then was that the two sets of fans were united against police and firemen who had come to put out the fires they had started, and this rare show of solidarity between the two sets of spectators has helped confirm the view that it was not until after the First World War that they became bitter enemies. The inter-war years and into the 1940s were punctuated by crowd troubles, but there were no riots to match the 1909 or 1980 Cup Finals. Like sectarianism, however, they have a history that extends back well before 1914 or even 1912, the year given by Maley as the beginning of the troubles.

Crowd Troubles Before 1914

It would have been surprising if there had been no trouble. In the early days of football in Scotland crowd break-ins were so common that they were hardly news. Usually these break-ins were provoked by an event on the field, but sometimes quite simply to stop the game and so avert defeat, for when there was only a rope restraining spectators such intervention was a constant temptation; at other times restraining the crowd could be impossible, for officials were often unwilling to turn away paying customers. On the other hand rushes at the gate and over (or through) the fence could result in the presence of thousands of non-paying customers.

As grounds improved and controls on the numbers allowed in were more stringently applied, break-ins became less frequent, especially with increasing police vigilance, leaving fans to fight among each other on the terracings or on the streets outside the ground. Neither football, nor Glasgow, nor Scotland was unique in this. Every country where football was spreading in the late nineteenth century faced the same problems, until the top teams with their better-policed grounds and bigger crowds became safer for players and spectators alike than the games being conducted in parks or village greens.

Bottles were being thrown at referees and players as early as the 1880s, and rivets were popular missiles in the shipyard regions. But mud and stones were the most common means of assault other than fists and boots: in the first years of this century it was the Hearts and Aberdeen fans who seemed to come in for the most unwanted publicity, and it was said in condemnation of the latter that stones, like the haddock, were becoming freely associated with the northern city. In Glasgow the Queen's Park fans were most unpopular in certain quarters, and McLaughlin of Celtic, in his Athletic Notes for the *Glasgow Examiner*, frequently berated the 'covered standites' and even the gentlemen known as 'pavilionites'. It was as true then, as it is today, that the Glasgow football fan,[1] or the Glasgow working class, was not any more violent, in relation to the size of population, than the rest of Scotland. And just as Scottish fans since the late 1960s have had little by way of violence to teach their English counterparts, so in the years before World War I the *Scottish Referee* could editorialise on 'another of these disgraceful football riots which are becoming far too common in England'.[2]

This said, however, the particular violence and bitterness of Rangers/Celtic confrontations sets them apart: fans with no religious animus will fight as violently as do catholics and protestants, but before the racial overtones recently introduced into some crowd troubles in England, religion, as always, gave these battles a unique odium. This fundamental conflict has kept alive the longest-running blood feud in the history of any two sporting teams: in the years between the wars and into the 1940s and 1950s, when matches being played throughout the rest of the country appeared to be generally peaceful, Rangers/Celtic games were frequently marked by crowd troubles.[3]

Rangers had been playing Celtic for nearly ten years before the first reports of trouble were reported between the two clubs—a remarkable enough feat since both had been involved in incidents of varying seriousness with other clubs. In 1896 *Scottish Sport* noted that bad blood had crept into recent games between the two teams and cautioned them against allowing such displays to continue, as they would affect their interest.[4] The bad blood built up, but more people were attracted than put off by this. In 1898 Celtic allowed nearly 50,000 people to crowd into Parkhead for the New Year's Day game with Rangers, and with Rangers pressing for the winner with the score at 1–1 the crowd, which had interrupted play frequently, finally brought the game to a halt. A major problem at this game was the absence of mounted police, only forty ordinary constables being charged with the control of the 50,000 fans inside the ground.[5] The Celtic club, at the same time as it did its best to make sure Rangers didn't get the increased share that a game declared a friendly would entail, excused the employment of so few police on grounds of cost.

In 1902 Celtic Park was the scene of 'one of the most disgraceful exhibitions that has ever been witnessed in a Scottish football arena', and the *Scottish Referee* which condemned the game in these terms indicated that bitterness between the two clubs was not new; it went on to talk about the 'past deplorable incidents between Celtic and Rangers' and asked rhetorically why rat pits should be illegal and such exhibitions tolerated.[6] Two factors which were to be behind many of the riots that followed were blamed for the troubles of that day: poor refereeing and violence on the field. Celtic officials insinuated that it was not so much poor refereeing as biased refereeing, and this was how some of the players saw it, reacting with referee baiting that 'almost amounted to violence'.[7] Finally Sandy McMahon, a great Celtic favourite, and claimed in the catholic press as the 'fairest and most sportsmanlike player ever known', tripped the referee as he walked away from him, and was sent off.[8]

The first three months of 1905 saw two field invasions at Old Firm games: the first, the Ne'erday game, at Ibrox, was little more than a break-in caused by a crowd overflow, but the second involved a physical attack on the referee. At the former it seems there was 'a rush of youths' at a time when Celtic were asserting themselves in a scoreless game, but there were no serious accusations that the game was brought to a premature finish to save Rangers. The *Glasgow Star* rather self-righteously blamed the break-in on the greed of the Rangers officials, who, despite the recent memory of the Ibrox disaster, allowed too many people through the turnstiles: however, 'the money's the thing', it concluded.[9] Celtic supporters had less reason to be self-righteous about the riot in March, a cup semi-final at Parkhead, where a violent game was brought to an end eight minutes from time, with Rangers winning 2–0. This was the infamous 'Quinn/Craig game', where Quinn was ordered off after appearing to kick the Rangers fullback. A section of the spectators broke through the fence, taking the iron-spiked palings with them as weapons, and set on the referee. Only Hay, the Celtic captain, saved the incident from becoming worse as he protected the referee from the fury of the crowd. Celtic director Glass came out to appeal to the fans, and for his trouble was hit over the eye with a stone which inflicted a bad cut. An attempt was made to restart the game, but players were attacked again, and so the match was abandoned. Another familiar complaint was prominent in this riot, as it had been in the January break-in and other crowd disturbances: the leading role played by boys and youths. After the January break-in the *Referee* had suggested that the boys' gate be closed, now the Celtic officials claimed that of the 100 to 150 (out of 35,000) spectators who trespassed on to the field, most were boys. They thought they could secure a replay and were just engaging in horseplay.[10] The other major complaint was the absence of mounted police, just as when Rangers supporters brought the 1912 cup game with Clyde to an end when Rangers were down 3–1.

One complaint that appeared only in the catholic press, however, was that of religious bigotry. As Quinn was leaving the field, one of the Rangers players said: 'Serves you right, you Papish -------!' This was reported in the *Glasgow Observer*,[11] which was deluged with letters from irate readers anxious to know who the insulting Rangers player was. Graciously the *Observer* refused to release his name, but did add that a postcard to Quinn, c/o Parkhead, might have the desired result.[12] Apparently there was little that was new in this. Just under ten years earlier McLaughlin had blasted a section of the Rangers support for unfair abuse of the Celtic players. He claimed that there was an 'unreasonable and bitter hostility—perhaps I might even call it bigotry—in some quarters against the Parkhead team'.[13] About the same time *Scottish Sport* had warned about an 'accumulation of incidents' and 'spice of bitterness' being added to the rivalry of the two teams.[14] If McLaughlin had occasion to complain about the Rangers support, so too had Rangers about Celtic: in October 1896 Rangers players leaving

Celtic Park were attacked by a 'crowd of ruffians' who let fly a hail of mud and stones at the Rangers' brake. Nick Smith was hit dangerously close to the eye by one of the stones, but luckily suffered no more than a cut face.[15]

Clearly, then, relations between the two clubs and their respective supporters before 1912 were not as harmonious as Maley, and following him various other commentators, have suggested since. The managements were involved in several disputes, and this was reflected on the field and on the terracings. What is true is that Rangers were less likely than certain other clubs to be singled out for abuse by the catholic press. Indeed for McLaughlin writing in the *Examiner* it was Hearts, but more particularly Queen's Park, who were the main villains. This was doubtless for the middle-class bias which the working-class Celts had to suffer, for it was Queen's Park and not Rangers who then represented middle-class respectability. Disagreements between Celtic and Queen's Park had resulted at least twice in their snubbing each other after disputed victories in the Glasgow Cup Final. The links between Queen's Park, the SFA, amateurism and Scottish respectability fuelled McLaughlin's anger as he pointed out how

> The Hampden covered standites, with whom I regret to have to associate also a great number of pavilionites, are rapidly securing for themselves the unenviable position that used to be allocated to the Tynecastle habitués. Rabid and bigoted partisanship is an exceedingly mild term to apply to their ferocious ebulations [*sic*]. Were they of the working-class there might be a little excuse for them, but the most of them at any rate are dressed like gentlemen. I am afraid the resemblance ends there. A worse exhibition than these gents favoured us with has never been given in Scotland. It was worthy of a band of drunken cannibals.[16]

A few months later he claimed that 'rabid and disgraceful partisanship' was becoming a feature at Hampden, with stone-throwing at players and the referee often winding up proceedings, while the officials refused to do anything about it.[17]

This was McLaughlin retaliating at the abuse and prejudice he believed his club was suffering from the Scottish press and public. But the influence of Queen's Park, in the corridors of power as on the field of play, declined as rapidly as that of Rangers rose. By the time of the First World War Celtic and Queen's Park would become the greatest of friends, with the latter on several occasions having reason to be grateful to Celtic, generally for their refusal to poach the amateur players[18] and, more recently, for trying to keep Hampden alive.

At the turn of the century Queen's Park still retained the prestige of having been the premier club in Scotland, but by then they had lost the prestige that is gained by winning trophies. That had passed to Celtic and Rangers. Matches between Celtic and Rangers, as standard bearers for their respective societies, were supercharged with a bitterness that heightened the tensions present in any local derby. Bad refereeing, violent play on the field, inadequate policing, the role of youngsters: some or all of these factors were present in blow-ups between the two teams before the First World War, and they would reappear right down to the present day. But because of the peculiar position of the two clubs, these inevitable problems take on inflated importance. And yet none of these was present in the mixture that caused the explosion of April 1909 which resulted in the Scottish Cup being withheld for that year.

Another unusual feature of that riot was that both sets of fans were equally condemned by their respective managements, while neither catholic nor secular press sought excuses for or assigned blame to one set of supporters rather than the other. Such unanimity, however, was not a sign that sectarianism had suddenly disappeared from the Scottish sporting scene: rather it was one of the few, but not unknown, instances of middle-class horror at working-class violence transcending other fears.

Seventy thousand people saw the first drawn Cup Final in 1909, most of them paying a hard-earned shilling to do so, particularly hard as the previous two years had seen one of the worst recessions in the history of industrial Glasgow, particularly bad since it interrupted the prosperity that had generally marked the years before World War I. Another 61,000 paid to see the replay the following week. Naturally they wanted to see a result and, noting the plethora of draws at that time, at least one newspaper had given them the idea that extra time would be played if there was still no result after ninety minutes. When, at the end of normal time, the teams were still level, the fans refused to move, encouraged in their belief that there would be an extra half-hour played by the sight of members of both teams staying on the field. The fans waited, tension grew, suspicions were raised—without basis, although not without reason—that the clubs and the authorities wanted another draw so that they would share another gate. Tension was broken and anger boiled over when an official strode out and ostentatiously removed a corner flag.

The events that followed have often been described: the burning of the goalposts and nets, the wrecking of the pay-boxes, the cutting of the hose-pipes to prevent the firemen putting out the fires. The battles went on until seven o'clock that evening. In the final tally nearly a hundred were injured, six seriously, including policemen and firemen. Only three arrests were made—that is to say actually taken into custody, for there were many more arrests but the police were forced to release their captives.[19]

The papers had a field day, with the *Glasgow News* heading a cartoon depicting 'King Hooligan', 'Seeing Red', the latter trying to link the uproar the previous week at the Trades Council and Town Council meeting as part of the same event.[20] The *Glasgow Observer* tried to exonerate the ordinary football enthusiast by claiming that it was criminals and professional thieves who had started it all,[21] but overlooked the absence of 'professionalism' that left the Scottish Cup and £1,400 in gate money untouched in a tenement across the road. Letters to the editor blamed the clubs, the authorities, football itself, hooligans; other reports commented on the number of 'well dressed respectable men who got carried away and threw stones'.[22] Attempts were made to blame 'a few dozen ruffians who can disorganize anything', and inevitably the main culprits were 'undisciplined youths of from 16 to 20 years of age' or 'hundreds of hare-brained boys and thoughtless youths scenting a huge lark'.[23]

In the official outcome neither the authorities who had not had the foresight to arrange extra time (and so gave rise to the belief that they wanted to squeeze extra gate money out of the spectators), nor the newspapers who had led the public to believe extra time would be played, were included in the tally of causes. It is always easier to blame a few ruffians or a handful of youths; if only it were so, the job of the police would be so much easier.

The Inter-War Years

The years after the end of the Great War saw boom crowds and further outbreaks of spectator troubles. This was the period when the brake clubs were furiously denounced as a 'menace' to the game. These precursors of today's supporters' club buses dated back to the 1890s. The oldest Celtic Brake Club was St Mary's, founded in 1889,[24] but many others followed. The first annual social gathering of the United Celtic Brake Clubs was held at the Grand National Halls on 31 January 1896,[25] while the second, in December of that year, was 'crowded to suffocation'. The number of clubs had grown from four to thirteen in that time, and the position of the brake clubs 'was now assured'; from 'scant recognition they were now vying with each other in display of banners'.[26] The Rangers brakeists would soon accept the challenge of such displays.

"SEEING RED."

[The spirit of disorder manifested at the Trades Council and Town Council meetings last week culminated in the disgraceful riot at Hampden on Saturday evening.]

King Hooligan. *Glasgow News*, 19 April 1909

The brake clubs continued to grow until just after the First World War, when they had become a big enough nuisance for the law to clamp down on them. By this time, of course, they were motorised, and so larger and more mobile. During the football season Monday was becoming a regular day at the local police courts for the sentencing of youths who had got into trouble the previous Saturday. At one such session at the Ayr Police Courts following an Ayr United v Rangers game, the fiscal, Mr L. C. Boyd, commented on how

... at the corresponding match last year similar scenes of a disgraceful character took place on the part of the Rangers club. It was a singular fact that supporters of other clubs, with only occasional exceptions, behaved like ordinary citizens. The Rangers followers came to the town in brakes, char-a-bancs and motor lorries. They were composed of a large number of young hooligans whose object seemed to be not to enjoy the football match but to create pandemonium wherever they went.[27]

There were troubles inside the grounds, too, and one of the worst of such incidents was at Celtic Park on 26 April 1920 when Celtic fans broke on to the field during a Monday evening game against Dundee and attacked the referee as well as some Dundee players, one of whom was hit on the head and another taken off unconscious. As a result Celtic had to close their ground for four weeks. This was one of many disturbances at this time, made easy by the absence of police, but given its own peculiar twist in that some Celtic fans believed Dundee had allowed Rangers to beat them on the previous Saturday and so maintain their three-point lead in the league race. The *Weekly Record* commented:

We have been passing through a few black days in football. Again the game is liable to suffer, at least in the eyes of certain people, and the whole cause of the trouble is a few irresponsible youths who haven't the slightest respect for law and order. The trouble has been brewing for some time. One could see it at different grounds. Referees, if they weren't actually assaulted, were undoubtedly threatened ...[28]

Two weeks later it wrote on 'The Menace to Football' and urged that an effort be made to stop the brake clubs. It claimed that the football season had come to a disgraceful end, and that the game was in danger as respectable people were turned away from it by brakes which drove through the streets with fans waving flags and making hideous noises with their terrible rattles. This particular outburst was brought on by the Queen's Park team being abused by their own supporters and by the 'nasty business' at an Old Firm game at Ibrox, when Rangers disputed a Celtic penalty, and then Celtic were denied one they should have got. This was followed by incidents in which Gordon of Rangers hit Watson, who did not retaliate, but was avenged by a team-mate, McKay, who hit Gordon and walked off without waiting for the referee to send him off. Watson, who had not retaliated when hit by Gordon, was also sent off.[29]

Football was going through one of its periodical crises with attacks on, and defence of, the character of the people who followed their football teams week in week out. Back in 1908 the brake clubs had been accused in the press of being made up of 'hooligans' and 'weedy' or 'rickety' youths. At the Celtic Brake Clubs' Supper of that year President Gowans replied to the 'slanders' by saying that his members were respectable working-class men, earning an honest living and, in addition, 'pledged teetotallers'.[30]

The years after the war through to about 1925 were turbulent times, with young men trained to kill returning to peacetime lives and a shortage of jobs. From the mud of the trenches and the taste of death, the fear of shellshock and blinding by mustard gas, they returned to find that those who had not been abroad had little time for heroes; they were, after all, ten a penny and the routine life of earning a living had to go on. In Ireland warfare still raged until 1922, and this provided an outlet for some: more timid souls who perhaps preferred the symbolic and less lethal confrontations of the football stadiums, could adjust to life by following Rangers or Celtic. The wonder of this period, in Scotland especially, with proportionately higher casualties in the holocaust, is not that there were so many incidents between rival fans, but that there were so few: in Germany, France and Italy readjustments to civil life saw bloody riots and changes of government by violence; Red Clydeside saw windows smashed and skulls cracked, but there was never any serious threat that the machine guns placed around George Square during the strike riot of 1919 would ever have to be used. The worst violence in Glasgow was still along the Paisley Road after a match at Ibrox and in the vicinity of Janefield Street or Bridgeton Cross when Celtic were playing at home. Towards the end of 1920, the year in which Celtic Park had been closed for a month, a Celtic game against Clyde at Shawfield was marked by violence from the fans, who pelted the players with 'brickbats and jagged fragments of dirty slag'. 'Man in the Know' exonerated both Clyde and Celtic fans (Celtic were losing 2–1 at the time, so there would have been little to upset the home supporters), blaming the trouble on 'barbarians, mostly boys', members of the 'cut-throat class with which the war had deluged the big cities'. In the crowd of 25,000, he claimed, there had been only two or three dozen miscreants. Since they belonged to neither Clyde nor Celtic, where could they be from? 'Man in the Know' suggested the answer: they belonged to 'the same class of criminals who have killed football in Belfast', and so would be better off going to Ireland to join the Black and Tans.[31]

Anxious eyes were cast on the approaching Ne'erday game at Ibrox, and for the first time it was decided to control the approaches to the ground, with Celtic supporters following one route and Rangers another, while both sets of fans were segregated at different ends of the ground. Celtic won 2–0, and there was no trouble, the rival brakeists not seeing each other. Flags and banners were banned, although some were smuggled into the ground, as well as at least one revolver and a hatchet, which prompted one reporter to note, somewhat sadly, that he could foresee the day when fans might have to be searched at the turnstiles. If the colour was absent, the songs were there, the Celtic choir in full voice with: 'Hail Glorious St Patrick', 'God Save Ireland', 'Slievenamon', 'The Soldier's Song', 'There is a Happy Land', improvised with the name of Celtic favourites, and the inevitable 'Keep the Green Flag Flying'. If there was any mistaking the nature of the conflict, it was recorded on brakes with the score: Rebels 2 Black and Tans 0; or Sinn Fein 2 League of Nations 0. All this was reported by 'Man in the Know' with the heartiest acclaim, as was the noisy and colourful homeward procession, for who could possibly take offence at such lovely singing and associations with such a noble cause?[32]

Whether or not 'Man in the Know' and fellow spirits in the Celtic camp were aware of it, the Celtic brakes, with their colours, bugles and banners were a source of nuisance and often provocation. Equally so were those of the blue brigade. In 1923 one incident among many involved the driver of a Celtic Supporters' Club bus (motor charabanc) being forced by police to drive it into a police station, where all its occupants were arrested. This was after a game at Ibrox, and the bus was hired by the 'Sally Boys', not a recognised brake club. Licensed to carry twenty-five, the bus was carrying nearly twice that number as it proceeded from Ibrox to the city, with the boarders yelling threats, brandishing poles and—worst of all—yelling filthy epithets against the Rangers hero Alan Morton. At the police station thirty-nine arrests were made, and bottles, loaded sticks, hammers and stones were found in the charabanc. The defence lawyer claimed rather weakly that the incriminating weapons had been thrown into the vehicle by a Rangers brake, but also claimed, with perhaps more justification, that while the Celtic brakes were followed, those of the Rangers were not.[33]

It was not just contact between Celtic and Rangers fans that resulted in flare-ups. When, in April 1922, Celtic, in need of one point to win the League flag, went to Cappielow Park to play Morton, the outcome was one of the worst riots Greenock had ever seen. The Celtic fans went in their brakes blowing bugles and sporting their colours, but also waving Sinn Fein flags. They were met by the local fans, many of whom came from the strong Orange areas in Port Glasgow, with their pockets stuffed with rivets. Twenty-three thousand fans crowded into the ground, thousands were left outside; banners were forbidden, but the police might as well have told the tide to stay out. Fighting at the 'Wee Dublin' end broke out during the first half. Then at the interval, with Celtic losing by one goal, there was an explosion of violence from the west terracing and the field was taken over by rioting fans. Eventually the pitch was cleared and the match completed. Celtic got their point, with a few minutes remaining, but their fans had to fight their way back to the special trains, and incidents occurred throughout the district, most notably the burning of captured Celtic banners.[34] 'Man in the Know' commented on 'the Port Glasgow scalliwags mobilised in their thousands' who attacked the numerically weaker Celtic brake clubs, adding that 'The Belfast touch was in evidence here'.[35] Earlier, however, a correspondent of the same paper, calling himself 'a Celtic admirer', had complained about the Sinn Fein flag which had 'as much connection with the Celtic F.C. as it has with the open golf championship'. He thought the Celtic rowdies got what they deserved and suggested that manager Maley contact the owners of charabancs and ask them to refuse hire to any club that carried bugles or banners.[36]

It has been a healthy feature of the Celtic football support that it has always had individuals who were prepared to speak out in criticism of the less admirable activities of the club and its associates. Late in 1924 a Celtic supporter took exception to the provocative behaviour of the various brake clubs. He noted those of the Rangers in passing but was more concerned about Celtic supporters who had sung 'ugly stuff' at Brockville and Dens Park. At these grounds there had been no excuse for hymns, political songs and other emblems. He went on to make several practical suggestions for combating such behaviour, basically a concerted attempt by respected catholic youth bodies to influence such fans in the right way, pamphlets encouraging them to a more positive support, and the appointment of leaders to take action against offenders.[37]

Catholic community leaders had every right to concern themselves with the behaviour of Celtic fans: only the most wilfully blind could convince themselves that Celtic were merely a sporting body. In his report on the 1923 Cup Final between Celtic and Hibs, 'Man in the Know' was anxious to portray the meeting of these 'two Irish teams' as a social and political, as much as a sporting triumph. The conduct of both the players and the fans stood out in 'striking contrast to the previous year's all blue final' (Morton v Rangers), and the presence of the police at the game was 'not only a superfluity, but an insult'. In conclusion he pointed out that the behaviour of all concerned had made the 'recent anti-Irish mouthings seem the frothy bubble of imbeciles'.[38] This was his response to the 'menace of romanism' debate that was then such an agitated subject of discussion in more intellectual circles.

On the windy slopes of Glasgow's football grounds, and the roads leading to them, that debate was continued at a much more basic level.

In October 1925 the *Daily Record and Mail* reported:

FOOTBALL ROWDIES
121 Brake Club Supporters Fined in Glasgow
BANNERS, RATTLES AND BOTTLES

This followed a Glasgow Cup semi-final played at Ibrox the previous Tuesday, and the accused were made up of Rangers and Celtic brakeists who had been arrested either on their way to the game or on the way back, deliberately, it seems, driving their vehicles through rival territories, where they shouted, swore, waved banners and sang party songs.[39] Whether or not it was the tougher attitude of the magistrates, whether it was the increasing popularity of trains over brakes to take fans to the games, thus stopping them wandering through streets of their choice, or whether the antagonists had simply exhausted their hatreds for the time being, football was about to enter a quieter period. This seems to have been the last headline-grabbing Old Firm disturbance for several years.[40]

The Fans on the Terracing

To look at crowd photographs of the pre-war years, or even up to the 1950s, it is easy to get the impression that games then were played before sombrely dressed spectators who were equally sombre in their behaviour, and that it was difficult to tell one lot of supporters from another. This is in marked contrast to today's shots of supporters with waving banners, outstretched scarves and wearing jerseys as worn by the teams themselves. All this in glorious colour, and sharply focused, with wide-angle lenses and telephoto lenses catching action in the mass and in close-up. At home, television captures it all as a kaleidoscope of colour and noise. It is likely, given the greater affluence and wider variety of ways to show your allegiance to one team or another, that today's games *are* more colourful; it is less certain that they are any noisier. However that may be, it is easy from reading the newspaper accounts of games, before the days of cheaper colour reproduction and saturation picture coverage, to believe that little has changed. At least so far as Old Firm games are concerned. The crowds of the first years of the century, and for every decade after, have been reported by contemporary sports writers as presenting a spectacle of colour and noise such as had never been seen (or heard) before. Perhaps they were right!

In 1955 Kenneth Wolstenholme came up from England to act as commentator at the televised Scottish Cup Final of that year between

Clyde and Celtic. He says he was amazed at the banners, flags, whistles and songs, and claims never to have heard such a din. Nearly twenty years previously he had been equally astonished when he came up for the final of the Empire Exhibition Cup Final, played between Celtic and Everton:

> ... my first taste of the Scottish fervour ... especially the brand turned on by the Celtic fans. They waved their banners, they waved their flags, and they sang their revolutionary songs and their special war cry of 'the Dear Little Shamrock'.[41]

Thirty years prior to that the *Glasgow Observer* described how the goal that won the Glasgow Cup for Celtic against Rangers, in October 1909, turned a 'black and white study' into a green festival 'as if by magic the heights were decorated with green banners and flags', the fans splitting ears with their ricketties (rattles).[42] In the same fixture three years later Celtic were beaten 3–1 by Rangers, and a Celtic supporter wrote to the catholic press complaining about 'the usual crowing, jeering and boastful flag-waving inseparable from a Celtic reverse'. This 'amazing outburst of bigoted exultation' came from a 'travelling menagerie of supporters whose bestial howls make the day hideous wherever the Rangers happen to be playing'.[43]

In the late 'twenties a letter to the catholic press criticised those Celtic supporters who gathered at the Janefield End at Celtic Park for their noise, their language and their singing of 'Hail! Glorious St Patrick', commenting that he certainly would not have approved of them singing triumphantly about wading 'knee deep in Orange blood'. This was particularly insulting, as many players and supporters of Celtic were protestants. The writer went on to complain about the waving of tricolours, pointing out that green and white were Celtic's colours and the correct place for the Irish flag was with other national flags above the grandstand, and not to be waved provocatively among the crowd. In a game against Hearts the continued singing and chanting was particularly condemned, as it did not have the excuse of provocation from a rival 'choir'.[44] The admonitions had no effect. Two years later the same paper made an appeal in thick black type for the Celtic followers to behave themselves:

> ... They are asked to cut out all provocative and unmannerly displays and leave such discreditable tactics to crowds supporting teams less illustrious and distinguished than Celtic ... ignore the taunting challenges and silly flag-waving of the opposition ... cut out singing at matches [and the] chanting of childish ditties varied—and this is the most objectionable feature—by verses of a hymn. It merely gives an excuse for the enemy to reply with their ribald doggerel and insulting challenges.[45]

Shortly after this John Thomson was killed diving at the feet of Rangers' Sam English, and the next time the teams met 'not a vestige of colour was to be seen, hardly a sound heard ... no singing, no flag-waving, no provocative challenges'.[46] As after an even sadder occasion nearly forty years later, the peace did not last long. Even on the day of the tragedy the real hooligans were in evidence: Meiklejohn, who had had to silence his own fans shortly after the accident, later had to approach the referee to complain about the barracking of English by Celtic followers.

One reason the catholic press condemned bad behaviour from their fans was that it incurred the prejudice, as they saw it, of the police. After a riot against Motherwell, with 10,000 fans spilling on to the track to avoid the fighting, leaving a familiar 'no man's land' on the terracing, the *Glasgow Observer* reporter chastised the hymn singing and flag waving as much in sorrow as in anger, for the fans seemed incapable of realising that this was the excuse the police waited for. Celtic fans, because of the colours they sported, could not expect impartiality when the powers moved in.[47]

One of the most famous descriptions of Rangers fans in this period is in George Blake's *The Shipbuilders*, where Danny Shields goes off to what Blake calls the industrial substitute in Scotland for clan warfare. Blake took it for granted that Danny, not a violent man, was 'as ready as the next man to fight a supporter of the other team' and categorised the Rangers/Celtic conflict as more

> than the simple test of relative skill. Their colours, blue and green, were symbolic. Behind the rivalry of the players, behind even the commercial rivalry of limited companies, was the dark significance of sectarian and racial passions. Blue for the Protestants of Scotland and Ulster, green for the Roman Catholics of the Free State; and it was a bitter war that was to be waged on that strip of white-barred turf. All the social problems of a hybrid city were to be sublimated in the imminent clash of mercenaries.[48]

About the same time the journalist 'Gulliver' recorded his impressions of an Old Firm Ne'erday game at Parkhead.[49] 'Gulliver' admitted that he was not a football enthusiast, but since New Year's Day, a holiday with everything closed, promised to be even more dismal than the traditional Scots Sabbath, he decided to go to the big game. He found himself at the Rangers end, with gum-chewing, bunneted fans. 'Blue was the predominant colour, and innumerable blue handkerchiefs were in evidence, and soon began to wave defiance at the other end of the field, where green handkerchiefs were soon answering'. 'Gulliver' found the crowd good-humoured and knowledgeable, but the conditions were primitive, even dangerous, with ambulance men constantly removing spectators who had fainted in the crush. As the language became bluer than the handkerchiefs, and bottles were emptied and casually smashed on the ground, he found it all too much. He fought to get out, passing one man who swore that although he had paid a shilling to get in he would pay two to get out, but he had one particularly anxious moment when a drunken fan

> grabbed my arm in a vice-like hold, looked at me with glassy eyes and said 'Hauf a meenit, mate'. I felt sure he was about to pick a quarrel for I suddenly realized that I was wearing a blue tie, and his was green, and partisan feeling was running high. I need not have worried. He merely wished to ask a question, and his question was so astounding that I could hardly believe that I was hearing aright. 'Mate', he said, tightening his grip, and swaying, 'wha' was the name o' the island tha' the great Napoleon was sent to—y'know, after the ba'le o' Wa'erloo y'know?'
>
> 'St Helena, wasn't it?' I answered.
>
> His face grew grim. 'St Helena, St Helena, tha's place mate, tha's place. Well, that's were that ??? So-and-so (one of the players) should be sent. See!' And he released my arm and collapsed.

The years between the wars were bad years for Celtic, and it is likely that their fans were more often in trouble than those of Rangers. The team had a lean run on the field, and their supporters, mainly catholic working class, suffered more than their protestant counterparts in the Depression. The Rangers followers, of course, were no angels. It seems they were no better in 1940 than they had been in 1920 when they had been condemned by the Ayr County Court fiscal. In a rare letter published in the course of the football riots of 1940, a fan from the East wrote an 'Indictment of Rangers fans' which appeared in the *Sunday Mail*.[50] He had been to Firhill for a Partick Thistle v Rangers game where the home supporters were outnumbered by ten to one. He claimed that the language was bad enough, but the 'bigotry and ignorance' were so great that he would not have believed it if he hadn't witnessed it himself: 'It is a subject which is usually absent from reports of football matches and yet is the one thing that brings out the very worst in the type of spectator who was there beside me'. It was always the same where Rangers played, and if Celtic were as bad, then it would be better for football if both clubs went out of existence. Having made the point about bigotry that the secular press was usually too coy to mention, he went on to point out another unpalatable fact, namely that the Rangers hooligans, far from being an insignificant minority, were 'I am afraid a big section of the crowd'.

HI! Hi! Step up and hear the news, This
interests all you men,
The firm of Green and Blue goes into
Business once again;
"The same old brag," Pittodrie says.
"We're silent—and more wise.
"When they come here, they'll find it
doesn't
"Pay to advertise." OLO.

Back in Business. *Daily Record and Mail*, 26 November 1934

The Bottle Parties

Normal football was suspended in Scotland for the duration of the
Second World War, and the competitions that were organised were
artificial affairs, played before crowds reduced by law, and by such
players as were available. War service deprived many clubs of their
players, and teams were sometimes made up at the last minute after
appeals to the crowd for someone to fill a gap, but one consolation to be
derived from the rule allowing 'guest' players was the spectacle of a
Matthews/Lawton combination playing for Morton. This added to, but at
least helped make up for, the unreality of the competition of those years.
In other ways, however, and this in regard to The Old Firm, the game
continued as before: while catholics and protestants fought together in
Europe, opposing fans at Ibrox and Parkhead continued their own
particular warfare. After a riot at Ibrox in May 1940 the *Glasgow Herald*
announced that 'Times were back to normal at Ibrox last night—at least

so far as football as played between Rangers and Celtic is concerned'.[51] 'Rex' of the *Sunday Mail* remarked that while many commentators had noted what these two clubs had done *for* the game, not enough had said what they had done *to* the game, and that if a balance were drawn up it would have to include 'the many disgraceful scenes on terracing and field created by meetings of these clubs'.[52] Alan Breck pointed out that you didn't have to go to France to see some fighting and declared in exasperation that 'if the appeal of these two teams is to be based on such scenes the future of the game is a dismal one indeed'.[53]

The game was a Charity Cup semi-final, played before a restricted crowd of 30,000. Poor refereeing and violence on the field sparked off the trouble. In one incident Venters of Rangers kicked the ball away in disgust, bringing a shower of stones from the Celtic end. He refused to go and collect the ball when told to by the referee and walked off the field instead. The following year it was the same again, this time in the first Old Firm game of the 1941–42 season, before 65,000 fans at Ibrox. Delaney and Crum of Celtic were stretchered off the field, with the referee taking no action against the culprits. The incident that provoked the riot was when Dawson pushed Delaney and had a penalty awarded against him. He protested vigorously, but saved the penalty in any case. Then came the bottles, with the players taking shelter in the nets. The upshot was that Celtic's ground was closed for one month, an action that drew a howl of protest from the catholic press and an indignant outburst from Patrick Dollan, Lord Provost of Glasgow, who claimed that this was 'the most cockeyed judgement I have ever read—more like Nazi policy than British fair play', adding that the Scottish football authorities had always been lopsided in their judgement. The Celtic director, Col. Shaughnessy, noted that Celtic supporters had done nothing until the bottle throwing.[54] One incident that the catholic press did not raise, however, was the waving of a tricolour during the playing of the National Anthem[55]—this during one of the darkest periods of the war, while the Irish Republic remained aloof from the fight against Nazism and some of its activists had recently been engaged in terrorism on British soil.

In the spate of correspondence that followed it emerged that Celtic fans had been involved in several nasty incidents: a pitch invasion at Broomfield in a match against Airdrie, bottles against Hearts, and bottles and stones in two Rangers games. 'Rex', who made no secret of his disgust with with both sets of spectators, pointed out that the Rangers toughs had had it easy for the past few years, and then he went on to strike closer to the heart of the matter. Chief Inspector Sillitoe had made veiled references to the problem when he had urged both clubs to 'clean up their Augean stables', but 'Rex' came straight to the point:

> The most utter piffle has been written about the Rangers–Celtic disturbances. Onus is put on the players, the spectators, the police— everybody except the real culprits, the respective club managements. They have done nothing to reduce the religious heat which brings huge crowds to these games—one would almost think that they encouraged it to ensure such crowds, the game itself seems now to be merely a thin cover for the 'Billy or a Dan' challenge.[56]

The battles continued throughout the 'forties, culminating in the 'Great Flag Flutter' of 1952. In the Ne'erday game at Ibrox in 1943 Celtic lost two players ordered off and were beaten 8–1. The fighting was confined to the terracing. To celebrate the end of the Second World War a Victory Cup was organised. Rangers and Celtic met in the semi-final, drew, and in the replay at Hampden the following Wednesday evening 'a hard and sporting game' became a fiasco following Celtic protests at a penalty award to Rangers twenty minutes from the end. Celtic players surrounded the referee, and Paterson, the Celtic captain, who had been warned in the first half, was ordered off. Celtic continued to protest, and when Young placed the ball to take his kick, Mallan kicked it away, so he joined Paterson on the way to the pavilion. When Young scored from the spot, a spectator burst on to the field, to be arrested before he could reach the referee, but not before he threw a missile at him: three further arrests were made of fans invading the field. Celtic, with two men injured, one of whom was eventually carried off on a stretcher, finished the game with seven men and a cripple, but Rangers eased up and scored only one more goal.[57] In some ways the most remarkable outcome of the game was the booking of Lynch, the one Celtic player who had kept well clear of the trouble, and whose booking came after the match. Despite this, the defence of Lynch by Duncanson who was his opponent at the match, and the reasonable doubts about the fitness of the referee to be in charge of the game, the SFA refused to investigate and upheld the committee's four-week suspension of Lynch.

Three years later The Old Firm troubles brought the *Picture Post* photographers and reporters to Scotland to report on the 'sempiternal Battle of the Boyne' 'or Irish civil war'.[58] 1949 had been the year of the bottle parties, with a minor shower at the Ne'erday game and a veritable hail of missiles at the League Cup game at Ibrox in August. This followed the notorious Cox/Tully incident in a League Cup game at Ibrox. On 27 August Sammy Cox got the ball clear from the chief joker in the Celtic pack, Charlie Tully, then stepped back and kicked him in what was euphemistically called 'the groin'. As 'Rex' reported it: '95,000 gasped when the ref waved play on'.[59] Immediately a shower of bottles emerged from the crowd, raining down on the field, track and just as often fellow-supporters, but a thick cordon of police prevented a mass invasion of the pitch. The game was ruined from then on and a shuttle service of ambulancemen was necessary to cart away the fallen from the numerous battles on the terracing. The two teams met again a fortnight later in a Glasgow Cup match at Celtic Park, and the *Glasgow Herald* report could not hide its opinion of the referee's performance at that game. It claimed that Rangers' winning goal, scored three minutes from the end, started with a handball that was not, and a free kick that was taken while the ball was moving, to be scored by Findlay from an offside position. All this time the Celtic players were protesting, and Tully urged his team-mates to leave the field. On the restart Boden kicked the legs from Waddell and no action was taken. By this time the track around the ground was thick with policemen.[60]

In nearly all of these incidents in the 1940s it was the Celtic fans who were at the heart of the trouble, but in addition to the normal provocation of the Rangers support, it does seem that they were at the receiving end of bad refereeing decisions and tough, even unjust, punishment from the SFA. Following the incident at Celtic Park when Tully urged his team-mates to leave the field, the Celtic management requested that the forthcoming league game with Rangers at Ibrox be postponed: the clubs were meeting too frequently for their own good. This request was refused and the Celtic Supporters Association, representing 12,000 members, decided to boycott the next Old Firm game—this was the one that *Picture Post* came up to record. Only 65,000 attended, and *Picture Post's* Denzil Batchelor was disappointed: they turned out to be 'the best behaved crowd in the world'. However, he noted that 'After all, there was a wee bit breathing space now and then, even in the Battle of the Boyne'.

Throughout all these disputes the newspaper columns were filled with solutions to the problem: both clubs should be dissolved; these games should be played behind closed gates (described by 'Rex' as the 'looniest solution'); clubs should swop strips; the matter would resolve itself as the decent fans stayed away; and of course many suggestions as to what should be done to the 'hooligan minority'. The SFA decided that the real cause of the trouble was the Irish tricolour flying over the 'Jungle'—the covered enclosure facing the stand—at Parkhead. What prompted this decision was an Old Firm riot in which the Celtic fans seemed wholly to blame—even the *Glasgow Observer* admitted that Rangers deserved to win. It was at Parkhead, the Ne'erday game of 1952, and Rangers were winning comfortably when bottles were thrown from the Celtic end and crowds flocked on to the track from the covered enclosure.

The result was an inquiry into The Old Firm troubles by the Glasgow magistrates, who made several recommendations to the Scottish Football Association and the Scottish League. These suggestions included the ending of Old Firm games on New Year's Day, limits on the crowd at these games, which should be all-ticket, and the discouragement of the display of flags 'which might incite feeling among the spectators'. It was this last recommendation that resulted in The Great Flag Flutter,[61] when the Referee Committee of the SFA told the two clubs to take down from their grounds 'any flag or emblem that has no association with the country or the sport'. There was no doubt that this was aimed at Celtic: they had shamrocks on their corner flags, and occasionally wore strips with a shamrock on the breast, but the real cause of the heart-burning was the flying of the Irish flag over the Jungle, albeit alongside the Union Jack and other flags.

Many, perhaps even most, visitors to Celtic Park had been unaware of the Irish flag fluttering above them, and to suggest that it had been in any way responsible for the crowd troubles was ridiculous. In the Ne'erday match under discussion, as in previous disturbances that had served as background to the dispute, Celtic supporters had been to blame: it could hardly be said that *they* were in any way moved to anger by the flag. On the other hand there had been crowd troubles at Hampden and Ibrox without the flag. This is not to play down the importance of symbols, but in this case it was a symbol not of what fired the fans, but rather of what fired the prejudices of particular officials in high office. In this case at least Celtic had reason to suspect that they were suffering from bigotry, but they could not accuse the entire Scottish press of complicity, as Cyril Horne waged a pointed campaign against the legislators of the game in his regular column in the *Glasgow Herald*.[62] Celtic were to survive the attacks, but it was the self-interest rather than the enlightenment of the other clubs that saved them.

When the matter came to be discussed by the Referee Committee of the SFA, Celtic chairman Robert Kelly resolutely refused to remove the tricolour, since it in no way contravened any of the rules of the Association. To some people's surprise he was supported in his stand by Wilson of Rangers, but when the representatives of the other clubs saw that Kelly was serious, and they counted up the cost in terms of rearranged fixtures and losses at the gate if Celtic withdrew or were expelled from Scottish football, they granted Celtic a stay of execution.

G

CELTIC

Official   Programme

An Appeal

The Directors of Rangers Football Club and Celtic Football Club are very seriously perturbed by the fact that in recent years the games between the Clubs have been spoiled by the misbehaviour of certain spectators, and they now make a very earnest appeal to all their followers to do everything in their power to prevent any kind of disturbance in the future and to assist the Police in every manner possible.

Robert Kelly,   John F. Wilson,
Chairman.   Chairman.

SCOTTISH LEAGUE DIV. "A"

CELTIC v RANGERS

Friday, 1st January, 1954

Kick-off 2 p.m.

No. 12   PRICE THREEPENCE

An Appeal. Celtic Programme, 1 January 1954. (Pat Woods collection)

Crowd trouble in the mid-1950s. Fans escape the fighting on the terracing at Ibrox. *Glasgow Herald* and *Evening Times*

This gave them time to chew over principles that were eventually digested.

Some Scots continued to harbour grievances about the Irish flag flying over Parkhead; more probably appreciated the triviality of the affair. But for Scottish catholics there was nothing trivial in what they saw as further proof that they had not yet been wholly accepted into Scottish society. The half dozen or so years after the Second World War were probably the worst in Celtic's history: success on the field was scarce, and this was reflected in the crowd troubles of those years. Then there was the treatment meted out to Celtic by some sections of the press and elements within the Scottish football authorities. Despite sacrifices in two World Wars catholics had still not been accepted as Scots by all sections of the Scottish public. The catholic followers of Celtic were Scots of several generations by the 1950s; they were no longer the Irish nationalists of the early century, but their Church had not given up its hopes of converting Scotland to the true faith, and the cause of Ireland still tugged at many hearts, as shown by the waving tricolours any Saturday. Whether they liked it or not, Rangers and Celtic were still tied to their history and their society, and it was as respective spokesmen for influential sections of that society that Robert Kelly refused to take down the Eire flag and George Graham, secretary of the SFA, 'High Mason and Grand Master of the Orange Lodge',[63] seemed bent on forcing a humiliating capitulation.

Celtic in 1952 were on the defensive in more ways than one: their playing record was poor and the conduct of their fans was an embarrassment. Although this is the fate of most clubs at some time or other in their history, Celtic were also put on the defensive through their association with what were seen as symbols of sectarianism. Certainly as a result of the recommendations of the Glasgow magistrates both clubs were ordered to take all possible steps to prevent their spectators flaunting provocative flags or emblems, and to do what they could to prevent them expressing sectarian sentiments, but while Celtic had to undergo the inquisition over the flag, no one questioned the Rangers Board about their attitude to catholics. It would be well over a decade before the Rangers club, on the defensive about its playing performance and the behaviour of its fans, also found itself on the defensive about sectarianism at the highest levels.

NOTES

1. See especially the McElhone Report and the statistics on troubles at or near major football grounds in Scotland. Statistics can be notoriously unreliable, and the table of arrests in this report was for home matches in one season (1975–76): Motherwell and Kilmarnock had much worse figures than Celtic's (0.67 and 0.62 arrests per 1,000 at game, against 0.31 for Celtic, 0.14 for Rangers); Ayr United (0.49), St Johnstone (0.35) and Partick Thistle (0.32) were slightly worse. It should be added that it is more often the travelling fans who cause trouble. Most of the offences included above are minor, and the official conclusion was that 'the concern expressed by the media about hooliganism at football matches is out of proportion to the level of hooliganism which actually occurs at these matches' (p. 26). *Report of the Working Group on Football Crowd Behaviour*, Edinburgh, 1977.

2. *Scottish Referee*, 12 February 1906. Since the mid-1960s hooliganism at English football grounds has become a 'cause for national concern'. For just one comment comparing the scene in Scotland today with that in England, see James McKillop's article in the *Glasgow Herald*, 'English football hooligans who make our fans look tame' (28 August 1978).

3. On this, however, some caution must be urged. Recent research into soccer hooliganism shows that there was much more crowd trouble in those supposedly quieter times than is generally believed. Before television, coverage of the game

was spread much thinner, and so long as trouble didn't spill over onto the pitch it was often ignored. It would appear that football hooliganism has increased from about 1960, with an increasing spiral after 1966, but not so drastically as some people believe. Although the period between the wars and for a decade and a half thereafter does appear to have been comparatively free from crowd trouble, there were many incidents reported. Whether a systematic study would reveal further episodes, enough to change the picture, or how many incidents passed unreported, is an open question. This subject has been thoroughly investigated by a Leicester University team of sociologists, whose results should soon be made public. In the meantime they have published several papers indicating their results so far. I have summarised part of this in a paper I gave to the third History of Sporting Traditions Conference, at La Trobe University, Bundoora, Victoria, August 1981: 'Soccer hooliganism: the case of Celtic/Rangers between the Wars'. I am most grateful to the Leicester group, especially John Williams, for keeping me informed of their research and sending me a copy of their End of Grant Report: E. G. Dunning, P. J. Murphy and J. M. Williams, Department of Sociology, University of Leicester, 'Working-class social bonding and the sociogenesis of football hooliganism'. SSRC End of Grant report, September 1982.

See also: R. Ingham *et al*, '*Football Hooliganism*', the *Wider Context*, London, 1977, which has a critique of previously published commentaries. R. Carroll, 'Football hooliganism in England', *International Review of Sport Sociology*, 1 [15], Warsaw, 1980, pp. 77–92, has a very good critique of Taylor, Marsh, Ingham and others. For a foretaste of the Leicester group's findings, see E. G. Dunning, J. A. Maguire, P. J. Murphy and J. M. Williams, 'The social roots of football hooligan violence: some preliminary notes' (University of Leicester). To be published. J. Hutchinson, 'Some aspects of football crowds before 1914', *Society for the Study of Labour History Conference*, Sussex University, 1975, has some excellent material, much of it drawn from Scottish sources. Wray Vamplew, 'Sporting crowd disorder in Britain, 1870–1914: causes and controls', *Journal of Sports History*, vol. vii, no. 1 (Spring, 1980), pp. 5–20.

4. *Scottish Sport*, 13 October 1896.
5. *Glasgow Examiner*, 8 January 1898.
6. *Scottish Referee*, 3 January 1902.
7. *Ibid*.
8. *Glasgow Examiner*, 4 January 1902, p. 4.
9. *Glasgow Star*, 7 January 1905.
10. *Scottish Referee*, 27 March 1905.
11. *Glasgow Observer*, 1 April 1905.
12. *Glasgow Observer*, 8 April 1905.
13. *Glasgow Examiner*, 28 November 1896.
14. *Scottish Sport*, 11 August 1896.
15. *Scottish Sport*, 13 October 1896.
16. *Glasgow Examiner*, 7 November 1896.

17. *Glasgow Examiner*, 6 March 1897.

18. *The Bulletin*, 19 May 1917, p. 4. This special report on the eve of a Glasgow Charity Cup Final also pointed out that the two clubs accepted the honesty of the home team in games with each other and so the visiting team did not check the gate takings.

19. There has been no thorough study of the riot itself, but Terence Delaney has included the *Scotsman's* account in his anthology, *The Footballer's Fireside Book*, London, 1963, pp. 123–9. My comments are drawn from a reading of several newspaper accounts of the time. Note too that John Burrowes, in *Frontline Report*, Edinburgh, 1981, p. 22, cites someone who claims to have been there and that Rangers supporters 'were grabbing Celtic fans and giving them a quiet doing' while both sets of fans were taking on the police. Since that person also claims that the Billy Boys were involved, his memory looks decidedly at fault. The story is far from improbable, however.

20. *Glasgow News*, 19 April 1909.

21. *Glasgow Observer*, 24 April 1909.

22. *Glasgow News*, 19 April 1909, p. 6.

23. *Glasgow Observer*, 24 April 1909.

24. *Glasgow Observer*, 16 June 1906.

25. *Glasgow Examiner*, 8 February 1896.

26. *Glasgow Examiner*, 19 December 1896.

27. *The Press* (Govan), 24 December 1920, p. 4.

28. *Weekly Record*, 1 May 1920, p. 16.

29. *Weekly Record*, 15 May 1920, p. 16.

30. *Glasgow Star*, 15 February 1908. In the mid-1920s the *Scots Observer* published an article claiming that football had ceased to be a pastime and had become a mob fetish, followed by urban dwellers of the blighted areas of central Scotland. To such people bread, milk and potatoes were simply things that came out of shops and a field was associated only with goalposts and striped jerseys. Letters in reply counter-claimed that football was a blessing and that most fans were decent, honest and upright working men (*Scots Observer*, 9 and 16 October 1926).

31. *Glasgow Observer*, 27 November 1920.

32. *Glasgow Observer*, 8 January 1921. 'Man in the Know' concluded his report of the homeward procession: 'Of course, the flags, bugles, ricketties, etc., forbidden in the park, got full show on the homeward journey. It was a delight to see the boys so thoroughly enjoying themselves. It was their turn and they made full use of it. Good luck to them and to the team which gave them ample cause for rejoicing'. On many other occasions 'Man in the Know' railed against the crowing and catcalling of Rangers supporters when Celtic lost. Such rejoicing was bigoted 'exultation', but he took consolation in that the club and its supporters were worthy of each other (see especially *Glasgow Observer*, 19 October 1912). 'League of Nations' is a jibe at Rangers acquiring players of other clubs and of different nationalities. See also p. 129 above.

33. *Evening Citizen*, 30 October 1923.

34. This riot is reported in the Morton centenary history: Tom Robertson, *Morton, 1874–1974*, Greenock, 1974, pp. 24–5.

35. *Glasgow Observer*, 27 May 1922.

36. *Glasgow Observer*, 6 May 1922.

37. *Glasgow Observer*, 18 October 1924.

38. *Glasgow Observer*, 7 April 1923, p. 10. This is the year in which *The Catholic Menace* was published.

39. *Daily Record and Mail*, 8 October 1925.

40. This does not mean that Celtic/Rangers matches suddenly became peaceful affairs. On 10 October 1927, for instance, the *Leicester Mercury* reported details of a disturbance outside Hampden after an Old Firm cup-tie, in which 'rival factions clashed' and had to be separated by mounted police. The trouble began when Watson, a Rangers supporter, rushed at a man who was wearing a green scarf and had a green handkerchief in his pocket.

41. K. Wolstenholme, *Sports Special*, London, 1955, pp. 82–3.

42. *Glasgow Observer*, 16 October 1909.

43. *Ibid.*, 19 October 1912.

44. *Ibid.*, 24 August 1929.

45. *Ibid.*, 8 August 1931.

46. *Ibid.*, 3 October 1931.

47. *Ibid.*, 20 February 1932.

48. George Blake, *The Shipbuilders*, London, 1936, p. 100. For Blake's description of Danny's preparation for the match, his experience of it, and the return journey, see *ibid.*, pp. 97–107.

49. 'Gulliver' (Colin Milne), *So This Is Glasgow?*, Glasgow, 1938, pp. 31–39.

50. *Sunday Mail*, 2 June 1940, p. 19.

51. *Glasgow Herald*, 23 May 1940, p. 10.

52. *Sunday Mail*, 26 May 1940, p. 19.

53. *Evening Times*, 23 May 1940, p. 5.

54. *Glasgow Herald*, 18 September 1941, p. 4.

55. *Sunday Mail*, 28 September 1941, p. 15.

56. *Sunday Mail*, 14 September 1941, p. 15.

57. *Glasgow Herald*, 6 June 1946. For the controversy surrounding the game, see Kelly, *Celtic*, pp. 43–6, chapter entitled 'Cruel punishment'.

58. *Picture Post*, 15 October 1949, pp. 20–24.

59. *Sunday Mail*, 28 August 1949, p. 19. In addition there were reports and photos on the front page of the *Mail*.

60. *Glasgow Herald*, 14 September 1949, p. 9.

61. The Celtic histories treat this subject in great detail, Handley devoting a chapter to 'The Great Flag Flutter'. There is a concise and (as always) well-balanced account in T. Campbell, *Glasgow Celtic, 1945–1970*, pp. 46–52.

62. *Ibid.* Campbell's account uses the *Glasgow Herald* extensively.

63. He is thus described by Celtic chairman Desmond White in his foreword to McNee's *The Story of Celtic*, p. 7.

PART THREE

Traditions under Challenge

The first years of peace after the Second World War, like those after 1918, saw the biggest aggregate crowds in the history of the game, although unlike those after 1918 the boom lasted for a decade and more. From 1946, most workers had the whole of Saturday off, and coach travel became cheaper than it had ever been, but this was also a decade of tightened belts, rationing and the near collapse of sterling, before the consumer revolution from the mid-1950s. As the standard of living rose, attendance at football declined: television, cheaper travel, higher wages and longer holidays helped to widen horizons, and the average fan was led to expect greater value for his entrance money than in the past. From the mid-1960s what seemed a new element to many entered the scene, with an apparent upsurge in hooliganism, and this in turn has been added as a cause of the declining attendance that have marked all but the big games ever since. Scotland, ever at the mercy of the richer southern clubs, was particularly hard hit by the lifting of restrictions in English football in the early 1960s, abolishing the maximum wage and liberalising player contracts. After that even Rangers and Celtic were in trouble trying to keep their star players in Scotland, and the decline of the game as a spectator sport seems to have continued ever since.

The two decades after 1946 were also unusual in that they were not dominated by The Old Firm, as the honours in Scottish football were distributed in a way that had not previously been known this century. From the mid-1960s Celtic re-established a dominance they had not known since the Six Flag team of 1905–10, and Rangers came under pressure from management and terracing to do something to break the stranglehold of their arch-rivals. This was a battle fought out mainly on the football field, but it had significant repercussions elsewhere. Just as England from the mid-1960s has been caught up in a spiral of spectator trouble, so was Scotland, particularly through the antics of frustrated Rangers fans. Before this time crowd troubles had tended to be passed over or ignored by the press, but television—omnipresent and sensation-seeking—highlighted and in turn helped escalate the problem, albeit with moral condemnation and calls to investigate its root cause. This meant going beyond the football stadium to the society that created the troublemakers, and in the case of Rangers and Celtic to the allegedly sectarian policies or practices of the clubs. By the 1970s Celtic and Rangers had behind them the richest and longest unbroken traditions of any two football clubs, developed to a significant extent out of rivalry with each other. In basic practices and policies the two clubs had changed little over the previous fifty years, but the world had, particularly in regard to various social issues: nations that had previously tolerated massive abuses in regard to silent minorities found themselves under the international microscope. In Scotland the position of catholics had ceased to be that of economic underdog, and the scale of the mistreatment of catholics could in no way compare to that of racial minorities in other countries or of catholics in Ulster. But in Scotland itself there were concerned groups who took as an insult to basic Scottish tolerance the apparent exclusion from employment of catholics by the Rangers Football Club. All these factors came together from the late 1960s to focus attention on The Old Firm in a way that had never happened before.

CHAPTER 8

Two Clubs, Two Traditions

On 3rd October 1965 a short, sarcastic article appeared in the *Sunday Mail* berating former Rangers player Ralph Brand for 'lifting the lid' on Ibrox in an unnamed newspaper. The newspaper was the English-based *News of the World*: the articles, written more in exasperation than anger or even hatred, condemned the Ibrox club for its feudal attitude to the players; criticised its antiquated training routine; commented on the tense atmosphere in the club generally; and even went so far as to denounce the management for its '100% protestantism' policy. The condemnation of Brand, written by Allan Herron, criticised him for accepting the club's hefty salary for twelve years, but came down on him most heavily for breaking the unwritten law of the Rangers: that what happens behind the dressing-room door or at the top of the marble stairs is the business of Rangers alone and is not to be discussed outside. To be a Ranger was to be a Ranger for life. Other players who had left the club with grievances had refused to break these traditions and had remained silent. As for the Ibrox Board, it was furious but was maintaining a dignified silence. The club had closed its doors on Brand for ever, and so too had Herron, though in a more metaphorical way, for he never could bear the guy who carried tales out of school.[1]

About a year before Brand 'blew the lid' on Ibrox, an underground magazine had been circulating around Celtic Park and the away grounds where Celtic were playing: called *The Shamrock*, it was put out anonymously by some Edinburgh Celtic supporters unhappy about the performance of the club, which they attributed to the policies of the management. It was also radical in its politics, in regard to football administration as much as the nation: it thought the SFA should be run by players and clubs by the supporters, and in Irish affairs it supported the policies of the nationalists.[2] The *Shamrock* did not last beyond about 1963–4, possibly into 1965. Changes by Celtic at the top level were followed by improved performances by the team, and from 1965 *Celtic View* was launched, a magazine run by the club, but always open to the opinions of the supporters.

The Brand articles and the underground *Shamrock* are perhaps minor ripples beneath the storms that are faced weekly by most football clubs. Players are never going to be absolutely happy with the management, especially when they get dropped, and supporters are not always going to accept the decisions of the management, especially when the team is on a losing run. But the episodes just mentioned are symptomatic of deeper issues which lie at the very heart of the two clubs. Rangers' response to criticism was silent anger that their sanctity should be breached, their authority questioned; non-official protest came in the Herron article and a barrage of abuse from *News of the World* readers, in the correspondence columns of that paper. The appointment of Jock Stein as manager of Celtic and the introduction of *Celtic View* had nothing to do with the *Shamrock*, but the very appearance of that newspaper was typical of a more democratic, critical spirit between Celtic management and supporters, the supporters feeling that the club in some way belonged to them, not as a distant god, but as part of their daily life. The Celtic Board has been every bit as authoritarian as that of Rangers, and the treatment of the staff just as ruthless on occasions—witness the forced resignation of Billy McNeill as manager at the end of June 1983 after a loyal and almost unbroken association with the club—but somehow these Celtic incidents have seemed more like disputes within a family than *ex cathedra* judgements. Rangers and Celtic grew in opposition to each other as representatives of two communities in Scottish society; by the 1960s they were two teams which represented two long and very different traditions.

The 'Rangers tradition' and the 'Celtic spirit' are two phrases that appear frequently in the vocabulary of the two clubs. What this means is not always spelled out, being accepted as holy writ by the faithful, but it is a reality just the same. The most obvious image of the clubs is that which they portray on the football field, their style of play and their reaction to victory and defeat, while more solid and silent reminders are there in the shrines that are the football stadiums themselves. Less tangible but not less real ingredients in the making of the 'tradition' or 'spirit' are in the relations between management, players, supporters and the general public, as revealed in the clubs' policies and performances, interpreted in official and semi-official publications, and in their handling of public relations. In all these aspects the two clubs show traditions as consistent as they are different.

Playing Styles

The image of Rangers that comes across to the impartial observer is of a proud, dour and uncompromising machine, bred on success which it has come to see as a birthright. Any team which threatens this is challenged or mown down with a ruthless efficiency which emphasises teamwork, strength and commitment rather than skill and delicacy. This has been built on almost unbroken success since the end of World War I and a dominance that lasted through to the mid-1960s. Before the last two decades, on the other hand, Celtic's success was never so regular or long-lasting as that enjoyed by Rangers between the wars, and their record in the two decades after 1945 was their worst ever, marked by their only threat of relegation, but enlivened as always by successes out of the blue such as the winning of the Coronation Cup in 1953 and a never-to-be-forgotten 7–1 thrashing of Rangers in the League Cup Final of 1957. Celtic, then, could not boast of their consistency in those years, and indeed made a virtue of less polished performances which relied on individual cheek and artistry. Percy Young, in his history of British football, refers to the 'tribal animosities by now wrapped up in religious colours' of the two clubs, and in comparing their stylistic contrasts refers to the 'virtues of efficiency on the one hand and inspiration on the other'.[3] A more homely contrast is given in Gordon Williams' *From Scenes Like These*, where the main character admits that

> ... he'd never really *liked* Rangers, although he was a Protestant. Celtic had always seemed more friendly, somehow. Look at Charlie Tully. Rangers went in for strength, like granite. Charlie Tully had bowly legs and was bald and didn't look strong enough to beat carpets yet he had more personality in his little finger than Rangers had in their whole team. Charlie Tully would jink towards the Rangers defence—you'd need guts to take on big Geordie Young and Willie Woodburn and Sammy Cox and Jock Tiger Shaw—and when they came at him, ready to hammer him into the ground, he'd bamboozle them, pointing the way he pretended to pass the ball, sending them chasing in the wrong direction, or running on without the ball but still pretending to dribble so cleverly they'd follow him, trying to make a tackle.[4]

Others might be less impressed by such Tully tricks as bouncing the ball off an opponent's back after he had handed him the ball for a throw in, or 'cheating' from the corner flag as he did to score direct against Falkirk, but it showed a cheeky individualism that would not have been tolerated by Rangers. In players like Torry Gillick, Ian McMillan, Jim Baxter and Willie Henderson, Rangers had classy individuals, but Henderson was unhappy for a long time at the club and Baxter's refusal to conform played its part in his leaving the club. Brian Glanville expressed his views in a novel called *The Rise of Gerry Logan*,[5] in which the hero, born in Scotland, moves to England then Italy. His opinions of

Glasgow and The Old Firm are harsh, but he comes down heavier on Rangers, perhaps because the period in which he placed the novel was a period of Rangers dominance:

> When we were young in Glasgow, we were always hearing about the Scottish tradition, how the only real football was Scottish football, ball control and short passes and keeping the ball on the ground, but as we grew up we found there *was* no Scottish football, or at least nobody was playing it in Scotland. Rangers were the worst of all; the great club with a great history, Alan Morton and Davie Meiklejohn and all the rest of it—and out on the field it was nothing but power and speed, big strong wingers and long balls. They were a team I hated to play against, because everything was physical, you never learned anything.[6]

In 1955 Tom Dougray, a Scot and veteran referee of eleven Cup Finals, who was at the centre of many Old Firm battles from the early 1900s, claimed that the Celtic team of his young days, that of Shaw, McNair and Dodds, was the best he had ever seen, and commented on the Celtic players as the princes of 'patter merchants', constantly chattering away to put their opponents off.[7] To this Irish blarney Rangers contrasted their 'gaffers', senior players directing strategy from the middle of the field in voices that brooked no dissent, even if that dissent was a decision made by the referee. Rangers were said to dominate referees and the officials of the SFA as much as they did their opponents on the field.

The Rangers players of the late 1940s and early 1950s were indeed a formidable combination. Led by George Young in many stirring encounters, they earned themselves the reputation of the team with the Iron Curtain defence. This was the heyday of spectator support for football in Scotland, with attendance records set that will never be broken, and many of which were not made at matches featuring Rangers or Celtic.[8] Rangers had reigned supreme in the inter-war period, and intended to continue their run thereafter. They were less successful than in their pre-war years, however, and opposing teams and referees often had to pay the penalty for this. Violence on the field and badgering of referees reached such a pitch that in March 1953 Cyril Horne of the *Glasgow Herald*, commenting on the 'Alarming Reputation of Ibrox', demanded an inquiry into Rangers. He commented on the 'moral—or amoral—support' of their tens of thousands of fanatical followers, and concluded that since the management refused to make any public comment 'on the 'repeated misconduct of their players', they could only be condoning it.[9] Few other newspapers were prepared to go so far in condemning Rangers' players, supporters and management: it is significant that the newspaper that printed the article did not rely on its sports pages for sales.

The Celtic players were no angels in their attitude to opposition players, and in this time their supporters were frequently in some trouble or other. But since this was often caused by a referee's decision for which they were severely punished, giving them the occasionally correct impression that they were not having much luck with the man in charge of the game or the attitude of its administrators, the management had less inclination to condemn them for it. Since their early days Celtic had often suspected the fairmindedness of the SFA, and little that happened in the 1940s or early 1950s gave them cause to think that times had changed. Rangers, from their position of strength, successfully maintained the silent belligerence of their 'Wha daur meddle wi' me!' attitude.

If the fun in football comes from winning, then Rangers should have been the happiest club in the country, but the discipline in the club seems even to have deprived it of overt expressions of such enjoyment. Charlie Tully, in his *Passed to You*, enjoyed the happy atmosphere at Celtic Park and claimed: 'That's what's wrong with Rangers for instance. They have some decent lads on their playing staff, but they go around as if they had a toothache. Not laughing, or even smiling. Dunno how they do it'.[10] Tully, of course, is neither an insider nor an impartial observer, but there would be few who would deny his claim. George Young agrees that they were 'a greeting faced lot' and tells the story of Struth belting Cox across the backside with his stick following a quarrel with Woodburn as a result of which Struth told Cox to strip and take a bath.[11] In the 1960s Brand commented on the 'tensions that exist at Ibrox, the underlying 'atmosphere' between some of the players and management',[12] and the following year Willie Henderson issued his *Forward with Rangers* in which he devoted a chapter to his rivalry with Alex Scott, one of a 'powerful clique of first team players' who made his life miserable there.[13] Struth's 'iron discipline' is often said to have been the secret of Rangers' success, a discipline nowhere more obvious than in the rules he set up regarding standard of dress. Perhaps this did inspire pride in the club, but there is something rather pathetic in the spectacle of a player of Torry Gillick's class having to come to training with a paper bag into which he dropped his bunnet before donning the bowler that was *de rigueur* within sight of Ibrox. Certainly there was more to be proud of in seeing your team arrive at the stadium well dressed and neat than scrubby and smoking 'jaw-warmers',[14] but to insist that players put their shorts on last to avoid spoiling the crease[15] is verging on the ludicrous.

The players are the most obvious features of the two clubs, but the

Bill Struth in the place of honour in the Ibrox trophy room. Photograph
Malcolm R. Hill. Courtesy the Third Eye Centre and the Scottish Arts Council

two traditions are equally obvious in other ways: in the club newsletters and magazines; in the official histories; and also, though less obviously, in the two men who, more than any others, dominated their development—Bill Struth and Willie Maley.

Handbooks and Histories

Celtic were issuing a fairly comprehensive Handbook in the early 1890s, while Rangers were putting out their Blue Book from 1889. By the 1920s both clubs issued an annual handbook for the information of supporters, particularly of the coming season's fixtures. For Rangers the handbook was little more than that, save for the occasional chastisement of the language of sections of their support, words of praise for the Alliance Eleven, a listing of the club's not insubstantial achievements on the playing field, and the odd comment that if other clubs did not like the Rangers' dominance, then it was up to them to do something about it. The Celtic handbooks, on the other hand, were a much more substantial affair, 50 pages and more compared to the Rangers' 30, although admittedly much of this was taken up by advertisements. But it was also given much more to comments often berating the fans for their behaviour, sour remarks about the referees, and frequent reminders of the prejudice the club had had to suffer in its early days, and which had not quite disappeared. The tone of many of these Celtic handbooks is not pleasant; they reflect the bad times the club was going through, but they also reflect a more human touch absent from the Rangers publications.

Programmes were not a regular feature of club matches before the Second World War, but since then they have seldom been much more than a public relations exercise, welcoming the visitors and listing the probable teams. In 1963, however, Celtic were unable to prevent their frustrations leaking out, and they came in for censure by the SFA for some 'acid passages' in their official programme, slating Rangers in an attack which was said to have taken neutrals aback.[16] Rangers would never have allowed such an indiscretion, preferring a diplomatic silence.

Supporters started to organise themselves on a more formal basis at this time, too, and sought recognition from the club itself, but their publications were mainly of the great-moments-relived type of entertainment. The first comprehensive newspaper for supporters was put out by the management of Celtic when they launched *Celtic View* in 1965. When Rangers caught up with Celtic in this respect in August

1971, the early promise of *Rangers News* soon faded, and it has never achieved the more mature content of its Old Firm rival.

The staple diet of The Old Firm newspapers is, not surprisingly, match reports, club notes, interviews with staff and playing personalities, and reminiscences of great moments in the clubs' histories: famous victories and salutes to star players. *Rangers News*[17] started off as a high quality paper, with some excellent illustrations. Appearing every Wednesday for 5d, it was good value. But the traffic is pretty well all one-way, with the manager and editorial staff regaling the readers with statements of what a fine club they have and what a grand bunch of supporters they are. Occasionally the fans would be abused for their behaviour, but it would be difficult for a reader of *Rangers News* to believe that the Rangers support includes some people whose language is not of the purest, that the sentiments some express contain a certain amount of blasphemy and incitement to violence, and that indeed it has been known for some fans to express their hatred in a more physical fashion. Every now and then the management might be jolted out of its complacency. This happened in 1972 when the club was beset by trouble from its supporters, and manager Willie Waddell appeared in order to broadcast an appeal to the fans. More typical, however, was the reaction to the Cup Final riot of 1980, when it was dismissed in one small paragraph.[18] By refusing to acknowledge the existence of persistent troublemakers, perhaps Rangers hoped they would disappear. Alternately they would take the attitude that it was their own problem, and no one else had the right to stick their noses in.

The reader of *Celtic View* is left in no doubt that Celtic have followers who are not an adornment to the club, as just about every incident involving crowd troubles involving Celtic supporters is discussed and condemned. The nature of their offences is not glossed over, and the foulness of the language and the offensiveness of sectarian sentiment are clearly spelled out. The club recognises its sentimental and historical attachment to Ireland and that the majority of its supporters are catholics, but it has no wish to alienate Scots who do not share these religious beliefs. Moreover such fans are denounced as a blot on the religion they profess to believe in, and the waving of tricolour flags is condemned as a prostitution of a cause which has nothing to do with football.[19] That Celtic continually berate their fans for their bad behaviour is no reflection on the greater degree of hooliganism among their followers: merely Celtic's comparative honesty.

In certain other aspects, too, *Celtic View* reveals a greater maturity. *Rangers News* started off with a regular 'Letters to the Editor' column, but this never became a significant part of the paper. It promised a great deal in the early numbers, but then became a forum for adulation of players and club, and virtually faded away. 'Letters to the Editor' in *Celtic View* has been one of its features, with pointed and well-directed criticism of management, players and supporters as well as the inevitable hero-worship and mutterings about conspiracies on the part of the Scottish press and public. Through *Celtic View* the management show a much greater willingness to abide by the guidelines suggested by outside bodies, while Rangers are more inclined to dismiss this as unwarranted interference. Rangers have consistently maintained that what Rangers do is their business, and that they will not be dictated to by public pressure or official criticism, be it in regard to the behaviour of their fans or how they run the affairs of the stadium.

When one comes to a comparison of the official histories of the two clubs, a similar pattern emerges. Several potted histories of Celtic have appeared in the press, but the first major history was *The Story of the Celtic*, written on the eve of the Second World War by Willie Maley. It is more a collection of reminiscences than a serious history, but it is nonetheless valuable for that, as no other individual had had such a long and unbroken association with the club. It is also typified by the petty quibbling approaching paranoia that I have discussed earlier. In 1960 James Handley produced a second major history. Well written and thoroughly researched, it has a decidedly catholic bias. This means, however, that the club is not spared its early desertion from charitable principles to become a business, and while Handley praises the club for its continued subscription to some charities, he is not loathe to point out that the directors did very well for themselves at the same time. Chairman Kelly's book, *Celtic*, came out in 1971, badly scarred by the bitterness of a director with a lifelong association with the club who could not forget what he considered the shameful treatment that had been meted out to it throughout its history, not least in the two decades when he had been its chairman.

Shortly before this a Celtic supporter, Tom Campbell, wrote an unofficial history of the club since the Second World War. This is essentially an account of the games played by Celtic in this time based on original sources, but typically it does not flinch the wider issues, and Campbell acknowledges that the team he loves is not without its flaws. In 1970 Celtic were merely in the middle of their great run, but Campbell does not dwell on the succession of victories, dismissing them instead since 'the price of monopolistic success in a narrative is boredom'.[20]

The best known of the Celtic histories is that by journalist Gerry McNee, which the club asked him to write after his paean of praise of the Celtic supporters, *And You'll Never Walk Alone* (1972), and a sensitive biography/autobiography of Jimmie McGrory, *A Lifetime in Paradise* (1975). McNee's official history had achieved a certain notoriety even before it was published, thanks to the judicious release of certain extracts for serialisation in the *Daily Express*. The furore raised by McNee's criticism of Stein for the 1970 European Cup Final defeat in Milan diverted attention from the more important criticisms in the book: the reassertions of anti-catholic bias, masonic manipulation of the SFA, and diatribes against Rangers. The book is well written, but since it is based on the earlier histories by Maley and Handley, and carries their biases and complaints into the 1960s and 1970s, it is guaranteed to help keep alive the persecution complex still felt by some Scottish catholics.

The Celtic histories, then, have aroused controversy, among both supporters of the club and others; they are outspoken and do not ignore the social context within which football matches are played. Celtic acknowledge that they are part of a larger society. The same cannot be said about the Rangers histories, the first of which was written by John Allan in 1923, with sequels in 1934 and 1951, and all of which are little more than pedestrian chronologies written by the faithful for the faithful. The Rangers histories by Hugh Taylor (1961), John Fairgrieve (1964) and Ian Peebles (1973) are written by the slightly less faithful, but still for the faithful, and although only Peebles' was an official history, the other two had the club's approval.

In *We Will Follow Rangers* Hugh Taylor points out that he is 'a neutral supporter', but his opinion of the club comes through in an extended military metaphor, praising Rangers as 'the Scots Guard of football in this country'. To Scottish football Rangers contributed 'courage, determination, spirit: crazy qualities it is true, but essentially Scottish'.[21] The last remark could be seen as a jab at Celtic. Present-day readers of Fairgrieve's remarks about The Old Firm in the *Sunday Mail* might be somewhat surprised by his declaration early in *The Rangers, Scotland's Greatest Football Club:*

> Rangers are the greatest football club in Scotland, have been so for many years, and very probably always will be, as long as the game is played. This is a fact of football life, and cannot reasonably be argued with.[22]

Peebles produced a most lively book for the Rangers centenary year (well, nearly; they were a year late), which they celebrated by winning the European Cup Winners' Cup in Barcelona (1972), and defeating Celtic 3–2 in the 1973 Scottish Cup Final. Peebles tells his readers that the Ibrox management did not ask him to withdraw a single word of what he had written:[23] the disclaimer is somewhat superfluous, however, as there is barely a word of criticism in the entire book.

These three books have the advantage of everything else written on Rangers in that they are readable and aimed at an audience beyond school age. But they are uncritical; they see the club as it sees itself: supreme, unflinching and impervious to all attacks. They do include the odd reference to other factors that have shaped Scottish football, token references to worthy opponents and even a recognition that their fans are not always welcome everywhere they go, but it is a world in which all revolves within the confines of Ibrox Park.

Allison's history, *Rangers: the New Era* (1966), admits, however briefly, that some hooligans attach themselves to Rangers, but dismisses them as an insignificant minority. Fairgrieve, however, suggests the uncomfortable truth that the hooligans might be a minority, but not a small one, and that in the choir of thousands there were more potential and actual hooligans than the club would admit. He goes on to give an outline of the sectarianism attached to The Old Firm, and although he does not discountenance the part played by the 'strong body of Orange workers' who arrived from Ireland and settled around Govan, he squarely blames Celtic: 'The origin of Rangers was non-denominational, but the origin of Celtic was not'.[24]

Fairgrieve's vision of football extending beyond the stadium is also enhanced by a more humane spirit absent in other writings on Rangers. This is in his chapter entitled 'John Thomson', where he gives due recognition to this 'prince of goalkeepers', the legendary Celt who died in the course of an Old Firm game. The tragedy of 5 September 1931 does not warrant a single mention in any other history of Rangers, although one can read in the official history of how 'a cloud hung over Ibrox in November [1932] for on the 9th of that month ex-Bailie Joseph Buchanan passed away in a nursing home'.[25] 'Tragedy' is a word that had lost meaning in Rangers literature, referring as it so often did to odd games lost. In the genuine tragedy of that September day Sam English in particular was totally blameless, and as the Movietone newsreel of the incident clearly shows, his immediate reaction after the collision was to limp painfully and in obvious distress towards the prostrate 'keeper. Thomson had suffered serious injuries before that fatal day, and the photos of the incident show his head in an alarmingly exposed position. Moreover the crowd, when it realised the extent of the injury, grew silent. Rangers had nothing to be ashamed of in that incident, except, perhaps, in their refusal, but for Fairgrieve, to record it in their official histories.

Through to the 1960s Rangers were gorged on success and were respected by large sections of the public for a proud tradition that embodied courage, efficiency and refusal to be 'pushed around'.[26] Where Rangers laud tradition and discipline, Celtic laud spirit and improvisation. The fostering of this spirit is attributed by James Handley to Willie Maley, a spirit which he claims permeated all its triumphs and which was as palpable in 1887 when the club was founded as it was in 1937 when Maley celebrated fifty years of unbroken association with the club.[27] But if Maley had more to do with the creation of the Celtic tradition than any other individual, Rangers had in Bill Struth an individual who lived for Rangers and whose name was synonymous with the club for thirty years and more. In character and personality Struth and Maley were cast in the same mould: those who knew them usually regarded them with awed respect, and refer to the kind heart behind the cold or hard exterior, or a temperament that did not suffer fools gladly. Both were disciplinarians, both lived for their respective clubs, and both were instrumental in guiding their destinies. Despite the similarities, however, their careers highlight essential differences in the traditions of the two clubs.

Struth

William Struth[28] was born in Edinburgh, about 1876. He later moved to Fife and became a stonemason by trade. His interests were more in professional running, however, and a fanatical devotion to fitness brought him to the attention of Clyde. It was with Struth as their trainer that the 'Bully Wee' had some of their best days, reaching the Scottish Cup Final in 1910 and 1912. In this latter year Struth was approached by Rangers, but it was not until 1914 that he moved across to Ibrox, after the Rangers trainer, Jimmy Wilson, died. Struth knew very little about football, but after the death of William Wilton on 2nd May 1920, it was he who was asked to become Rangers' manager. He inherited great players, such as you would expect the richest club in the country to be able to buy, or attract, and whatever one may think of his dictatorial hold over them, and an attitude to dress that amounted to a fetish, Rangers had an unprecedented run under his tutelage. When he retired in 1954, aged seventy-eight, Rangers had relentlessly carried all before them, particularly in the inter-war period, when the big and the wealthy found it easier to weather the economic disasters of that time.

Struth was said to have an eye for good players and the ability to get the best out of them, not because of any football genius, but because of a gift for psychological appraisal. What this amounted to is never clearly spelled out, as he ruled the players from afar and never discussed tactics, which he left to the players on the field; any words of inspiration seem to have been a veiled threat to get to bed earlier or a whispered warning to smarten up their dress. Struth ruled the team through a hierarchy of older players, encouraging some to regard themselves as superior to the others and entitled to petty privileges, and so he created the atmosphere that Willie Henderson found so distasteful when he joined the club in the 1960–61 season. Respect for Struth was inspired by fear: fear not so much that one might lose one's job, but that one would not be accepted into the holiest tabernacle in Scottish football.

Perhaps Struth had something of that indefinable quality called 'charisma', something which can only be felt by personal contact. But for an impartial observer assessing the man through nothing more than the written word, far from the magic aura of the marble staircase, the excitement of a packed Ibrox, or the sparkling spectacle of the trophy room, a different man emerges. A story, with Struth 'chuckling as he related it', is lovingly retold by Willie Allison, who claimed that 'it reveals the man who was Bill Struth'.[29] It was a handicap race, in which Struth stole twenty yards on his competitors and, on breasting the tape, grabbed his voucher and went straight on to the bank where he cashed it and caught the first train out of town before enraged officials and competitors caught up with him. Allison thinks that the £5 later repaid to the Porthcawl sports meeting 'ten times' over makes up for the anger and resentment of the time. But then Allison several times praises the free enterprise system, of which he sees Rangers as a prime examplar. The motto for both, perhaps, was to win at all costs and the devil take the hindmost.

The story of McPhail and the 'canteen of cutlery' is better known: at least it is open to two interpretations. Clearly Struth was living in a different world from his players, and when in the mid-1930s, in the depths of the Depression, he offered them the above-mentioned silverware if they beat Arsenal in what promised to be a massively attended friendly, he turned their resentment into action. Veteran McPhail and a more tremulous newcomer, Jerry Dawson, marched up the magic staircase and presented the players' grievances with the memorable observation: 'There's no much use having a knife and fork, Boss [sic], if ye canny afford a steak'.[30] At least he did agree and made amends.

Struth expected to be obeyed, and could not understand that there might be some individuals who refused to be overawed by the might of Ibrox. One of these was Jimmy Simpson, who had gained fourteen full international caps while playing for Rangers between 1928 and 1939. He was coaching Buckie Thistle in 1947 when he was offered the job of trainer with Rangers. It was soon made clear why he had been offered the job: Rangers had their eye on Simpson's son, Ronnie, and they wanted his father to apply pressure on him to come to Ibrox. In a book written while he was having a superb Indian summer career with Celtic, Simpson says that Struth was stunned by his father's refusal to influence him.[31]

With his grip over the club strengthened by a substantial shareholding—the largest of any individual (1,097)—Struth showed that he could be as ruthless towards his directors as he was to players or staff. At the 1947 AGM, on one of the occasions when the domestic affairs of the club were liable to be aired in public, Struth effectively engineered the downfall of James Bowie, a former player like the two other directors, Morton and Brown, and chairman for the previous twelve years. Director Brown categorised Struth's takeover as 'a carefully organized coup', while Struth justified his action by declaring before a packed extraordinary and annual general meeting of shareholders that 'The efficiency of Rangers has not been achieved because of the present directors, but in spite of them.' Bowie himself saw the issue as a 'fight for the right of the voice of the small shareholder, as well as the large, to have a say in the administration of a great football club which is to all of us a great deal more than a financial investment'. In the event Bowie was defeated, and Struth entered the Board along with W. R. Simpson and J. F. Wilson.[32] Bowie is not heard of after that.

As a 'football dictator', regardless of how much he was respected, Struth would not accept criticism, or even advice. And for one who, wherever else his genius lay, was not a soccer tactician, the times were catching up. The Rangers that Brand criticised in 1965 were still the Rangers as formed by Struth: Scot Symon was Struth's chosen successor, a man as remote from the players as Struth, and even more remote from the press. Symon at least had been a player. As manager he carried on in the style for which he had been renowned as a player, and which was firmly entrenched as part of the Rangers tradition; as Ian Peebles says in his centenary history: 'When Scot Symon tackled a player ... he stayed tackled! ... A man tackled by Symon rarely sought a repeat performance, especially if he had been foolish enough to foul another Rangers player at any time in the game'.[33] Looking back proudly to the Struth era, Willie Allison, speaking as the Director of Publicity, boasted of it as 'one of grim, no-team-is-our equal conviction'.[34] By the 1960s such a style was not enough, but while the Boss remained the Boss in most football clubs, the claims of the players to be respected as individuals went beyond the wage demands and contract freedoms being worked out in England. Alan Morton had been a superstar who accepted the Ibrox tradition to the extent that he became a director; Torry Gillick hated the discipline, but had to put up with it; Jim Baxter was the first player whose talents allowed him to subvert the Ibrox tradition of dress and what it signified in other terms. His dress and attitude to training riled the management, and he committed the sin, no more kindly looked on by Kelly of Celtic, of mixing socially with Celtic's Pat Crerand.[35]

By the late 1960s Rangers' days of divine command were over, and the criticisms of Brand, Henderson and some others were proving to have been of some substance, despite the outraged reaction of writers like Allan Herron. In 1970 Ian McColl, one of the stars of the 'Iron Curtain' defence, suggested that Rangers' troubles had begun with Struth. He pointed out that even when English teams had been encouraging coaches for some years, Struth refused to let anyone at Ibrox, whether players or staff, have anything to do with coaching. McColl still remembered when Saturday was the only time he saw the ball, and remarked somewhat ironically that at least this helped him improve his badminton.[36] By then Stein's revolutionary methods were having magical results at Parkhead, and something akin to panic set in among the normally stoic custodians of the game at Ibrox. Symon was sacked, his successor David White did not last long, while Waddell brought some cheer but no salvation.

Struth presided over the greatest successes the Ibrox club has ever known, and as such must be associated with them, although his personal contribution must be measured alongside the wealth and glamour that made Rangers the mecca for every football-mad youth in Scotland who was not a catholic. His only rival in football was Willie Maley of Celtic, whose club did not have the same money but did spell glamour for any football-mad youth who was a catholic. Maley's personality and character bear many similarities to Struth's, and his hold over the club was almost as absolute, his attitudes identical. But he was working inside a different tradition, and in the world he was living in this set limits to his success.

Maley

Willie Maley[37] was not yet twenty when some Celtic scouts came out to Cathcart to try to persuade his brother Tom to join the newly constituted club. They signed up the two brothers, but it was the younger one who was to prove the greater asset: a useful player, who represented Scotland on two occasions in full internationals, it was nevertheless as secretary and later as manager that Willie Maley made his mark. He ended his playing career while still young, in part to concentrate on the hosier's and sports outfitter's shop which he bought while only twenty-six, and although Celtic remained his first love, he combined this with success in business, coming to own the Bank Restaurant. No doubt the saddest day in his life was when he was dropped from the position of manager of the club he had served for fifty-two years, a decision which he said 'robbed me of the very tang of life'.[38] Unlike Struth, who virtually died in harness two years after he relinquished the manager's job, Maley had a further eighteen years to live, in which time he never returned to the club in any official capacity.

In an autobiographical series written for the *Weekly News* in 1936, Maley claimed that but for a political rising in Ireland and the capture by his father of a young Fenian seeking to flee the country, he might never have come to know the Celtic Football Club. His father, born in Ennis, Co. Clare, had a distinguished career in the British Army, and it was towards the close of this career, when stationed in Dublin, that he captured a Fenian trying to escape the country after the abortive uprising of 1867. The youth probably appealed to the old soldier's Irish patriotism, and was allowed to continue on his way to Scotland. The two kept in touch, and when Maley was discharged in 1870 he accepted the invitation of the young rebel, Pat Welsh, to join him in Glasgow. Welsh, doing well as a master tailor, looked after the Maleys, who included the eldest son born in the West Indies, Tom, born in Portsmouth, and the infant Willie, born in Newry. The retired soldier was appointed drill instructor in Thornliebank, and from there he moved to Cathcart, where the family settled down. It was there, in 1887, that Pat Welsh took Brother Walfrid and John Glass to persuade Tom to join Celtic.

From this time on Maley's life and the history of Celtic become inseparable. Like Struth, Maley was devoted to athletics, and turned Celtic Park into a great sports venue in the 1890s, as Struth, following Wilton, would do for Ibrox in the 1920s.[39] And like Struth, Maley was a stern disciplinarian, distant and unfriendly except to close friends. He did not have the good fortune to see the club through unbroken success, however, for although he played with the team that rocked Scottish football from 1888, and managed the all-star eleven that dominated the game from 1904 to 1910, Celtic were constantly in the shadow of their Old Firm rival throughout the inter-war period. Maley did not react well in adversity, and some of his reports in the official Celtic Handbook for this period are petty in the extreme, castigating the supporters for drops in attendance and censuring sections of those who did come for abusing the management. Frequently he would bemoan the 'vile luck which has hounded us this year in our Rangers games' (1926–27), and blame defeats on bad luck and poor refereeing.[40]

When the press criticised Celtic for transferring so many players, he replied that 'the club has never sold a man without his asking for same'.[41] Just two years earlier Maley had tried to perpetrate what could only be described as a shabby deal on one of the best and most loyal footballers any club could want to have on its books. This was the attempt to sell Jimmy McGrory to Arsenal against the young centre-forward's wishes. What made this all the more reprehensible is that the transfer was attempted while Maley was taking McGrory on the annual pilgrimage to Lourdes, and yet the manager said nothing about the attempted deal to him. Perhaps he was acting under instructions from the directors, but he did little to ease the youngster's feelings. Moreover Maley allowed McGrory to play through most of his career for £8 a week, £1 less than the rest of the team.[42] Such, it seems, were the rewards for a loyalty that asked no questions.

No more than with Struth could it be said of Maley that he was a shining light when it came to sportsmanship. When McGrory left Celtic at the end of his playing career to become manager of Kilmarnock, the new manager soon saw his team pitted against his old club. Beating Kilmarnock 6–0 at half-time, Maley warned his players not to let up in the second half, and Celtic went on to score two more goals. When the two teams next met, in a cup game, however, Kilmarnock beat Celtic 2–1 and went on to the final. An understandably elated McGrory went to see his old manager after the match to thank him for a sporting game. But Maley would have nothing to do with him: he refused to acknowledge McGrory's presence, and all the time he was in the room kept his eyes firmly fixed on the papers on his desk.[43]

Celtic later made amends to McGrory when they appointed him manager in 1945, and kept him on even when it was apparent that the qualities that distinguished him on the football field—he was the epitome of gentlemanly conduct—were drawbacks as a manager. But the rift with Maley was never healed. It seems to have occurred over a dispute concerning the venue for the club's Jubilee Dinner, with Maley piqued that they ate at the Grosvenor instead of his Bank—later described by present chairman Desmond White as 'a glorified public house frequented by bookmakers and others'.[44] He was also angry that he had to pay tax

This photograph shows the Scottish pilgrims returning to the Rosary Square
during the procession of the Blessed Sacrament. In the foreground is Mr W.
Maley, J.P. (with umbrellino) and Dr Maguire, of Glasgow.

Willie Maley and Lourdes. *Glasgow Observer*, 22 July 1938

on the club's gift of 2,500 guineas in recognition of his fifty years'
service. Struth had been a difficult person to deal with, but he had a
substantial shareholding in the club and he had almost unbroken success
on the field. Maley had taken Celtic to great heights, especially in the
first decades of the club's existence, and at the time of the Jubilee Dinner
Celtic were League champions and had just won the prestigious
Exhibition Trophy. But his success on the field did not equal that of
Struth. More crucially, he had no control over the management, and this
affected his dignity.

When Celtic went to America in 1931, he claimed to be too sick to
continue, in what was apparently a ploy to force the club to invite his
brother Tom along. He was successful, and Tom joined the touring party
a week later, Maley's sickness having in the meantime disappeared. Maley
had his own version of the event, however: 'On the journey across the
Atlantic the directors had a very happy thought. Recalling that my
brother Tom was so very closely identified with the inception of the club
and played such a prominent part in its early struggles, they decided to
invite him to join the party, and he crossed in the next steamer that sailed
a week later'.[45]

However old-fashioned Struth's methods were later shown to be, he had the support of the management and a team which picked itself. Maley never had the same control over his players, many of whom were sold or sought transfers. Beyond his control was a depression that hit catholic workers harder than any others, and this affected gates, but also beyond his control were the directors who employed him and owned the shares. Success was the only weapon he had against them, as it was the only counterweight against his own stubborn personality. His 'retirement' in January 1940 was not a happy moment for the club (which made only the briefest mention of the dismissal in its official organs), nor for the long-serving manager, who had a further eighteen years to live with his disappointment.

Neither Struth nor Maley, however, could rise above the traditions they inherited, and to which they contributed. Struth was the embodiment of the Protestant ethic, succeeding with success and accepting it with a grim satisfaction that had the stamp of the elect. His social and political credentials were impeccable. Maley, on the other hand, was of an Irish father who fought in the army but allowed his discipline to weaken under political sympathies. Maley's brother Tom was involved in a fall from grace with the Manchester City bribery scandals,[46] and Willie, as seen in the American tour incident, let affection weaken his own discipline. These were faults, but they were human faults. The Celtic players might not have been as well dressed as Rangers, but they had more laughs, even in adversity. Above all, however, it would have been unthinkable for Rangers to allow as manager the owner of a 'glorified public house frequented by bookmakers and others'.

By the end of the 1950s Struth and Maley were dead, and Scottish football was on the verge of great changes as it at last tried, like English football, to catch up with the rest of the world. England's humiliation in the World Cup in Brazil in 1950 and Scotland's disgraceful refusal to participate were added to in 1954 when both countries were outclassed in Switzerland and thousands of Scottish supporters, crammed into any tenement house that had a television set, wished as Uruguay walked all over Scotland that Eurovision had not been established in time for the World Cup. In 1953 the Hungarians taught England a football lesson at Wembley and seven years later Real Madrid came to Hampden to do the same before an appreciative crowd and a mesmerised Eintracht Frankfurt in the European Cup Final.

But big changes were underway with The Old Firm, too, although this was not immediately apparent: it is easier to change playing techniques than it is the traditions of generations. Rangers bestrode the early years of the 1960s with a class that had Baxter stamped all over it, but with the departure of this player of genius, the team lost its brilliance. This might not have been so disastrous in football terms but for the regeneration of the fortunes of Celtic in 1965. Before 1967 Rangers had performed great feats in Europe, but it was left to Celtic to take the plum trophy. In 1967 they won the European Cup, the first British team to do so, and thereafter their stranglehold in Scotland hardly slackened, and when it did, this was not always due to the challenge of Rangers.

Celtic's triumph in Europe won over many Scots who liked to believe that it was their own countrymen and not a team of Irish catholics who were able to beat the best that England or Europe could put against them. Celtic, never a closed club, opened up and increasingly were seen for what they are: a Scottish club of Irish and catholic origins. Rangers, on the other hand, remained what they had become: a club closed to certain members of the Scottish community, believing themselves to be of the elect, and followed by supporters pledged to 'Follow, follow ...' But changes were underway in the 1970s: Rangers' sectarian policies were no longer accepted passively or proudly by the public, nor were they ignored in the press; and while thousands of their supporters refused to 'Follow, follow ...', the club had reason to wish that many of those who did had stayed at home. Rangers were still the biggest club in Scottish football throughout the 1970s, witness the huge turnover from Rangers Pools and their always impressive stadium. They were certainly big in purely material terms, but this is not the only measure of the term. By the late 1970s the elect had become a beleaguered minority.

NOTES

1. The Brand articles, appearing under the title 'The Lid Off Ibrox', are in the *News of the World*, 26 September 1965, 3, 10, 17, 24, 31 October 1965; Herron's rejoinder, 'Come off it, Ralph', appeared in the *Sunday Mail*, 3 October 1965.

2. Extracts from *The Shamrock*. Courtesy of Pat Woods.

3. P. M. Young, *A History of British Football*, London, 1973, p. 190 (Arrow edition).

4. G. Williams, *From Scenes Like These*, London, 1968, p. 42.

5. B. Glanville, *The Rise of Gerry Logan*, London, 1965, p. 73 (Corgi edition).

6. *Ibid.*, p. 73.

7. *Evening Citizen*, 26 January 1955, in interview with Malcolm Munro. It should be noted, however, that he thought football so bad at that time that it wasn't worth going to see. This condemnation was not just of Scottish football

in 1955, but included the all-conquering Hungarian team with Puskas, Kocsis and Hidegkuti!

8. Compare the following, taken from *Rothmans Football Year Book: 1976–77*:

2 January 1950	Hibs v Hearts	Division 1	65,840
2 January 1950	East Fife v Raith Rovers	Division 1	22,515
11 March 1950	Stenhousemuir v East Fife	Scottish Cup, Round 4	12,500
26 January 1952	Raith Rovers v Hibs	Scottish Cup, Round 1	30,000
10 February 1952	St Johnstone v Dundee	Scottish Cup, Round 3	29,972
23 February 1952	Queen of the South v Hearts	Scottish Cup, Round 3	24,500
7 February 1953	Raith Rovers v Hearts	Scottish Cup, Round 2	30,000
13 March 1954	Aberdeen v Hearts	Scottish Cup, Round 4	45,061

Although this shows a healthy relief from The Old Firm stranglehold, it has to be admitted that nearly every other attendance record involves either Celtic or Rangers.

9. *Glasgow Herald*, 9 March 1953.

10. C. Tully, *Passed to You*, London, 1958, p. 83.

11. *Sunday Mail*, 14 March 1976.

12. *News of the World*, 26 September 1965.

13. W. Henderson, *Forward with Rangers*, London, 1966, pp. 14–19. Only the sympathy shown by Baxter and Shearer helped to keep him 'reasonably happy'.

14. In placing the sartorial reputation of Rangers back in the days of Wilton, Peebles cites the oral evidence of a Mr Irvine, who was a neighbour of Wilton's when he was a young boy, and then trained at Ibrox on Thursday nights as a member of the Bellahouston Academy FP team. Mr Irvine remembers the Celtic team arriving with bunnets and Quinn smoking a 'jaw warmer': Rangers arrived with soft hats or bowlers, and many carried an umbrella. I. Peebles, *Growing with Glory*, Glasgow 1973, p. 11.

15. The 'crease in the pants' story come from Jerry Dawson in *Rangers News*, 19 January 1972. Dawson thought Struth was years ahead of his time in psychology, and cited other examples of this: players were not allowed to use the subway; they were not allowed to attend late sessions at the cinema; fresh water bathing was banned; tennis was forbidden as a summer pastime because it tightened the muscles.

16. *Scottish Daily Mail*, 19 August 1963.

17. I am indebted to Peebles Publications for allowing me access to their complete file of *Rangers News*.

18. The club does denounce 'foul chants', and the troubles of mid-1972 were met by threats from Waddell that Rangers would be ruthless and that the foul mouths would be chased off the terracing (esp. 9 August 1972). In the issue of 23 August 1972 *Rangers News* got closer to the heart of the matter when it mentioned for the first time 'political bias' and 'religious bigotry'. The photo of Waddell addressing the crowd is in the edition of 16 August 1972. It took the more spectacular violence of 1972 and 1976 to shake the club out of its complacency in regard to its support, which for the most part it looks on with benign complacency and occasional adulation. (See p. 228, below).

19. It would be tedious to attempt to list all the occasions when *Celtic View* discussed the behaviour of Celtic fans, but in general the condemnation of the morons is mixed with appeals to the rest of the support to assist in upholding the club's image. Nor does it hedge the political and sectarian issues. An early appeal to supporters asked them to help get rid of touts who were selling pictures of the late John F. Kennedy outside the ground. This would not be tolerated inside the ground, but they were equally concerned about what happened in the vicinity, and deplored that Kennedy's religion should obscure the fact that he had nothing to do with Celtic or Scottish football (1 December 1965). After the Liverpool disturbances of 1966 *Celtic View* asked supporters' clubs to help overcome the disgrace at Liverpool (27 April 1966), and shortly after that a fan who had signed a pledge in blood with several other fans ('Celtic Forever', but with no violence), wanted to rid the club of 'these louts, who make Celtic and the Catholic Church something for the general public to despise' (2 May 1966). After trouble at Easter Road in 1968 'Kerrydale' warned against excuses on the ground that another club or clubs had its hooligans, and dismissed the usual fiction about these hooligans being 'a small minority' (24 January 1968). The *View* called on supporters who did not like the National Anthem to remain silent and not to prevent other Celtic supporters, who had no objection to it, from singing it; asked that obscene and sectarian songs be drowned out by other club songs; and in an article, 'War on the Wreckers', spelled out in unambiguous terms that those who thought they were fighting a holy war in Celtic's name had better think again (9 August 1972). This last warning came with the troubled start to the 1972–73 season that also saw so many disturbances at Rangers games. Like Waddell, Stein felt moved to take more direct action against troublesome fans, only in his case he waded straight into them at halftime during a game at Stirling, to give them a tongue lashing (16 August 1972). Shortly after this the club issued a full-page spread explaining 'Why the Tricolour is still flying at Celtic Park'. This included the letter sent to the Glasgow magistrates, in which Celtic acknowledged the Irish associations of the club and its supporters, but dissociated it from any sectarian, political or religious organisation. It promised to co-operate with the civic and football authorities on the problem of football hooliganism, and while stating its belief that the Irish flag had nothing to do with this, promised to take it down should the contrary be proven (30 August 1972).

20. T. Campbell, *Glasgow Celtic: 1945–1970*, Glasgow, 1970, p. 140.

21. H. Taylor, *We Will Follow Rangers*, London, 1961, p. 13.

22. J. Fairgrieve, *The Rangers. Scotland's Greatest Football Club*, London, 1964, p. 15.

23. Peebles, p. 152.

24. Fairgrieve, pp. 26–7.

25. J. Allan, *Eleven Great Years. The Rangers, 1923–1934*, p. 69.

26. Cf. Taylor, p. 24, referring back to Rangers' refusal to replay the 1879 Cup Final against Vale of Leven: 'Rangers, never a team to be pushed around by anyone, had resolved not to play in the Scottish Cup any more that season'.

27. Handley, *The Celtic Story*, p. 123.

28. There has been very little written on or by Struth, beyond what appears in the official histories. 'The Bailie' ran one of his sketches of famous people on Struth in the *Weekly Herald*, 29 February 1936.

29. Allison, *The New Era*, pp. 23–24.

30. Peebles, *Growing with Glory*, pp. 45–6.

31. R. Simpson, *Sure It's a Grand Old Team to Play For*, London, 1967, pp. 152–3.

32. *Daily Record*, 10, 11, 12, 13 June 1947.

33. Peebles, p. 79.

34. *Scots Book of Football*, London, 1969, p. 71.

35. On the subversion of the Rangers tradition, and for an excellent portrait of this talented footballer, see Bob Crampsey, *The Scottish Footballer*, pp. 56–9. See also Brand's sarcasm about having to turn up for training 'dressed suitably for lunch in a posh restaurant', and how Baxter ignored this ruling. Brand commented on how the club would have looked rather foolish if it had forced a showdown with their biggest star 'on the explosive issue of whether he wore a tie or not'. When Brand himself turned up for training in a casual shirt, trainer Kinnear told him in no uncertain terms never to repeat the offence (*News of the World*, 10 October 1965). It should be noted that Patsy Gallagher was a law unto himself at Celtic Park: he owned a pub, which was forbidden to other players, and received a much higher salary. This seems to have been accepted by the rest of the Celtic team (McGrory, pp. 24, 26). Brand criticised Rangers for not giving Baxter a higher wage than the rest of the team.

36. Article: 'Did the Ibrox trouble start with Struth?' in *Football Scot*, 25 April 1970.

37. There have been a few potted biographies and character sketches of Maley, other than those in the official histories. Most useful of these are: 'Fifty Years in Football. Willie Maley's Life Story', told by himself in the *Weekly News*, weekly from 23 May 1936 to 29 August 1936; 'Maley of the Celtic', by brother Alex, in *The Scottish Field*, March 1940.

38. *Evening News*, 25 May 1940.

39. By the late 1920s the Ibrox Sports had superseded the sports meetings at Celtic Park. Maley had been to the fore in instituting the many improvements that made Celtic one of the most progressive clubs of the 1890s, but above all in athletics meetings. The folding of these meetings in the 1920s is just one other instance of how the Ibrox club was better able to weather the economic difficulties of the inter-war period.

40. Compare especially the Handbook for 1930–31, where he bemoans the loss of the Ne'erday game against Rangers: 'Their usual good luck held, and an off-side goal at the end gave them victory'. Later, referring to the Charity Cup, he blamed bad refereeing, but added: 'However we have tasted in this wise a few times and are getting quite used to it, but even this sort of thing must have an end'. In the Rangers Handbook for the same year Struth commented that guessing the correct toss of the coin in a Charity Cup Final was the only luck

H

they had had the previous season. So much for the big clubs accepting bad breaks gracefully!

41. Not only did Maley claim this, in the Handbook for 1930–31, but the previous year he had the gall—in view of the treatment of McGrory—to attack McInally for transferring to Sunderland, seeing this as treachery to 'the team that made him'.

42. The transfer attempt is told in McGrory's *A Lifetime in Paradise*, pp. 30–2; that of being 'cheated' of £1 a week on p. 26 (although McGrory describes it as 'a rather amusing story').

43. Interview with Jimmy Cairney in *Celtic View*, 25 August 1971.

44. McNee, *The Story of Celtic*, p. 7.

45. See *ibid.*, pp. 6–7 for the first story and Maley, *The Story of the Celtic*, p. 168 for the other. Tom died four years later.

46. It seems from the *Glasgow Observer*, 9 June 1906, that Tom got Meredith of Manchester City to try to bribe Leake of Aston Villa to throw the match for £10. When Meredith looked like becoming the scapegoat, he started to talk and an Inquiry followed. Maley was then banned by the FA, and returned to Scotland, where he became a sports journalist with the *Glasgow Star*. He returned south a few years later, when the ban was lifted, to manage Bradford City.

CHAPTER 9

Sectarianism in the 'Seventies

It has long been the claim of the Celtic Football Club that they are not a sectarian club, that they welcome to their playing staff or any other aspect of club activity people of any race, creed or colour. The cynics will argue, with some truth, that Celtic would not be half the team they are without their protestant players. The fact remains that they practise no discrimination. It is also a fact that they are a catholic club of Irish origins, but one which has evolved with the descendants of the early immigrants to become as Scottish, despite their religion and origins, as any protestant born of long Scottish lineage. Today they are accepted as such by most Scots, particularly since 1967 when they won the European Cup in Lisbon. Some Scots were understandably perturbed then by the plethora of Irish flags dwarfing the few obviously Scottish symbols, but despite the tricolours this was unquestionably a triumph for Scottish football, and that is how it was seen by all but a few.

Spectator Troubles, Sectarianism and the Public Reaction

Celtic's victory in Lisbon was matched by the conduct of their fans: indeed since then their behaviour, with the perpetual exceptions and one or two spectacular lapses, has generally been a credit to the club. This was particularly underlined by the reaction to defeat in Milan in 1970, when over-confident fans saw their heroes fail miserably before a much underrated Feyenoord of Holland. Dutch and Scottish supporters exchanged scarves and banter before making their respective ways home, even if in some cases to the wrong destination due to airport officials loading drunken fans on to planes according to colours rather than accents.[1] Indeed the record of Celtic fans in Europe, at a time when the visits of British clubs are coming to be regarded as a new barbarian invasion, has been exemplary. At home, too, in visits to England where provocation and a lower flashpoint are more in evidence in face of the Auld Enemy, Celtic—although the citizens of Liverpool and Burnley might wince at the thought—have more to be proud of than to decry, making them the most sought after club for benefit matches.[2] Unfortunately the same cannot be said about Rangers, whose fans

217

throughout the 'seventies seemed to proceed from disgrace to disgrace. One result of this has been that the sectarian policies of the club have come under heavy fire for the first time.

The invasion of St James Park, Newcastle in 1969 sounded the first alarm bells. Rangers fans, when they saw their hopes of proceeding to the final of the Inter-Cities Fairs Cup vanishing, invaded the field bent on stopping the game or venting their outrage on the home fans. A shocked Willie Waddell, then a reporter with the *Scottish Daily Express*, claimed never to have been so ashamed or to have seen anything so frightening. It was something he hoped never to see again.[3] Unfortunately it was something he was to see again—many times. Three years later, then manager of the club, Waddell watched as his fans showed that they had problems in handling victory, when a magnificent performance by Rangers in the final of the European Cup Winners' Cup in Barcelona was marred by rioting fans. Certainly Franco's police, unaware that a Glasgow football fan is less likely to accept submissively a baton or a boot than the locals who had lived most of their life under a police state, were largely to blame for this. However, it does seem that large contingents of Rangers fans had behaved deplorably before the game as they were to do afterwards. Cheap wine and the knowledge that they were in a catholic country added venom to the various incidents.

Fresh from bringing disrepute on Scotland in Spain, Rangers supporters brought disrepute on Glasgow three months later after a pre-season defeat by Hibs in a Drybrough Cup game at Easter Road. This time it was British Rail and some of its travellers who had to face the fury of fans unable to accept a setback against their Edinburgh rivals. But this was a mere skirmish, sandwiched between the 'Battle of Barcelona' and the 'Battle of Birmingham' in 1976. In the latter case religion or fascist police could in no way be blamed for provoking the events that brought a 'friendly' between Rangers and Aston Villa to a premature halt. Certainly the local fans knew how to taunt the visitors from the north, and the English police do not have the skill or tact of their Glasgow counterparts, but this can in no way diminish responsibility for wanton violence that was condemned throughout the British press. Nor could the Rangers management continue to hide its head in the sand—although it tried hard!—about the nature of a large section of its support. Nor would the press let the management escape blame for the sectarianism of the club that so many now found intolerable. The many attacks on the club's sectarianism led to Waddell being forced into proclaiming that Rangers would sign a catholic if one who was good enough came along. The club thus dissociated itself from policies whose

Crowd trouble in the mid-1960s, during an Old Firm match at Ibrox. *Glasgow Herald* and *Evening Times*

existence they had denied. Clearly the Scottish press and others concerned about Scotland's reputation were no longer prepared to put up with what was a standing indictment of Scottish tolerance; it was not just the Rangers Football Club, but Scotland as a whole, that was being disgraced.

Before the mid-1960s Celtic supporters had had a poor reputation. As we have seen, they were frequently in trouble throughout the 1940s and 1950s; they brought little credit to themselves in the first year of the 1960s, booing during the playing of the National Anthem, cheering when Davis of Rangers was stretchered off at Hampden, and reacting to their defeat by Dunfermline in the replayed Cup Final of the 1960–61 season with what one of their own supporters called a mood of 'overt intimidation';[4] at the Scottish Cup semi-final against St Mirren at Ibrox in March 1962 they tried to save their team, losing 3–0, with a pitch invasion, leading to brawls on the field and on the terracing; the following year their reaction to defeat was less violent but no more impressive when they walked out *en masse* from the replayed Cup Final against Rangers long before the final whistle, with the score 3–0; in 1965

Celtic fans were in trouble at Sunderland, and Liverpudlians will still tell you of the scenes that followed the referee's decision that put Celtic out of the European Cup Winners' Cup in April 1966.[5] From about this time, however, the pendulum of public opprobrium started to swing towards the Rangers supporters.

Rangers supporters' most spectacular battles (with one exception) were in England and on the Continent, but throughout the 1960s and 1970s they had been involved in a whole series of unsavoury incidents—and few would claim that before this they were renowned for being generous and open-hearted towards the opposition. In 1960 Rangers fans disrupted the peace of the border town of Berwick after a Scottish cup-tie; at Wolverhampton the following year various disturbances accompanied Rangers' qualification for the final of the European Cup Winners' Cup; in May 1963 obscene chants against a dying pope were heard at the Scottish Cup Final replay, and in November of that year the religion of the American President was remembered when jeering interrupted the minute's silence to commemorate President Kennedy's death (just as in 1952, these same fans had mocked the silence respecting the premature death of the young Celt, John Millsopp); in October 1965 Celtic players faced an invasion of Rangers supporters when they tried to show the League Cup to their fans shortly after they had won it, effectively putting an end to 'laps of honour' for many years; in February 1967 bottles were thrown at a friendly in Leicester, and at Dundee six months later the Rangers game against Dundee was brought to a stop by bottle-throwing. Very little of this was new; what was new was that such behaviour was getting greater publicity through television, and the changing climate of public opinion was refusing to tolerate it.

The 1960s, particularly the latter half, were a time of great change in the western world, with long-held values being exposed to doubt and possible revision: the Pill revolutionised private morality, the Vietnam war made people examine their political consciences, and pope John XXIII upset many catholics with the reforms of Vatican II. Blacks, homosexuals and women were among 'oppressed' groups who refused to endure further discrimination and sought 'liberation' by drawing public attention to their cause. By doing so they helped push back the frontiers of bigotry that had lain for generations on whole groups of silent victims. In Scotland the most senseless bigotry was one that most western nations had come to terms with: religion. It was as a monument to such bigotry that the Rangers Football Club found itself increasingly isolated by a more enlightened press and public.

Before 1969 Rangers' attitude to catholics had seldom been raised, and never openly or in isolation from Celtic's Irish connections. Back in 1925, as a result of the riots that had marked many of the games in previous years, 'John o'Groat' of the *Weekly Record* commented that Rangers and Celtic were 'rivals not only in football, but bitterly opposed in other aspects of life as well'.[6] He did not expand on that topic. In 1938 'Rex' commented wryly on the exaggerated displays of friendship between officials of the two clubs at the Celtic Jubilee dinner: 'If the 'Old Firm' want to draw the crowd they'll draw a deep breath before they repeat those loving speeches',[7] but three years later he let his real feelings come to the surface following the riots of that year when he blasted the managements of the two clubs for 'doing nothing to reduce the religious heat which brings huge crowds to these games'.[8] At the first Old Firm game after the Great Flag Flutter he commented on the slashing and bottling after the game, and while there was no trouble inside he did point out that Celtic fans obeyed the 'no banners' order and reacted to the Rangers' flouting of it by a well-drilled slow handclap,[9] but it was not until the following week that he reported the disgust he had felt at the 'shameless and filthy shouts that brought the one minute silence for John Millsopp to an abrupt end'.[10] Ten years later he raised the question of 'The problem we'll never solve', and claimed that Celtic and Rangers were paralysing the game, but did not mention religion.[11] The most sustained criticism of Rangers in this time came from Cyril Horne, writing (usually anonymously) in the *Glasgow Herald*. Indeed when the *Herald* issued a special colour supplement to celebrate its two hundredth anniversary he was described by Alastair Burnet as 'the sternly jawed, close-cropped Cyril Horne, locked, it seemed in unremitting war with the directors of Rangers F.C. about whose performances he was a well known agnostic'.[12] However, these attacks did not openly raise the question of religion.

At this time it was always Celtic who had to defend themselves against charges of sectarianism. No-one asked Rangers to sign a catholic when Celtic were told to take down the tricolour in 1952; Willie Maley, when interviewed by Jack House in 1955,[13] was at pains to list the non-catholics who had played for Celtic, while Rangers' 'protestants only' policy was ignored; in his condemnation of The Old Firm 'Rex' seldom singled out Rangers; when Jock Stein, a protestant, was appointed manager of Celtic in 1965, the religious issue was raised without reference to the policy operating at Ibrox.[14]

The Scottish dailies and Sunday papers generally left Rangers in peace, and criticism of their policies was left to fringe journals like *Goal*,[15] or 'foreign' newspapers like the *News of the World* which published the

Brand articles in 1965. On a visit to Canada in 1967 Rangers vice-chairman, Matt Taylor, was questioned about Rangers' refusal to sign catholics, and answered that 'It is part of our tradition. We were founded in 1873 as a Presbyterian Boys' Club. To change now would lose us considerable support'.[16] It seems that the Scottish *Daily Express* was the only paper to give this publicity.

Celtic players, supporters and officials have always been less reticent about discussing sectarianism, as they have never practised it, and even in some of the autobiographies by players that seldom get more controversial than discussing methods of training or the hobbies of their colleagues, Celtic stars have let their readers know what they think about Rangers' policies—thus no doubt confirming the 'bitter' image held by some protestant diehards. McNeill and Simpson claimed that they enjoyed The Old Firm games, while Bobby Murdoch said that he would not walk the length of London Road or Copland Road to see one, and that if he was injured he would rather stay home with his family. But these players blamed troubles on the spectators. Not so Jimmy Johnstone, whose *Fire in My Boots* came out in 1969: he accused the Ibrox Board of pandering to bigotry and declared that there would be no solution 'until the Ibrox board drop their silly and insulting rule and sign a catholic'.[17] In *Playing for Celtic, No. 2* (1970) Celtic player Jim Brogan blamed Rangers as the main offender in The Old Firm troubles because of 'their policy of not signing Catholics for their team'. About the same time Pat Crerand, then with Manchester United, wrote in his autobiography that when there was trouble at Rangers/Celtic games 'the real culprits are not the drunks who fight on the terracing but the bigoted men at Ibrox who deliberately make their team a religious symbol'.[18]

So when Danny McGrain wrote his *Celtic: My Team* in 1978, attacks on sectarianism in Scottish sport were far from new, but his opening chapter on 'Religion' was a scathing indictment of the Rangers' policies, showing that they were not only an insult, but that they were petty and stupid for the way they cost them potential star players. McGrain had been a Rangers-daft youngster, but the Rangers scout who came to see him assumed from his name that he was a catholic. Kenny Dalglish was another Rangers-daft youth who ended up with Celtic, for different reasons—one can only speculate on the difference these two players might have made to the Rangers teams of the 1970s! When Derek Johnstone issued the companion volume to McGrain's book, *Rangers: My Team*, he spent an agonising chapter on the religious issue: he stated that he was not happy about the club's policies, and even criticised the management for remaining silent on the issue, but blamed the Scottish education system as a more serious cause of sectarianism. He was only too glad that the problem was one for the manager and not for him.[19] That a Rangers player should go to such lengths discussing the matter is in itself an indication of the progress the issue had made in the 1970s.

Rangers under Fire

The turning point was 1969. It was then, after the Newcastle troubles, that certain of the Scottish dailies started to campaign against sectarianism in Scottish sport, particularly the *Daily Express* and the *Daily Record*. Alex Cameron demanded 'a vigorous clean-out of inbred bigotry which coincidence no longer begins to explain or excuse' and called on Rangers to change their policies and sign a catholic. Any fan who stayed away from their games because of this they would be well rid of.[20] It was in 1969, too, that the Rev. Robert Bone of Ibrox Church denounced Rangers before a congregation of 700: he said that he was dissociating himself from Rangers because of the filthy language and filthy conditions at the ground. He added that until one or two catholics were fielded at Ibrox, religious hatred would continue to flare up on the terracing. This provoked an angry response and a sarcastic reply from the Rangers chairman, John Lawrence, about the minister setting himself up as a soccer expert, and for accepting the free tickets the club gave him each year when he knew the club's policies. Lawrence, in a rare moment of indiscretion, said that the policy of not signing catholics had been with the club since it was formed. However, he refused to acknowledge that sectarianism had anything to do with the hooliganism. The *Daily Express* reported this as a 'distressing statement for anyone to make in June 1969 in Scotland ... It came all the harsher from the chairman of Rangers'.[21] The policy, admitted in Lawrence's statement, was praised by former Rangers trainer, Jimmy Smith, who made the claim that Rangers were a strong protestant team with a strong protestant following, and that the only way to avoid cliques was to have players of the same religious faith[22]—this from a team notorious for its factions and pettiness compared with a club whose greatest performances had been with teams made up of both protestants and catholics.

On 2 January 1971 Scottish football suffered its greatest ever tragedy when 66 fans leaving Ibrox by Stairway 13 were crushed to death and a further 145 were injured. It had been the fourth accident on that stairway in the previous ten years: two people were killed and 44 injured in 1961, eleven people were taken to hospital after crushing in 1967, and two

Orange march arriving at Ibrox Park, July 1970. An estimated 15,000 took over an hour to pass by the saluting base outside the stadium. The Rev. William Downie, Grand Chaplain, conducted the divine service inside the stadium. *Glasgow Herald* and *Evening Times*

were seriously injured among 30 victims in 1969. None of this was thought of in the tragic aftermath of that gloomy January evening, however, and no match-saving goal other than that scored by Colin Stein in the last few seconds could have been more miserably celebrated when its terrible consequences became known. For it was the response to this late equaliser that resulted in some fans tripping and others falling over them in a horrific human avalanche.[23] It happened at the Rangers end, but this was irrelevant in the upsurge of sympathy that swamped any sectarian feeling. How could anyone's religious upbringing be of any consequence in such circumstances? Supporters' associations and ordinary fans of the two clubs came together to support fund-raising schemes for the victims and their bereaved, and at the funeral services Rangers and Celtic footballers stood together inside the same church walls.

The minister of the Pollokshields–Titwood Parish Church, Arthur H. Gray, appealed to the directors of Rangers 'to continue what you have begun, that the rivalry, still keen, will be bereft of bigotry: a triumph for human relationships which, at the end of the day, are the only things that matter'.[24] *Celtic View* headlined its issue following the tragedy

BLACK SATURDAY: The Old Firm Match that Didn't Matter

and in a black-lined editorial concluded that there were 'no Billys or
Dans lying still under these shrouds at Ibrox on Saturday. Only dead
people with families and friends'. If only this could be realised, it went
on, 'then perhaps something of value might emerge from this, the most
heartbreaking day our Scottish game has ever known'.[25] The club gave
£10,000 to the Lord Provost's Disaster Fund and promised full co-
operation for any proposed game involving a Celtic–Rangers select.

The moment was not seized, unfortunately. Even while the
brotherhood of mourning was still strong, Clifford Hanley could remark
how ridiculous it was for so much fuss to be made over a football match
when thousands were regularly being killed on the roads, at home, or at
their places of work.[26] Such sentiment was not as extreme as the
outpourings of the notorious leader of the Church of the Twentieth
Century Reformation Movement, Pastor Glass, whose opinions, at least,
are generally confined to his little-known *Scottish Protestant View*. He
attacked the *Daily Express* for mentioning that two of the dead had
strong Orange connections and that one of them had served two years
for arson of a Roman Catholic church. His worst rage, however, was
reserved for Archbishop Scanlan's Requiem Mass which he saw as an
insult 'to the memory of the Protestant dead'.[27] On the other hand the
degree of paranoia still apparent among some Celtic supporters was
revealed in the corridors of the Southern General Hospital as the dead
and dying were being brought in. Among the less seriously injured at the
match that day was a Celtic supporter who was presumably recognisable
by the colours he wore. As doctors and nurses dashed around him
treating the more serious cases, he believed he was being deliberately
ignored and had to be restrained as he yelled at the nursing staff:
'Protestant _____'.[28]

When the horror passed out of the headlines it remained in the lives of
those who had been affected, and Rangers were left with the claims for
damages. As a result of this and the official inquiry Rangers suffered
further at the hands of the press, who reported the findings as they
became known.[29] Out of this emerged the conclusion that the club had
been reluctant to take expert advice on ground safety, despite the three
major warnings in the decade before 1971, and Sheriff Irvine Smith in his
judgement, after the fourteen-day hearing, severely criticised the men
who ran Rangers at the time of the disaster. He stated that Rangers
director Hope's evidence, confused and contradictory, had to be read to

An opportunity lost? Rangers directors David Hope, John Lawrence (Chairman) and Matt Taylor pictured outside St. Andrew's Roman Catholic Cathedral, Glasgow, with the cathedral administrator, Canon John McGuckin, after requiem mass for Ibrox Disaster victims, January 1971. *Glasgow Herald* and *Evening Times*

be believed, while that of ex-manager White became increasingly unimpressive as his cross-examination progressed. He concluded:

> Rarely can an organisation of the size and significance of Rangers Football Club have succeeded in conducting their business with records so sparse, so carelessly kept, so inaccurately written up and so indifferently stored.[30]

The events of 1972—Barcelona and then a troubled start to the 1972–73 season—brought further attacks on Rangers. Certainly some of the attacks were 'even-handed', but it was now Rangers' turn to feel that it was they who were being picked on. Headlines in the *Daily Express* on 16 August 1972 challenged The Old Firm to STAMP OUT THE BIGOTRY, and in the article that followed publicised the Glasgow magistrate's request, following a meeting with Celtic and Rangers, that Willie Waddell make a public statement saying that Rangers were not sectarian, and that Celtic take down the Eire flag. Waddell had denied the sectarian charge and hotly refuted an outsider's right to dictate club policy. On page 6 of the same paper Waddell's statement about sectarianism clashed rather discordantly with Rangers director George Brown's explanation of 'Why we will not sign a catholic'. Brown said that he had accepted 'with resignation' the religious exclusiveness of Rangers and thought the day would never come when Rangers signed a catholic: Rangers had always been *the* protestant team, and such it always would be. It was a tradition going back over a hundred years. The *Express* had to publish an embarrassed declaration from Brown the next day that what he had said he had said as a private individual, and not as a Rangers official.[31]

The usual storm of letters to the editor followed, but the most sensational aspect of the August 1972 discussion was the details leaked to the press concerning what had been said at the meeting. It was reported that Bailie Michael Kelly, a nephew of the late Celtic chairman and in his private life a Celtic supporter, asked why Rangers were not prepared to play catholics, and the reply came as recorded in the minutes:

> Mr Waddell (raising voice): Are we here to justify how we run Rangers football club or to curb hooliganism? There is never any talk of sectarianism within Ibrox Stadium. If people come in and make use of sectarianism [*sic*] then that is their responsibility, but I can assure you that there is no talk of sectarianism at board level, management level, or player level.[32]

It could of course be said in criticism that the issue of sectarianism *should* have been discussed at Ibrox, but this was not how the press saw it, claiming instead that Rangers had dissociated themselves from sectarianism. The *Glasgow Herald*, however, lent its columns in condemnation of Rangers. It praised Bailie Stevenson for cutting through 'the platitudes, humbug and trite nonsense which is usually produced on this subject' and came right to the crux of the matter: 'bigotry and the hostility it generates will never be stamped out until the major clubs end the official sanction which they lend to it'.[33] In an editorial a week later, after a further spate of correspondence on the issue, the *Herald* widened its accusations when it condemned the clubs for being totally out of touch with the fans, unaware, in the directors' boxes, or unconcerned, about 'the primitive conditions and sanitation of club grounds'. But it came back to the central issue: it criticised both clubs for refusing to grant Bailie Stevenson's request that Celtic take down the Irish flag and that Rangers issue a statement about sectarianism. This at least would have proved their critics wrong; their refusal to do so remained as 'an earnest of their lofty detachment from the problem'.[34]

The Celtic management were no more pleased than Rangers by the leaked details of the discussions with the Glasgow magistrates, and were

Willie Waddell appeals to Rangers fans after troubled start to 1972–73 season.
Glasgow Herald and *Evening Times*

no doubt more annoyed by the flag issue being raised again. In a lengthy
statement, chairman Desmond White pointed out that Eire was, after all,
a friendly country, and that while Celtic had historical associations with
that country, their loyalties were entirely to Scotland, and that as an
organisation their 'sole object is to play football in a sporting and
entertaining fashion'. He repeated that Celtic were not a sectarian,
political or religious organisation, that they were primarily a Scottish
club, proud of their Scottish heritage, that they had brought great
distinction to Scotland, that the people of Scotland were also proud of
these exploits, and that 'we will endeavour in the future to continue to

WHY I DID IT

Jock Stein explains that foray into the crowd at the Stirling game

'The wreckers are chanting about things that have nothing to do with football'
JOCK STEIN

I DON'T LIKE criticising Celtic fans. But I have to take odds with at least a section of them. What I did on Saturday was something I've felt like doing for quite a while.

It's my sincere wish that it will have a lasting effect, as I'm sure that the vast majority of our fans do. Celtic supporters have enjoyed a lot of good times during the past few years, and all of it was due to hard work—by the players, the backroom boys and the directors.

The fans, too, have played a major role and we don't want to see it all ruined now by the bad element who have recently emerged. Nor do we want to see the fans of long standing who followed us through the lean years discouraged from watching us play.

FLASHBACK . . . . Manager Jock Stein climbs out of the crowd after delivering his half-time tongue lashing to the chanting section of fans at Annfield.

This bad element—or the wreckers as the View called them last week—are singing and chanting about things which have nothing to do with football.

Surely there are enough Celtic songs without introducing religion or politics or anything else.

OFFERS

These offensive songs and chants could damage Celtic's hard-won reputation built up by good football and sportsmanship.

Offers to play all over the world keep arriving at Celtic Park.

Last year we took part in the Bobby Moore testimonial. Next month we play in Bobby Charlton's benefit match.

This is an indication of our high standing in world football.

The club don't want to lose all this. Neither, I'm sure, do any of our real supporters.

Continued on Centre Pages.

Jock Stein makes a more direct appeal, August 1972. *Celtic View* bring fame and prestige to the name of Scotland'. The statement also referred to their two players who had won Victoria Crosses, and the last pre-war captain who had won the Military Cross, and added that two of 'our present directors served in the armed forces throughout the last war'. So far as the Irish flag was concerned, White thought it would be an insult to those of their followers who were proud of their Irish ancestry if that flag was singled out for removal among the others flying over the stand. He did not believe the flag was the cause or focal point of any hooliganism, but if this could be demonstrated, then his Board would be prepared to reconsider the issue. In the meantime the precipitate action of the magistrates had 'rendered it impossible for the Celtic Board to accede to their demand'.[35]

There is a suggestion here that Celtic had considered removing the flag. This would have had little effect on Celtic's hooligans, but it would have put pressure on Rangers to reciprocate with some gesture or other. And while Celtic fans in this period were not involved in any incident as spectacular as Newcastle, Barcelona or Birmingham, they had been involved in many incidents throughout the 1960s, most notably at Liverpool in 1966, when a last-minute goal that would have kept Celtic in the European Cup Winners' Cup was disallowed, resulting in a flare-up. There was also serious rioting in Dublin in October 1970 at half-time in a European Cup Winners' Cup game against Waterford, when Celtic were walking over the locals, and leading 4–0 after 37 minutes. The only other time they hogged the hooligan headlines, however, was in 1978 during an Anglo-Scottish Cup game in Burnley. In Scotland Celtic fans caused trouble at many of the grounds they visited and upset towns where their supporters' club buses stopped for drinks, but they were little different in this respect from the fans of other clubs. However, the louts do draw attention to themselves, and this reflects on everyone wearing the same colours, so that neutrals often have good reason to wish a 'plague on both your houses' so far as the fans of The Old Firm are concerned.

On one issue a section of Celtic supporters stand clearly condemned, and this is their apparent loyalty to Ireland rather than Scotland. A British national anthem is not Scottish, so Celtic fans can hardly be condemned as anti-Scottish for refusing to sing it with any enthusiasm, but the more wholehearted hatred that greets it is more because it symbolises for them what they believe to be the oppression of Ireland. For the same reasons Rangers supporters sing it with great gusto. On this point, too, the Union Jack does for the eye what the national anthem does for the ear, and moderate Scots might well wonder what all this has

Celtic manager Billy McNeill with police during trouble involving Celtic fans at Burnley, September 1978. In background is no-man's land separating rival fans on the terracing. *Glasgow Herald* and *Evening Times*

to do with their country! More objectionable, though less visible (or audible) is the failure of many Celtic supporters—the proportion has been estimated to be as high as 90 per cent—to support the Scottish national team. Again much of this antagonism, or mere apathy, arises because they believe Scotland is Rangers-dominated, and although this connection is getting harder to see, and although claims of prejudice over the selection of Celtic players for internationals are now generally baseless, there have been occasions when out-of-form Celtic players wearing the national colours have been abused by Scottish fans—most notably Jimmy Johnstone and Davie Hay. But the most obvious and understandable aspect of some Scots' dislike of Celtic supporters is their association of the colours of the IRA with Celtic, their tricolours often making this allusion specific: green and white are Celtic's colours, not the green, white and gold of the Vatican and Irish nationalism, and Scots who find objectionable what the IRA terrorists are doing in Ireland have reason to dislike such associations, just as the waving of such colours at Lisbon detracted from the 'Scottishness' of that victory.

The Celtic management has often denounced these political associations. The riot at Waterford was not provoked by Scottish fans, nor did it even involve them. Blaming political provocateurs from the north, Jock Stein, speaking for the management, said: 'If they have dislikes and hatreds that they associate with politics and religion they have got to understand that we want no part of them or their views', and the club went on to withdraw from its registers one of the supporters' clubs that had been identified in the rioting.[36] The support of these thousands of Irish followers, although including only a minority of political activists, was certainly not for a club which they considered Scottish: it is likely, then, that the Celtic management underestimates the power of symbols and what the tricolour flying over Celtic Park does stand for— not just to Scottish bigots, but the Irish nationalists, and even ordinary Scots! If they can't take it down, they could at least replace it with the original all-green flag (with a golden harp), which would remove the present-day political connotations and retain the historical links.

One of the features of the press attacks on hooliganism in the 1970s is that although the fans have taken the brunt, the directors of the clubs have not escaped censure so easily as they did in the past. In the various suggestions to combat the problem, however, the thrust was usually on repression rather than education. The outcome of the 1972 discussions was various point plans, with bans on drinking, control of supporters' club buses and other schemes at least as old as 1962 and mainly proven failures.

Scarcely had Rangers recovered from the shocks of 1972 than its Board managed to draw attention to itself without the help of the fans. In May 1973 rumours were in the air that the Board had blocked Lawrence's nomination of David Hope as chairman. Lawrence proposed Hope in view of the work he had done building up the Rangers Pools and the Social Club, indeed doing more to add to Rangers' off-the-field business success than any other individual. It was believed to have been decided, however, that his indiscretion of 43 years previously, when he had married a catholic, overrode these other considerations. Hope, whose wife had been dead fifteen years, was chairman for seventeen minutes, and two years later he was not even on the Board.[37]

The Hope episode, however shabby it might have appeared to outsiders, had no obvious effect on supporters, for whom success on the field is more important than contributions to other aspects of a club's growth. In 1973 Rangers were enjoying a good spell, coming a close second to Celtic in the League, but avenging that with a thrilling victory over them in the Scottish Cup Final. Success continued thereafter for a

Street vendor outside Celtic Park, 1982. Photograph Malcolm R. Hill. Courtesy the Third Eye Centre and the Scottish Arts Council

few years, and it seemed that Rangers were about to regain their proper place in the football firmament. Some supporters, however, thought it was time to introduce some stern material at Board level, and this came in April 1976 when the Ibrox Board was rocked by a massive share deal which saw Lenzie garage owner Jack Gillespie in a position to claim entry to the fortress: with 36,300 shares, at £8.15 per share, he was easily the biggest shareholder.[38] The incumbents repelled the intruder that year, but the following March they gave in and so avoided all the publicity that had accompanied his unsuccessful bid. This also prevented the likelihood of his becoming the first director actually to be elected by the shareholders.

In the meantime the club had more familiar problems to deal with when in October 1976 its fans went on the rampage at Birmingham. This followed the abrupt end to Rangers' friendly against Aston Villa with only 53 minutes played, the visitors losing at the time. The Scottish press waded straight into Rangers without any side issues about the tricolour flying at Parkhead. This time the reaction in the press was enough to shake the Ibrox management out of its complacency: the *Daily Record* gave a full page to the issue and queried the claim of the Ibrox management that they had done 'everything'. They printed Waddell's refutation of the charge that he had not acted on the Minister for Sport's Working Party recommendations for combating hooliganism, but were more insistent on pointing out that Rangers' anti-catholic employment policies encouraged 'the bigoted, lunatic fringe of their so-called support'. They brought Celtic briefly into their attack on bigotry, but pointed to the uniqueness of the Rangers Board, who supported a policy 'as despicable as it is intolerable'.[39] The *Evening Times* declared that 'The Rangers bosses have to change their die-hard, blue-nosed Protestant policy',[40] and even the ultra-conservative protestant *Sunday Post* added its voice, however tremulously, to the chorus of criticism. But the clearest condemnation of Rangers came from one of Scotland's top football writers, Ian Archer, then with the *Glasgow Herald*:

> ... As a Scottish football club, [Rangers] are a permanent embarrassment and an occasional disgrace. This country would be a better place if Rangers did not exist.
>
> They are a permanent embarrassment because they are the only club in the world which insists that every member of the team is of the one religion. They are an occasional disgrace because some of their fans, fuelled by bigotry, behave like animals.
>
> I am Scottish and love football. Everyone else who is Scottish and loves football should insist in every possible way that the root cause of the Rangers sickness is broken—that the club should say *now*, that they will have no part in bigotry and discrimination.[41]

A bemused Willie Waddell, who had called out in despair that 'These louts are crucifying a great club!', must have found the criticism in the press even harder to comprehend. Worse was to come when he had to read out a statement from the management that Rangers *would* in the future sign a catholic player if one good enough came along. The press changed to congratulating Rangers, but some of their fans were not so amused, the Larkhall branch of the Rangers Supporters Club in particular.[42] The *Sunday Post's* 'Our Man in the Crowd' joined the Rangers fans at Ibrox to test reaction to the Rangers statement about signing a catholic and reported: 'Yes, Mr Waddell, You've Got Problems', for the fans he mingled with and spoke to made it clear that they did not want the honour of the club besmirched with a catholic signing.[43]

Despite the Rangers management's denunciations of the 'louts' and 'hooligans' who 'attached themselves' to the Rangers FC, it has been said that they were not so anxious to drive them away that they would actually carry out their declared policy after Birmingham and sign a catholic. At the end of 1983 Rangers had still done nothing about signing a catholic, despite the availability on the transfer market of several top-class catholics.[44] Attendances at Ibrox have dropped alarmingly since 1976, and while this is certainly part of the generally depressing decline in spectator interest, the Rangers' slump is comparatively drastic. There are some who say that thousands of Rangers fans refused to return to the ground after the Birmingham declaration. If so—and there is no hard evidence—Rangers must see themselves as caught in an ironic dilemma, for they have not won back the fans chased away by the club's sectarianism.

Rangers and the Church of Scotland

By this time the Church of Scotland had shown itself to be much more progressive than its sporting acolyte. Indeed within the church there was an active group who were so incensed about its being linked with Rangers and bigotry that they sought either to break the link or have Rangers get rid of their sectarianism. They were responding to the changes of the mid-1960s, especially since 1964 and the decisions of Vatican II when the catholic church came such a long way towards catching up with the modern world. Encouraged by Pope John XXIII, the catholic church relaxed many policies that made it easier for catholics to enjoy fuller and freer relations with non-catholics. Not all sections of the catholic church approved of what was decided in 1964,[45] but the liberals in the church were given official approval.

The Church of Scotland has welcomed the gestures of 1964, although not without problems with the more fractious members who feared the machinations of their arch-enemy in Rome. At the General Assembly of the Church of Scotland on 26 May 1967, the Moderator, Right Reverend Dr W. Roy Sanderson, rose to address his fellow ministers and noted the absence of the television cameras that had been so obvious on previous days: with a smile he informed the gathering that they had left to cover 'the homecoming of a football team from Lisbon'. He registered his accord with this decision and went on to extend his congratulations to the Celtic Football Club on their splendid achievement in becoming European champions. The Assembly acclaimed his statement with an immediate and prolonged burst of applause.[46] Two years later their moves in an ecumenical direction were vociferously opposed, and the day before Rangers fans rioted at Newcastle, the General Assembly of the

The *Protestant Telegraph* on sale outside Ibrox Park, 1982. Photograph Keith Ingham. Courtesy the Third Eye Centre and the Scottish Arts Council

Rangers fan outside Hampden Park, 1982, prior to Scottish Cup Final. Photograph Keith Ingham. Courtesy the Third Eye Centre and the Scottish Arts Council

Church of Scotland was brought to a halt by a 'sash-waving mob' incensed by the invitation to Father Dalrymple to attend the meeting.[47] Prominent among the protesters, and bearing a petition expressing his outrage, was Rev. Ian Paisley, then on the threshold of national notoriety. In the meantime Rangers fans knocked him off the front page, and as inquests into the Newcastle debacle continued, Rangers received a most unkindly cut when the Rev. Bone announced his refusal to continue to support them. He admitted that he had accepted the free passes given by the club, and that he had heard of their attitude to catholics when he returned from Africa five years previously: what he hadn't known was that the policy was 'hard and fast'.[48]

The issue lay low for a while, but in October 1974 a report by the Presbyterian Church and Community Committee condemned religious segregation in sport in the same way as it 'would oppose and deplore any other form of discrimination'. A copy of this report was sent to the clerk of the Glasgow magistrates' committee and to the secretary of the Rangers Football Club, but it did not receive much publicity.[49] As the decade grew to a close, however, and Rangers seemed as unwilling as ever to open their doors to a catholic, the Church struck again, first through *The Bush*, the news journal of the Glasgow Presbytery, and then on the radio programme *Crossfire*. The warm-up for these two events was speculation that the career of Rangers' players was under threat if they became too friendly with catholics. Rumours had abounded of the reasons for Graham Fyfe's fluctuating fortunes at Ibrox, and the player later did say he believed he had suffered for marrying a catholic.[50] Later it was said that Bobby Russell was under pressure because he married a catholic. In neither case was the wedding even celebrated in a catholic church and the wife in each case was a non-practising catholic. In an exclusive interview with the *Glasgow Herald* intended to squash such stories Russell claimed that he had been under no threats whatsoever and that his wife was welcome at Ibrox.[51]

The *Herald* interview came in response to the most blistering attack the Rangers Football Club had had to face until that time. This was the special *Bush* issue with its front page given to an attack on Rangers. Headed

THE BLUE BARRIER

it opened: 'ARE you a Catholic? That's the big disqualifying question to an applicant for any job at Ibrox' and went on to claim following its investigations, that 'Rangers Football Club is more anti-Catholic than it

THE BLUE BARRIER

DEAR JOHN GREIG

"ARE you a Catholic?" That's the big disqualifying question to an applicant for any job at Ibrox.

SECTARIANISM CONDEMNED

Four years ago this Presbytery condemned that sectarianism. Rangers said it didn't exist. Two years later they changed their non-existent policy. "We'll sign a Catholic," said their general manager. Two weeks ago they still hadn't. Nor are they likely to. Blind prejudice is no respecter of football skills alone.

QUESTIONS AND QUOTES

Over the summer we investigated the Ibrox situation. We unearthed stories of people applying for advertised jobs who were asked their religion as almost the first question. We have a quote from a director that boldly states why Catholics should not play for Rangers. We looked at the career of some players who were unfortunate enough to fall in love with Catholic girls. We retraced the story of how a man lost the Rangers chairmanship because his late wife had been a Catholic. And we conclude that far from changing anything with a new policy, Rangers Football Club is more anti-Catholic than it ever was.

NEXT STOP PARLIAMENT

So instead of publishing what we discovered and getting the usual "no comment" from Ibrox we have passed our dossier on to higher authority. A Scottish MP will raise the matter in the House of Commons. A Scottish peer will raise it in the Lords. This cancer in the heart of the warmest, friendliest city on earth must finally be rooted out. Parliament in this instance may be mightier than the pen.

DISTRUST

We add two comments. The first is that we distrust Willie Waddell. His is a role that Ibrox should clarify. From being an undistinguished journalist he has in a few years become seemingly all-powerful at Rangers. Unfortunately for the club, this Presbytery knows he does not always mean what he says.

SCOTTISH SPORTS PRESS

The second comment must be on the sad state of the Scottish sports press. It's running scared of Rangers. Ally MacLeod becomes an easy target when the knives are out. But how many of the same journalists have bravely tackled the bigotry that lies behind the facade of Edmiston Drive. If more of them had, this editorial might never have been written.

We like you. A lot of people like you. That's why they subscribed some £75,000 to your testimonial before you even decided to leave! Probably its because of the things you represent: guts, strength, fairness, skill and a typically Scottish resilience. Rangers have kicked too many people in the groin before this for you to be unaware of that.

Our main concern is a religious one. That the club you now manage practices religious discrimination. Before long parliament will have its say about that.

We wonder where you stand on the issue. We aren't asking whether you would play a Catholic but whether you will? And if you won't is it because your bosses on the Ibrox board won't have one on the staff?

We would like an answer as direct and uncompromising as your tackles used to be. Or perhaps you cannot answer. Your general manager has said he speaks for Rangers and no-one else. The role of being Willie Waddell's puppet ill becomes you.

You've always struck us as being your own man. I hope you prove us right in that you have something to say on the most fundamental issue that faces Rangers.

And we look forward to hearing from you.

THE BUSH EDITORIAL GROUP

'The Blue Barrier'. *The Bush*, September 1978. Courtesy the Presbytery of Glasgow. Views expressed in *The Bush* were not necessarily those of the Presbytery of Glasgow ever was'. After a strong attack on Waddell it commented on the sad state of the Scottish press which was 'running scared of Rangers'. Otherwise, it concluded, its editorial might not have had to be written.[52]

A *Glasgow Herald* editorial of 25 August 1978 pointed out that the time was surely right for everyone at Ibrox to take note, that it was beside the point for the Scottish Football League to say that the church should be more concerned about its own membership than the affairs of the Rangers, for if Rangers were setting a bad example of sectarian behaviour, then it was the duty of the church to do something. Gillespie of the Rangers commented sarcastically that 'these people don't seem to have much to do with their time',[53] and an MP thought the 'confrontation approach' had set the cause back.[54] In view of Rangers having done nothing, it is difficult to see what had been set back. In the meantime readers of the *Bush* protested by refusing to buy further copies of the paper, and the Glasgow Presbytery's Bath Street office had to suffer abusive phone calls. The issue died down again and it was decided that the dossier would stay under wraps because of the damage it could cause to past and present members of the Ibrox staff.

Then came the *Crossfire* programme in November 1978 which subjected Rangers' sectarianism to withering criticism. Ministers on the programme claimed that Rangers players had been under pressure from the club because of their association with catholics, one of them being ill-treated because he wanted to attend the catholic funeral of a lifelong friend. Rev. Graham would not name the players 'for obvious reasons', Ian Archer expressed doubts about the sincerity of the post-Birmingham declaration, and Brian Wilson hinted at a latent fascism in the behaviour of some of the fans and referred to the National Front graffitti he had seen at Eindhoven, where Rangers had played a European Cup match. Rangers refused to be drawn into the discussion and revealed a great deal about themselves and their estrangement from a democratic society with the comment by Waddell that radio, television and newspapers were not the places to discuss important issues![55]

Rangers did have someone to defend them on the programme, however—the Rev. James Currie, well-known wit and Rangers supporter. He classified stories about Rangers having a sectarian policy as 'absolute balderdash' and as proof offered the facts that Waddell was a good Christian and Pastor Glass had been refused permission to hand out anti-catholic pamphlets at Ibrox. He objected to a 'Presbyterian clique' investigating Rangers, and described them as a 'strident minority'. The *Daily Express* highlighted his defence of Rangers and questioned whether 'it is normal for a BBC minister-producer to boast he has been investigating Rangers for 6 years? But Rangers still have some friends in the Kirk and one of them is the Rev. James Currie, a life-long Rangers fan'.[56]

Rangers did indeed have many friends in the Kirk. For its attack on Rangers the *Bush* newspaper was threatened with extinction, as its subscribers dropped from 13,000 to 8,000, making it scarcely viable.[57] (It has since folded.) And when the issue of Rangers and sectarianism was brought up by an enthusiastic young minister, the Rev. John Ostler, at the General Assembly in 1980, the result was somewhat ambiguous: in an appeal to the Rangers Football Club to 'publicly disclaim a sectarian bias in management and team structure' 386 commissioners supported the motion, 186 disapproved. Presumably the 400 or so who abstained were not dissatisfied with Rangers and their association with religious bigotry.[58] Clearly the responsible elements in Scottish society were still offering their support, however tacit, to bigotry: the silent majority that by saying nothing thereby approves.

Concern about sectarianism in Scotland, as can be seen by the attacks on Rangers' sectarianism in the seventies, has advanced from the days when it was accepted as a fact of life. Indeed criticism was coming in from many quarters, and in late 1979 comedian Rikki Fulton could include a lampoon of the club and its policies in his late-night television show. But there is a certain inertia in Scottish society that manages to let the waves of criticism lap harmlessly around it: Rangers have remained unmoved by the attacks on them, secure in the support of a silent majority that either does not see sectarianism in sport as a serious matter, or which tacitly or openly supports it. The first years of the 1980s have not been altogether auspicious for those who would like to see a Scotland in which bigotry is a thing of the past.

NOTES

1. The story surrounding the chaos at Milan airport comes from the entry on Celtic in the Marshall Cavendish *Book of Football*, an encyclopedia in 75 weekly parts: part 3 published 1971. Like many other stories of this type, such as those arising out of the epic journeys to Lisbon and Barcelona, fact often disappears in myth, and solitary episodes are expanded to become the general rule. Rangers' supporters have still to find a historian, and impartial observers have not been kind to them, but for an entertaining account of the behaviour of Celtic supporters, written from a frankly partisan point of view, see Gerald McNee's *And You'll Never Walk Alone*.

2. Cf. especially the reaction of Arsenal fans and players to the six thousand Celtic fans who travelled to London for the Sammy Nelson benefit match in late November 1980. Apart from the boost to the gate given by the travelling support, the good humour of the crowd won over everyone there, not least Sammy Nelson himself, who admitted that the reception they gave him left him near to tears. See the press of this time, also *Celtic View*, 3 December 1980. Ipswich fans, players, management and police were equally ecstatic about the Celtic fans' 'sporting attitude and general good behaviour' during the Allan Hunter testimonial game on 3 November 1981. Again see press of this time, and for a copy of the Chief Superintendent Eric Shields' congratulatory telegram, see *Celtic View*, 11 November 1981.

3. *Daily Express*, 22 May 1969. (All references to the *Daily Express* are to the *Scottish Daily Express*.)

4. Campbell, *Glasgow Celtic, 1945–1970*, p. 100.

5. In the early 1960s Labour MP for Thurrock, Hugh Delargy, had advocated the liquidation of Celtic. This followed a game in Dundee in 1961 during which 50 people were allegedly bottle-slashed and one man later died in gaol. Delargy claimed that 'Riots like this have been going on for 50 years. Admonitions, by-laws and action by the police and club management have been in vain. The club should liquidate itself—as Belfast Celtic did years ago'. (Reproduced in *Celtic View*, 12 July 1967, as an example to Celtic supporters of the sort of abuse to which they had been subjected.) Subsequent crowd troubles involving Celtic fans are discussed later.

6. *Weekly Record*, 28 March 1925.

7. *Sunday Mail*, 19 June 1938, p. 40.

8. *Ibid.*, 14 September 1941, p. 15.

9. *Ibid.*, 21 September 1952.

10. *Ibid.*, 28 September 1952, p. 17.

11. *Ibid.*, 28 January 1962, p. 22.

12. *Glasgow Herald* colour supplement, 27 January 1983, p. 37. In the correspondence that was provoked by his reporting of a Rangers v Red Star Bratislava game at Ibrox in November 1959, one letter writer said that 'for some years now Mr Horne has made it very plain that he cannot report any match in which Rangers are involved with any sense of fairness', while another pointed out that Horne's criticism merely balanced the bias of other sports writers (*Glasgow Herald*, following match report 12 December 1959, p. 9). It should be noted that he accused Rangers merely of rough play.

13. *Evening News*, 3 February 1955.

14. McNee, *The Story of Celtic*, p. 14.

15. *Goal* was a publication put out by young Scottish journalists chafing under the restraints on what they were allowed to discuss in the major papers. It came out in 1965 with a few youthful blasts, including one on 'The Meatball of Bias', claiming that reformers of Scottish football would get more joy campaigning for civil rights in Alabama than they would getting Rangers or Celtic to change

their policies. It claimed that both managements knew that by encouraging the bigotry 'that nearly every Glasgow kid is made to swallow or choke on' they were 'onto a good thing' (issue of November 1965, p. 9).

16. *Daily Express*, 10 May 1967.

17. Jimmy Johnstone, *Fire in My Boots*, London, 1969, pp. 88–91. See also Billy McNeill, *For Celtic and Scotland*, London, 1966; Ronnie Simpson, *Sure It's A Grand Old Team to Play For*, London, 1967; Tommy Gemmell, *The Big Shot*, London, 1968; Bobby Murdoch, *All The Way with Celtic*, London, 1970.

18. *On Top with United*, pp. 31–2.

19. Derek Johnstone, *Rangers: My Team*, London, 1979.

20. *Daily Record*, 27 May 1969, p. 28 (all references to *Daily Record* are to *Scottish Daily Record*).

21. *Daily Express*, 3 June 1969, pp. 8–9.

22. *Ibid.*, see also *Daily Record* of this time.

23. There is an excellent evocation of the disaster and the events leading up to it in J. Burrowes, *Frontline Report*, Edinburgh, 1982.

24. Reproduced from *Life and Work*, magazine of the Church of Scotland, in *Scottish Protestant View*, February 1971.

25. *Celtic View*, 7 January, 1971.

26. He repeats this in Archer and Royle (eds.), *We'll Support You Ever More*, London, 1976, p. 75.

27. *Scottish Protestant View*, February 1971.

28. *Evening Times*, 4 January 1971.

29. The article 'Falling Masonry', in *The Foul Book of Football*, claims that the press, afraid of being thought anti-Rangers, relegated the findings 'to page 5 of the *Daily Record* and page 8 of *The Scotsman*'.

30. Mitchell Library file on disaster and *Daily Express*, 24 October 1974, pp. 1, 11.

31. *Daily Express*, 17 August 1972.

32. *Daily Express*, 23 August 1972, p. 4.

33. *Glasgow Herald*, 16 August 1972, p. 8.

34. *Glasgow Herald*, 23 August 1972, p. 8.

35. *Daily Express*, 23 August 1972. See also *Celtic View*, 30 August 1972, which reproduces the letter to the magistrates.

36. McNee, *And You'll Never Walk Alone*, pp. 78–80.

37. For one of the clearest statements on the rumour surrounding Hope's troubles with the Ibrox Board, see *Sunday Standard*, 5 July 1981, article by Jack Webster and William Robertson.

38. *Glasgow Herald*, 21 April 1976.

39. *Daily Record*, 11 October 1976, p. 2, 13 October 1976, p. 2.

40. *Evening Times*, 11 October 1976, p. 3.

41. *Glasgow Herald*, 11 October 1976, p. 3.

42. *Sunday Mail*, 5 December 1976.

43. *Sunday Post*, 17 October 1976, p. 31.

44. The *Sunday Mail*, 18 May 1980, ran a two-page colour article with comments from 'good catholics' who had been playing since Rangers 'signed the pledge' in 1976, some of them even having come on the market. Among the star Scots were Billy Bremner, Joe Jordan, Arthur Graham, Frank McGarvey, Frank Gray and Paul Hegarty.

45. On the struggles of the liberals inside the catholic church see Cooney, *Scotland and the Papacy*, particularly the chapter on ecumenism, 'Romeward bound'. For an entertaining but even more insightful appreciation of the effects of the reforms of Vatican II in the lives of ordinary catholics see David Lodge's novel *How Far Can You Go?*, London, 1980.

46. This is neatly summarised in Campbell, *Glasgow Celtic: 1945–1970*, p. 7.

47. This was front-page news in the *Daily Express* and *Daily Record*, 21 May 1969.

48. *Daily Express*, 2 June 1969.

49. 'Church and Community Committee Report', October 1974. It concludes: 'Finally, Presbytery will hardly need reminding of the unique factor in our local situation where the religious affiliations of Rangers and Celtic supporters become a very real part of the problem of hooliganism. It has been suggested that Rangers Football Club has a practice if not a policy, of refusing to sign players who are Roman Catholics. The club itself is equivocal as to whether or not this is the case. Should it be the case, then it must be said clearly and openly that such a practice or policy would receive no support whatsoever from this Presbytery. Whilst it is not Presbytery's role to dictate policies to a football club, religious segregation in sport is deplored by us in exactly the same way as we would oppose and deplore any other form of discrimination'.

50. See p. 252.

51. *Glasgow Herald*, 26 August 1978, p. 1.

52. *The Bush*, September 1978, No. 51.

53. *Glasgow Herald*, 25 August 1978, p. 1.

54. *Glasgow Herald*, 28 August 1978, p. 3.

55. *Glasgow Herald*, 28 November 1978.

56. *Daily Express*, 29 November 1978, p. 3.

57. *Daily Record*, 10 April 1980: 'Kirk paper in closure threat after row over 'Gers''.

58. *The Scotsman*, 22 May 1980, p. 1. Also private correspondence with the Church of Scotland. The *Daily Express*, 22 May 1980, reported the Kirk's 200 majority as a condemnation of 'sectarian bias' in headline: 'Ban on Catholics condemned in shock Assembly vote ... KIRK RAP FOR RANGERS'.

CHAPTER 10

Into the 'Eighties

On 10 May 1980 sports viewers throughout the world saw an entertaining Scottish Cup Final between Rangers and Celtic end in unprecedented scenes of spectator violence as the arena was taken over by brawling fans, to be cleared eventually thanks only to mounted police. Yet of all the riots involving the supporters of Celtic and Rangers, there are surely few that could have been more easily averted: the game had been relatively trouble-free, played in a sporting spirit and with no serious disputes with the referee's decisions. Perhaps it was this very calm, and misplaced confidence in the spectator fencing, that influenced the decision to send policemen from inside the ground to help patrol the fans on their way home from the match. But for the Glasgow police this was an incredible error of judgement. They have a superb record, as well as the respect of those who have least reason to like them. Better than anyone else they know that while an Old Firm game is not over until hours after the final whistle, nevertheless the crucial moment is just before and after that very whistle. Yet there they were, as extra time at Scotland's premier game drew to a close, with a presence around the perimeter of the Hampden track that would hardly have been adequate for an inconsequential league game. As such they were unable to push back the trickle of Celtic fans who jumped the fence to congratulate the players and to celebrate their team's victory. Had these first fans been kept behind the fence, the scenes that followed would have been avoided.

At the Rangers end of the field the presence of the green and white celebrants of victory was insult added to yet another setback, and hundreds of Rangers supporters swarmed across the field to vent their spite on the jubilant enemy at the other end. Celtic supporters were later condemned for their part in the brawls, and certainly they stood fist to fist, boot to boot, and bottle for bottle with the enemy, but what would have been thought of them if, at the sight of the charging Rangers supporters, they had turned and fled? There is no way they could have stood their ground and patiently explained to the advancing blue brigade that all they were doing was saluting their team and no insult was intended to worthy opponents. They were Glaswegians and Scottish, and they were being challenged: honour dictated only one course of action. It could be said that the Celtic fans' victory dances were also a challenge,

244

Hampden Riot, 1980. *Glasgow Herald* and *Evening Times*

Hampden Riot, 1980. *Glasgow Herald* and *Evening Times*

and certainly that is how the Rangers' faithful would have seen it, but there are challenges and challenges. And whatever the error of the police in not nipping the trouble in the bud, their reaction afterwards was courageous and efficient, earning them the applause of those who watched the battles from the stands and terracing: they undoubtedly saved the skin, bones and possibly lives of countless numbers of fans. It was also a reminder that without these same police nearly every Old Firm battle would be a bloodbath, and that it is only their skill, patience and presence that makes these games possible at all.

1980 Riot and Repercussions

Naturally the papers were full of the riot, and the game itself tended to get forgotten. Celtic blamed the police, the police blamed the Celtic players for rushing to their fans in triumph at the end of the game, everybody blamed drink, but Secretary of State for Scotland George Younger preferred to use the police statement to blame the Celtic players (as did Rangers), and the SFA inquiry blamed all these factors. The most significant feature of the SFA executive committee report was that perhaps for the first time in the history of Old Firm battles the leading authority in Scottish football came off the fence to make a stinging attack on sectarianism, particularly that of Rangers.[1] Concerning the two sets of spectators, the report admitted that the Celtic fans

> invaded the track and goal area for the purpose of cavorting around and generally celebrating with the Celtic players who had chosen to run to that end of the stadium, on the final whistle, to demonstrate to their supporters their exuberance at victory. At that stage of events there was nothing violent in the exchanges between players and fans. Rather it was a spontaneous, if misguided, expression of joy.

The thoughts that filled the minds of the Rangers fans were quite different:

> ... There was no question of celebration in the minds of the fans who invaded from the West end of the ground. They had violence in mind and no sooner was it offered than it was returned with enthusiasm. The brutal and disgusting scenes which followed as bottles flew and drunken supporters charged and countercharged from one end of the field to the other, brought disgrace upon the two clubs concerned, upon Scottish football generally, and were an affront to Scotland as a nation.

The SFA committee claimed that it was far from satisfied that each

club had done everything in its power to dissociate itself from
sectarianism, which it claimed to be 'the root cause of the hatred and
bitterness which has existed between the two sets of supporters for
decades', but regretted that on legal advice it had no 'authority to insist
that the clubs should renounce any act or policy which could be said to
encourage political or religious bigotry'. On the reaction of the two clubs
the committee noted that Celtic were willing to co-operate, but that the
Rangers club 'insists that its present policies are in keeping with the
Association's wishes. The committee is not satisfied with the latter's
assertion'.[2] David Miller, secretary of the Rangers Supporters Association,
went further in answer to the charge of sectarianism by saying: 'It is Rangers'
prerogative who they sign and I think the majority of Rangers supporters are
quite happy with things the way they are'.[3]

Neither club was pleased with the £20,000 fine imposed on it but the
general opinion in the press was that they had got off lightly. Indeed,
with gate money, sponsorship, and live television coverage fees, neither
club suffered hardship. Some papers reminded their readers that the
Highland League club Huntly had been banned for two months for
crowd troubles at one of their games, while their fine of £100 was harsh
enough in view of their average gate of 300. Admittedly that field
invasion had been directed at the referee, but certainly the economic
power of Celtic and Rangers puts them on a different level: a ban on
The Old Firm clubs would hit more than Celtic and Rangers. Although
leading figures like Willie Harkness of the SFA and George Younger in
the House of Commons used the police statement to blame the Celtic
players for setting off the riots,[4] most journalists highlighted the role of
sectarianism and therefore came down more heavily on Rangers. Rangers
Chairman Rae Simpson held himself loftily aloof from such suggestions.
He claimed that a number (unknown) of catholics (unnamed) were
employed by Rangers in 'responsible' positions (unspecified), and that
Glasgow was polarised and this was not Rangers' fault. Desmond White
of Celtic was 'appalled' that his club should continue to be accused of
sectarianism, and listed the number of Celtic captains, including Bertie
Peacock whom he claimed could have been called an Orangeman, who
had played for Celtic, and again mentioned the offer of a position on the
Board to Jock Stein two years previously. There were six protestants in
the 1980 cup-winning team, and there could have been one more but for
injury.

The issue of sectarianism had never been long out of the news before
the Hampden riot. At the start of the year 'Green Eyes' Alex Cameron of
the *Daily Record* was accused of self-righteousness for his attitude to

J

rugby in South Africa and slamming Rangers' 'club policy', which one writer characterised as a 'little idiosyncrasy'.[5] John Fairgrieve published a couple of extracts from the mail he had received following his comments on the Hampden riots: one from Mr N. O. Surrender (U.D.A., Class of 1690) threatened:

> I would like you to get it into your thick papist head that while there is the Orange Order, Black Order, Apprentice Boys of Derry, and the Rangers Supporters Club, Ibrox will stay Protestant. We are just about fed up with your kind attacking the Rangers' policy.[6]

Hampden continued to be in the news at this time, though mainly over its fate as Scotland's national stadium. What should have been regarded as one of Scotland's first national monuments, at one time the largest sports stadium in the world and scene of many moments of grandeur, grit and tragedy, was threatened with demolition because of the cost of bringing it up to modern standards. Queen's Park could not afford the upkeep, the SFA could not offer more than a promise to finance the cost of bringing the ground to minimum safety requirements, and the Tory government reneged at the last moment on a commitment to subsidise the bulk of the £12 million needed for renovation. One of the clubs that did not support the renovation of Hampden was Rangers, who said that they wanted to see the big games shared out among the other Scottish clubs. It was believed that a letter from Rae Simpson to a swithering Tory government, expressing this point of view, helped them in their decision to go back on the promise of money for Hampden.[7] Clearly Rangers had visions of the newly modernised Ibrox taking over from Hampden, but they underestimated the reaction that such a proposal would cause: the choice of either Ibrox or Parkhead for internationals and big cup games was certain to drive a sectarian wedge through Scotland's support. Moreover, despite the drastic fall in attendances at Scottish football, the big matches still draw at least 20,000 more than an all-seated Ibrox can hold. Above all, however, no other ground stands out so obviously as a bastion of sectarianism.

In August Celtic hit the sectarian headlines when Chairman White, still smarting from the accusation of sectarianism following the Hampden riot, spoke at the Danny McGrain benefit dinner and opened his remarks by pointing out that McGrain was a protestant. He was greeted by a slow handclap and walkout by some of the guests, two from the main table and others from the floor. An unnamed politician described his speech as offensive and an insult to McGrain, while 'a leading Glasgow businessman' later complained to Joe Beltrami, chairman of the McGrain

testimonial committee, about White's remarks.[8] McGrain himself had
made his feelings on sectarianism known in no uncertain terms in his
Celtic: My Team, and the press had not been slow in criticising Rangers
in recent months, so perhaps White's comments were out of place. But
he had good reason to feel angry at the response to his remarks.
However, while the charge of sectarianism cannot stick when levelled at
Celtic, their religious associations are always there to help cloud the issue.
At the McGrain dinner they were there in the presence of the Archbishop
of Glasgow, Thomas Winning. He was a patron of the McGrain
Testimonial Committee, but it is hard to see what he had to do with
either McGrain or football.

Celtic were briefly in the news again in September when Dr Michael
Kelly, in his first year as Lord Provost of Glasgow, was accused of going
to see only Celtic games. In the event he stopped going to any games for
a while. Then came the world lightweight title fight at Glasgow's Kelvin
Hall in November, between the reigning champion Jim Watt, and an
American called Sean O'Grady. The known sympathies of some of
Watt's supporters, and the suspicious-sounding name of the challenger,
gave the bout a sectarian edge, and this boiled over in a pre-match
controversy. Promoter Mickey Duff was approached by the editor
of *Celtic View* concerning a promotional visit to Parkhead, and he is
reported to have agreed that this would be a great idea. In the event
Watt couldn't make it, because he was training in London, and so
O'Grady went to the Celtic/Kilmarnock match alone. He was presented
with a Celtic jersey as a souvenir of his visit, but was misguided or
innocent enough to wear it when presented to the crowd at half-time. He
was accused of flaunting the club's colours, with Celtic as his willing
accomplices, and an angry Duff said shortly after the bout: 'It was clearly
an effort to drum up Catholic support'. As a final irony it turned out
that the O'Gradys, despite their name, were not catholics, but members
of the Millwood Baptist Church in Oklahoma City![9] There are more
than Rangers scouts, it seems, whose lives are made unnecessarily
difficult!

At least this helped distract attention from Rangers for a while. On
3rd September star winger Willie Johnston was sent off after an alleged
attack on Aberdeen's John McMaster which resulted in the Dons player
needing a medical check-up for injuries to his neck.[10] This was Johnston's
thirteenth sending-off in a controversial career. A tight-lipped John Greig
claimed: 'We have our own code of conduct at Ibrox. Every Rangers
player is aware of it and are [*sic*] equally aware of the consequences'.[11]
Whatever that code is, Johnston was soon back in the game, and two

months later he was back in the headlines for an incident involving Hearts' young full-back Steve Hamilton. As a result of a clash Hamilton had to leave the field with stud marks on his stomach, and to injury was added insult when Johnston gestured his contempt to abusive Hearts fans. Only one bottle was thrown. Scottish sports writers were furious, but since the referee did not see this off-the-ball incident, and the SFA received no official complaint, they could do little more than express their outrage.[12] As for Rangers, they had made their opinion on such incidents known.

In October 1980 Rangers were in the news when their fans went down to England and did *not* cause any trouble. This was for the Anglo-Scottish Cup game against Chesterfield, Rangers' first visit south of the border since Birmingham four years previously. The Rangers management and citizens of Chesterfield looked to the anticipated invasion with some trepidation, and some locals, with an eye to the quick quid, offered their services to small businessmen in the area, boarding up the vulnerable parts of their premises.[13] All fears were misplaced, and money spent on protective covering was wasted. The Rangers fans, in co-operation with their club, disgraced no one, although their team embarrassed Scotland when the third division English eleven easily defeated the visitors 3–0.

The most notable event of 1980 concerning the two Old Firm teams, however, other than the Hampden riot, was the broadcast in November by London Weekend Television of their *Credo* programme dealing with the sectarianism of The Old Firm. This was the second time the two clubs had come in for such treatment in the one year. Shortly after the Hampden riot and just before the England/Scotland international, *Current Account* presented a programme on football hooliganism, arriving at Hampden 1980 via Barcelona 1972, Wembley 1977, and the local Scottish scene in 1977–78 featuring Rangers fans in fights and a field invasion at Fir Park, Motherwell, during what was effectively the League championship decider and Celtic fans disturbing the peace against Hibs.[14] In regard to hooliganism in general the programme highlighted the McElhone recommendations: the right to search fans entering grounds; bans on taking drink onto supporters' buses; the erection of spectator barriers; the provision of more seating; the introduction of organised pre-match entertainment; experiments in serving beer inside the ground from plastic cups; and finally the granting of draconian powers to the SFA.

Inevitably the issue of sectarianism was brought up, with Brian Wilson launching a vitriolic attack on Rangers and the spinelessness of the SFA. Rangers were presented as a 'business ... posing as a football club ...

making money out of a policy of religious apartheid'. The SFA was called on to act on this 'cancer in Scottish society'. The SFA, unfortunately, but not surprisingly, was not there to answer charges of inaction but Rangers allowed Rae Simpson to appear on the programme. He expressed some amazement that his club should be accused of sectarianism, for after all other clubs had hooligans, and the Hampden riot was no different from that at Wembley in 1977. In any case Rangers were doing all they could about the problem, installing an all-seated stadium—this, apparently, would solve all the problems. From such empty optimism the discussion went over to ex-Ranger Jim Baxter's pub, where the problem was reduced to drink and hatred, the latter based on religion. At least here there was an essential honesty.

The *Credo* programme, being a religious broadcast, dealt solely with sectarianism, and was assured a good coverage by the suggestion that there was an attempt to prevent the Scottish viewing public from seeing it. Scottish Television denied accusations that its refusal to show the programme, beamed throughout England, but only through Border Television in Scotland, was a form of censorship, and eventually STV put the show on the air—at 9 a.m. on a Sunday morning, seven weeks later! The programme appeared without cuts, despite the pleas of at least one MP, Govan's Andy McMahon, that 'the more inflammatory scenes involving youthful football supporters' be edited out. He was concerned about the effect on potential employers.[15] The advance publicity promised hatred and bigotry, and viewers were not to be disappointed, with clips of fans in vicious punch-ups, the singing of sectarian songs, and quieter discussions between fans who linked one side with Ulster and the UDA and the other with Ireland and the IRA. More prosaically one fan said it was simply a matter of 'Proddies' beating 'Kah'licks', and another admitted knowing very few catholics, but felt he had to hate them because he was a Rangers supporter. Not surprisingly, Rangers refused to appear on the programme and indeed refused all co-operation with its producers. Celtic thought it inadvisable to appear since Rangers were not represented, and the SFA seem to have judged that the programme had little to do with them. Spokesmen for the clubs were there, however, Rangers through Rev. James Currie who, in an analysis which, though delivered with clearer diction than that of the fans in Jim Baxter's pub, did not add anything to what they had said, pooh-poohed any association of Rangers with sectarianism and blamed all the troubles on drink. Other presbyterian ministers attacked Rangers, with one of them claiming that Rangers made a handsome profit out of bigotry. Rev. Donald Macdonald, a seasoned critic of Rangers and speaking from a well-informed knowledge of the growth of The Old Firm, condemned his church for not taking a stronger stand. He pointed to the number of abstentions on the Ostler motion at the General Assembly condemning sectarianism in football, and suggested that this was partly because there were a large number of ministers in Scotland who were offered and accepted free stand tickets to Ibrox. Another long-standing critic of Rangers, freelance journalist Brian Wilson, added his pungent comments, as powerful as Macdonald's for the way they cut through the cant, and, like his, based on solid foundations.

The aspect of the programme that received widest publicity, however, was the revelation by former Ranger, Graham Fyfe, about the club's interference in the private lives of their players. The former Rangers player stated in public what everyone connected with the game had always believed was the case: that any Ranger who became emotionally involved with a catholic could expect to come in for questioning by the management. He told how, when it was known that he was marrying a catholic girl, he was called into the manager's office and asked about it. Even when he assured the manager that he was getting married in the Church of Scotland, which the couple did, after the wedding he felt he was under 'tremendous pressure'. He stayed on another four years with Rangers before leaving and eventually emigrating to the States. Although his wife had long since given up her catholicism, and indeed by marrying in the Church of Scotland demonstrated this, Fyfe felt that he had to go, saying: 'Deep down I think I had to move from Rangers because I married a catholic'.[16]

There was a more or less predictable defence of Rangers by Allan Herron, who claimed to have been 'astounded' at Fyfe's remarks and concluded: 'The real reason why [Fyfe] left Rangers was that he wasn't quite good enough. And Graham knows it'.[17] Certainly it was four years before Fyfe made his move, and he only 'thought' he had to move because of his wife's former religion. Moreover he enjoyed a good press in the *Rangers News* at this time.[18] But the questioning about who he was to marry was never denied, and in no other sporting organisation could such a triviality have been blown up to such proportions.

Two years later Rangers player Gordon Dalziel announced that he was going to marry a catholic, carefully pointing out that 'I have already had the all-clear at Ibrox'. Moreover he assured reporters (no doubt to quell the fears of Rangers followers) that 'I'm not going to get married in the chapel or anything like that', and eased any worries he might himself have been feeling by pointing out that Bobby Russell had married a catholic and yet his career had not been affected.[19] Rangers were not exactly signing on a catholic, nor were they even allowing a player to stay on who was marrying one, but they were allowing one to stay on despite his marrying someone who *had been* a catholic. If this was progress, then it is a sad comment on the mentality of the men who run Ibrox.

Most of the Scottish press accepted the *Credo* programme as necessary viewing, with Charles Graham of the *Evening Times* demanding: 'Let us see the truth about ourselves'.[20] That 'truth' was not pretty, but it is difficult to dress up bigotry in acceptable garb. The producers of the programme did not invent the problem, they merely highlighted it, and so one can only reflect sadly on the attitude of one of the men who more than most others should have been concerned about what it had to show: Willie Harkness, President of the SFA. Living in Dumfries, he was able to see the first showing on Border TV, but could only comment that 'The programme disgraced Scottish football'.[21] Whoever, or whatever, disgraced Scottish football, it was certainly not London Weekend Television.

The Debate Continues

If 1980 had been a bad year for Rangers, 1981 was only marginally better. The Scottish public was blessed with the arrival of a new Sunday paper, the *Sunday Standard*, in the spring of that year, and while it was a welcome addition to Scots folks' Sunday reading, it offered no comfort to Rangers, particularly since its leading sports writer was Ian Archer. Scottish radio, too, persisted in disturbing the peace out Ibrox way, with an assessment of The Old Firm by William McIlvanney, broadcast on Radio 4 and Radio Scotland on 15 February, shortly before another Celtic/Rangers confrontation.

This programme criticised the reluctance of Scots to talk about the reality of what was happening at Old Firm matches, and dismissed claims that it was 'only a game', for the results kept spilling out of the sports pages into the hard news. McIlvanney emphasised that Glasgow is a city of marvellous warmth and variety, a 'twenty-four hour cabaret', but added that 'anyone inviting you to come to that cabaret who pretends that there isn't something harshly unique about the Rangers/Celtic rivalry should be sued under the trade descriptions act'. Using a variety of well-informed contributors, he reviewed the situation in Scotland even before the two clubs were formed, through the development of industry, particularly in the shipyards, mentioned the part of the two clubs in fuelling sectarian hatred, and inevitably came to concentrate on Rangers' unwillingness to sign a catholic. From there the spread of sectarianism through the so-called educated classes was discussed, as well as the role of education and the effect of the troubles in Northern Ireland. Spokesmen for the supporters' associations of the two clubs appeared, Miller for Rangers and Delaney for Celtic, but none for the managements: Simpson of Rangers and White of Celtic refused to appear. This was a pity, for no better discussion of The Old Firm problem had previously been put on the air or expressed in the press. The depth of analysis surpassed anything else that ever had been said on the subject.

McIlvanney pointed out that there was a great need for discussion on the subject as a 'means of dissipating the fog of prejudice and half-thought that seems to obscure some Glaswegians from themselves'. 'Out of that historical fog', went on McIlvanney, 'can come humour and lucid intervals of mutual understanding, but at its thickest it remains an unhealthy part of Glasgow's environment, a sort of cultural pollution that can help to foster distorted attitudes, brute prejudice, and for some a battled[?] despondency.' The failure of the two clubs to contribute to this discussion reflects badly on their social conscience or consciousness. With such 'leaders', who can blame the lapses of the followers?

In May of that year the extra-sporting associations of The Old Firm made another of their recurrent appearances when supporters of an Ulster Loyalist demonstration sought to counter a demonstration by supporters of the IRA hunger strikers. The demonstrations were to be in Edinburgh on a Sunday, and since Rangers were playing Dundee United in the Scottish Cup Final the day before, leaflets were to be distributed among the Rangers supporters. As the organisers said: 'We are trying to reach people who could reasonably be expected to sympathize with our cause: there was no time to pass it on by word of mouth.'[22] In fact for a long time since, and right up to the present day, peddlers of sectarian propaganda have found a good market in or near either of the two Old Firm grounds on match days.

Later that year, in one of the many inquests into the poor performance of the team,[23] the *Sunday Post* asked David Miller of the Rangers Supporters' Association what was going wrong. Miller blamed the scouting system which allowed young talent bred in the West to go elsewhere.[24] Not once did he mention the weakest aspect of that policy: Rangers' refusal to have anything to do with any youngster who exuded the slightest aroma of catholicism. Ian Archer, in an article pointing the way to how Rangers could regain their former glory, went straight to the point: Rangers were 'prisoners of their prejudice'. Ending the ban on

IRELAND'S WAR

NEWSPAPER OF THE GLASGOW IRISH FREEDOM ACTION COMMITTEE   ISSUE No. 2 (38-8)

20p

14 YEARS

OF IRISH

RESISTANCE

● Derry's Francis Hughes and Maguire/McBrearty bands, turned out in smart military-style uniforms.

DEMONSTRATION
SATURDAY 1 OCTOBER 1983
• LONDON •
•Complete British withdrawal from Ireland!•
•Self-determination for the Irish People!•
•The right of repatriation for all POWs•
ASSEMBLE 1pm BIDBOROUGH STREET
(nearest tube and rail station Kings Cross/St Pancras)
Write for leaflets and posters to
GIFAC, Box 27, 488 Great Western Road Glasgow.

CONFERENCE
SUNDAY 2 OCTOBER 1983
• LONDON 9.15–5.30 •
BUILD A UNITED IRISH SOLIDARITY MOVEMENT
One Day National Conference
Caxton House, St John's Way Archway London N19
Nearest tube Archway
For leaflets, posters and further information, contact
GIFAC, Box 27, 488 Great Western Road Glasgow.

Pamphlet on sale outside Celtic Park before Old Firm game, 3 September 1983

SCOTTISH LOYALISTS

LEST WE
FORGET

THE S.L. ARE HOLDING THIS PARADE TO
HONOUR LORD MOUNTBATTEN WHO WAS
BRUTALLY MURDERED BY THE I.R.A. IN
AUGUST 1979. EVERY LOYALIST IS INVITED
TO ATTEND TO SHOW THEIR RESPECT FOR
THIS GREAT BRITISH LEADER AND ALSO TO
REGISTER THEIR UTTER CONTEMPT FOR
THE I.R.A. AND THEIR R.C. FOLLOWERS -
THROUGHOUT BRITAIN.

> SCOTTISH LOYALISTS
>
> LORD MOUNTBATTEN MEMORIAL PARADE
>
> ALL LOYALISTS WELCOME
>
> TO PARADE
>
> ON SATURDAY 3RD SEPTEMBER 1983
>
> LEAVING DEVON STREET 10.30 A.M.
>
> FLUTE BANDS IN ATTENDANCE.

— FOR GOD AND SCOTLAND

Leaflet distributed inside Ibrox Park during Wednesday evening League Cup match, Rangers v Clydebank, 31 August 1983. Rangers were due to play Celtic the following Saturday catholics would be no cure-all, but it would be a start, besides which it would make the club more respectable. He cited two stories, one of a former Rangers scout who told them to 'stuff the job' when he was ridiculed for recommending a boy who was a catholic, and another of a scout from a less wealthy club who would ring around Rangers' scouts asking if they had come across any talent they couldn't sign themselves. He claimed to have got many good players that way.[25]

Amidst the more familiar complaints came one story that was (in all senses) out of the blue. In normal times the sexual goings on of the rich are standard fare for the readers of Sunday morning newspapers. Such trivia are totally divorced from football, and this should have been so in the case of the mistress (or wife) of Jack Lawrence, son of the former Rangers chairman. Except that she was a catholic. As part of her case to have a share of the Lawrence inheritance for her daughter, as wife of Jack 'by habit and repute', she offered the evidence that Jack had taken her, a catholic, into the directors' box at Ibrox.[26] Despite such evidence her case was rejected.

The unwelcome publicity of the 'mistress left out in the cold' was in no way of Rangers' making; but at the same time the directors showed that they were still capable of drawing unkindly light on themselves when they were accused of 'sacking' Willie Waddell from his job as consultant to the board of directors.[27] Hugh Taylor headed his story 'Oh, So Shabby', and commented on how sad it was that Rangers should so brusquely send packing 'one of their most famous sons'. He noted that Waddell had received his dismissal notice through the post and asked:: 'Will Rangers never find the human touch?'[28] When Celtic brought universal condemnation on themselves for the way they got rid of manager McNeill in June 1983, at least one critic commented that they were 'acting like Rangers'.[29]

In the event it turned out that Waddell had not been sacked, but the rumours, denials, accusations and counter-accusations fed on the silence that Rangers believe is their best policy. In this case, however, Waddell successfully sued the *Sunday Mail* whose front page 'exclusive' had broken the story. In the meantime Tom Dawson, Rangers' third largest shareholder, had to admit: 'Rangers make their image worse by repeatedly shrouding Ibrox in secrecy during crises. Nothing comes out well in the wash there'.[30] When the Rangers Board came back with a clear-cut rebuttal of the allegations, explaining the circumstances of Waddell being given a generous early retirement pension—he had not been in good health—the club's image was only partly restored. The issue resurfaced briefly at the AGM later in the year when the directors came under fire from irate shareholders. Beyond the talk of power struggles, payments to Waddell and the club's profits one speaker brought everything back into perspective: 'It's tragic,' he said, 'that a team in the East End of Glasgow, I won't even mention its name, is heading for its thirteenth League within 16 seasons'.[31]

Politics and the Pope's Visit

If Rangers were still 'prisoners of their prejudice', they were also to some degree prisoners of the society in which they operated, for in areas totally divorced from football, bigotry was still refusing to lie low. In March 1982, at the Hillhead by-election, the fate of Roy Jenkins and the Social Democrats was the main issue, but the Tories fielded a catholic candidate and so raised the sectarian issue. It was not the first time sectarianism had played a role in Scottish politics in recent times. At the 1959 General Election the safe Labour seat of Coatbridge and Airdrie was nearly lost when Labour nominated a catholic who was opposed by the sister of Alan ('Wee Blue Devil') Morton. She lost by only 759 votes. The only other seat at that election where Labour did badly was the marginal one of Glasgow Kelvingrove, where an Irish-born catholic, Mary McAllister, lost the seat that she had won in a by-election in 1958. This was against a background of spectacular successes by Labour everywhere else in Scotland. The Tories also were liable to run into trouble when they fielded catholics. Back in 1940 sitting Tory MP, Sir John McEwan, converted to catholicism and lost what had been the safe seat of Berwick and Haddington in the next election. In fact the Tories never elected a catholic in Scotland before 1974, but—shade of McGrain and O'Grady— protestant voters rejected the Tory candidate for the safe seat of Pollok in 1964 because of the suspicious ring to his name: Robert Kernohan.[32] Although the nomination by the Tories, until the 1950s an exclusively protestant party, of catholic lawyer, Gerry Malone, for Hillhead aroused comment in the Scottish press, sectarianism in Scottish politics was clearly on the wane. Some cynical catholics claimed Malone was nominated because the Conservatives anticipated a drubbing, but although beaten in 1982, he was successful in the 1983 General Election in Aberdeen South. Moreover in 1982 Mrs Thatcher appointed Michael Ancram, a catholic, as chairman of the Scottish Tories, and in June 1982 Labour fielded a catholic candidate in a by-election for Coatbridge and Airdrie. There was no repeat of the 1959 cliffhanger, and Labour held the seat comfortably.[33]

1982, however, was above all the year of the papal visit:[34] or at least it would have been but for the unforeseen tragedy (mixed with some triumph) of the Falklands War. Inevitably there were a few hitches with the pope's visit, not least when for a while it looked as though his organisers regarded Scotland as a northern extension of England. The pope soon rectified this insensitivity, however, with his declaration that the Church was intricately involved in the struggle for national independence, and making his traditional blessing of the ground on arrival on Scottish soil.

Protestant schoolchildren were to be given a day off for the visit, but this was met by a protest from concerned protestants, and so only one third of Scotland's divided youth were freed from the schoolroom for the day. Rev. Ian Paisley promised to lead a demonstration against the visit and Pastor Glass made the usual spectacle of himself, but the Moderator of the General Assembly of the Church of Scotland said he would welcome the pope as he would any other visiting church leader. The church's official organ, *Life and Work*, predicted that protestants would welcome the pope 'courteously as John Paul but not as Peter', and in May the General Assembly in Edinburgh gave its Moderator permission to meet the pope. The wilder men of the Free Kirk and other fundamentalist sects on the other hand voiced their hatred of Romanism, but the Orange Order, although it could not be expected to be ecstatic about the visit, generally advised its supporters to 'Keep the heid'.

The pope came, was seen, and on a certain level conquered. He was received with the enthusiasm usually reserved for pop stars and football matches, and while this meant the inevitable accompaniment of slickness and commercialism, there could be no denying his populist appeal and hard-hitting Christian message, delivered straight from the Bible with a passion that would have done the most fervent fundamentalist proud. Whether the wildly cheering youths were being massaged by the media rather than charmed by the message is another matter, but when the pope had gone and the sun went down, Scots of whatever Christian persuasion were left with a feeling of fellowship which did no harm as regards future relations.

Scotland survived the papal visit virtually unscathed. There were no riots and Pastor Glass had to suffer the indignity of being ignored. Whether this was because of the distraction of the war in the South Atlantic, or whether it was because the police, by whatever methods, kept tabs on the bigots, we can never be sure. What we do know is that hundreds of thousands of catholics joined in rapturous welcome for their spiritual head, and Scotland discovered that there had been little to fear in the first-ever visit by a reigning pope.

Outside Celtic Park, 1982. Photograph Keith Ingham. Courtesy the Third Eye
Centre and the Scottish Arts Council

Celtic Park, 1982. Forfar, a second division side, had recently held Rangers to a
0–0 draw in the Scottish Cup semi-final. Photograph Keith Ingham. Courtesy
the Third Eye Centre and the Scottish Arts Council

A proud young Rangers fan poses outside Hampden Park before the 1982 Cup Final. Photograph Malcolm R. Hill. Courtesy the Third Eye Centre and the Scottish Arts Council

With the exhiliration of the pope's visit only a memory, Scots were left with two conclusions: the first was the progress made towards interdenominational harmony in Scotland. No such visit could have been contemplated even two decades before. But second is the unbridgeable gap that still divides protestants and catholics on the religious level, for behind the benign smile and the welcoming arms that make pope John Paul everyone's ideal of a benevolent grandfather lies a mind that would be more at home in the Middle Ages. Any reunification of the Christian Church would still have to be on Rome's terms. This was brought out in two different interpretations of the visit. The first, by Archbishop Thomas Winning,[35] who was instrumental in bringing the pope to Scotland: talked about the Church transcending the political and earthly to judge things as Christ judges them; about rising above differences in loving brotherhood; about the mutual love of those who believe in the Gospel of Peter; and about the pope bringing the light of Christ to illuminate our path through life. In addition he criticised those who had discarded the Christian code of morality. He spoke as though these were facts rather than hopes for the future, blithely or blindly overlooking two centuries and more of bigotry and sectarianism whose origins lie, as much as anywhere else, in the attitudes of the hierarchy of the Roman Catholic Church.

The Archbishop, in addition to the above platitudes, referred to the century and a half of Scottish catholics being a minority, and how this had sapped their potential as a vigorous Christian community. Did he mean by this their failure to convert Scotland to catholicism? Who made up this Christian community? Was this community composed of those catholics who knowingly or otherwise, but acting on the dictates of the hierarchy, have devoted their lives to antagonising protestants? Is it composed of those so full of the hereafter that they neglect the social and material needs of their flock in the here and now? It is most unlikely that he was referring to those catholics who seek above all else to live in peace and mutual understanding with non-catholic Christians, or who wish to come to terms with the modern world.[36] If the Celtic Football Club is to be taken as an example of catholic Christian community, then this was a community that scarcely lacked vigour. And while its record is not unblemished, the good that belongs to it owes more to basic brotherhood and humanity than it does to following the commands of those in authority.

Pope John Paul, and presumably Archbishop Winning, are anxious to stem or even reverse the liberalising trend begun in the mid-1960s. Their fears in this regard are based on solid theological ground, for the catholic church can only be weakened in its power by any diminution in the central authority of the papacy. While emphasis remains on the need for this central authority, the hopes of the liberals, both catholics and protestant, must remain frail, while diehard protestants can continue to point an accusatory finger at the Vatican. This was highlighted by the Rev. William Downie of Dumbarton, who, in a letter to the *Glasgow Herald* in June 1982, pinpointed two fundamental problems regarding protestant/catholic relations.[37]

The first of these is the relationship between the pope and ecumenism. Downie challenged the sincerity of the pope's message of reconciliation and tolerance, suggesting that this involved a reconciliation to Roman authority and a tolerance of the advancement of Roman Catholicism. Would the Roman Church, he asked, allow a Protestant Minister to dispense communion in a Roman Church without being ordained by a Roman Bishop? Or would he be allowed to conduct the wedding service of a Roman Catholic without denying the right of that person to partake of the eucharist in a Roman Catholic Church? Second, Downie expressed his concern about the pope's conservatism: the stress and unhappiness his teaching created in family life, the social divisiveness of separate catholic schools, and the insult to government schools which, catholics claimed, could not educate the whole child.

Theological disputes about the spiritual powers of priests or the nature of the eucharist have nothing to do with football; nor do the private beliefs of practising christians. But the dividing line between the practice of religion and the expression of sectarianism is often difficult to draw, and sectarianism creates the atmosphere in which The Old Firm exists. Sectarianism today is a much simpler problem than it was at the turn of the century when it was inextricably lined with politics, social class and nationalism as well as religion. Today it is more simply an issue of religion. There are catholics who are wealthy and vote Tory, there are catholics who have succeeded in most walks of life, and the Scottish National Party has been urged to make itself a front runner in ending discrimination against catholics.[38] In Scotland today the two most obvious examples of sectarianism, and as such its propagators, are the Scottish education system and the Rangers Football Club. The defenders of the one are the catholic church and the defenders of the other are the protestant establishment. Both have come under attack, and both are resisting strongly, but at least neither is as secure in the assumption of infallible righteousness as it once was.

K

NOTES

1. Minutes of the Scottish Football Association's Executive and General Purposes Committee's meeting, held 1 July 1980. Most newspapers made extensive quotes from this report when it was released.

2. Ibid., pp. 19, 20, 22. As regards the SFA's inability to act against Rangers, it should be pointed out that, article 2 of the Statutes of FIFA, approved and adopted by Congress 1961 and altered by subsequent Congresses, states that: 'There shall be no discrimination against a country or an individual for reasons of race, religion, or politics'. Sub-clause 4.5 states:

> A National Association which tolerates, allows or organizes competitions marked by discrimination or which is established in a country where discrimination in sport is laid down by law should not be admitted to F.I.F.A. or should be barred if it was. A National Association, when applying to take part in a competition, or deciding to organize one, shall give assurances to the Federation, that its provisions will be respected.

This clearly bans South Africa. Rangers' case is more difficult, as all the evidence against them is circumstantial. Short of finding an article of association in the Rangers constitution banning catholics, or official correspondence supporting such a policy, there is little the SFA can do. Even if such evidence is available somewhere in the Rangers archives, the likelihood of an SFA investigator finding it is not very high, given the difficulties encountered by the official courts of the land following the investigations into the Ibrox disaster.

In April 1983 it was claimed on a BBC 'Nationwide' programme that Scotland should be banned from the World Cup and European tournaments because Rangers would not sign a catholic. When confronted with 'Nationwide's' claim that Rangers were 'openly sectarian', the general secretary of FIFA, Mr Joseph Blatter, said that they would be 'sending a team to investigate the club's policy'. These claims were dismissed by Rangers officials, and the vice-president of FIFA, Northern Ireland's Harry Cavan, described them as 'utter nonsense'. Blatter also refuted them (*Daily Record*, 27, 28 April 1983). FIFA sent to the SFA the dossier supplied to them by the 'Nationwide' reporters, but Cavan indicated that this was a formality and that FIFA would not be ordering Rangers to sign a catholic. In June, SFA secretary, Mr Ernie Walker, revealed the contents of his reply to FIFA. He said the SFA saw no reason why it should explain itself to the BBC and acquiesce in its 'passing desire for another mildly sensational headline'. Whereas it would not pander to 'media whims', it would conduct an inquiry if ordered to do so by FIFA (*Glasgow Herald*, 15 June 1983, *Evening Times*, 14 June 1983). Echoes here of Waddell and the role of the media in a democratic society.

3. *The Scotsman*, 2 July 1980.

4. Some papers did not miss the chance to point out that Mr Younger, Secretary of State for Scotland, had family associations with a well-known brewing company.

5. *Daily Record*, 5 January 1980.

6. *Sunday Mail*, 13 July 1980.

7. See especially *Daily Record*, 25 November 1980, 12, 15, 16, 19 December 1980.

8. *Sunday Mail*, 10 August 1980.

9. See especially the *Sunday Mail*, 2 November 1980 and *Celtic View*, 5 November 1980.

10. The *Scottish Daily Express*, 5 September 1980, featured the issue on its front page, asking: 'Is this the end for Willie?' and devoted most of its back page to an article by Ian Archer demanding that players who step out of place be put back into line.

11. *Scottish Daily Express*, 5 September 1980, article by Jim McLean.

12. Again the *Express* gave the matter headlines, referring to it as 'A Kick in the Guts!' (24 November 1980), with Jim McLean demanding: 'Let's Have Justice' (25 November 1980). Hugh Taylor, in the *Evening Times* (24 November 1980) asked sadly: 'Will Bud never learn?' Rangers were later in trouble over a player who was on the sidelines and not even stripped getting in trouble with the referee at Dundee, and in March 1982 Gregor Stevens was suspended for six months after a tackle which resulted in Kilmarnock defender Albert Morrison being carried from the field with a double fracture of the right leg. The incredible outcome of this incident was that the Players' Union regarded the suspension as too harsh, despite the fact that Stevens had been ordered off five times and booked on 19 occasions since joining Rangers from Leicester three years previously. See *Daily Record*, 9 March 1982.

13. The *Sunday Post* (26 October 1980) reprinted a copy of the advertisement under the heading: 'The Town That's Scared of Rangers'.

14. 'Current Account', broadcast by BBC, 20 May 1980. The field invasion at Fir Park unsettled a Motherwell team which had been winning comfortably 2–0. After the resumption Rangers came back to win and take the two points that they needed to keep ahead of Aberdeen (see J. Webster, *The Dons*, London, 1978, pp. 203–4).

15. *Daily Record*, 21 November 1980.

16. See especially the *Daily Record*, 20 November 1980, where Jim Laing reported an exclusive telephone interview with Fyfe, who was in Cleveland, Ohio.

17. *Sunday Mail*, 23 November 1980. Nevertheless Herron has made some scathing attacks on Rangers. In July 1983 he referred to 'the odious religious sanctions at Ibrox' and welcomed and encouraged any 'real effort to lift their shabby sectarian policy' (3 July 1983).

18. Fyfe is an accomplished singer and was popular in this capacity at the Rangers Social Club. See especially *Rangers News*, 30 August 1972, 13 September 1972, 24 July 1974, 26 March 1975 (with photograph of wife and two children).

19. *Evening Times*, 31 August 1982; *Daily Record*, 1 September 1982, but omits quote about 'chapel' (in Glasgow, it should be noted, this word is used to denote a catholic church).

20. *Evening Times*, 20 November 1980.

21. *Daily Record*, 24 November 1980.

22. *Glasgow Herald*, 7 May 1981.

23. A 2–0 defeat by Partick Thistle had fans baying for Greig's blood, and unflattering comparisons were made with Celtic supporters who had waited outside the St Mirren ground to cheer their players after they had lost the League to Aberdeen in 1980. Commenting on another incident involving Ranger fans, John Fairgrieve thought it a bit much that they should boo their players before they had even taken the field (*Sunday Mail*, 1 November 1981).

24. *Sunday Post*, 8 November 1981.

25. *Sunday Standard*, 27 September 1981.

26. *Daily Record*, 25 June 1981.

27. *Sunday Mail*, 28 June 1981.

28. *Evening Times*, 29 June 1981.

29. *Sunday Standard*, 3 July 1983.

30. *Sunday Standard*, 5 July 1981.

31. *Glasgow Herald*, 11 December 1981.

32. For sectarianism in Scottish politics, see especially Tom Gallagher, 'Catholics in Scottish politics', in *The Bulletin of Scottish Politics*, issue no. 2, Spring 1981, pp. 21–43. Most of the above paragraph is taken from this article.

33. Tom Gallagher, 'Scotland quietly bridges sectarian divide', in *The Weekend Scotsman*, 2 April 1983.

34. On the pope's visit to Scotland, see in particular Cooney, *Scotland and the Papacy*.

35. Article in *Evening Times*, 31 May 1982.

36. On 24 April 1983 the Scottish *Sunday Standard* released details of a poll conducted by them in conjunction with the BBC on the religious state of Scotland. Archbishop Winning's reaction to the liberalism of Scottish catholics as revealed in this poll was to condemn 'the corrupt society in which we live' and to blame 'the age of the easy way out', accusing some catholics of succumbing 'to the pressures of the permissive society' (article by Jack Webster, 'Keeping the Faith').

37. *Glasgow Herald*, 9 June 1982.

38. See in particular the article by Tom Gallagher in which the author urges action by the SNP against sectarianism and communal quarrels which he sees as 'one major symptom of a wounded society'. *79 Group News*, June 1982.

CONCLUSION

Continuity, Change and Challenge

On 28th May 1988 Celtic will celebrate the centenary of their first game of football. That game was against Rangers, and it would be fitting if The Old Firm also celebrated its centenary on that date. Much will depend, however, on how the public judges these games. From the earliest days of The Old Firm the pundits have argued over the good or ill that Rangers and Celtic have done for or to Scottish football. On the one hand it is argued that they have attracted to football people who otherwise would not have been interested, and that the money this has brought in has constantly subsidised the game. Until 1960, when they could offer players pay and conditions as good as those of most English clubs, they kept many of the best players in Scotland. In the early days Celtic in particular, but later Rangers, brought many talented Scots back across the border. As a result both Rangers and Celtic have at various times laid claim to be the best in the world, albeit for the most part a football world much more restricted than the one we know today.

On the other hand the Old Firm monopoly can be seen as a drain on other clubs, with the less prosperous unable to retain young stars whose ambition is set on one or other of the Big Two. More seriously, fans who should be supporting the local clubs can be seen filling buses packed with green or blue-bedecked supporters on their way to Glasgow, passing their home-team ground with hardly a glance. The Scottish Cup has offered a chance of glory for the locals, but the League for most of the twentieth century, with the solitary exception of Motherwell in 1931, a sprinkling of clubs in the two decades after the Second World War (notably Hearts and Hibs), and Aberdeen and Dundee United in 1980, 1983 and 1984, has belonged to Rangers or Celtic. The success of Aberdeen and Dundee United, however, promises to be no mere flash in the pan, and there is optimism in some quarters that a New Firm, based on the east coast and free from sectarianism, is in the making. However welcome this break with the old-time monopolists may be, the effect in terms of attracting big crowds is not yet encouraging.[1]

Within ten years of the foundation of Celtic the press were making sarcastic comments about the drawing power of the Glasgow giants, and querying the overall benefits of disproportionate support. Within a couple of decades the smaller clubs were becoming dependent on the home games with Celtic or Rangers to keep their books balanced. In answer to the critics of Rangers' monopoly in the inter-war period Struth would point out that if other clubs did not like the Rangers' monopoly, then it was up to them to get together a team good enough to beat them. It was, he would hint, a free world, and other teams were as free as Rangers to make themselves champions.

This was nonsense, as the basis of Rangers' success, and Celtic's, was their position as respective champions of Scotland's religiously divided society. Newspapers earlier in the century were usually too discreet to make direct reference to this, and through to the 'fifties and early 'sixties it was virtually a taboo subject. 'Rex' raised the issue in anger after the riots of 1941, but just over twenty years later when he made another attack on The Old Firm, suggesting that it was a bloodsucker blighting the development of all other clubs, he did not mention religion.[2] Had he been living a couple of decades later, he might have called them the 'Upas Tree' of Scottish football, the phrase adopted by Sydney Checkland for his economic history of Glasgow, a history which he sees as being dominated by heavy industry, with this industry, like the Upas Tree of Indian legend, killing all that fell under its shade.

Such an analogy has a certain appeal, but it mustn't be taken too far, as it would imply that The Old Firm are as ineluctably tied to their sectarian origins as a tree is to its roots. Celtic were the original sectarian team, but today it is Rangers who carry this stigma. It is said that Rangers will not change their attitude to catholics because it would lose them thousands of their supporters, and in financial terms, both at the gate and in the vast returns from Rangers Pools and other accessories, it would be a disaster. One thing is certain, and that is the commercial success of Rangers' enterprises unrelated to success on the field. Less certain is whether Rangers' playing a catholic or in other ways making it clear that they had dissociated themselves from sectarianism would have as disastrous an effect on their support as some people say. They would lose thousands from the terracing, but thousands they could well be rid of. In turn they might see the return of thousands of fans who have been chased away from Ibrox by the foul language and loud-mouthed bigotry that are an affront to any decent supporter; language and sentiments, too, as prevalent in or near the expensive seats in the stand as in the cheaper parts of the ground.

Criticism of sectarianism—and today that means criticism of Rangers—is based on the moral issue of whether or not it is right to practise discrimination on religious grounds. If Rangers want to continue this practice, then. they must expect to draw on themselves the opprobrium of those who deplore such divisiveness. They must also expect that each time their fans are in trouble the religious issue will be raised, and the management will be rightly criticised for fostering the hatreds that make these riots so odious.

Since coming under attack, Rangers have denied having a policy of refusing to employ catholics, but it is clear that they have such a practice: some players, notably Brand and Fyfe, have said so, and chairmen and directors as diverse and well established as John Lawrence, Matt Taylor and George Brown have all admitted this publicly, even saying that it is as old as the club itself. But since a practice is harder to act against than a policy, no laws can force Rangers to change. All that remain are sanctions and moral pressure. In recent years the press, important sections of the public, and some in the Church of Scotland have criticised the club, with no noticeable effect other than the declaration after Birmingham and the anguish induced by the resignation of Greig in October 1983. In April 1983 a team of 'Nationwide' reporters brought the issue to the attention of FIFA for the SFA to investigate. Both bodies appear to have shelved it,[3] leaving Rangers with the comfortable thought that the leading authorities in the game are unconcerned about their attitude. Free from official sanctions, so far Rangers have resisted all moral pressures, and their best defence here is a successful team and well-behaved fans, for it is only when the team is performing poorly and the fans react violently that the issue of sectarianism is resurrected in the press.

It is one of the unfortunate facts of the modern game that paying spectators are no longer as important to the financial underpinning of a football club as they once were. The drastic decline in gates at Ibrox does not appear to be putting the club under any great financial strain, thanks in part to the income it receives from pools and lotteries, the most lucrative in Great Britain: in September 1983 these amounted to a turnover of over £6 million, of which £1 million was clear profit. Rangers seemed unconcerned about the failure of the Spaceshot venture—an attempt to combine with Manchester United to draw on the financial resources of two of the most fanatically supported clubs. Administrative problems were given as the official reason for the failure, but unofficial opinion is that some Rangers supporters wanted their money to go only to Rangers, while others objected to what they saw as an association with a catholic team.[4] The dismal prospect of football spectators becoming redundant, however, is still very much in the future, and the success of off-field perks must rely ultimately on a successful team attracting people to watch it play. This could present an even more dismal prospect for some hardline Rangers supporters than an empty stadium, for it appears to be a fact of present-day football life in Scotland that no club can afford to ignore the talent that is coming out of catholic schools. Whether Rangers face up to this remains to be seen, as would the reaction of its fans to what many of them would consider a fate worse than relegation. Recent developments might indicate, despite some anxious moments, that those fans need not have much to worry about, at least on the former score.

Within weeks of the opening of the 1983–84 season Rangers were desperately struggling to find the form their fans demand and that their history has led them to expect. As a result, John Greig's position as manager was becoming increasingly intolerable, with fans baying for his resignation and the Board unwilling to give him an unqualified vote of confidence. Eventually he offered his resignation on 28 October 1983: it was accepted, and Rangers had to find a new manager. The sectarian issue was immediately raised, and while speculation raged as to whether the job would go to Alex Ferguson of Aberdeen, Jim McLean of Dundee United, or Jock Wallace of Motherwell, sections of the press took the opportunity to press Rangers to seek a new image along with a new manager by making a clean break with their sectarianism.[5] The sectarian issue continued to be raised in the press as it watched every move Rangers made to secure a new manager, and headlines indicated that the new manager would be receiving a salary of about £60–70,000 and a free hand in the signing of players.

Despite this, Rangers' first two choices for manager, Ferguson and McLean, in decisions that would have been unbelievable twenty years previously, refused the offers. Ferguson was reported to have stipulated, when unofficially approached before Greig's resignation, that he would not consider the position unless he could sign catholics, and as a former player he knew what he was talking about, while McLean, in the midst of the debate, was signing Clydebank's Tommy Coyne, a catholic and a prolific goalscorer. In view of the published statements that the two managers approached would be free to sign whom they wished, it must be assumed that this was not a factor in both of them declining the offer, that indeed both saw loyalty to the clubs that they had made and which had made them as more important than a lucrative financial reward. As for the Rangers Board, it never made an explicit statement that it was breaking with old traditions or policies. Chairman Simpson's attitude throughout was that Rangers had never been a sectarian club, so there was nothing to change.[6] When the job eventually went to third choice, Wallace, many Rangers fans, for whom Wallace had always been *first*

"Does it huv tae be blue smoke afore we know if we've a new manager ?"

The Faithful Await. *Daily Express*, 9 November 1983

choice, could breathe a sigh of relief, believing that the club was not about to surrender its most deeply held tradition.

Jock Wallace had been a Rangers fan since he could remember, although his birthplace should have had him supporting one of the Edinburgh teams. He was one of Rangers' most successful managers, seeing the club enjoy great domestic success, including two trebles, before he suddenly quit in May 1978. He left under a cloud: some said it was because of a personality clash with Waddell and that he resented the restrictions placed on him as team manager by Waddell remaining as club manager; others said he was not satisfied with his financial remuneration. Whatever the reasons, they have remained a closely guarded secret. One thing Wallace had never made a secret of, however, was his continuing love of Rangers, with photos of his successful Rangers teams gracing his manager's office at Leicester, and so when the offer of the Rangers job came he accepted it with unalloyed joy. Here he was, back with the club his heart had never left, the epitome of the Rangers stalwart, the man who had urged his players to roar out 'No surrender!' on their way up the tunnel at Ibrox, the man who preferred the guts of a Tom Forsyth to the skills of a Glen Hoddle: the qualities, in short, that had made the great Rangers teams at least of the 1920s through to the 1950s.

In view of his known sympathies, and in view of the promises made to Ferguson and McLean that they would be free to sign catholics, it was inevitable that one of the first statements Wallace would have to make on accepting the job was what his attitude was in this regard. The *Daily Star* ran an interview by John Mann headed 'Religion and Me', which was a masterpiece of diplomacy. To all those who wanted to see a change in Rangers policies Wallace sent out assurances that all he wanted from any player was that he was good enough and could do the job Rangers required. He also repeated what Simpson had 'spelled out [that] we are a non-sectarian club'. The Rangers faithful, however, could take comfort in reading between the lines of his further comments that any player he signed would have to have 'really wanted to play with Rangers'. He also pointed out that he wasn't going to be stampeded into signing a catholic because of a campaign 'by a lot of people who should know better', and concluded with comments that everyone could agree with, but which would have been superfluous except for the reputation of the club whose manager he had become: 'Let's not have religion up front. Let's get the emphasis back where it should always be, on football ability and nothing else'.[7]

At the Rangers AGM on 20 December 1983 three new directors were appointed: Tom Dawson, John Robinson and Hugh Adam. Willie Waddell, who had announced his retirement just before the appointment of Wallace, was made an honorary director. On the same day as the AGM was due to meet, Alex Cameron urged in his column in the *Daily Record* that one of the shareholders call for confirmation from the Board that Rangers would sign players regardless of creed. When a 77-year-old shareholder, William Campbell, did just this, he turned what had been a peaceful meeting into an uproar. His intervention was greeted with booing and jeers, and after the meeting he had to face the wrath of several angry shareholders.

On 10 January 1984 the Rangers Board underwent extensive changes with the retirement, as chairman, of Rae Simpson (who remains a director); he was replaced by John Paton, while Tom Dawson replaced Paton as vice-chairman. There was no room at the top for Jack Gillespie, who had been succeeded as vice-chairman by Paton in November 1983. For those anxious to see a more open Rangers, there was perhaps a glimmer of hope in this. Perhaps also in the new chairman's early comments. Inevitably he had to face the question of Rangers and

Catholics. Just as inevitably he said that Rangers' doors were open to players of all creeds, adding that this had been made clear to everyone who had been interviewed recently for the manager's job in succession to Greig. But he also expressed his belief that the arrival of a catholic at Ibrox seemed inevitable. One would think so ... As the bemused Scot replied to the incredulous foreigner who suggested that a Maradona scoring a hat-trick for Rangers every other week would win the praise of the Rangers faithful, you *would* think so, wouldn't you...?

While Wallace settles into his new job, the sectarian image of Rangers appears to be only slightly clouded over: whether the appointment of Ferguson or McLean would have resulted in a change of policy we will never know; perhaps it will come with Wallace. In the meantime Rangers have once again lost the chance to make a clean break with sectarianism. Throughout the whole affair the Rangers Board made no explicit statement about signing catholics, and while the press publicised the promises to prospective managers that they could sign catholics if they wanted to, none of this was repeated in the official *Rangers News*. Here, before their own fans, is where the true will of the management is made known. When all the dust has settled we are left with a sense of *déjà vu*, and the uncomfortable feeling that Scottish football is still no further forward than it was in October 1976. The pressures exerted on Rangers at the end of 1983, however, are more pressing than in October 1976. Then it had merely been rioting fans, today it is the status of the club as a first-rate playing combination that is under threat. Thus Rangers, secure in the knowledge that FIFA and the SFA seem unconcerned about sectarianism in Scottish football, and reassured in their faith that press and public indignation are as the breath of the unclean, remain nevertheless under the pressure that comes from being unable to produce the results where they count. The way in which this pressure is removed remains to be seen. A strong Rangers team is needed for the good of Scottish football; a non-sectarian Rangers is necessary for its good reputation.

Ironically the power to force a change at Ibrox is in the hands of one of its greatest critics so far as sectarianism is concerned: the Celtic Football Club. It was Celtic who refused to play against communist countries after the invasion of Czechoslovakia in 1968 (although they had toured the United States the same year when American bombers were devastating Vietnam), and which has maintained an unflinching attitude in regard to sporting contacts with South Africa. If Celtic carried their justifiable anger against racial and political discrimination into the religious sphere, and acted in their belief that Rangers do discriminate against catholics, by refusing either to play against them or in any competition in which they took part, the consequences would be explosive. In 1952 at the time of the Great Flag Flutter such action by Celtic might well have been disastrous for the club, and it is possible that it would have gone out of existence as Belfast Celtic did in 1949 (a sad loss with repercussions in regard to the defusing of sectarian hatred in Ulster that can only be guessed at). In the 1980s it would be unthinkable that Celtic would go out of existence. The Scottish public is much more enlightened than it was thirty years ago, and direct action by Celtic might win as much praise as it would blame.

To be realistic, of course, Rangers and Celtic are too closely dependent on each other: the business peace that dates back to the inception of The Old Firm is still a commercial reality. It was Rangers who supported Celtic in the fight over professionalism in the 1890s, as it was in the Great Flag Flutter of 1952; and today it is one of the exquisite ironies of commercial sponsorship that the only way Celtic and Rangers could cash in on the financial bonanza of those aesthetic atrocities known as shirt logos, was to combine. Because of the odium it would arouse, no sponsor could risk his product being advertised on one or other club jersey, and so the two clubs have had to find joint sponsorship—appropriately enough with the Scottish Co-operative Society. There is one other perfectly good reason why Celtic should not be interested in Rangers changing their policies: no club benefits more from them than Celtic!

Ideally any change would come from within Ibrox. A few catholics in the ground or ancillary staff, the signing of a catholic or two would not suddenly change Rangers into a mongrel/papist eleven. They would be as protestant as Celtic are catholic, but the hard edge of sectarian hatred would be softened. They would still see their fans involved in terracing troubles, the air would still be thick with obscenities, but, without the slur of religious discrimination, they would be no worse than Liverpool and Everton, Manchester City and United, or Arsenal and Spurs. And they would remain *the* protestant team of Scotland. But not a sectarian team, merely a protestant one.

Neither Rangers nor Celtic can easily discard nearly a hundred years of history. In the early days the only things about Celtic that were not catholic and/or Irish were certain star players: management, supporters and the catholic press saw the success of the club as a vindication of catholic life and the virtues of Irish nationalism. Today catholics need no such demonstrations or vindications, and Celtic, with catholic connections unbroken but Irish sympathies more historical than real, represent an important aspect of Scottish character. Another aspect of Scottish character is that proud sense of achievement of the Scottish Protestant that has contributed so much to a better way of life around the world. The less desirable types have been portrayed in the soul-destroying morality of the characters in the novels of A. J. Cronin; nearer the present time we have the swaggering bravado of Bill MacWilliams, who stars in Hector MacMillan's play, *The Sash*. Unfortunately these have too often been the images of Scottish protestantism that have been projected most widely. Recently the world has seen another aspect of that character in one of the stars of the film *Chariots of Fire*, where Scotland's champion rugby player and athlete, Eric Liddell, epitomises the highest values of sportsmanship and personal morality.

Celtic and Rangers represent two sides of Scottish society that can be seen as complementary rather than contradictory. Their differences can be worked out in healthy rivalry rather than sharpened by constant conflict. They act on society, as society acts on them, and this limits their choices. Scotland's segregated education system is still the biggest hurdle to overcome in the elimination of sectarianism, and from this standpoint there is a hollow note of hypocrisy in the condemnation of Rangers' sectarianism by Archbishop Winning.[8] No supporter of Scotland's segregated system of education has the right to condemn the Rangers Football Club or anyone else for promoting religious antagonisms. While the catholic church insists that its children must be educated in isolation from other Scots—and this can only be based on their belief that education must be a catholic education—then it must expect that other Scots will harbour certain suspicions about them. By the same token protestant groups that support the exclusion of catholics from any aspect of public life have no right to criticise an education system that promotes religious exclusiveness. Bigotry is based on suspicion and thrives on ignorance; on the other hand it can be diminished or disappear with more open social relations and personal interaction. Catholics need not like protestantism, or protestants catholicism, but this should not prevent the one liking protestants or the other catholics. With an end to bigotry they need not even like each other, but the basis of their disagreements might at least be more rational.

While catholics are stuck with a hierarchy committed to sectarian education, protestants are stuck with the Rangers Football Club. Enough has been said about their sectarian practices. Both clubs could still do something to eliminate their religious associations. Celtic have every right to fly their Irish flag; it is part of their history. But they should remove the tricolour and replace it with the original all-green Irish flag. At least that would eliminate its associations with terrorist movements active in

Ireland today. Otherwise there is not much else Celtic can do, except persist in getting a prominent protestant on their Board, and so quell the rumours that the invitation made to Jock Stein was more a gesture than a serious offer. They could also stop issuing free passes to priests, and certainly could do well to stop inviting the catholic archbishop to official club functions. Similarly Rangers could stop issuing free passes to protestant ministers. On the other hand both clubs could make a determined effort to invite clerics from across the religious divide, so that we would have the Moderator of the General Assembly of the Church of Scotland at the next testimonial dinner for a star Celtic player and priests being invited to help fill the seats at Ibrox. Both Archbishop Winning and the Moderator have allowed themselves to be seen in more or less formal association with the clubs of whose religious persuasion they hold the highest rank.[9] They have certainly not held themselves aloof from the issue. A catholic in a Rangers jersey is probably the first step, preferably while they are on a winning run and not before: one day we might hope to see a catholic on the Rangers Board—or even someone who was married to a catholic. In wilder fantasies we might imagine Archbishop Winning being invited to address the Rangers Supporters Association!

When Celtic celebrate the centenary of their first game, let us hope that they will celebrate by playing against their opponents at that first match. Let us hope, too, that that game will be played in the spirit that marked that first game, which, though sectarianism was present in the Celtic club, was not marked by sectarian hatred. Celtic and Rangers are important parts of Scottish history, incorporating much of its greatness and the worst aspects of its religious warfare. They have served as outlets for social and political frustrations, communal rejoicing and the reduction of boredom in a world without work or where that work was not satisfying in itself. They have more often been prisoners of society than agents of change within it, although the presence from the beginning of protestants playing for Celtic has been a dilutant of sectarian hatred on the catholic side: with protestants like Jimmy Hay, John Thomson and Jock Stein, how could *all* protestants be bastards? Rangers have virtually never had that mellowing influence. Perhaps they never will, although it is hard to believe that they can continue without some softening of their attitudes. Rangers have always boasted what a great club they are. At present they have no better chance to show just how great they could be. This would be by overcoming the bigotry on the Board and on the terracing by acting on their declarations, however belatedly, and breaking with their practice of religious apartheid. The Old Firm would survive, but more as big city rivals than religious adversaries. This would not get rid of the hooligans who would continue to attach themselves to the clubs, but it would change the nature of the hooliganism.

The very character of football, based on tough, competitive clashes of mind and body, the tribal antagonisms of its followers, and the commercial greed of some of its sponsors, means that football as played in Scotland will never be a picnic. That is not how Scots would want it. Much of this we can tolerate. But not gratuitously injected hatreds, like religious bigotry. This has been the source of success of the two clubs; it has brought them the best players in Scotland, the most supporters and consequently the biggest profits. Today they are securely enough established to purge themselves of the worst elements of their past. The two clubs have met many challenges in their long careers; it would be to the benefit of Scotland and Scottish football, as much as to the honour of the two clubs, if they were to overcome this moral challenge with the same determination as they have shown on the field of play.

NOTES

1. Although sectarian sensitivites might be removed, others are liable to reappear. At the start of the 1983–84 season the managers of these north-eastern clubs revealed a pettiness that did not reflect well on their positions: Alex Ferguson of Aberdeen refused to allow Willie Miller to receive a well earned 'man of the match' award because a guest of the match sponsors was said to have called his players hooligans, while Jim McLean of Dundee United banned a *Sunday Mail* reporter from an after-match press conference out of anger at that newspaper's coverage of the club's affairs. Then there was the unreported incident at Dundee, where the Third Eye Centre Exhibition on Scottish Football was due to open for its first provincial tour on 10 September 1983. Among the memorabilia on sale at that exhibition were facsimiles of postcards that were popular early in the century, highlighting Scottish teams. Dundee United, of course, were not founded until 1923, so there was no facsimile featuring them, but the organisers of the opening made the unfortunate mistake of using one featuring Dundee as their invitation card for the opening. The result was a virtual boycott of the exhibition by Dundee United, who did not come to the opening or allow their League trophy to be put on display. Perhaps they had other reasons for this than the offending invitation card, but it was also rumoured that they had threatened to withdraw their bank account from the sponsors of the exhibition, the Clydesdale Bank.

2. *Sunday Mail*, 28 January 1962, p. 22, see also above, p. 221.

3. See note 2, p. 264. For the most pungent comments on the response by FIFA's Harry Cavan and SFA secretary Ernie Walker, see Brian Wilson, 'Falling Masonry?' in *Streets Ahead* (Glasgow), issue 5, 24 June/7 July 1983. Noting Cavan's position with the Northern Ireland FA, Wilson commented that it would be unlikely that Cavan would be at ideological odds with the Rangers boardroom, adding: 'It may even have occurred to him that if FIFA start taking an interest in club sectarianism, just about the only other place on earth where they will find it is in the President (*sic*) of FIFA's own backyard'.

4. *Sunday Post*, 1 May 1983, 'Football's spaceshot takes a tumble', where these speculations are raised.

5. The events set in motion by Greig's resignation on 28 October 1983, through to the appointment of Wallace on 11 November, were closely followed in the Scottish press. On 31 October 1983 the *Evening Times* headed a black-lined editorial: 'Time to put an end to the Ibrox bigotry'; the *Glasgow Herald* urged the club to 'Put a few things right off the park' in an editorial: 'Hard truths at Ibrox' (9 November 1983); from Edinburgh, Ian Wood in *The Scotsman* thought that a Rangers team in danger of foundering 'on the rocks of their own misguided religious commitment' had reached the 'time to cure an old ailment' (9 November 1983); while Patrick Glenn in the *Observer* commented that the most astonishing aspect of the whole affair was the Rangers Board's 'willingness to allow the new man to sign Catholic players', risking in doing so 'partial dismemberment' (6 November 1983). In the *Sunday Mail* John Fairgrieve saw the likelihood of a revival of Rangers' playing fortunes with the appointment of Wallace and welcomed 'the possibility, even the probability, of a new era ... in which there will be no more bigotry, no more sectarianism, at the biggest football club in the land' (13 November 1983). For an excellent summary of the '13 days that rocked Scottish football', see Jim Morrison's 'Anatomy of a Crisis' in the *Evening Times*, 9 November 1983, written on the eve of the appointment of Wallace.

6. When Wallace was appointed, Simpson stated: 'Rangers are a non-sectarian club. I say that publicly here and now. This is our policy. Our new manager has the power to sign any player he wishes' (*Daily Express*, 11 November 1983). This would be an unambiguous declaration except for the record of the club in regard to public pronouncements and the action that should follow them.

7. *Daily Star*, 16 November 1983. In the *Rangers News* (16 November 1983) Wallace's reported comments were more reassuring to the faithful. There he referred to 'men who are desperate to put on that famous blue jersey', players with 'passion, character and commitment', who played 'for the jersey—EVERY TIME THEY WEAR IT'. This could exclude most catholics, in view of what they would, with reason, believe Rangers' colours stood for.

8. See in particular the front-page article in the *Scottish Daily Express*, 29 May 1980: 'Rangers under fire as Catholic leader steps into Old Firm row ARCHBISHOP HITS OUT'.

9. Archbishop Winning's Celtic associations have been referred to. In September 1983 the Right Reverend Dr J. Fraser McLuskey, Moderator of the General Assembly of the Church of Scotland, was photographed in the directors' box at Ibrox, alongside Gillespie and Paton (*Sunday Mail*, 25 September 1983, back page).

The Old Firm Monopoly

Compiled by Pat Woods

These figures highlight the Old Firm domination of Scottish football, based on the major competitions won by Celtic and Rangers since the formation of Celtic, the younger club. The period covered spans the seasons 1888/89 to 1983/84.

SCOTTISH LEAGUE CHAMPIONSHIP
1890/91–1983/84

87 seasons (competition suspended during Second World War, seasons 1939/40–1945/46).	Celtic	33 titles
	Rangers	36 titles
	*1st title (1890/91)	1 title
Both clubs have always played in top division of Scottish league.	shared by Rangers and Dumbarton	
	Others	17 titles
		——
		87
		——

*Rangers usually credited with 37 titles as result of 1890/91 shared championship—technically correct, but only outright wins taken into account here.

Summary Old Firm thus share 69 title wins (i.e. won outright), amassing approx. 80% of the championships. Between seasons 1904/05 and 1938/39 only Motherwell (1931/32) broke the monopoly, and in recent years only Aberdeen (1979/80 and 1983/84) and Dundee United (1982/83) have broken it since Kilmarnock's 1964/65 title win.

SCOTTISH CUP
1888/89–1983/84

84 seasons (competition suspended during wartime seasons 1914/15–1918/19 and 1939/40–1945/46)	Celtic	26 wins
	Rangers	24 wins
	*Cup withheld	1
	Others	33 wins
		——
		84
		——

*After 1909 Old Firm replay which ended in the Hampden Riot

Summary Old Firm share 50 wins (approx. 60%). During this period there were only 17 finals (approx. 20%) in which either member of The Old Firm did not compete.

SCOTTISH LEAGUE CUP
1946/47–1983/84

38 seasons

Celtic	9 wins
Rangers	12 wins
Others	17 wins
	—
	38
	—

Summary Old Firm share 21 wins (just over 50%). There have been only 12 finals (approx. one third) in which either member of The Old Firm did not compete.

Final summing-up The Old Firm have shared 140 wins (roughly two-thirds) in the 209 competitions since 1888.

Select Bibliography

This book is based mainly on primary sources, particularly the press, but since it covers a period of nearly one hundred years the use of these sources has had to be selective. The full range of texts consulted can be seen from the notes, and works listed here are only those which were most frequently used.

Primary Sources

Scottish Athletic Journal, from 1 September 1882, weekly
Scottish Umpire, from 21 August 1884, weekly.
Scottish Sport (merger of above two), from 6 November 1888, twice weekly.
Scottish Referee, from 5 November 1888, weekly.

Although the main content of the above was football, there were few specifically football publications in the pre-1914 period, and complete sets of the following are not readily available:

Scottish Football Association *Annual*, from season 1875–76 to 1899–1900 (?).
Rangers F.C. Handbook, from 1889.
Celtic F.C. Handbook, from 1892 (?).
The *Shamrock*, 'underground' paper *circa* 1964–5, copies courtesy of Pat Woods.
Celtic View, from August 1965 weekly during football season
Rangers News, from August 1971 weekly during football season.
The Celt, from August 1983, quarterly.

Club programmes do not reveal much and are of interest more to the collector than the social historian.

Stanley Paul (London) issue an 'annual' dealing with each club, aimed at the younger fans:

Ken Gallacher (ed.), *Playing for Rangers*, from 1969 (although at least one number under this title appeared in 1964)
Rodger Baillie (ed.), *Playing for Celtic*, from 1969

The Mitchell Library's holdings of Glasgow newspapers is vast, although it does not always have the sporting editions. Moreover the sports pages of these dailies, weeklies and later the Sunday papers, as seems to be the fate of such publications, are heavily vandalised. Nevertheless what remains is more than any one individual could cover easily. For the purposes of this book I found the catholic press most useful, not just because of its concentration on Celtic (and therefore its relationship with Rangers), but because it raised issues that the secular press preferred to pass over:

Glasgow Observer, from April 1884 weekly
Glasgow Examiner, from 16 March 1895 weekly, which merged with *Glasgow Star and Examiner*, from March 1903, which in turn merged with *Glasgow Observer* in July 1908, but continued to come out with separate banner

Secondary Sources

As background to the history of Glasgow, in addition to the literary and other sources mentioned in Chapter 5, I consulted mainly:

J. H. Muir, *Glasgow in 1901*, William Hodge and Company, Glasgow and Edinburgh, 1901
C. A. Oakley, *The Second City*, Blackie and Sons, Glasgow, 1946, also revised edition 1970
C. Brogan, *The Glasgow Story*, Frederick Muller Ltd., London, 1952
J. Cunnison and J. B. S. Gilfillan (eds.), *The Third Statistical Account of Scotland*, Glasgow, Collins, Glasgow, 1958
S. G. Checkland, *The Upas Tree: Glasgow, 1875–1975*, University of Glasgow Press, Glasgow, 1976, with second, enlarged edition 1981

For the Irish in Scotland, in addition to the various articles cited, I used mainly:

J. E. Handley, *The Irish in Scotland*, John S. Burns, Glasgow, n.d. [1964] (single volume based on Handley's studies of the Irish in Scotland of 1943 and 1947)
D. McRoberts (ed.), *Modern Scottish Catholicism*, John S. Burns, Glasgow, 1979

Scottish Football

Scotland's football obsession has not been reflected in serious writing on the subject: it still awaits a good general history, let alone a social history like Tony Mason's *Association Football and English Society: 1863–1915*, Harvester Press, Brighton, 1980. (This book should also be consulted for its bibliography of sport in general, but football in particular, for the pre-1914 period.) Nevertheless there has been some brilliant writing in short articles, most notably:

Ian Archer and Trevor Royle (eds.), *We'll Support You Evermore. The Impertinent Saga of Scottish "Fitba"*, Souvenir Press, London, 1976
—while Bob Crampsey's *The Scottish Footballer*, William Blackwood, Edinburgh, 1978 is short, but full of superb insights

In addition to the various club histories, whose quality varies from the excellent to the execrable, see:

John Rafferty, *One Hundred Years of Scottish Football*, Pan Books, London, 1973

Mike Aitken (ed.), *'When Will We See Your Like Again?' The Changing Face of Scottish Football*, EUSPB, Edinburgh, 1977

John Hutchinson, *The Football Industry. The Early Years of the Professional Game*, Richard Drew Publishing, Glasgow, 1982. (Although dealing with football in Great Britain, it draws heavily on Scottish sources.)

Kevin McCarra, *A Pictorial History of Scottish Football* (due to be published in 1984)

Most player biographies seem more intent on saying what the players (or their 'ghost') thought ought to be said than what they wanted to say, although there are notable exceptions; these and the club histories are discussed in Chapters 4 and 8.

Celtic F.C.

Club histories:

Tom Campbell, *Glasgow Celtic, 1945–1970* (published by author, Glasgow, 1970)

James E. Handley, *The Celtic Story* (Stanley Paul, London, 1960)

Robert Kelly (Sir), *Celtic* (Hay, Nisbet and Miller, Glasgow, 1971)

Gerald McNee, *And You'll Never Walk Alone* (Impulse Publications, Aberdeen, 1972)

Gerald McNee, *The Story of Celtic, an Official History, 1888–1978* (Stanley Paul, London, 1978)

Willie Maley, *The Story of the Celtic* (printed for author at Villafield Press, Bishopbriggs, 1939)

Pat Woods, *Celtic F.C. Facts and Figures, 1888–1981* (Celtic Supporters Association, Glasgow, 1981)

Celtic have a video of a film produced in 1967: 'The Celtic Story, 1888–1967', a joint Celtic F.C./Take Two Video Ltd. production, Glasgow, 1982, obtainable in VHS and Betamax versions.

Player Biographies

Pat Crerand, *On Top with United* (Stanley Paul, London, 1969)

Tommy Gemmell, *The Big Shot* (Stanley Paul, London, 1968)

Jimmy Johnstone, *Fire in my Boots* (Stanley Paul, London, 1969)

Bobby Lennox with Gerald McNee, *A Million Miles for Celtic* (Stanley Paul, London, 1982)

Danny McGrain, *Celtic: My Team* (Souvenir Press, London, 1978)

Jimmy McGrory, *A Lifetime in Paradise*, ed. by Gerald McNee (published by authors, Glasgow, 1975)

Billy McNeill, *For Celtic and Scotland* (Pelham Books, London, 1966)

Bobby Murdoch, *All the Way with Celtic* (Souvenir Press, London, 1970)

Ronnie Simpson, *Sure It's a Grand Old Team to Play For* (Souvenir Press, London, 1967)

Charlie Tully, *Passed to You* (Stanley Paul, London, 1958)

Rangers F.C.

Club histories:

John Allan, *The Story of the Rangers, Fifty Years of Football, 1873–1923* (Rangers F.C., Glasgow, 1923)

John Allan, *Eleven Great Years, the Rangers, 1923–1934* (Rangers F.C., Glasgow, 1934)

John Allan, *Rangers' Eventful Years, 1934–1951* (Rangers F.C., Glasgow, 1951)

Willie Allison, *Rangers, the New Era, 1873–1966* (Rangers F.C., Glasgow, 1966)

John Fairgrieve, *The Rangers: Scotland's Greatest Football Club* (Robert Hale, London, 1964)

Ian Peebles, *Growing with Glory*. Centenary History (Rangers F.C., Glasgow, 1973)

Hugh Taylor, *We Will Follow Rangers* (Stanley Paul, London, 1961)

A video film history of Rangers is available.

Player Biographies:

Jerry Dawson, *Memoirs, 1929–1949* (*Scottish Daily Record* and *Evening News*, Glasgow, 1949)

John Greig, *A Captain's Part* (Stanley Paul, London, 1968)

Willie Henderson, *Forward with Rangers* (Stanley Paul, London, 1966)

Willie Johnston, *On the Wing!* (Arthur Barker, London, 1983) (with Alex Hosie)

Derek Johnstone, *Rangers: My Team* (Souvenir Press, London, 1979)

George Young, *Captain of Scotland* (Stanley Paul, London, 1951)

Index

Abercorn FC   15, 116
Aberdeen   93
Aberdeen FC   7, 36, 55, 81, 164, 179, 213n, 265n, 267
Adam, Hugh   272
Adams, Davie   54
advertising   *see* commercialism
Airdrie   94, 145, 258
Airdrie FC (Airdrionians)   14, 15, 117n, 180
Albion Rovers FC   36
Allan, John   77, 80, 108, 202
Alloa Athletic   84
Allison, Willie   77, 90n, 108, 202–3, 205, 206
amateurism   21, 23–4, 37, 167
Ancient Order of Hibernians (AOH)   71, 74, 128, 129
Ancram, Michael   258
Angus, William (VC)   126, 141n
Anson, Peter   139
anti-catholicism   2, 12, 93–6, 117n, 127–8, 136–9, 189n, 202; *passim*
Apprentice Boys of Derry   162n, 248
Arbroath FC   14
archbishops: 71
    Eyre   61, 70, 109
    McDonald   140
    Mackintosh   132
    Scanlan   225
    Winning   249, 262, 266n, 275, 276, 279n
Archer, Ian   234, 239, 253, 254, 257
Arsenal FC   35, 207, 209, 241n, 274
Askey, Arthur   118n
Aston Villa FC   216n, 218, 233
athletics   20, 28, 215n
Ayr United   170, 186n

Bailie, The   49
Baillie, Doug   79
Barcelona   45, 218, 240n, 250
Barlinnie (prison)   153
Barry, Kevin   74
Batchelor, Denzil   181
Battles, Barney (senior)   71, 106, 119n
Battles, Barney (junior)   86
Baxter, Jim   195, 207, 212, 213n, 215n, 251
Bayern Munich FC   1, 162n
Bearsden   138, 146
Begg, James   112
Belfast   118n, 124–5, 136, 172, 174
Belfast Celtic FC   66, 241n, 274
Beltrami, Joe   248
Bennett, Alex   83, 91n
Berwick   220

Billy Boys   *see* gangs
Birmingham   81, 100
'Birmingham Declaration'   76, 81, 92n, 234–5, 239, 269, 273
Black and Tans   74, 125, 126, 172, 173
Blackburn Rovers FC   48, 81
Blairs College   64
Blake, George   144, 177
Blyth, Laurie   72
Boden, Alex   182
Boer War   71
Bone, Rev. Robert   223, 237
Bo'ness United FC   91n
Bowie, James   206
Boucicault, Dion   108
Boyle, Jimmy   144
Boyne, Battle of the   137
Boys' Brigade   52, 90n, 92n, 98, 128, 135
Braby, F. J., & Co. Ltd.   15–6
Bradford City FC   84, 216n
brake clubs   25–6, 59, 67, 69, 70, 71, 74, 169–75 *passim*
Brand, Ralph   90n, 193, 197, 206, 207, 215n, 269
Breck, Alan   180
Bremner, Billy   243n
Bridgeton   144, 149, 152
British Legion   135
Brockville   *see* Falkirk FC
Brogan, Colm   95
Brogan, Jim   222
Broomfield   *see* Airdrie FC
Brown, George   206, 227, 269
Brown, William   83
Buchanan, Joseph   203
Buckie Thistle FC   206
Burnet, Alastair   221
Burnley   84
Burnley riot   230–1
Burns, Robert   78
Busby, Matt   6, 119n
Bush, The   75–6, 237–9, 240

Caledonian Society   128
Cameron, Alex.   223, 247–8, 272
Cameron, Rev. Duncan   127
Campbell, John   72,73
Campbell, R. G.   83–4
Campbell, R. W.   90n
Campbell, Tom   201, 219
Campbell, William   272
Canada   5, 8, 94, 99, 210, 222

Cardiff 94, 100, 147
Carfin Shamrock FC 22
Cargill, Sir John T. 103, 157
Carson, Edward 125, 134
Catenian Association 128
Cathkin Park (Third Lanark) 29, 35
Catholic Action 128
Catholic Brains Trust 89n
catholic church
in Ireland 134–5
in Scotland 60–1, 128, 130–1, 262
assimilation/segregation 96–8, 127–31, 262
and civil liberties 133, 135, 220
and politics 98–9, 131–5
and priests 95, 100, 128, 132, 140, 159n
influence of 69, 97, 113, 129, 130, 135
and Celtic FC; 61–3, 129, 276; and
Manchester United; 118n; *passim*
catholic community 2, 12, 65–6, 75, 96–100,
106, 128–9, 174, 194 *see also* anti-
catholicism
catholic guilds 128
Catholic Young Men's Society (CYMS) 63,
140
Cavan, Harry 264, 278n
Celtic FC *see also* crowds, riots, supporters
formation and early days 9–10, 17–21, 32n,
60–6
and charity 18, 21, 24–5, 27, 60, 63, 65–6,
201
and limited liability 24–7, 106
and religion 18–19, 60–6, 110, 214n
and Ireland 19, 31, 66–75, 98, 110, 228,
230–2
disputes with Irish community 21–2, 25–6,
71
disputes with authorities 22–4, 27–8, 33n,
105, 115–6, 181–4
paranoia/bigotry, bias against 21–4, 45,
104–16, 119n, 165, 166–7, 171, 173,
177, 183, 185–6, 197, 201, 231
and publicans 24, 25, 26, 103–9 *passim*, 112
and non-catholics 26–7, 63, 64, 176, 221,
247, 276
friendship with Rangers 27–9, 221, 274
disputes with Rangers 31, 37, 54
directors 31, 34n, 63, 65, 70, 71, 103–4,
115, 181, 182, 184, 194 (*see also*
individual directors)
and historians 33n, 105, 113, 201–2
publications 64, 105, 199–201, 209
shareholders 103–4
'tradition' 193–204, 207–11
Celtic Handbooks 64, 105, 199, 209, 215–6n
Celtic Jubilee Dinner 209–10, 221
Celtic Park 9, 20–1, 35, 39, 44, 45, 70, 208
Celtic programmes 199
Celtic supporters' clubs (*see also* brake
clubs) 182, 199, 254

Celtic View 193, 194, 199–201, 214n, 224–5,
249
Chariots of Fire 275
Charles, Prince, 'The Young Pretender' 91n,
93
Chesterfield FC 250
Church of Scotland 95, 96, 99, 126–7, 139,
156, 235–40, 259, 269, 276, 279n
Church and football 51–2
Churchill, Lord Randolph 124, 134, 141n
Clyde FC 13, 23, 35, 55, 81, 119n, 166, 172,
176, 204
Clydebank 94
Clydesdale Bank 277n
Coatbridge 94, 145, 258
Colgan, Tom 68, 71, 72
commercialism 10–2, 21, 34n, 35–55 *passim*,
111
advertising 14, 24, 35, 50, 57n, 106
gate receipts 10, 31–2, 37–9, 53–5 (*see also*
crowds, attendance)
sponsorship 52, 268, 269, 274
Communism 3, 132, 136, 158
Condon, Captain Edward O'M. 72, 73
Conlon, Rev. J. 69
Conn, Alfie 84
Conway, Dr John 61, 68
Cormack, John 136–7, 142n
Coronation Cup 195
Cowlairs FC 9, 20
Cox, Sammy 181–2, 195, 197
Coyne, Tommy 270
Craig, Alex. 113–6, 166
Craig, Tom 89n
Craig, Tom 'Tully' 84
Craigavon, Lord 138
Crampsey, Bob 8, 31, 34n
Credo, TV programme 250, 251–3
Crerand, Pat 144, 150, 207, 222
Crichton, Walter 85
Cronin, A. J. 275
Crossfire, radio broadcast 237, 239
crowds
attendance 5–6, 10, 12, 13, 19, 31, 36–9,
55, 110, 164, 169, 180, 182, 183, 191,
196, 213n, 235, 248, 267, 268
description 59, 175–8, 188n (*see also*
supporters, symbols of sectarianism)
troubles 16, 21, 22–3, 31, 37–9, 81, 110,
111, 119n, 163–5 (*see also* riots)
Cruden, John 72, 73
Crum, John 180
Curragh Mutiny 125
Current Account, TV programme 250–1
Currie, Rev. James 239–40, 251
cycling 20

Daily Express 202, 218, 222, 223, 225, 226,
227, 239–40

Daily Record 56n, 138, 222, 233–4, 242n
Daily Telegraph 146–7
Dalglish, Kenny 222
Dalrymple, Father 237
Dalziel, Gordon 252
Daphne disaster 14
Davitt, Michael 70, 73, 74, 75, 89n
Dawson, Jerry 180, 205, 213n
Dawson, Tom 257, 272
Delaney, George 254
Delaney, Jimmy 180
Delargy, Hugh, MP 241n
Dens Park *see* Dundee FC
Denvir, John 112
Devlin, Joe 72, 74, 88n
Diamond, Charles 66, 106, 131
Docherty, Tommy 119n
Dodds, Joe 196
Dollan, Patrick 157, 180
Donnachie, Joe 82
Dorotheus, Brother 18
Dougray, Tom 196
Downie, Rev. William 263
Doyle, Dan 119n
Duff, Mickey 249
Duff, Tom 87n
Duke Street (shoot-out/prison van case) 126, 129
Dumbarton FC 13, 14, 17, 70
Dunbar, Michael 72, 82
Dunbar, Tom 82, 83
Duncan, Scott 84
Duncanson, Jimmy 181
Dundee 2, 7, 19, 97, 99, 136
Dundee FC 44, 55, 171, 174, 220, 277n
Dundee Burns Charity Cup 19
Dundee Harp FC 15, 18–9, 100, 109–10
Dundee United FC 254, 267, 277, 277n
Dunfermline FC 82, 219

East Fife FC 213n
Easterhouse project 147
Easter Rising 125
Easter Road *see* Hibernian FC
Edinburgh 2, 7, 139–40, 142n
education:
    Act, Scotland, 1872 47
    Act, Scotland, 1918 97–8, 126, 127, 138, 139, 148, 152
    catholic 73, 100
    separate schools 96, 98, 130, 131, 135
        (Eire), 151, 223, 259, 263, 275
    university 127–8
Eintracht Frankfurt FC 211
Elder, John and Co. 85
Empire Exhibition Cup Final 176, 210
English, Sam 177, 203
Eucharistic Congress (Edinburgh) 140

European Cup 202, 211, 212, 217, 231, 235
European Cup-Winners Cup 202, 218
Evening Citizen 39, 48, 138, 149–50, 151–2
Evening News 48, 51, 119n
Evening Times 22, 31, 48, 234, 253, 278n
Everton FC 19, 52, 100, 118n, 176, 274

Fairgrieve, John 162n, 202–3, 248, 278n
Falkirk FC 55, 112, 174, 195
Fascism 3, 132–4, 136, 138, 157–8
Ferguson, Alex 270, 272, 273, 277n
Fenian uprising (1867) 72, 208
Ferguson, John 71, 74
Ferguson, Provost (Govan) 15–6
Feyenoord FC 217
FIFA (Fédération Internationale de Football Association) 264n, 269, 273, 278n
Firhill Park *see* Partick Thistle
Flag controversy (1952) 113, 181–4, 221, 274
Flag Flutter *see* Flag controversy
flags and banners *see* symbols of sectarianism
Flood, Tom 68
Football Association (FA) 6, 34n
FA Cup 36
Forrester, Charlie 136, 138
Forsyth, Tom 272
Forward 36
Franco, General 133–4
Freemasonry 76–8, 89n, 128, 132, 133, 135, 186, 202
freemasons 63, 85, 87n, 132
Fullerton, William (King Billy) 145, 152, 153, 156–8, 161n
Fulton, Rikki 240
Fyfe, Graham 237, 252, 265n, 269

Gaelic Athletic Association 73
Gallagher, Patsy 123, 215n
gangs 2, 121, 143–58
    Baltic Fleet 148
    Billy Boys 145, 149, 151–8, 188n
    Calton Entry 149, 150, 151
    Liberty Boys 149
    Penny Mob 147, 148
    Redskins 148
    San Toy Boys 147
    South Side Stickers 149, 151
    Tim Malloys 147
    Tong 146
Garngad 144, 156
Geddes, Rt. Rev. John, Vicar apostolic 95
General Strike (1926) 129, 154, 157
Gibb, A. D. 139
Gillespie, Jack 233, 239, 272, 279n
Gillick, Torry 92n, 195, 197, 207
Gilmour, W. W. 138
Glanville, Brian 195–6

Glasgow
  Amnesty League 71
  anti-catholicism 93, 242n
  Association 22–3, 105
  character 1–2, 121–2, 253–4
  Charity Cup 10, 17, 19, 30, 61–2, 63, 65,
    180, 188n, 215n
  Corporation 43–4, 136, 147
  Cup 10, 17, 22–3, 29, 54, 63, 110, 167,
    175, 176, 182
  drunkenness 111, 112
  Eastern Standard 72, 86
  Examiner (absorbed by *Glasgow Star*, then
    Glasgow Observer) 24–5, 64, 70, 105,
    108, 119, 164, 167
  Free Press 97
  gangs 121–2, 143–54, 157–8
  Gas Supply Company 104
  Green 13, 136, 145
  Herald 130–1, 138, 179, 182–3, 227, 234,
    237, 239, 278n
  Hibernians 22, 26, 33n
  international exhibitions 9
  League 10
  magistrates 183, 186, 214n, 226, 227, 228,
    237
  municipal politics 135–8
  News 48, 169
  'No Mean City' image 121–62 *passim*
  Observer 22, 24, 26, 39, 50, 61, 64–5, 72,
    105, 106, 115, 119n, 126, 129, 131–4,
    166, 169, 176, 177, 182–3
  passion for football 7, 35–6, 51
  Presbytery 75, 237–9, 243n
  Star (becomes *Star and Examiner*, then
    absorbed by *Glasgow Observer*, but still
    appearing under its own banner) 72,
    105, 115, 166, 216n
  transport 43–5, 136
  University 8, 96, 128, 139
  Weekly Herald 136
Glass, Pastor Jack 80, 112, 137, 225, 239, 259
Glass, John 19, 26, 61, 64, 68, 71, 72, 73, 166,
  208
Glenn, Patrick 278n
Goal 221, 241–2n
Gorbals 121, 129, 137, 143–51 *passim*, 159n
Gordon, Jimmy 171
Goudie, George 14
Govan 15–6, 84, 91n
Gowans, James 171–2
Graham, Bishop 128
Graham, Rev. 239
Graham, Arthur 243n
Graham, Charles 253
Graham, George 186
Grant, James 72
Gray, Rev. A. H. 224

Gray, Frank 243n
Greenock 94, 95, 158n
Green's Playhouse 160n
Gregory, Professor J. W. 130
Greig, John 76, 78, 90n, 238, 249–50, 266n,
  269, 270, 273, 278n
Groves, Willie 108–9
Guardian 147
'Gulliver' (Arthur Milne) 177–8

Hampden Park 29, 35–6, 54, 167, 248
Handley, James E. (Brother Clare) 34n, 105,
  113, 119n, 141n, 201, 202, 204
Hanley, Clifford 225
Hannan, Canon Edward 19
Harding, Gilbert 89n
Harkness, Willie 247, 253
Harland and Wolff 59, 84–5, 91n
Havelin, Frank 25, 108
Hay, David 231
Hay, Rt. Rev. George, Vicar apostolic 95
Hay, Jimmy 166, 276
Heart of Midlothian FC (Hearts) 34n, 86,
  164, 167, 180, 213n, 250, 267
Hegarty, Paul 243n
Henderson, James 85
Henderson, Willie 195, 197, 205, 207
Hendry, Jack 83
Hendry, William 115
Henry, Stephen 68
Heron, Giles 63
Herron, Allan 193, 194, 207, 252, 265n
Hibernian FC (Hibs) 9, 18–9, 21–2, 31, 33n,
  43, 68, 70, 100, 106, 109–10, 111, 117n,
  174, 213n, 214n, 218, 250, 267
Hillhead by-election 258
Hillhead High School 98
Hind, Archie 147
Hitler 132, 133, 137, 158
hooliganism (*see also* supporters, gangs,
  riots) 123–4, 140, 141n, 158n, 186–7n,
  191, 232, 250
Hope, David 225, 232
Horne, Cyril 106, 183, 196, 221, 241n
Hunter, Allan 241n
Huntly FC 247

Ibrox Church 223
Ibrox disaster:
  1902 38–40, 166
  1971 223–6
  other deaths, serious injuries 223–4
Ibrox Park 10, 13, 15–7, 32, 35, 37, 44–6,
  208, 212, 248
Ibrox Sports 208, 215n
internationals 6, 29, 36, 37–9, 88n
Ipswich Town FC 241n

Irish Free State   98, 125, 126, 134–5
Irish Home Rule   71, 98–9, 124–6, 154, 155;
    see also Celtic FC and Ireland
Irish immigration   2, 85, 93–6, 127–31, 139;
    see also Celtic FC and Ireland
Irish National Foresters   73
Irish National League   63, 71
Irish Parliamentary Fund   70
Irish Weekly Independent   66, 73

Jackson, John   82
Jews   129, 133, 137, 162
Johnston, Willie   249–50, 265n
Johnstone, Derek   79, 89–90n, 222–3
Johnstone, Jimmy   222, 231
Johnstone, Peter   126, 141n
Jordan, Joe   243n
Juventus   1

Kearny   74, 92n
Kelly, Frank   64
Kelly, James   22, 24, 51, 68, 72
Kelly, Michael   227, 249
Kelly, Robert   105, 113–6, 119n, 183–6, 201,
    207
Kennedy, John F.   214n, 220
Kernohan, Robert   258
'Kerrydale'   214n
Kichenbrand, Don   82, 92n
Kilmarnock   136
Kilmarnock FC   36, 186n, 209, 249
Kinnaird, Lord   6, 57n
Kinnear, David   215n
Kipling, Rudyard   125
Kirkwood, Davy   121
Kivlichan, Willie   81, 83
Knights of St Columba   128
Knox, John   93, 100, 147
Ku Klux Klan   158
Kyle, Archie ('Punch')   81, 91n

Labour Party   98, 126, 138, 258
Lafferty, Pat   81
Lanarkshire   94
Law, Andrew Bonar   124
Lawrence, Jack   257
Lawrence, John   223, 232, 257, 269
Lawson, King   132
League Cup   181, 195
League of the Cross   24, 26, 108, 112
Leicester FC   220, 271
Leicester University study of football
    hooliganism   187n
leisure (other than football)   5, 9, 41–2, 57n,
    135–6, 150, 160n
Leith FC   116
Lennox, Bobby   90n
Liddell, Eric   275

Lisbon   45, 217, 231, 235, 240n
Liverpool   7, 94, 100, 118n, 147
Liverpool FC   1, 6, 100, 118n, 214n, 220, 230,
    274
Livingstone, George   83
London Caledonians FC   74
Lourdes   64, 209, 210
Lynch, Matt   181

Macadam, John   81
McAllister, Mary   258
McCall, James   23, 24
McCallum, Neil   22, 23
McCandless, Billy   90n
McColl, Ian   207
McDonald, Rev. Donald   251–2
McElhone Report   186n, 250
McErlean, Frank   72
McEwan, Sir John   258
MacEwan, Father Sydney   98, 129
McFadden, John   68
McGarvey, Frank   243n
McGinn, Ned   63
McGrain, Danny   79, 222, 248–9, 258
McGregor, William   6
McGrory, Jimmy   202, 209, 216n
McGuinness, Wilf   119n
McIlvanney, William   4n, 253–4
McInally, Tom   86, 216n
MacKay, James W.   33n
McKay, James   26
McKay, Johnny   171
MacKenzie, Compton   139
McKeown, Mick   83
McKillop, William   29, 68, 71, 72, 73
McKitterick, Jock   162n
McLaughlin, John H.   25, 27, 29, 34n, 37, 44,
    64, 68, 70–1, 105, 108, 116, 164, 166,
    167
McLean, David   84
McLean, Jim   270, 272, 273, 277n
McLuskey, Rt. Rev. Dr J. F.   279n
McMahon, Andy, MP   251
McMahon, Sandy   71, 165
McMenemy, Jimmy   73
McMenemy, Laurie   119n
MacMillan, Hector   275
McMillan, Ian   195
McNair, Alex   196
McNee, Gerry   105, 113, 202
McNeil, Moses   13
McNeill, Billy   119n, 194, 222, 231, 257
McPhail, Bob   205
MacRory, Father   129
McShane, Harry   132
Mail   48
Mainds, Colin   80
Maley, Alec   72, 208

Maley, Charles 72, 208
Maley, Tom 55, 65, 72, 207–8, 210, 211, 216n
Maley, Willie 31–2, 33n, 34n, 38, 59, 64, 68, 69, 72, 73, 90n, 105, 113, 123, 163, 167, 174, 199, 201, 202, 204, 207–11, 215–6n, 221
Mallan, Jimmy 181
Malone, Gerry 258
'Man in the Know' 26, 44, 65, 74, 82, 129, 172–4, 188n
Manchester 7, 94, 100
Manchester City FC 65, 83, 211, 216n, 274
Manchester 'Martyrs' 72, 89n
Manchester United FC 1, 19, 100, 118–9n, 144, 269, 274
Mannion, Wilf 86
Marr, John S. 29
Mathew, Father 112
Meechan, Peter 106
Meiklejohn, David 123, 177, 196
Mellish, John 29
Meredith, Billy 216n
Merry, Colonel 61, 63
Miller, David 247, 254
Millsopp, John 220, 221
Morrison, Jim 278n
Morrison, Sergeant T. 152
Morton, Alan 123, 173, 196, 206, 207, 258
Morton FC 33n, 55, 173–4, 179
Mosley, Oswald 137
Motherwell 94
Motherwell FC 177, 186n, 250, 265n, 267
Muirhead, Tommy 86
Murdoch, Bobby 89n, 222
Murphy, Arthur 25, 72, 73
Murray, Tom 80
Mussolini 132, 158

National Front 162n, 239
Nationwide, TV programme 264n, 269
Ne-erday (New Year's Day) games 12, 29, 111, 115, 172, 177–8
Nelson, Sammy 241n
Ne temere decrees 97, 127
Newcastle United FC 6, 81
News of the World 193, 194, 221
Nicholas, Charlie 35
Noble, Graham 147
No Mean City 143–4, 146, 150–1, 160n
Nottingham Forest FC 14

O'Brien, Father 132
Observer 147, 278n
Observer, Glasgow, see *Glasgow Observer*
O'Callaghan, John 72, 73
O'Connor, T. P. 71, 88n

O'Farrell, Frank 119n
O'Grady, Sean 249, 258
O'Hara, John 61
Old Renton Affair 23–4, 105
O'Neill, Hugh 92n
Orange Order 3, 78–80, 94, 128, 134, 135, 138, 161n, 162n, 186, 259
Orangemen/ism 59, 84–5, 99, 101–2, 117, 124–5, 132, 136, 139, 150, 173–4, 203, 225, 247, 248
Orange Walks 94–5, 145, 150, 154–6
Ostler, Rev. John 240, 252
Our Boys (Dundee) 15

Paisley, Rev. Ian 237, 259
Park, T. R. 23
Parkhead see Celtic Park
Parkhead Forge 104
Parkhead Juniors 81
Partick Thistle FC 112, 149, 178, 186n
Paterson, George 181
Paton, John 272, 279n
Peacock, Bertie 87n, 247
Peddie, Rev. J. C. 149, 150–1, 153, 154, 159–60, 161n
Peebles, Ian 202–3, 206
Phillimore, Professor John S. 127, 141n
Picture Post 181, 182
Pigott, Richard 70
Pittodrie see Aberdeen FC
police 31, 110, 144, 147–56 *passim*, 164–171 *passim*, 173, 177, 181, 182, 218, 244–6
Popes 63, 64, 76–7, 128, 131–5, 136–7
  John XXIII 235
  John-Paul II 77, 259, 262
  Pius XI 128
Papal visit to Scotland 258–9, 262–3
press (*see also* individual newspapers and journalists)
  catholic 64–5, 66, 129, 141n, 165, 166, 167, 176–7, 180
  sporting 14–7, 47–50, 105–8
  other 48–50, 87, 90n, 91n, 138, 141n, 155, 218–9, 238–9, 242n, 267–8, 269, 278n
Preston North End FC 6, 16
Primrose, Sir John Ure 85, 103
professionalism 10, 15, 23–4, 25, 27–9, 32n, 34n, 51, 105, 108, 111, 274
Protestant Action 136
Protestant League (see 'Scottish Protestant League')
Protestant Vanguard 137
protestantism (*see also* under specific heading, e.g. Church of Scotland)
  'respectability', 100, 112–3, 211, 275;
  suspicion of catholics, 98, 131 (*see also* anti-catholicism)

Queen's Park FC   10, 12–15, 20, 22–3, 27, 29, 32n, 48, 52, 83, 110, 111, 164, 167–8, 171, 248
Quin, D. J. M.   106
Quinn, Jimmy   73, 113–6, 123, 166, 213n

Rafferty, John   86
Raith Rovers FC   213n
Rangers FC (*see also* crowds, riots, supporters)
  formation and early days   12–17, 32n
  Board   75–81, 85–7, 103–4, 156, 181, 184, 186, 193, 194, 196, 200, 201, 206, 218–9, 223–4, 225–7, 232–4, 237–40, 242n, 257, 270, 272–3, 276 (*see also* individual directors)
  friendship with Celtic   27–9, 221, 274
  disputes with Celtic   31, 37, 54
  shareholders   45, 103–4, 206, 233, 257–8, 273
  and historians   32n, 77, 118n, 201–3
  and catholics   2, 75–6, 81–3, 84–7, 92n, 218, 221, 234–5, 247, 251–3, 264n, 269, 270–3
  and Freemasonry   76–8, 89n
  and Orange Order   79–80, 156–7
  and Billy Boys   145
  'tradition'   193–207, 211–2
  criticism of their religious exclusiveness
    by press   218–9, 220, 221–2, 223, 226–7, 233–4, 249–50, 253, 255, 257, 270, 278n (*see also* Horne, Cyril)
    by radio   239, 250, 253–4
    by television   240, 250–3, 264n, 269
    by Celtic players   222
    by church groups and individuals   223, 224, 235–40, 243n, 275
Rangers Blue Book   199
Rangers Handbooks   199, 215–6n
Rangers News   200–1, 213n, 252, 273, 279n
Rangers Pools   212, 232, 268, 269
Rangers Social Club   232, 265n
Rangers Supporters' clubs   199, 234, 247, 248, 254, 276
Ratcliffe, Alexander   137–9, 142n
Real Madrid   1, 7, 211
Red Clydeside   2, 120–1, 172
Red Star Bratislava FC   241n
Reformation   93, 95, 155
Renton FC   19, 23–4, 32n
Restoration of Catholic Hierarchy   63, 80, 95
'Rex' (*Sunday Mail*)   180–2, 221, 268
Reynolds, Jerry   22, 106
riots (*see also* crowds, hooliganism, gangs)
  Rangers v Celtic   113, 140, 166, 180–5, 220
    Hampden, 1909   168–9, 170
    Hampden, 1980   162n, 200, 244–7, 250
  involving Celtic   167, 171, 172, 173–4, 180, 219–21, 250

  involving Rangers   166, 171, 218, 220
    Newcastle, 1969   218, 235, 237
    Barcelona, 1972   218, 250
    Birmingham, 1976   76, 218, 233–4
  other football riots   116, 164–5, 250, 251
  other riots   94–5, 101–2, 124–6, 139–40, 142n, 155–6, 172
Robertson, G. G.   144
Robinson, John   272
Rosebery, Lord   71
Rotary clubs   135
Rouse, Nathan   51
Russell, Bobby   237, 252

Saint Aloysius High School   127
Saint Johnstone FC   186n, 213n
Saint Joseph's College (Dundee)   82
Saint Mirren FC   15, 55, 81, 219
Saint Mungo Halls   72, 115
Saint Patrick's Day
  Dinner (1936)   69
  festivals   71
Saint Vincent de Paul Society   60, 63
Sanderson, Rt. Rev. Dr W. Roy   235
Scarff, Peter   64
Scots Observer   127, 188n
Scotsman, The   242n, 278n
Scott, Alex   197
Scott, Sir Walter   6
Scottish Amateur Athletic Association   27
Scottish Athletic Journal   14–5, 19, 32n, 34n, 47, 50, 105–6
Scottish Co-operative Society   274
Scottish Cup   10, 13, 17, 19, 20, 36, 54, 63
Scottish Football Association (SFA)   6, 21, 23–4, 27, 29, 71, 105, 113, 115, 167, 181–6, 196, 197, 199, 202, 246–7, 248, 250–1, 264n, 269, 273, 278n
SFA *Annual*   13, 32n
Scottish League   6, 10, 17, 20, 34n, 108, 183, 239
Scottish Loyalists   256
Scottish National Party   263, 266n
Scottish Protestant   96
Scottish Protestant League   136–8, 139
Scottish Protestant View   225
Scottish Referee   10, 11, 23–4, 37, 48, 53, 54, 106–7, 111, 119n, 164, 165, 166
Scottish Sport   17, 23–4, 27, 31, 37, 45, 47–8, 50, 53, 65, 108–10, 119, 165
Scottish Television (STV)   251
Scottish Temperance Alliance   160n
Scottish Umpire   14–6, 47
scouts   128
'Senex'   93
Sexton, Dave   118–9n
Shamrock, The   193, 194
Shankly, Bill   6

Shaughraum, The 108
Shaughnessy, Col. 180
Shaughnessy family 68
Shaw, Jock ('Tiger') 79, 195
Shaw, Charlie 196
Shearer, Bobby 213n
Sheffield 152
Sillitoe, Percy 149, 152, 154, 159–60n, 161n, 180–1
Simpson, Jimmy 206
Simpson, Rae 76, 247, 248, 251, 254, 270, 272, 278–9n
Simpson, Ronnie 206, 222
Simpson, W. R. 206
Sinn Fein 106, 129
Sleigh, Major Hume 138
Smith, Alex 83
Smith, Sheriff Irvine 225–6
Smith, Jimmy 79, 223
Smith, John 118n
Smith, Nick 167
South Africa 5, 264n, 273
Southern General Hospital 225
Spanish Civil War 132, 133–4
Spier, Major M. 153
Sporting Chronicle 65
Spurs *see* Tottenham Hotspur
Stein, Colin 224
Stein, Jock 63, 202, 207, 214n, 221, 229, 232, 247, 276
Stenhousemuir FC 213n
Stevenson, Bailie 227
Stern 90–1n
Stevens, Gregor 265n
Stirling Albion FC 214n
Stockport riots 94, 95
Stonyhurst College 25
street football 51
street games 145–6
Struth, Bill 17, 85, 86, 92n, 123, 197, 198, 199, 204–7, 208–12, 213n, 215–6n, 268
Sullivan, T. D. 73
Sunday Mail 178, 193, 257, 277n
Sunday Post 234, 254
Sunday Standard 253
Sunday Times 146
Sunderland FC 6, 216n, 220
supporters (*see also* brake clubs, crowds—descriptions, riots)
  Celtic 19, 61–3, 65–70, 74, 109–10, 111, 200, 214n, 217, 219–21, 230–2, 240–1n, 266n
  Rangers 12, 13, 45, 76, 78–80, 117n, 145, 157, 161–2n, 196, 200, 203, 212, 213n, 218–9, 266n, 268
  both 1, 2, 39, 41, 59, 90–1, 103–4, 267
  other 5, 39–40, 44, 51–2, 143

symbols of sectarianism (flags, banners, chants, etc.)
  Celtic/Rangers 59, 172–3, 175, 177–8, 188n, 227, 230–1, 276
  Celtic 64, 66, 68–9, 74, 90n, 173–4, 176, 177, 180, 182–6, 189n, 214n, 217, 226, 228–30, 232
  Rangers 79–80, 91n, 145, 222 (*see also* Rangers FC)
  other than football 3–4, 129, 136–7, 145, 154–6, 249, 258
Symon, Scot 78, 206, 207

Tanner, C. K. D. 73–4
Taylor, David 84
Taylor, Hugh 92n, 202, 257
Taylor, Matt 222, 269
Third Eye Centre Exhibition 277n
Third Lanark FC 13, 14, 20, 35, 80, 86
Thomson, John 80, 177, 203, 276
Thomson, Malcolm George 127
Torrence, John 139
Tottenham Hotspur FC 36, 84, 274
transport 9, 42–5, 191
  bus 42, 44
  charters 45
  Clyde Tunnel 44, 45
  Cluthas 44, 45
  ferries 41, 44
  'specials' 43, 45, 57n
  subway 42, 44, 45
  trains 42–3, 45
  trams 42, 43, 45, 136
Tully, Charlie 181–2, 195, 197
Tutty, James 81
Tweedsmuir, Lord 140

Ulster 1, 79, 80, 85, 90n, 91n, 96, 124–6, 134–5, 154, 155, 156, 162n, 192, 274
Ulster Covenant 125
Ulster Defence Association (UDA) 59, 80, 125, 251
Ulster Volunteer Force (UVF) 80, 162n
Unionist Party 134, 138, 154
United Irish League 71, 72, 73, 106
United Irish League (America) 72
United States of America 5, 66, 80, 86, 94, 99, 116, 136, 210, 274

Vale of Leven FC 13, 14, 116, 214n
Vallance, Tom 15
Vatican II 131, 235, 243n
Vaughan, Frankie 147
Venters, Alec 180
'Veteran' 22
Veuillot, Louis 131
Victory in Europe Cup 181
Vietnam War 220, 273

Waddell, Willie   76, 92n, 182, 200, 207, 213n,
        214n, 218, 226–7, 228, 234, 238–9, 257,
        264n, 271, 272
Walfrid, Brother   18–9, 60, 68, 87n
Walker, Ernie   264n, 278n
Walker, William   116
Wallace, Jock   78, 79, 270–2, 273, 278n
Warnes, Rev. S. H.   152
Waterford (riot)   230, 232
Watson, Charles   171
Watt, Jim   249
Weekly News   208
Weekly Record   171, 221
Welsh, Pat   208
West Bromwich Albion FC   157
West of Scotland Economic League   157
Wheatley, John   132
White, David   78, 207, 226
White, Desmond   72, 189n, 209, 228, 247,
        248–9, 254
White, Tom   65, 68, 72–3, 91n, 115
William of Orange (King Billy)   13, 136, 154,
        155
Williams, Gordon   195
Williamson, Billy   85, 92n
Wilson, Brian   162n, 239, 250–1, 252, 278n
Wilson, John F.   183, 206
Wilton, William   17, 204, 208, 213n

Wolstenholme, Kenneth 175–6
Wolverhampton   220
Wood, Ian   278n
Woodburn, Willie   85, 195, 197
workers
    and football   5–7, 13, 16, 32n, 35, 41–5,
        51–2
    and unemployment/Depression   85–6, 117n,
        136, 143–4
    living conditions   143–54
    working conditions   41–2, 53–4, 56–7
    and trade unions   99
    and Industrial Revolution   9, 41–5, 99–100,
        130
    and shipyards   84–5, 124, 125
    and Church   99–100, 132
    and middle-class fears, snobbery   9, 32n, 41,
        100, 111–2, 143, 146, 168
World War I   84, 125–6, 141n, 172, 185, 230
World War II   179–80, 185, 191, 230
Wylie, Tom   82–3

Yarrow Shipbuilding Company   3–4
Young, George   181, 195, 196, 197
Young Ireland Society   71
Young Men's Christian Association
        (YMCA)   51, 52
Younger, George   246, 247, 264n